A

CLASSED CATALOGUE

OF THE

LIBRARY

OF THE

CAMBRIDGE HIGH SCHOOL;

WITH

AN ALPHABETICAL INDEX.

TO WHICH IS APPENDED

A LIST OF THE PHILOSOPHICAL AND OTHER APPARATUS
BELONGING TO THE SCHOOL.

CAMBRIDGE:
JOHN BARTLETT.
1853.

CAMBRIDGE:
METCALF AND COMPANY, PRINTERS TO THE UNIVERSITY.

TO

THE TEACHERS AND SCHOLARS

OF

THE CAMBRIDGE HIGH SCHOOL,

AND TO

THE CHERISHED MEMORY OF THOSE WITH WHOM THE AUTHOR
WAS THERE CONNECTED AS A TEACHER,

THIS LABOR OF LOVE

IS DEDICATED.

PREFACE.

The Library of the Cambridge High School owes its origin partly to the liberality of a private individual, and partly to encouragement afforded by the Legislature of the State of Massachusetts. The nature of this encouragement may be learned from the following Resolve, which was approved March 7, 1843.

"*Resolved*, That the provisions of the Resolve of March third, eighteen hundred and forty-two, concerning school-district libraries, be, and the same are hereby, extended to every city and town in the Commonwealth, not heretofore divided into school districts, in such manner as to give as many times fifteen dollars to every such city or town as the number sixty is contained, exclusive of fractions, in the number of children between the ages of four and sixteen years in said city or town; *provided* evidence be produced to the Treasurer, in behalf of said city or town, of its having raised and appropriated, for the establishment of libraries, a sum equal to that which, by the provision of this Resolve, it is entitled to receive from the school fund."

The School Committee of Cambridge, in their Report for the year 1843, recommended to the town to raise the sum necessary to authorize it to draw an equal amount from the State Treasury. This recommendation was not adopted. But, in the spring of 1850, the present Master of the High School, Mr. Elbridge Smith, generously offered to place at the disposal of the City Council a number of suitable books, selected from his private library, of sufficient value to enable the city to avail itself of the patronage of the State. The offer was accepted. The books presented to the City Council were appropriated to the High School, and an order was drawn by the Mayor on the State Treasurer to the amount of $ 825. This money was expended for the purchase of books, under the direction of the School Committee.*

The value of the Library at its commencement, it thus appears, was $ 1,650. Since that time, considerable additions have been made. Several hundred volumes have been given by Mr. Smith, and valuable donations of books have been received from other individuals, among whom may be mentioned the Hon. Edward Everett, George Livermore, Esq., Prof. Benjamin Peirce, Prof. C. C. Felton, Prof. Henry W. Longfellow, the Rev. George R. Noyes, D.D., John Sargent, Esq., Charles Folsom, Esq., John E. Horr, Esq., Zelotes Hosmer, Esq., and Master William Everett. The city has appropriated $ 75 for the purchase of books and for binding, and has procured a book-case at an expense of $ 115. The present value of the Library, which now contains about sixteen hundred volumes, may be estimated at not far from $ 2,400.

---

* For a list of the books presented and purchased, see the Report of the School Committee of Cambridge for 1850.

A GOOD *alphabetical* catalogue of a library will be entirely satisfactory to one who knows all the books which may be useful or interesting to him, and who, accordingly, wishes simply to ascertain whether certain works are to be found in it. But, as such extensive bibliographical knowledge was hardly to be presupposed in the members of the Cambridge High School, I could not doubt that for them, at least, a *classed* catalogue, one which should guide them to the sources of information on particular subjects, would be far more valuable. It is hoped that the use of such a catalogue may promote the formation of those habits of investigation and research, which are essential to success in the pursuit of truth, — without which even genius may only mislead and bewilder its possessor. When the curiosity of the student is excited, it is most desirable that he should have every facility for pursuing the inquiries to which he is led, that he may thus be encouraged to examine and think for himself.

One who has become acquainted with the books of a well-selected library of one or two thousand volumes, and has learned how to turn them to account, will find this knowledge and experience of very great service to him, should he afterwards have access to larger collections. And if the classification adopted be not unnatural and arbitrary, the use of a classed catalogue, and the habit to which it leads of referring books to their proper place in a systematic arrangement of the different departments of literature, cannot be without value as a means of mental discipline. It may be, also, that, to those who are just beginning to traverse the vast fields of literature and science, a survey, as if from some eminence, of the territory that lies before them, will enable them to understand better the relations of its different parts to each other, will give them new conceptions of the varied objects of interest which it presents, and animate them to press cheerfully through the somewhat tangled and thorny paths by which it is to be entered.

THE *Classification* here adopted may be seen in the synopsis prefixed to the Catalogue. It is necessarily imperfect. The different branches of human knowledge are so intimately connected, that no scheme of classification can be devised, in which the several classes will not run into each other; and in the practical application of any system it will be found that some books belong equally to two or more different divisions. When such is the case with respect to any work, its title has usually been recorded in full under only one of these divisions, and briefly noticed under the others, with a reference to the complete entry. The affinities between different classes have often been pointed out by notes, which will also, it is hoped, aid the student who wishes to find what the library contains on a particular subject.

The *Alphabetical Index* at the end of the volume will show at once whether a particular work belongs to the library.

IN each Class, the titles of the works belonging to it are entered alphabetically under their *authors' names*, when these are known; or, in the case of *anonymous* publications whose authors are not ascertained, under *the first word of the title, not an article or a preposition.* (See INTRODUCTION, p. 39.) *Pseudonymous* works, if the true name of the author is not known, are entered under *the assumed name.* (See BROWN, p. 202.) Care has been taken to make such references from the most important words in the title, and from the assumed name, as will enable one readily to find the entry of any anonymous or pseudonymous work which is placed under the name of its author. (See PENITENTIAL, p. 28; PARLEY, p. 2.) — There is one important exception to the rule given above. In Class XXIV. Part II. (INDIVIDUAL BIOGRAPHY) the names of the *subjects*, not the *authors*, of the works contained in it are prefixed to their titles; and, as the authors' names all appear in the Index, it has not been thought necessary to make cross-references from them in this Part.

Works *published by any organized society*, using the term in its most comprehensive sense, if the production of its officers or agents in their official capacity, and also if anonymous, or *polyonymous* (that is, bearing the names of several authors), are entered under *the name of the society.* The first word of that name, not an article, is made the leading word in the heading. This rule is intended to include documents published by national, municipal, and other governments. (See CENTRAL SOCIETY, etc., p. 21; MASSACHUSETTS, p. 26; CAMBRIDGE, p. 11.) In cases not comprehended in the preceding statement, if the author's name is prefixed to a work published by a society, the work is entered under his name. (See MALKIN, p. 168.) All the works, however, published by a society are noticed under its name in the Index.

Periodical publications, except those issued by societies, are entered under *the first word of their titles, not an article*, with cross-references from the names of editors, and from other words under which they might naturally be looked for. (See AMERICAN Annals of Education, p. 16; COMMON SCHOOL Journal, p. 22.)

Collections embracing the works of several authors under a general title, except such as may be included in the two preceding rules, are entered under *the name of the editor.* (See SPARKS, p. 125; BRANDE, p. 199.)* If the editor's name does not appear, such a collection is treated as an anonymous work, unless the authors' names are given on the title-page, in which case it is catalogued under the first of these. (See SMALL Books, p. 208; CRABBE, p. 99.)

When any work forming part of a collection has an independent title-page and pagination, it is also catalogued separately under the class to which it belongs, its place in the collection, however, being indicated by a reference, within parentheses, at the end of the title. (See BARLOW, p. 1; DE MORGAN, p. 33.)

In accordance with the spirit of this rule, though it is not strictly required by its letter, the tracts composing Chambers's "Miscellany," "Papers for the People," and "Repository of Instructive and Amusing Papers," have all been classed and entered as distinct works. There was a special reason for doing this in the present Catalogue, as these tracts are admirably adapted to the wants of those for whose use it is chiefly intended. They were all, it is also to be observed, originally printed and paged independently. (See p. 202.)

In like manner, the titles of the various treatises contained in the first thirteen volumes of the Encyclopædia Metropolitana, with the exception of some anonymous portions of the first volume, have been inserted in their proper places in the Catalogue under the names of their authors. The articles in these volumes are not arranged alphabetically, as they are in the remainder of the work, and many of them have been published independently. (See SMEDLEY, p. 200.)

A similar course has been pursued in respect to the different works which are comprised in the four volumes entitled "Natural Philosophy," published by the Society for the Diffusion of Useful Knowledge. (See SOCIETY, etc., p. 42.)

In some instances, a reference has been made under the proper Class to a particular treatise of especial interest or importance included in the collected writings of an author, which are entered under a different Class. (See MILTON, p. 13; CHANNING, p. 22.)

All the more important *biographical collections*, not alphabetical, which belong to the library, have been *analyzed;* that is to say, in Class XXIV. Part II. references are made to the biographical sketches contained in them, under the names of those to whom they relate. (See p. 126.) This course has been pursued with the thirty-one volumes of Lardner's "Cabinet Cyclopædia" which are devoted to biography, Sparks's "Library of American Biography," twenty-five volumes, Belknap's "American Biography," Brougham's "Historical Sketches of Statesmen" and his "Lives of Men of Letters and Science," Mrs. Jameson's "Memoirs of Celebrated Female Sovereigns," "St. John's Lives of Celebrated Travellers," and many other collections.

In some cases it has appeared advisable to specify the *contents* of particular works. For the mode in which this has been done in the case of biographical collections not

* According to this rule, the second entry under PHÆDRUS, p. 91, should have been placed under CAREY.

analyzed, see FÉNELON, p. 121; PLUTARCHUS, p. 124. For examples of another kind, see PALEY, p. 8; AMERICAN INSTITUTE, etc., p. 17; MACAULAY, p. 207.

SOME explanations may now be given respecting the *headings* of the titles, or the words which determine their place in the alphabetical arrangement.

These consist, for the most part, of the *surnames* of authors, which, as well as their Christian names, appear in their *vernacular form*.

There are a few exceptions to this rule. The works and biographies of *canonized* persons, as Thomas Aquinas, are entered under their *Christian* names. *Sovereigns* are also designated by their Christian names, in the form in which they are commonly written in English. The names of *ancient Greek authors*, of *the Fathers of the Church*, and of *authors of the Middle Ages who wrote wholly in Latin*, with a few others, as Confucius, Copernicus, Grotius, are given in their *Latin form*.

In respect to surnames *with prefixes*, the following rules have been observed. In English names, the prefix is treated as a part of the surname. Accordingly, in the alphabetical series, De Morgan and D'Israeli are placed under *D*. — In all other languages except the French, surnames are entered under the letter following the prefix; as Von Humboldt, under *H;* Las Casas under *C;* Della Valle, under *V*. In French, also, this rule applies to names preceded by the preposition *de;* thus De Monts is placed under *M*. — French surnames preceded by *Le*, *La*, *L'*, are entered under *L*, as Le Vaillant, La Fontaine, L'Épée; if preceded by *Du* or *Des*, under *D*, as Du Bois, Des Cartes, more commonly written Dubois, Descartes.

Compound surnames, except English, are generally entered under the *first part* of the name, as Calderon de la Barca, Cubi i Soler, Merle d'Aubigné, Simonde de Sismondi. But it has not been thought expedient to put Fénelon under *Salignac*, though the rule has been carried to this extent by Lelong, in that monument of bibliographical industry and skill, the "Bibliothèque Historique de la France."

The works and biographies of English *noblemen* and *ecclesiastical dignitaries* are catalogued under their *family names*, not their titles, even though they may be more generally known by the latter. The Duke of Marlborough accordingly appears under *Churchill*, Lord Chatham under *Pitt*, and Lord Mahon under *Stanhope*. There can be little doubt that this is the best rule for *English* names, and perhaps it should be made universal, as it is in the new Catalogue of the British Museum and by Professor Jewett of the Smithsonian Institution. But partly from a doubt of the expediency of putting Buffon under *Leclerc*, Condorcet under *Caritat*, Lacépède under *La Ville*, Mirabeau under *Riquetti*, Richelieu under *Du Plessis*, Madame de Genlis under *Ducrest de Saint-Aubin*, and, as would seem to be required, Lafayette under *Motier*, to give no more examples, — and partly from the impossibility of determining with confidence, in some cases, whether a particular name is to be regarded as a family name or only as part of a title, — I have enrolled *all noblemen except British* under their *titular appellations*. This accords with the general usage in French and German biographical and bibliographical works. The necessary cross-references have been made from name to title, and *vice versâ*.

Family names and prefixes to them, which, for any reason, do not stand in the heading of the title as a part of the surname, but are placed after it in a parenthesis with the Christian name, are printed in *small capitals*. This rule includes the case of names changed by the assumption of a new surname, when the original name is also retained; as, SIGOURNEY (*Mrs.* Lydia HUNTLEY); TOOKE (John HORNE). The maiden name of a married woman, if not known to be retained, is likewise printed in small capitals, but in *brackets*. (See LOWELL, p. 25; HALL, p. 107.) The works of an author whose name has been changed are all entered under his *last-adopted* name, with the necessary cross-references.

Some persons who have two or more Christian names are generally designated by only one of them, and no more than this may appear on the title-pages of their works.

In such instances, this name is distinguished by being printed in s p a c e d l e t t e r s. When the initial only is used, as in cross-references and in the Index, it is *italicized.* (See SCHLEGEL, p. 2; VILLAGE Mayor, p. 110.)*

The heading of a title is inclosed in *brackets* when it does not appear in any form on the title-page.

In transcribing titles, no alteration has been intentionally made in the language of the author, and even the orthography and punctuation have been scrupulously preserved. The following *abbreviations* have, however, been used: "Ed." for "Edition"; "1st," "2d," "3d," etc. for "first," "second," "third," in designating the number of the edition; and, not unfrequently, the *initial* only of a name is given in the title, when that name appears in full in the heading. I now, however, doubt the expediency of this use of initials.

In works consisting of several volumes, it occasionally happens that their *titles differ.* Such differences are sometimes pointed out in a note. More frequently, after giving the title of the first volume, it has been found convenient to add the peculiarities in the titles of others, indicating the transition from the title of one volume to another by the sign | . For examples, see ARNOLD, pp. 6, 7; AMERICAN Annals, etc., p. 16; AMERICAN Almanac, p. 111; BANCROFT, p. 183.

For illustrations of the course which has been pursued in the case of volumes with *double titles*, one general and the other special, or one engraved and the other printed, differing from each other, see BUTLER, CHALMERS, p. 3; WARE, p. 9; EWBANK, p. 192.

Additions to a title are inclosed in *brackets;* any *omission*, except of the mere designation of the author's name when that appears in the heading, is denoted by *three dots.*

The abbreviation N. D. is used for "*No date.*" It must be mentioned, that no reliance can be placed on the date of *stereotyped* books printed in this country, as affording evidence of the time of their publication. The common booksellers' trick of affixing false dates to the works which they issue, with the view of promoting their sale, and, especially, of *postdating* them by three or four months, if published so near the end of the year, is to be reprobated as a falsification of literary history, with which all other history is so intimately connected.

In accordance with general usage, the terms *folio, quarto, octavo*, etc., or rather their abbreviations, have been used in designating the *form* of books. They denote, as every one knows, the number of leaves into which the printed sheet is folded. But this is what the best bibliographer cannot always determine, without knowing the size of the sheet. The signatures often fail him, because they may be the same in several different forms; for example, they are eight leaves apart in an ordinary octavo and in a 16mo printed in half-sheets; six leaves apart in a duodecimo printed in half-sheets and in a common 18mo. All that can be stated with certainty is the number of leaves intervening between the successive signatures. In the more doubtful cases, I have added this, within parentheses, after the ordinary designation of form, which, in general, is only given as *probable.*

It must be distinctly understood that the terms *folio, quarto*, etc. afford very little indication of the actual *size* of a book. A large duodecimo may be twice the size of a post octavo. If it is the purpose of the cataloguer to state the size, the only satisfactory mode is that recommended by Professor Jewett, namely, to give the measurement of the full printed page in inches and tenths of inches.

Another point must be noticed. Many stereotyped books have *two sets of signatures*, one usually consisting of letters, the other of Arabic figures, — in order that

* For other examples, see ARAGO, p. 47; HUMBOLDT, p. 53; SMITH, p. 59; FOLLEN, p. 72; BUTTMANN, p. 73; GOETTLING, HERMANN, JACOBS, p. 74; MATTHIAE, p. 75; SPITZNER, PASSOW, p. 76; GROTEFEND, p. 77; DOEDERLEIN, RAMSHORN, p. 81; HEMANS, p. 101; GUARINI, p. 141; LULLI, p. 147; THIERRY, p. 173; SCHILLER, p. 174; GUIZOT, p. 175; RANKE, p. 188; BOJESEN, p. 189; WACHSMUTH, p. 191. I refer to a considerable number of examples, though by no means all which the Catalogue affords, because this is a matter which has been seldom attended to in works of this kind. It is evident, however, that error and confusion may arise from neglecting it.

they may be printed in different forms at the pleasure of the publisher. Thus there happen to be in the High School Library two copies of Keightley's History of Rome, one printed at Boston in 1839 as an octavo, the other printed at New York in 1848, from the same stereotype plates, as a duodecimo. It has, accordingly, two sets of signatures, in one of which they occur at intervals of four, in the other of six leaves. Examples of a similar kind are numerous. They are noted in the Catalogue by the abbreviations "4. and 6.," "8. and 6.," and the like, within parentheses, immediately following the designation of form. (See [GOODRICH], p. 2.)

In other cases the signatures succeed each other at intervals, it may be, of eight and four, or twelve and six leaves, *alternately*. This is indicated in the Catalogue by the abbreviations "8. 4.," "12. 6.," etc. (See BARLOW, p. 1.)

In works consisting of but a single volume, *the number of pages* is stated as it is noted in the book, if less than 100, or more than 600. The sign + is added when the volume contains several pages not numbered, and therefore not taken into account.

SOME explanation is necessary respecting the titles of the volumes belonging to Lardner's "Cabinet Cyclopædia." The late re-issue of that work having been ordered for the library, though not yet actually received, it was thought desirable to catalogue it. But the titles given cannot be relied on as perfectly accurate, having been taken, not from the books themselves, but from the publishers' advertisement. A blank space has been left for the date. The references to the different volumes are adapted to the set in the library of Harvard College. As the work is stereotyped, they will probably suit the new impression.

One accidental omission, of considerable importance, under Class XXIV. Part I. must be noticed. The first three volumes of the "Cabinet Library" (see p. 203) should have been there entered under [GOODRICH]. — Though much pains has been taken to secure completeness and accuracy, other oversights and inconsistencies will doubtless be detected. It is hoped, however, that they will not be found numerous.

In two or three Classes a different course would have been pursued had not the number of volumes belonging to them been so small as to make it hardly expedient. In a classed catalogue of a more extensive library, it would be of great advantage, if, under the heads of "Voyages and Travels," and of "Geography," the names of the *countries*, etc. to which the works contained in these Classes relate should appear in their alphabetical order, as in a geographical dictionary, with references to the works in the library descriptive of each. Thus, in the present Catalogue, under Class XXIII. we might have the entry: — "**Italy.** *See* GOETHE (J. W. VON); — MORGAN (*Lady* S. [O.])." In such a case, it would be well to have the names of countries, etc. printed in a different type from that of the headings of the titles.

THE List of Apparatus appended to this volume was prepared by Mr. John Emory Horr, the present Sub-master of the High School.

IN compiling this Catalogue, I have derived useful hints and information from sources too numerous to be here specified. I wish, however, to express my particular obligations to the much-abused "Catalogue of Printed Books in the British Museum" (Volume I.), published under the superintendence of Mr. Panizzi, and to the Rules of Professor Jewett, whose enlightened zeal is doing so much for the extension of bibliographical knowledge and for the interest of public libraries in this country.

EZRA ABBOT, JR.

CLASSIFICATION AND CONTENTS.

Note. It will be perceived that the thirty-one Classes which follow are comprised in eight more general divisions, not numbered, but distinguished by a larger type.

SCIENCE OF MIND, AND OF MAN IN HIS HIGHER RELATIONS.

MATHEMATICAL SCIENCE.

PHYSICAL SCIENCE.

THE ARTS.

LANGUAGE; WITH AN APPENDIX.

APPENDIX TO "LANGUAGE."

WORKS OF IMAGINATION AND FANCY, WIT AND HUMOR.

Note. For *Ancient Greek and Latin Authors*, see Class XVI. Parts II. and III.

HISTORY OF MAN, IN HIS HIGHER RELATIONS.

Note. For the *Physical* History of Man, see Class XIII. Part V.

ENCYCLOPÆDIAS AND POLYGRAPHY.

CATALOGUE.

SCIENCE OF MIND, AND OF MAN IN HIS HIGHER RELATIONS.

(Classes I. — V.)

CLASS I. MENTAL PHILOSOPHY; LOGIC; ÆSTHETICS.

Note. The term "Mental Philosophy," as here used, includes Pure Metaphysics as well as Psychology. — For the *History* of Philosophy, see Class XXVIII. For *Æsthetics*, compare Class XIV. Part V. and Class XVII.

ABERCROMBIE (John), *M.D.* Inquiries concerning the Intellectual Powers, and the Investigation of Truth. ... From the last Edinburgh Ed. New-York. [1833?] 18° (HARPER's Fam. Libr., **37.**)

——— *The same.* With Additions and Explanations to adapt the Work to the Use of Schools and Academies, by Jacob Abbott. Boston, 1846. 12°

ANIMAL Instincts and Intelligence. (CHAMBERS's Papers, *etc.* XI. no. 82.)

[BARLOW (*Rev.* John)]. The Connection between Physiology and Intellectual Philosophy. *See* Class XIII. Part V. § 1.

——— On Man's Power over himself to prevent or control Insanity. Communicated to the Members at the Royal Institution of Great Britain, ... May 26th, 1843. ... Philadelphia. 1846. 24° (8. 4.) pp. 54. (SMALL Books, *etc.* I. no. 3.)

BERKELEY (George), *D.D.*, *Bp. of Cloyne.* The Works of G. B. ... . To which are added, An Account of his Life, and several of his Letters to Thomas Prior, Esq., Dean Gervais, Mr. Pope, &c. ... London. 1837. 8°

BOWEN (*Prof.* Francis). Lowell Lectures, on the Application of Metaphysical and Ethical Science to the Evidences of Religion. *See* Class II. Part I.

COLERIDGE (Samuel Taylor). ... Treatise on Method. (ENCYCL. Metrop., I. 1 – 28.)

[GOODRICH (Samuel Griswold)]. A Glance at Philosophy, Mental, Moral and Social. By the Author of Peter Parley's Tales. Boston. 1849. 16° or 18° (8. and 6.) (CABINET Libr., **16.**)

LOCKE (John). Locke's Essays. An Essay concerning Human Understanding. And a Treatise on the Conduct of the Understanding. ... With the Author's last Additions and Corrections. Philadelphia. [183– ?] 8°

——— The Conduct of the Understanding. *See* Class III. BACON (F.). Essays, *etc.* 1847. 18°

MILL (John Stuart). A System of Logic, Ratiocinative and Inductive; being a connected View of the Principles of Evidence and the Methods of Scientific Investigation. New-York. 1848. 8° pp. xiii., 600.

PARLEY (Peter), *pseudon.* *See* [GOODRICH (Samuel Griswold)].

PHILOSOPHICAL Theories and Philosophical Experience. By a Pariah. From the 2d London Ed. Philadelphia. 1846. 24° (8. 4.) pp. 69. (SMALL Books, *etc.* I. no. 1.)

REID (Thomas), *D.D.* Essays on the Intellectual Powers of Man. ... Abridged. With Notes and Illustrations from Sir William Hamilton and others. Edited by James Walker, D.D. .... 3d Ed. Cambridge. 1852. 12°

SCHLEGEL (Karl Wilhelm Friedrich VON). Æsthetic and Miscellaneous Works. *See* Class XXXI.

——— The Philosophy of Life, and Philosophy of Language, in a Course of Lectures, by Frederick von S. Translated from the German by the Rev. A. J. W. Morrison, M. A. London. 1847. 8° (BOHN's Stand. Libr.)

SPECTRAL Illusions. (CHAMBERS's Miscel., IV. no. 70.)

SPECULATIVE Manias. *See* Class IV. Part II.

UPHAM (*Prof.* Thomas Cogswell), *D.D.* Elements of Mental Philosophy, embracing the two Departments of the Intellect and the Sensibilities. ... 2 vols. New-York. 1852 – 50. 12°

——— A Philosophical and Practical Treatise on the Will. Forming the Third Volume of a System of Mental Philosophy. ... New-York. 1849. 12°

——— Outlines of Imperfect and Disordered Mental Action. ... New-York. 1848. 18° (HARPER's Fam. Libr., **100.**)

WHAT is Philosophy? (CHAMBERS's Papers, *etc.* XII. no. 92.)

WHATELY (Richard), *Abp. of Dublin.* Easy Lessons on Reasoning. ... 3d American from 5th London Ed. Boston and Cambridge. 1852. 12°

——— Logic. (ENCYCL. Metrop., I. 193 – 240.)

——— Elements of Logic, comprising the Substance of the Article in the Encyclopædia Metropolitana: with Additions, &c. Stereotype Ed. Boston. 1845. 12°

WINSLOW (*Rev.* Hubbard). Elements of Intellectual Philosophy. ... Boston. 1850. 12°

WONDERS (The) of Human Folly. (CHAMBERS'S Papers, *etc.* VIII. no. 63.)

CLASS II. THEOLOGY.

PART I. GENERAL WORKS; NATURAL RELIGION; EVIDENCES OF REVELATION.

BERKELEY (George), *D.D.*, *Bp. of Cloyne.* Alciphron, or the Minute Philosopher: in Seven Dialogues. Containing an Apology for the Christian Religion .... (Works, 1837. 8° pp. 117 - 241. — *See* Class I.)

BONIFACE SAINTINE (Xavier). *See* SAINTINE.

BOWEN (*Prof.* Francis). Lowell Lectures, on the Application of Metaphysical and Ethical Science to the Evidences of Religion; delivered before the Lowell Institute in Boston, in the Winters of 1848 - 49. Boston. 1849. 8°

BUCK (*Rev.* Charles). A Theological Dictionary, containing Definitions of all Religious Terms; a comprehensive View of every Article in ... Divinity; an impartial Account of all the principal Denominations ... in the Religious World from the Birth of Christ to the Present Day: ... with an accurate Statement of the most remarkable ... Events ... in Ecclesiastical History. ... Woodward's new Ed., ... from the last London Ed.; to which is added, An Appendix, containing an Account of the Methodist Episcopal, and Presbyterian Churches, in the United States .... Philadelphia. 1832. 18° or 12° (6. and 12.) pp. 624.

BUTLER (Joseph), *LL.D.*, successively *Bp. of Bristol* and *Durham.* The Analogy of Religion, Natural and Revealed, to the Constitution and Course of Nature. To which are added, Two brief Dissertations: I. Of Personal Identity. II. Of the Nature of Virtue. ... A new and improved Ed. London. 1842. 12°

Note. To this volume, which is bound with another containing Butler's Sermons (see Part III.), is also prefixed the following title: — "The Whole Works of J. B. .... New Ed., complete in one Volume." London: Thomas Tegg. 1841.

CHALMERS (Thomas), *D.D.* On Natural Theology. ... 2 vols. New York. 1844. 12°

Note. Also with the title: — "The Works of T. C. .... 5th uniform Ed. Volume First — Second."

CHANNING (William Ellery), *D.D.* The Evidences of Revealed Religion. Dudleian Lecture, 1821. — The Evidences of Christianity, Part I. II. (Works, III. 105 - 136, and 315 - 398.)

CORRIE (*Prof.* George Elwes), *and* ROSE (*Rev.* Henry John). Outlines of Theology. (ENCYCL. Metrop., II. 857 - 904.)

CUDWORTH (Ralph), *D.D.* The true Intellectual System of the Universe: wherein all the Reason and Philosophy of Atheism is confuted, and its Impossibility demonstrated. A Treatise on Immutable Morality; with a Discourse concerning the true Notion of the Lord's Supper; and two Sermons on 1 John 2 : 3, 4. and 1 Cor. 15 : 27. 1st American Ed.; with ... an Account of the Life and Writings of the Author: by Thomas Birch ... . 2 vols. Andover. 1837–38. 8°

DUNCAN (Henry), *D.D.* Sacred Philosophy of the Seasons; illustrating the Perfections of God in the Phenomena of the Year. By the Rev. H. D. ... Ruthwell, Scotland. With important Additions and some Modifications to adapt it to American Readers, by F. W. P. Greenwood. ... Vol. I. — Winter. | Vol. II. — Spring. | Vol. III. — Summer. | Vol. IV. — Autumn. 4 vols. Boston. 1839. 12° (SCHOOL Libr., Vol. VII.–X.)

HOPKINS (Mark), *D.D.* Lectures on the Evidences of Christianity, before the Lowell Institute, January, 1844. ... Boston. 1846. 8°

NEWMAN (*Rev.* John Henry). Apollonius Tyanæus. Miracles. (ENCYCL. Metrop., X. 619–644.)

NORTON (*Prof.* Andrews). The Evidences of the Genuineness of the Gospels. 2d Ed. 3 vols. Cambridge. 1846–48. 8°

——— Inaugural Discourse [on the Extent and Relations of Theology], delivered before the University in Cambridge, August 10, 1819. ... Cambridge. 1819. 8° pp. 48.

PALEY (William), *D.D., Archdeacon of Carlisle.* Natural Theology. — Evidences of Christianity. — Horæ Paulinæ. (Works, *etc.* 1830. 8° Vol. I. II. IV. — *See* Part III.)

——— Paley's Natural Theology, with Selections from the illustrative Notes, and the Supplementary Dissertations, of Sir Charles Bell, and Lord Brougham. The whole newly arranged, and edited by Elisha Bartlett, M. D. With numerous Wood Cuts, and a Life and Portrait of the Author. ... 2 vols. Boston. 1839. 12° (SCHOOL Libr., Vol. II. III.)

——— Paley's Natural Theology, with illustrative Notes, &c. by Henry Lord Brougham ... and Sir Charles Bell ... . To which are added, Preliminary Observations and Notes. By A. Potter, D. D. ... . 2 vols. New-York. 1840–47. 18° (HARPER'S Fam. Libr., **96, 97.**)

——— ... Natural Theology ... . Illustrated by the Plates, and by a Selection from the Notes of James Paxton ... . With Additional Notes, original and selected, for this Edition. And a Vocabulary of Scientific Terms. Stereotype Ed. Boston. 1849. 12°

[SAINTINE (Xavier BONIFACE)]. Picciola, or the Prison Flower. (CHAMBERS'S Miscel., I. no. 7.)

WHATELY (Richard), *Abp. of Dublin.* Introductory Lessons on Christian Evidences. 1st American from the 10th London Ed. Boston. 1850. 18°

PART II. THE SACRED SCRIPTURES.

THE BIBLE.

English.

THE HOLY BIBLE, containing the Old and New Testaments, translated out of the Original Tongues .... New York: American Bible Society. 1850. 8° pp. 968, 304.

French.

LA SAINTE BIBLE, qui contient le Vieux et le Nouveau Testament; revue sur les Originaux, par David Martin .... New York: Société Bibliqué [*sic*] Américaine. 1852. 8° pp. 819, 261.

German.

DIE BIBEL oder die ganze Heilige Schrift des alten und neuen Testaments. [Translated by Martin Luther.] New York, herausgegeben von der Americanischen Bibel-Gesellschaft. 1852. 8° pp. 828, 273.

Italian.

LA SACRA BIBBIA, che contiene il Vecchio e il Nuovo Testamento: tradotta in Lingua Italiana, da Giovanni Diodati. Londra. 1850. 8° *Not paged.*

Note. In all these editions of the Bible, the New Testament has an independent title-page.

OLD TESTAMENT.

JOB. A new Translation of the Book of Job, with an Introduction, and Notes chiefly explanatory. By George R. Noyes. 2d Ed. With Corrections and Additions. Boston. 1838. 12°

PSALMS. A new Translation of the Book of Psalms, with an Introduction, and Notes, chiefly explanatory. By George R. Noyes, D. D. .... 2d Ed. Boston. 1846. 12°

PROVERBS. A new Translation of the Proverbs, Ecclesiastes, and the Canticles, with Introductions, and Notes, chiefly explanatory. By George R. Noyes .... Boston. 1846. 12°

ECCLESIASTES. *See* PROVERBS.

SONG OF SOLOMON, *or* CANTICLES. *See* PROVERBS.

PROPHETS. A new Translation of the Hebrew Prophets, arranged in Chronological Order. By George R. Noyes. Volume I. containing Joel, Amos, Hosea, Isaiah, and Micah. | Volume II. containing Nahum, Zephaniah, Habakkuk, Obadiah, Jeremiah, Lamentations. | Volume III. containing Ezekiel, Daniel, Haggai, Zechariah, Jonah, and Malachi. 3 vols. Boston. 1833-37. 12°

NEW TESTAMENT.

Greek.

ʽΗ ΚΑΙΝΗ ΔΙΑΘΗΚΗ. The Greek Testament, with brief English Notes, chiefly philological and explanatory, especially formed for the Use of Colleges and the Public Schools .... 3d Ed., ... enlarged, and ... improved; accompanied with a new Map of Judæa and part of Syria .... By the Rev. S. T. Bloomfield, D. D. .... London. 1843. 12°

English.

The New Testament of our Lord and Saviour Jesus Christ. By William Tyndale, the Martyr. The Original Edition, 1526, being the first vernacular Translation from the Greek. With a Memoir of his Life and Writings [by George Offor, recast by J. P. Dabney]. To which are annexed, the essential Variations of Coverdale's, Thomas Matthew's, Cranmer's, the Genevan, and the Bishops' Bibles, as Marginal Readings. By J. P. Dabney. Andover. 1837. 12°

SELECTIONS.

Everts (*Rev.* W. W.). The Bible Manual; comprising Selections of Scripture, arranged for Occasions of Private and Public Worship .... Together with Scripture Expressions of Prayer, abridged from Matthew Henry. With an Appendix consisting of a copious Classification of Scripture Text, presenting a Systematic View of the Doctrines and Duties of Revelation. ... New York. 1846. 12°

Note. The Appendix is paged separately, with the title: — "The Scripture Text Book. Scripture Texts arranged for the Use of Ministers, S. S. Teachers, and Families. ..." Compiled by the "Religious Tract and Book Society for Ireland."

Part III. Other Works belonging to Christian Theology.

Note. For *Ecclesiastical and Sacred History*, see Class XXVI.

Anderson (Christopher). The Annals of the English Bible .... Abridged and continued by S. I. Prime, *etc.* *See* Class XXIX.

Appleton (Jesse), *D.D.* The Works of Rev. J. A. ... embracing his Course of Theological Lectures, his Academic Addresses, and a Selection from his Sermons: with a Memoir of his Life and Character [by Prof. Alpheus S. Packard]. ... 2 vols. Andover. 1837–36. 8°

Arnold (Thomas), *D.D.* Christian Life, its Course, its Hindrances, and its Helps. — Sermons, preached mostly in the Chapel of Rugby School. ... 5th Ed. London. 1849. 8°

——— Christian Life, its Hopes, its Fears, and its Close. — Sermons, preached mostly in the Chapel of Rugby School. ... 5th Ed. London. 1849. 8°

——— Sermons. ... Vol. I. 6th Ed. To which is added, A new

Ed. of Two Sermons on the Interpretation of Prophecy. | Sermons, with an Essay on the right Interpretation and Understanding of the Scriptures. ... Vol. II. 4th Ed. | Sermons. ... Vol. III. 3d Ed. 3 vols. London. 1850 – 45 – 45. 8°

——— Sermons chiefly on the Interpretation of Scripture. ... 2d Ed. London. 1845. 8°

ASSEMBLY OF DIVINES AT WESTMINSTER. The Shorter Catechism. *See* NEW ENGLAND Primer.

[BUCKINGHAM (Joseph TINKER)]. Devotional Exercises for Schools and Families. New Ed., with Additions. Boston. 1844. 16°

BUTLER (Joseph), *LL.D.*, successively *Bp. of Bristol* and *Durham.* Fifteen Sermons preached at the Rolls Chapel; to which are added Six Sermons preached on Public Occasions, &c. ... A new Ed. London. 1841. 12°

CHANNING (William Ellery), *D.D.* The Works of W. E. C. ... . 11th complete Ed., with an Introduction. 6 vols. Boston. 1849. 12°

CHRISTIAN Doctrine and Practice in the Second Century. [Consisting chiefly of extracts from the writings of Clement of Alexandria.] Philadelphia. 1846. 24° (8. 4.) pp. 87. (SMALL Books, *etc.* II. no. 7.)

CHRISTIAN Sects in the Nineteenth Century. In a Series of Letters to a Lady. ... Philadelphia. 1846. 24° (8. 4.) pp. 91. (SMALL Books, *etc.* III. no. 11.)

[CLEMENS ALEXANDRINUS]. *See* CHRISTIAN Doctrine, *etc.* 1846. 24°

COLEMAN (*Prof.* Lyman), *D.D.* An Historical Geography of the Bible. *See* Class XXII. Part II.

COTTON (*Rev.* John). [Catechism, *or*] Spiritual Milk for American Babes, *etc.* *See* NEW ENGLAND Primer. ... [1843.] 24°

DEVOTIONAL Exercises for Schools, *etc.* *See* [BUCKINGHAM (J. T.)].

EDWARDS (*Prof.* Bela Bates), *D.D.* Writings ... with a Memoir by Edwards A. Park. ... 2 vols. Boston. 1853. 12°

FÉNELON (François DE SALIGNAC DE LA MOTHE), *Abp. of Cambrai.* Selections from the Writings of Fenelon: with a Memoir of his Life by Mrs. Follen. [Preface to the 1st Ed., by Henry D. Sedgwick; and Introductory Remarks to the 4th Ed., by W. E. Channing, D. D.] 6th Ed. Boston and Cambridge. 1851. 16°

[GOODHUGH (William)]. The Pictorial Dictionary of the Holy Bible: or a Cyclopædia of Illustrations, Graphic, Historical, and Descriptive, of the Sacred Writings, by reference to the Manners, Customs, Rites, Traditions, Antiquities and Literature of the Eastern Nations. [Edited by W. G., and, after his decease, by W. C. Taylor, LL.D.] 2 vols. London. 1845. Large 8° pp. viii., iv., 1432.

HENGSTENBERG (*Prof.* Ernst Wilhelm), *D.D.* Egypt and the Books of Moses, or the Books of Moses illustrated by the Monuments of Egypt: with an Appendix. ... From the German by R. D. C. Robbins ... . Andover. 1843. 12°

JAHN (*Prof.* Johann), *D.D.* Jahn's Biblical Archæology, translated from the Latin, with Additions and Corrections, by Thomas C. Upham .... 5th Ed., stereotyped. New York. 1849. 8°

JENKS (William), *D.D.* The Explanatory Bible Atlas and Scripture Gazetteer; ... containing [17] Maps ...; a Dictionary of the Natural History of the Bible, with Engravings; and Tables of Time, Weights, Measures and Coins, Tabular Views, etc. ... Boston. 1847. 4°

KITTO (John), *D.D.* The Popular Cyclopædia of Biblical Literature condensed from the larger Work. By J. K. .... Assisted by Rev. James Taylor, D. D., of Glasgow. Illustrated by numerous Engravings. Boston. 1852. 8° pp. viii., 800. + (3 copies.)

LEIGHTON (Robert), *D.D.*, successively *Bp. of Dunblane* and *Abp. of Glasgow.* The Works of R. L. .... To which is prefixed a Life of the Author, by James Aikman, Esq. Complete in one Volume. Edinburgh. 1840. 8° pp. iv., lii., 687.

LIVERMORE (George). Remarks on the Publication and Circulation of the Scriptures, *etc.* *See* Class XXIX.

MIMPRISS (Robert). The Gospel History of our Lord's Life & Ministry, *etc.* *See* Class XXIV. Part II. JESUS CHRIST, *etc.*

NEW ENGLAND Primer. The New-England Primer improved for the more easy attaining the true reading of English. To which is added The Assembly of Divines, and Mr. Cotton's Catechism. Boston: printed by Edward Draper ... and sold by John Boyle ... 1777. [*A fac-simile reprint.* Hartford, Conn. Ira Webster. 1843.] 24° (12.) *Not paged.*

——— *See* Class XXIX. [LIVERMORE (G.)]. The Origin, History and Character of the N. E. Primer, *etc.*

NORTON (*Prof.* Andrews). Tracts concerning Christianity. Cambridge. 1852. Large 12° (6.)

PALEY (William), *D.D.*, *Archdeacon of Carlisle.* The Works of W. P. ... comprising the Additional Volume of Sermons first published in 1825. With a Memoir of his Life [by G. W. Meadley]. ... 6 vols. (bound in 3). [Vol. I. – V.,] Cambridge. 1830. [Vol. VI.,] Boston. 1827. 8°

Vol. I. Memoir. Natural Theology.
II. Evidences of Christianity. Tracts.
III. Moral and Political Philosophy.
IV. Horæ Paulinæ. The Young Christian instructed. Clergyman's Companion.
V. Sermons on Public Occasions. Sermons on several Subjects. Tracts.
VI. *With the title:* — "Sermons on various Subjects. By William Paley, D.D. Originally published by Rev. Edmund Paley, A. M. in MDCCCXXV. First American Ed."

Note. This set has no title-pages for Vols. IV. and V.

PICTORIAL Dictionary (The) of the Holy Bible, *etc.* *See* [GOODHUGH (W.)].

[TAYLOR (William Cooke)], *LL.D.* *See* [GOODHUGH (W.)]. The Pictorial Dictionary, *etc.*

WARE (*Prof.* Henry), *Jr., D.D.* The Works of H. W., Jr., D. D. [Edited by the Rev. Chandler Robbins.] 4 vols. Boston. 1846–47. 12°

Note. Vols. I. and II. have also the title: — "The Miscellaneous Writings of H. W., Jr., D.D." Vols. III. and IV. have also the title: — "Sermons by H. W., Jr., D. D. Vol. I. | Vol. II. To which are added his Work on the Formation of the Christian Character, and his Sequel to the same, now first published. New Ed." These vols. are dated 1849.

WESTMINSTER ASSEMBLY OF DIVINES. *See* ASSEMBLY, *etc.*

WHEATLY (*Rev.* Charles). A rational Illustration of the Book of Common Prayer of the Church of England: being the Substance of every thing Liturgical in Bishop Sparrow, Mr. L'Estrange, Dr. Comber, Dr. Nichols, and all former ... Commentators ... upon the same Subject. ... London. 1848. 8° (BOHN's Stand. Libr.)

PART IV. VARIOUS RELIGIONS AND SUPERSTITIONS; MYTHOLOGY.

Note. Compare Class XVI. Part I. and Class XXVII.

ANCIENT Rites and Mysteries. (CHAMBERS's Papers, *etc.* X. no. 73.)

CONFUCIUS. (CHAMBERS's Papers, *etc.* X. no. 77.)

DWIGHT (M. A.) Grecian and Roman Mythology. With an Introductory Notice by Prof. Tayler Lewis, and a Series of Illustrations in Outline. New York. 1849. 12°

ESCHENBERG (*Prof.* Johann Joachim). Greek and Roman Mythology. (Part III. of his Manual of Classical Literature. *See* Class XVI. Part I.; also Class XXVII.)

GROTE (George). A History of Greece. I. Legendary Greece, *etc.* *See* Class XXV. Part II. § 2.

HINDOO Superstitions. (CHAMBERS's Miscel., IV. no. 66.)

JEWISH Life in Central Europe. (CHAMBERS's Papers, *etc.* V. no. 39.)

KEIGHTLEY (Thomas). The Fairy Mythology, illustrative of the Romance and Superstition of various Countries ... . A new Ed., revised and greatly enlarged. London. 1850. 8° (BOHN's Antiq. Libr.)

——— The Mythology of Ancient Greece and Italy: for the Use of Schools. ... 1st American Ed., enlarged and improved. New York. 1843. 18°

LAYARD (Austen Henry). Nineveh ... with an Account of a Visit to the Yezidis, or Devil-Worshippers, *etc.* *See* Class XXIII.

MORITZ (*Prof.* Karl Philipp). Mythological Fictions of the Greeks and Romans. Translated from the 5th Ed. in German, with Improvements, by C. F. W. J[aeger]. New-York. 1830. 12°

MUELLER (*Prof.* Karl Otfried). Introduction to a Scientific System of Mythology. By C. O. Müller ... . Translated from the German. By John Leitch. London. 1844. 8°

MYTH (The). (CHAMBERS's Papers, *etc.* I. no. 5.)

RELIGION of the Greeks. (CHAMBERS's Papers, *etc.* VI. no. 47.)

SCOTT (*Sir* Walter), *Bart.* Letters on Demonology and Witchcraft .... New York. 1848. 18° (HARPER's Fam. Libr., **11.**)

SMITH (William), *LL.D.* Dictionary of Greek and Roman Biography and Mythology, *etc.* *See* Class XXIV. Part I.

CLASS III. MORAL PHILOSOPHY.

Note. For the *History* of Moral Philosophy, see Class XXVIII.; for the *History of Morals and Manners*, Class XXVII.

ABERCROMBIE (John), *M.D.* The Philosophy of the Moral Feelings. ... From the last Edinburgh Ed. With Questions .... New-York. 1848. 18° (HARPER's Fam. Libr., **58.**)

ADDISON (Joseph). *See* SPECTATOR. Selections, *etc.*

BACON (Francis), *Baron Verulam, and Viscount St. Albans.* Essays, Moral, Economical, and Political. — The Conduct of the Understanding. By John Locke .... — With an Introductory Essay, by A. Potter, D.D. .... New-York. 1847. 18° (HARPER's Fam. Libr., **171.**)

CHANNING (William Ellery), *D.D.* Address on Temperance. Feb. 28, 1837. (Works, Vol. II. — *See* Class II. Part III.)

——— Slavery. — The Abolitionists, &c. — On the Annexation of Texas to the United States. (Works, Vol. II.) Remarks on the Slavery Question. (*Ibid.* Vol. V.) Emancipation. — The Duty of the Free States, Part I. II. — Address at Lenox, Aug. 1, 1842. (*Ibid.* Vol. VI.)

——— War: a Discourse. 1816. (Works, Vol. III.) War: a Discourse. 1835. (*Ibid.* Vol. IV.) Lecture on War. 1839. (*Ibid.* Vol. V.)

CUDWORTH (Ralph), *D.D.* A Treatise on Immutable Morality. *See* Class II. Part I. CUDWORTH (R.). The true Intellectual System, *etc.*

FOSTER (*Rev.* John). Essays in a Series of Letters. ... The 21st Ed. London. 1848. 16° (8.)

GRAVES (*Mrs.* A. J.). Woman in America; being an Examination into the Moral and Intellectual Condition of American Female Society. ... New-York. 1847. 18° (HARPER's Fam. Libr., **166.**)

HINTS to Workmen. (CHAMBERS's Miscel., X. no. 170.)

JOHNSON (Samuel), *LL.D.* The Life [by Arthur Murphy] and Writings of S. J. .... Selected and arranged by Rev. William P. Page. ... 2 vols. New-York. 1847. 18° (HARPER's Fam. Libr., **109, 110.**)

——— The Rambler. — The Idler. — Twenty-nine Papers in the Adventurer. (Works, 1837. 8° Vol. I.)

LOVE is Power. (CHAMBERS's Miscel., VI. no. 98.)

PALEY (William), *D.D.*, *Archdeacon of Carlisle.* Moral and Political Philosophy. (Works, *etc.* 1830. 8° Vol. III. — *See* Class II. Part III.)

SIGOURNEY (*Mrs.* Lydia HUNTLEY). Letters to Young Ladies. ... 10th Ed., with Revisions and Enlargements. New-York. 1844. 12°

SPECTATOR. Selections from the S.: embracing the most interesting Papers of Addison, Steele, and others. [With Lives of Addison and Steele.] ... 2 vols. New-York. 1840. 18° (HARPER's Fam. Libr., **181, 182.**)

STEELE (*Sir* Richard). *See* SPECTATOR. Selections, *etc.*

STEWART (*Prof.* Dugald). The Philosophy of the Active and Moral Powers of Man. ... Revised, with Omissions and Additions, by James Walker, D.D. ... . Cambridge. 1849. 12°

TEMPERANCE Movement (The). (CHAMBERS's Miscel., II. no. 23.)

WAYLAND (Francis), *D.D.* The Elements of Moral Science. ... 40th Thousand. Boston. 1850. 12°

——— Elements of Moral Science ... . Abridged, and adapted to the Use of Schools and Academies, by the Author. 26th Thousand, revised. Boston. 1849. 18°

WHEWELL (*Prof.* William), *D.D.* The Elements of Morality, including Polity. ... 2 vols. New-York. 1845. 12° or 16° (6. and 8.) (Harper's New Miscel., I. II.)

CLASS IV. POLITICAL AND SOCIAL PHILOSOPHY.

Note. For Political *History*, see Class XXV.; for Political *Antiquities*, Class XXVII.

PART I. GENERAL WORKS ON GOVERNMENT, POLITICS, AND THE CONSTITUTION OF SOCIETY, WITH OTHERS, NOT INCLUDED IN PARTS II. AND III.; INTERNATIONAL AND CONSTITUTIONAL LAW.

BOLINGBROKE, Henry, *Viscount.* *See* ST. JOHN.

CAMBRIDGE, *Mass.* City of C. Address of the Mayor [James D. Green], upon the first Organization of the City Government, May 4, 1846. ... Cambridge. 1846. 8° pp. 16.

——— The Mayor's [James D. Green's] Address at the Organization of the City Government, and Reports of the Committee on Finance, and the School Committee, of the City of Cambridge. ... Cambridge. 1847. 8° pp. 75.

——— City of C. The Mayor's [Sidney Willard's] Address ..., and Reports of the Committee on Finance, and the School Committee. ... Cambridge. 1848. 8° pp. 87.

——— ... The Mayor's [Sidney Willard's] Address ..., and Reports of the Committee on Finance, the Overseers of the Poor, and the School Committee. [1849, 1850.] 2 vols. Cambridge. 1849–50. 8°

Note. "The Overseers of the Poor" rightly appears on the printed cover, though not on the proper title-page of the vol. for 1849.

CAMBRIDGE, *Mass.* ... The Mayor's [George Stevens's] Address ..., and Reports ... [as above]. [1851, 1852.] 2 vols. Cambridge. 1851–52. 8°

——— ... The Mayor's [James D. Green's] Address ..., and Reports ... [as above]. Cambridge. 1853. 8°

CAMP (George Sidney). Democracy. ... New-York. 1845. 18° (HARPER's Fam. Libr., **138.**)

CONSIDERATIONS on some Recent Social Theories. *See* [NORTON (C. E.)].

CONSTITUTIONS (The) of the several States of the Union and United States, including the Declaration of Independence and Articles of Confederation. ... New York: A. S. Barnes & Co. 1853. 8°

DE LOLME (John Lewis), *LL.D.* The Rise and Progress of the English Constitution: the Treatise of J. L. De Lolme, LL.D. with an Historical and Legal Introduction, and Notes, by A. J. Stephens ... . 2 vols. London. 1838. 8°

Note. The two vols. are paged continuously.

DOD, *or* DODD (Charles R.). A Manual of Dignities, Privilege, and Precedence: including Lists of the great Public Functionaries, from the Revolution to the Present Time. ... London. 1843. 16° pp. 683.

DUER (William Alexander), *LL.D.* A Course of Lectures on the Constitutional Jurisprudence of the United States, delivered annually in Columbia College, New-York. ... New-York. [1843?] 18° (HARPER's Fam. Libr., **160.**)

[HALE (Nathan) *and* PICKERING (Octavius)]. Journal of Debates and Proceedings in the Convention of Delegates, chosen to revise the Constitution of Massachusetts, begun and holden at Boston, November 15, 1820, and continued by Adjournment to January 9, 1821. Reported for the Boston Daily Advertiser [by N. H. and O. P.]. New Ed., revised and corrected [by N. H. and Charles Hale]. Boston. 1853. 8° pp. viii., 677.

HART (John S.), *LL.D.* A brief Exposition of the Constitution of the United States. For the Use of Common Schools. ... Philadelphia. 1845. 12°

JUNIUS, *pseudon.* The Letters of J. From the latest London Ed. ... 2 vols. (bound in one). New-York. 1821. 12°

——— J.: including Letters by the same Writer under other Signatures; to which are added his Confidential Correspondence with Mr. Wilkes, and his Private Letters to Mr. H. S. Woodfall; a new and enlarged Ed., with new Evidence as to the Authorship, and an Analysis by the late Sir Harris Nicolas ... . By John Wade ... . Vol. I. containing the entire Work as originally published, with illustrative Notes. | Vol. II. containing the Private and Miscellaneous Letters, and a new Essay on the Authorship. 2 vols. London. 1850. 8° (BOHN's Stand. Libr.)

Note. The title of Vol. II. reads:—"*Extracts from* an Analysis by Sir Harris Nicolas."

LIEBER (*Prof.* Francis), *LL.D.* Essays on Property and Labour as connected with Natural Law and the Constitution of Society. [With an Introduction, by Alonzo Potter, D.D.] New-York. 1847. (HARPER's Fam. Libr., **146.**)

LOLME (Jean Louis DE). *See* DE LOLME.

MACHIAVELLI (Niccolò). The Prince. *See* Class XXV. Part IV. § 1. B. *Italy.*

MANSFIELD (*Prof.* Edward D.). The Political Grammar of the United States; or, A complete View of the Theory and Practice of the General and State Governments .... A new and revised Ed. .... Cincinnati. 1851. 18° (6.)

MASON (Charles). An Elementary Treatise on the Structure and Operations of the National and State Governments of the United States. ... 2d Ed. ... Boston. 1843. 12° (3 copies.)

MASSACHUSETTS. *Constitution. See* Part III. MASSACHUSETTS. The Revised Statutes, *etc.*; — *also*, Supplements, *etc.*

MASSACHUSETTS — *Convention for Revising the Constitution. See* [HALE (N.) *and* PICKERING (O.)]. Journal, *etc.*

MILTON (John). Areopagitica: a Speech for the Liberty of Unlicensed Printing. (Works, 1848. 8° II. 48 – 191.)

——— The Tenure of Kings and Magistrates. (*Ibid.* II. 1 – 47.)

——— A Treatise of Civil Power in Ecclesiastical Causes. (*Ibid.* II. 520 – 548.)

MURRAY's Official Handbook. *See* [REDGRAVE (S.)].

[NORTON (Charles Eliot)]. Considerations on some Recent Social Theories. Boston. 1853. 16°

POLSON (Archer). Law of Nations. (ENCYCL. Metrop., II. 716 – 734.)

[REDGRAVE (Samuel)]. Murray's Official Handbook of Church and State; containing the Names, Duties, and Powers of the principal Civil, Military, Judicial, and Ecclesiastical Authorities of the United Kingdom and Colonies; with Lists of the Members of the Legislature, Peers, Baronets, &c. &c. London: John Murray. 1852. 8°

ST. JOHN (Henry), *Viscount Bolingbroke.* A Dissertation upon Parties. (Works, 1841. 8° II. 5 – 172.)

SOCIAL Theories. *See* [NORTON (C. E.)]. Considerations, *etc.*

STEPHENS (Archibald John). *See* DE LOLME (J. L.). The Rise and Progress, *etc.*

STORY (Joseph), *LL.D.* A Familiar Exposition of the Constitution of the United States ... with an Appendix, containing important Public Documents, illustrative of the Constitution. ... Boston. [1840 ?] 12° (SCHOOL Libr., Vol. XIII.)

UNITED STATES. *Constitution.* *See* CONSTITUTIONS;—DUER (W. A.); —HART (J. S.); —MANSFIELD (E. D.); —MASON (C.); —STORY (J.); —WILLIAMS (E.).

WEBSTER (Daniel). The Works of D. W. [With a Biographical Memoir of his Public Life, by Edward Everett.] 6 vols. Boston. 1851. Large 12° (6.) *Large paper.*

WILLIAMS (Edwin). The Book of the Constitution. Containing the Constitution of the United States; a Synopsis of the several State Constitutions; with various other important Documents .... New York. 1833. 12°

——— The Statesman's Manual. *See* Class XXV. Part IV. § 4. B. *a. United States.*

WORCESTER, *Mass.* Town of W. Report of the Town School Committee. Supplementary Report on paving Main-Street. Report of the Overseers of the Poor. Report and Return of the Fire Department. Submitted at the April Meeting. Worcester. 1847. 8° pp. 20.

——— City Document No. 1. Valedictory Address of Hon. Levi Lincoln, Mayor ...: with the Reports of the Committee on Finance, the City Treasurer, the School Committee, and the Chief Engineer, for the Year ending March 31, 1849. ... Worcester. [1849.] 8° pp. 48.

——— City Document No. 2. Inaugural Address of Hon. Henry Chapin, Mayor ..., April 2, 1849: with the List of City Officers for the Year 1849-50. ... Worcester. [1849.] 8° pp. 12.

——— City Document, No. 3. Inaugural Address of Hon. Henry Chapin, Mayor ..., April 1, 1850, with the Annual Reports of the several City Officers .... Worcester. [1850.] 8° pp. 77.

——— City Document, No. 4. Inaugural Address of Hon. Peter C. Bacon, Mayor ..., April 7, 1851; with the Annual Reports of the several City Officers .... Worcester. [1851.] 8°

——— City Document, No. 5. Rules of the School Committee, and Regulations of the Public Schools of the City of W. Worcester. [1851.] 8° pp. 32.

——— City Document, No. 6. Inaugural Address of Hon. Peter C. Bacon, Mayor ..., January 5, 1852; with the Annual Reports of the several City Officers .... Worcester. [1852.] 8°

——— City Document, No. 7. Inaugural Address of Hon. John S. C. Knowlton, Mayor ..., January 3, 1853: with the Annual Reports of the several City Officers .... Worcester. [1853.] 8°

PART II. POLITICAL ECONOMY, TRADE, FINANCE.

Note. For the *Useful Arts*, see Class XIV. For *Statistics*, see Class XXII.

DWELLINGS and Schools for the Poor. *See* [NORTON (C. E.)].

EMPLOYER (The) and Employed. (CHAMBERS's Miscel., I. no. 4.)

HISTORY of the Slave-Trade. (CHAMBERS's Miscel., I. no. 19.)

INDUSTRIAL Investments and Associations. (CHAMBERS's Papers, *etc.* XI. no. 87.)

LIFE-ASSURANCE: a Familiar Dialogue. (CHAMBERS's Miscel., III. no. 44.)

LOWE (Joseph). Commerce. (ENCYCL. Metrop., VI. 77 – 128.)

McCULLOCH (John Ramsey). A Dictionary, Practical, Theoretical and Historical, of Commerce and Commercial Navigation. ... Edited by Henry Vethake .... 2 vols. Philadelphia. 1845. 8°

——— ... Principles, Practice, and History of Commerce. ... Published under the superintendence of the Society for the Diffusion of Useful Knowledge. London. [1833?] 8° (Libr. of Useful Knowl.)

[NORTON (Charles Eliot)]. Dwellings and Schools for the Poor. From the North American Review for April, 1852. Riverside, Cambridge. 1852. 8° pp. 28.

POTTER (Alonzo), *D.D.*, *Bp. of Pennsylvania.* Political Economy: its Objects, Uses, and Principles: considered with reference to the Condition of the American People. ... New-York. [1841?] 18° (HARPER's Fam. Libr., **183.**)

RAILWAY Communications. (CHAMBERS's Papers, *etc.* XII. no. 89.)

SANITARY Movement (The). (CHAMBERS's Papers, *etc.* II. no. 9.)

SENIOR (*Prof.* Nassau William). Political Economy. (ENCYCL. Metrop., VI. 129 – 224.)

SOCIAL Utopias. (CHAMBERS's Papers, *etc.* III. no. 18.)

SPECULATIVE Manias — the Darien Scheme, the Mississippi Scheme, the South Sea Scheme, the Tulipomania, Modern Manias. (CHAMBERS's Miscel., X. no. 172.)

WATER Supply of Towns. (CHAMBERS's Papers, *etc.* VII. no. 49.)

WAYLAND (Francis), *D.D.* The Elements of Political Economy .... 3d Ed. — improved. Boston. 1840. 12°

PART III. LAW.

Note. For *International* and *Constitutional* Law, see Part I.

CRIMINAL Law. *See* PRINCIPLES.

CUSHING (Luther Stearns). Manual of Parliamentary Practice. — Rules of Proceeding and Debate in Deliberative Assemblies. 2d Ed. Boston. 1845. 18° (6.)

GRAVES (*Prof.* John Thomas). Roman and Canon Law. (ENCYCL. Metrop., II. 735 – 790.)

JEBB (Richard). General Principles of Law. (ENCYCL. Metrop., II. 675 – 715.)

[MAINE]. An Act to provide for the Education of Youth. ... 1850. Augusta. 1851. 12° pp. 52.

[Massachusetts]. An Act to establish the City of Cambridge, approved March 17, 1846. [Boston. 1846.] 8° pp. 20.

——— The Revised Statutes ... passed Nov. 4, 1835; ... to which are prefixed, The Constitutions of the United States and of the Commonwealth of M. Printed and published ... under the supervision and direction of Theron Metcalf and Horace Mann. Boston. 1836. 8° pp. xvi., 1007.

——— Supplements to the Revised Statutes. Laws ... passed subsequently to the Revised Statutes: to which ... [is] prefixed ... The Constitution of the Commonwealth as revised, ... [with] the Amendments: ... and to which are appended, The Apportionment of Senators and Representatives under the last Amendment of the Constitution; [and various] Resolves ... . Edited by Theron Metcalf and ... Luther S. Cushing. Boston. 1844. 8°

——— ... Supplement to the Revised Statutes; being the General Laws of the Commonwealth of M. Session, 1845. Prepared and edited by Luther S. Cushing. To be published annually. Boston. 1845. 8°

——— *The same.* Session, 1846. Boston. 1846. 8°

——— " " " 1847. Boston. 1847. 8°

Note. These Supplements are paged continuously with the volume dated 1844.

Polson (Archer). English Law. (Encycl. Metrop., II. 791 – 856.)

Principles (On the) of Criminal Law. Philadelphia. 1846. 24° (8. 4.) pp. 91. (Small Books, *etc.* III. no. 10.)

Rhode Island. School Laws of R. I. — Acts relating to the Public Schools of R. I., with Remarks and Forms [by Elisha R. Potter]. ... Revised Ed. Providence. Dec. 1846. 8° pp. 79.

CLASS V. EDUCATION.

Note. For the *History* of Education, see Class XXIX.

Abbott (Jacob). The Teacher: or Moral Influences employed in the Instruction and Government of the Young; intended chiefly to assist young Teachers in organizing and conducting their Schools. ... Boston. 1834. 12°

[Alcott (William A.)]. Confessions of a Schoolmaster. *See* Class XXIV. Part II.

——— *Editor.* *See* American Annals of Education, *etc.* Vol. VII. VIII.

American Annals of Education and Instruction, for the Year 1831. Edited by Wm. C. Woodbridge. Vol. I. Being a Continuation of the American Journal of Education, comprising also the Numbers from August to December, 1830. | For the Year 1832 – 1835. Edited by William C. Woodbridge. Vol. II. – V. | For ... 1836. William C. Woodbridge, Editor. Vol. VI. | For ... 1837. Conducted by Wm. A. Alcott. William C. Woodbridge, Foreign Editor. Vol. VII. | American Annals of Education, for the Year 1838. [Vol. VIII.] Edited by William A. Alcott ... . [Aug. 1830 — Dec. 1838. Monthly.] 8 vols. Boston. 1831 – 38. 8°

Note. The title of Vol. I. is different in some copies, reading "for the Year 1831 and a Part of 1830," and omitting all that follows "Vol. I." The nos. of the "Journal" for Aug. — Dec. 1830 were published as the first part (but not so designated) of Vol. I. of the "Annals," by merely altering their titles, headings, paging, and signatures. Part II. of Vol. I. (comprising the nos. for Jan. — Dec. 1831) is paged independently, and was also published with an independent title-page.

——— *See* AMERICAN Journal of Education.

AMERICAN INSTITUTE OF INSTRUCTION. The Lectures delivered before the American Institute of Instruction ... August 1840 — August 1849; including the Journal of Proceedings, and a List of the Officers. Published under the Direction of the Board of Censors. | The Lectures ... Aug. 1850; including ... a General Index to the Volumes thus far published [viz. from 1830 to 1850], and a List of Members, Past and Present. ... 11 vols. Boston. 1841 – 51. 12°

Vol. for 1840. Lecture I. Intellectual Education in Harmony with Moral and Physical. By JOSHUA BATES. — II. On the Results to be aimed at in School Instruction and Discipline. By T. CUSHING, JR. — III. On the Duty of visiting Schools. By THOS. A. GREENE. — IV. On the Objects and Means of School Instruction. By A. B. MUZZEY. — V. On Courtesy, and its Connexion with School Instruction. By G. F. THAYER. — VI. On the Brain and the Stomach. By USHER PARSONS, M.D. — VII. Common Complaints made against Teachers. By JACOB ABBOTT.

1841. — I. On the best Mode of preparing and using Spelling-Books. By HORACE MANN. — II. On the best Method of exercising the different Faculties of the Mind. By WM. B. FOWLE. — III. On the Education of the Laboring Class. By THEODORE PARKER. — IV. On the Importance of the Natural Sciences in our System of Popular Education. By A. GRAY. — V. Moral Culture essential to Intellectual Education. By E. W. ROBINSON. — VI. On Simplicity of Character, as affected by the Common Systems of Education. By J. S. DWIGHT. — VII. On the Use of the Globes in teaching Geography and Astronomy. By A. FLEMING. — VIII. On the Elementary Principles of Constitutional Law, as a Branch of Education in Common Schools. By EDWARD A. LAWRENCE.

1842. — I. On Moral Education. By GEO. B. EMERSON. — II. On Universal Language. By SAMUEL G. HOWE. — III On the Girard College. By E. C. WINES. — IV. The Schoolroom as an Aid to Self-Education. By A. B. MUZZEY. — V. On the Moral Responsibility of Teachers. By WILLIAM H. WOOD. — The Teacher's Daily Preparation. [From the German.]

1843. — I. The Bible in Common Schools. By HEMAN HUMPHREY, D.D. — II. The Classification of Knowledge. By SOLOMON ADAMS. — III The Moral Dignity of the Teacher's Office. By PROF J. H. AGNEW. — IV. A few of the "Hows" of School-Keeping. By ROGER S. HOWARD. — V. Advancement in the Means and Methods of Public Instruction. By DAVID P. PAGE. — VI. On Reading. By CYRUS PEIRCE. — VII. Some of the Duties of the Faithful Teacher. By ALFRED GREENLEAF. — VIII. Some of the Defects of our System of Education. By R. B. HUBBARD. — IX. The Importance of our Common Schools. By S. J. MAY.

1844. — I. The Religious Element in Education. By CALVIN E. STOWE. — II. Female Education. By WILLIAM RUSSELL. — III. On some of the Obstacles to the greater Success of Common Schools. By CHARLES NORTHEND. — IV. Some of the Dangers of Teachers. By DANIEL P. GALLOUP. — V. On the Introduction of Natural History as a regular Classic in our Seminaries. By CHARLES BROOKS. — VI. On Classical Instruction. By A. H. WELD. — VII. On School Discipline. By JOSEPH HALE. — VIII. On Methods of teaching to read. By SAMUEL S. GREENE. — IX. The Duty of the American Teacher. By JOHN N. BELLOWS. — X. The Necessity of Education in a Republican Form of Government. By HORACE MANN.

1845. — I. Dignity of the Teacher's Office. By JOEL HAWES, D.D. —— Address on the Formation and Excellence of the Female Character. By JOEL HAWES. — II. The Duties of Examining Committees. By Prof. E. D. SANBORN. — III. On the Beau Ideal of the Perfect Teacher. By DENISON OLMSTED, LL.D. — IV. On the Necessity of the Study of Physiology. By EDWARD JARVIS, M.D. — V. On Intellectual Arithmetic. By F. A. ADAMS. — — VI. On County Teachers' Institutes. By SALEM TOWN. — VII. On the best Method of teaching Geography. By WM. B. FOWLE. — VIII. On Vocal Music in Common Schools. By A. N. JOHNSON. — IX. On the Connection between Geography and History. By GEORGE S. HILLARD.

1846. — I. Home Preparation for School. By JASON WHITMAN. — II. The Influence of Moral upon Intellectual Improvement. By H. B. HOOKER. — III. The Essentials of a Common School Education, and the Conditions most favorable to their Attainment. By RUFUS PUTNAM. — IV. The Education of the Faculties, and the proper Employment of Young Children. By SAMUEL J. MAY. — V. The Obligation of Towns to elevate the Character of our Common Schools. By LUTHER B. LINCOLN. — VI. Importance of cultivating Taste in Early Life. By ARIEL PARISH. — VII. On Phonotypy and Phonography .... By STEPHEN P. ANDREWS. — VIII. On the Study of the English Language. By D. HUNTINGTON.

1847. — I. On the Study of Language. By HUBBARD WINSLOW. — II. On the Appropriateness of Studies to the State of Mental Development. By THOMAS P. RODMAN.

1848. — I. Failures in Teaching. By JOHN KINGSBURY. — II. The Cooperation of Parents and Teachers. By JACOB BATCHELDER. — III. The Qualifications of the Teacher. By Rev. NATHAN MUNROE. — IV. On School Government. By J. D. PHILBRICK. — V. The Improvement of Common Schools. By WM. D. SWAN.

1849. — I. The Defect of the Principle of Religious Authority in Modern Education. By JOHN H. HOPKINS, D.D. — II. The Education demanded by the peculiar Character of our Civil Institutions. By BENJAMIN LABAREE, D.D. III. Earnestness. By ROGER S. HOWARD. — IV. The Essentials of Education. By THOMAS H. PALMER. — V. The Claims of Natural History as a Branch of Common School Education. By WILLIAM O. AYERS. — VI. Education — the Condition of National Greatness. By PROF. E. D. SANBORN. — VII. The Duties of Legislatures in relation to the Public Schools in the United States. By REV. CHARLES BROOKS. — VIII. Practical Education. By W. C. GOLDTHWAIT.

1850. — I. God's Plan for educating Man. By C. C. CHASE. — II. Political Economy, as a Study for Common Schools. By AMASA WALKER. — III. On the Importance of Early Training. By SOLOMON JENNER. — IV. Characteristics of the True Teacher. By JOHN D. PHILBRICK. — V. The Influence of the Social Relations in the West upon Professional Usefulness and Success. By EDWARD WYMAN.

AMERICAN INSTITUTE OF INSTRUCTION. ... Memorial of the Directors of the American Institute of Instruction [Geo. B. Emerson and six others, praying that provision may be made for the better preparation of teachers]. [Boston. 1837.] 8° pp. 18. (Mass. House Doc., Jan. 1837, No. 12.)

AMERICAN Journal of Education. For the Year 1826 - 1829. Vol. I. - IV. [Jan. 1826 — Nov. and Dec. 1829. Vol. I. - III., monthly; Vol. IV., two-monthly. Edited by William Russell.] 4 vols. Boston. 1826 - 29. 8°

———, for the Year 1830. New Series — Vol. I. [Edited, from Aug. to Dec., by Wm. C. Woodbridge.] Boston. 1830. 8°

Note. The nos. for June and July have the heading "The American Journal of Education *and Monthly Lyceum*," and those for Aug. — Dec. "American Journal, *and Annals* of Education *and Instruction*," to which the titles on their covers corresponded.

——— *See* AMERICAN Annals of Education, *etc.*, with the *Note.*

ANNALS of Education, *American*. *See* AMERICAN, *etc.*

[ASSOCIATION OF MASTERS OF THE BOSTON PUBLIC SCHOOLS]. Remarks on the Seventh Annual Report of the Hon. Horace Mann, Secretary of the Massachusetts Board of Education. [Prepared by a Committee of the "Association," viz. Barnum Field, William A. Shepard, Samuel S. Greene, and Joseph Hale, and signed by thirty-one Masters.] Boston. 1844. 8°

See BOSTON — *Primary School Committee*. Report, *etc.* 1844. 8°; — [EMERSON (G. B.)]. Observations, *etc.*; — MANN (H.). Reply, *etc.*

——— Rejoinder to the "Reply" of the Hon. Horace Mann, Secretary of the Massachusetts Board of Education, to the "Remarks" of the Association of Boston Masters, upon his Seventh Annual Report. [To which are appended, "Rejoinder to the Second Section of the 'Reply,'" by Wm. A. Shepard; "Rejoinder to the Third Section," *etc.*, by S. S. Greene; and "Rejoinder to the Fourth Section," *etc.*, by Joseph Hale.] Boston. 1845. 8° pp. 55, 56, 40, 64.

See MANN (H.). Answer to the "Rejoinder," *etc.*; — [WITHINGTON (L.)]. Penitential Tears, *etc.*

——— Report of a Committee of the Association ... on a Letter from Dr. John Odin, Jr., and in relation to a Report of the Special Committee of the Primary School Board. Boston. 1845. 8° pp. 18.

BARNARD (Henry). Normal Schools, and other Institutions, Agencies, and Means designed for the Professional Education of Teachers. ... Part I. — United States and British Provinces. Part II. — Europe. 2 pts. Hartford. 1851. 8° pp. 222, 435.

——— Reports on the Public Schools of Rhode Island. *See* RHODE ISLAND — *Commissioner of Public Schools.*

——— School Architecture, *etc.* *See* Class XIV. Part IV.

BARNEY (H. H.). Report on the American System of Graded Free Schools, to the [Cincinnati] Board of Trustees and Visitors of Common Schools. ... Printed by Order of the Board. Cincinnati. 1851. 8° pp. 72.

BENEDICT (Erastus Cornelius). An Address delivered at the First Anniversary of the Free Academy of the City of New York July 24 1850 ... . Published by Order of the Board of Education. New York. 1850. 8° pp. 38.

[BISHOP (Nathan)]. First — Second Annual Report of the Superintendent of Public Schools, *etc.* *See* BOSTON — *School Committee.* ... 1851, *etc.* 8°

BOSTON. ... Truants. [Boston. 1853.] 8° pp. 8. (City Doc., No. 21.)

BOSTON — *Primary School Committee.* Report of the Special Committee of the Primary School Board, on a Portion of the Remarks of the Grammar Masters. ... Boston. 1844. 8° pp. 13.

See ASSOCIATION OF MASTERS, *etc.* Report, *etc.* 1845. 8°

——— ... Report to the P. S. C., June 15, 1846, on the Petition of sundry Colored Persons, for the Abolition of the Schools for Colored Children. With the City Solicitor's [Peleg W. Chandler's] Opinion. ... Boston. 1846. 8° pp. 38. (City Doc., No. 23.)

BOSTON — *School Committee.* First — Second Annual Report of the Superintendent of Public Schools [Nathan Bishop], of the City of B. [To the School Committee.] ... 2 vols. Boston. 1851 – 52. 8°

Note. The title of the first vol. reads "First *Semi*-Annual Report," *etc.*

——— ... Normal School. [Report of Le Baron Russell, and two others.] Boston. 1852. 8° pp. 14. (City Doc., No. 40.)

[———] Organization of the Grammar Schools of the City of B. February, 1853. ... Boston. 1853. 8° pp. 18.

——— ... Reports of the Annual Visiting Committees of the Public Schools ..., 1845 – 1847. 3 vols. Boston. 1845 – 47. 8° (City Doc., No. 26, 28, 40.)

Note. The Reports for 1845 — that on the Grammar Schools, signed Theophilus Parsons, S. G. Howe, and Rollin H. Neale, and that on the Writing Schools, signed William Brigham, J. I. T. Coolidge, and Hiram A. Graves — gave rise to a controversy, and mark an era in the history of the Boston Schools. For extracts from them, with remarks by Mr. Mann, see "Common School Journal," VII. 289 – 368.

See [HOWE (M. A. D'Wolf)]. Review, *etc.* ; — HOWE (S. G.). To the Citizens of Boston, *etc.*

——— The Report of the Annual Examination of the Public Schools of the City of B. — 1848 – 1852. 5 vols. Boston. 1848 – 52. 8°

Note. The Reports for 1851 and 1852 form City Documents No. 52 and No. 50, for those years, respectively.

——— Reports ... relating to the Ventilation of the School Houses, *etc.* *See* Class XIV. Part III.

——— ... Rules of the S. C., and Regulations of the Public Schools of the City of B. ... Boston. 1844. 8° pp. 24. (City Doc., No. 27.)

——— ... Rules ... [as above]. ... Boston. 1848. 8° pp. 32. (City Doc., No. 6.)

——— ... Rules ... [as above]. ... Boston. 1853. 8° pp. 59. (City Doc., No. 12.)

——— *See* BOSTON — *Primary School Committee.*

BOSTON — *Superintendent of Public Schools.* *See* BOSTON — *School Committee.* First — Second Annual Report, *etc.*

BOSTON MASTERS, *Association of.* *See* ASSOCIATION, *etc.*

BRIGHTON, *Mass.* — *School Committee.* Thirteenth — Fourteenth Annual Report ... for 1850 - 51 — 1851 - 52. 2 vols. Cambridge. 1851 - 52. 8°

Bristed (Charles Astor). Five Years in an English University [Cambridge]. ... 2 vols. New York. 1852. 12°

Bristol Academy, *Taunton*. *See* Felton (C. C.). An Address, *etc.*

Brougham (Henry), *Baron Brougham and Vaux*. Discourses on the Objects and Uses of Science and Literature. By Henry Lord Brougham, Prof. [Adam] Sedgwick ..., and the Hon. G. C. Verplanck. With Preliminary Observations, &c., on Reading, by A. Potter, D.D. ... . New-York. 1848. 18° (Harper's Fam. Libr. **179.**)

——— Practical Observations on Popular Education. ... From the 20th London Ed. Boston. 1826. 8° pp. 36.

[Burton (*Rev.* Warren)]. The District School as it Was. By One who went to it. Revised Ed. Boston. 1850. 18°

Cambridge, *Mass.* Report of a Committee [James Hayward, and eight others], appointed August 4, 1834, to consider the Subject of a Reorganization of the Public Schools in the Town of Cambridge. [Cambridge. 1834.] 8° pp. 12.

Cambridge, *Mass.* — *School Committee.* Annual Report ... March 15, 1841 — March 6, 1843. [The Rev. Artemas B. Muzzey, Chairman.] | ... March 5, 1844 — March 3, 1846. [The Rev. William A. Stearns, Chairman.] 6 vols. Cambridge. 1841 - 46. 8°

——— Reports for 1847 - 1853. *See* Class V. Part I. Cambridge, *Mass.* ... 1847, *etc.*

——— Regulations for the Public Schools ... adopted ... May 1, 1844. Cambridge. 1844. 12° pp. 10.

——— City of C. Regulations of the Public Schools, adopted ... August 6, 1849. ... Cambridge. 1849. 12° pp. 32.

——— ... Regulations ... adopted ... June 19, 1851. ... Cambridge. 1851. 12° pp. 33.

Carter (James Gordon). Essays upon Popular Education, containing a particular Examination of the Schools of Massachusetts, and an Outline of an Institution for the Education of Teachers. Boston. 1826. 8° pp. 60.

Central Society of Education. The Educator. Prize Essays on the Expediency and Means of elevating the Profession of the Educator in Society. By John Lalor, Esq. J.[ohn] A. Heraud, Esq. Rev. E.[dward] Higginson. J.[ames] Simpson, Esq. Mrs. G. R. Porter. Under the Sanction of the C. S. of E. London. 1839. 12°

——— First Publication. Papers by Thomas Wyse, Esq. M. P. Dr. [David Boswell] Reid, F.R.S. Charles Baker, Esq. B.[enj.] Hawes, Jun. Esq. M.P. A.[ugustus] De Morgan, Esq. Alexander Allen, Esq. William Wittich, Esq. G.[eorge] R.[ichardson] Porter, Esq. Dr. [Arthur] Mower. B. F. Duppa, Esq. Also the Results of the Statistical Inquiries of the Society. London. 1837. 12°

CENTRAL SOCIETY OF EDUCATION. Second Publication. Papers by George Long, Esq. William Wittich, Esq. B. F. Duppa, Esq. A. De Morgan, Esq. William King, Esq. M.D. W. E. Hickson, Esq. Lady [Mildred] Ellis. Thomas Wyse, Esq. M.P. Mrs. G. R. Porter. Alfred Fry, Esq. G. R. Porter, Esq. F.R.S. Mons. [Emanuel] De Fellenberg. Rawson W. Rawson, Esq. Thomas Coates, Esq. Also, the Results of the Statistical Inquiries of the Society. London. 1838. 12°

——— Third Publication. Papers by C. Baker, Esq. B. F. Duppa, Esq. F.[rederick] Liardet, Esq. W.[illiam] S.[mith] O'Brien, Esq. M.P. George Long, Esq. Rev. S. Wood. William Smith, Esq. G. R. Porter, Esq. F.R.S. Thomas Wyse, Esq. M.P. London. 1839. 12°

CHANNING (William Ellery), *D.D.* Self-Culture. (Works, II. 347–411.) — Lectures on the Elevation of the Laboring Portion of the Community. (*Ibid.* V. 149–230.)

CHARLESTOWN, *Mass.* — *Board of Trustees of the Charlestown Free Schools.* Annual Report ... April, 1847. Boston. 1847. 8° pp. 16.

——— *See* CHARLESTOWN, *Mass.* — *School Committee.*

CHARLESTOWN, *Mass.* — *School Committee.* Annual Report .... February, 1848. Charlestown. 1848. Large 12° (6.) pp. 36.

CINCINNATI — *Board of Trustees and Visitors of Common Schools.* Twenty-first Annual Report ... to the City Council of C., for the School Year ending June 30, 1850. Together with ... various Supplementary Documents, exhibiting the Condition and Prospects of the Schools. ... Cincinnati. 1851. 8° pp. 95.

——— *See* BARNEY (H. H.). Report, *etc.* 1851. 8°

COMMON SCHOOL Controversy (The); consisting of Three Letters of the Secretary of the Board of Education, of the State of Massachusetts, [Horace Mann,] in Reply to Charges preferred against the Board, by the Editor of the Christian Witness [M. A. D'Wolf Howe] and by Edward A. Newton ...; [with the articles written by them;] to which are added Extracts from the Daily Press, in regard to the Controversy. Boston. 1844. 8° pp. 55.

COMMON SCHOOL Journal (The). For the Year 1839–1848. Vol. I.–X. Edited by Horace Mann .... 10 vols. Boston. 1839–48. 8°

——— New Series; for the Year 1849–1852. Vol. XI.–XIV. from the Commencement, and Vol. I.–IV. of the New Series. Edited by Wm. B. Fowle .... 4 vols. Boston. 1849–52. 8°

Note. Discontinued.

CONFESSIONS of a Schoolmaster. *See* [ALCOTT (W. A.)].

[CONGREGATIONAL BOARD OF EDUCATION]. Crosby-Hall Lectures on Education. [Delivered and published under the direction of the Board.] London. [1848?] 8°

I. On the Progress and Efficiency of Voluntary Education in England. By EDWARD BAINES, JUN.

II. On the Education of the Working Classes. By the Rev. ALGERNON WELLS.
III. On the Parties responsible for the Education of the People. By RICHARD WINTER HAMILTON, LL.D.
IV. On Normal Schools for the Training of Teachers. By Rev. ANDREW REED.
V. On the Non-Interference of the Government with Popular Education. By EDWARD MIALL.
VI. On the Progress and Efficacy of Voluntary Education, as exemplified in Wales. By the Rev. HENRY RICHARD.
VII. The Educational Position of the People of England, and the Position of Nonconformists in relation to its Advancement. By the Rev. ROBERT AINSLIE.

CONSIDERATIONS and Facts respecting a Public High School in the First School Society of Hartford. [Hartford? 184–?] 8° pp. 16.

CROSBY-HALL Lectures on Education. *See* [CONGREGATIONAL BOARD OF EDUCATION].

DICK (Thomas), *LL.D.* ... On the Improvement of Society by the Diffusion of Knowledge .... New-York. 1840. 18° (HARPER'S Fam. Libr., **59.**)

DISTRICT School (The) as it Was, *etc.* *See* [BURTON (W.)].

DORCHESTER, *Mass.* — *School Committee.* Annual Report .... Presented April, 1853. Boston. 1853. 8° pp. 23.

DWELLINGS and Schools for the Poor. *See* [NORTON (C. E.)].

[E. (G. B.)]. Observations, *etc.* *See* [EMERSON (George Barrell)].

EDGEWORTH (Maria *and* Richard Lovell). Practical Education. ... New-York. 1835. 12°

EDSON (Theodore), *D.D.* An Address, *etc.* *See* Class XXIX.

EDUCATION Movement (The). (CHAMBERS'S Papers, *etc.* V. no. 36.)

EDUCATION of the Citizen. (CHAMBERS'S Papers, *etc.* I. no. 4.)

EDUCATOR (The). *See* CENTRAL SOCIETY OF EDUCATION.

ELIOT (Samuel Atkins). A complete System of Education. A Lecture delivered before the American Academy of Arts and Sciences, January 19, 1853. Boston. 1853. 8° pp. 19.

[EMERSON (George Barrell)]. Observations on a Pamphlet [by the "Association of Masters of the Boston Public Schools"], entitled "Remarks on the Seventh Annual Report of the Hon. Horace Mann, Secretary of the Massachusetts Board of Education." [Signed "G. B. E."] Boston. 1844. 8° pp. 16.

——— ... The Schoolmaster. The Proper Character, Studies, and Duties of the Teacher, with the best Methods for the Government and Instruction of Common Schools, and the Principles on which Schoolhouses should be built, arranged, warmed, and ventilated. *See* POTTER (A.) *and* EMERSON (G. B.). The School, *etc.*

EVERETT (Edward). Importance of Practical Education and Useful Knowledge: being a Selection from his Orations and other Discourses, by E. E. Boston. 1840. 12° (SCHOOL Libr., Vol. XIX.)

FELTON (*Prof.* Cornelius Conway), *LL.D.* An Address delivered at the Dedication of the New Building of Bristol Academy in Taunton,

August 25, 1852, by C. C. F. . . . . With an Appendix, containing an Historical Sketch of the Academy, an Account of the Festival, and a List of the Trustees and Preceptors. Cambridge. 1852. 8° pp. 54.

[Field (Barnum)]. *See* Association of Masters, *etc.*

Fireside Education. (Chambers's Miscel., IX. no. 159.)

Foster (*Rev.* John). An Essay on the Evils of Popular Ignorance. New Ed., revised and enlarged. 15th Thousand. London. 1847. 16° (8.)

[Fowle (William Bentley)]. The Scholiast Schooled. — An Examination of the Review of the Reports of the Annual Visiting Committees of the Public Schools of the City of Boston, for 1845, by "Scholiast" [M. A. D'Wolf Howe]. By a Bostonian. Cambridge. 1846. 8° pp. 65.

——— The Teachers' Institute; or, Familiar Hints to Young Teachers . . . . 2d Ed. Boston. 1847. 12°

——— *Editor.* *See* Common School Journal. New Series, *etc.*

——— *See* Smith (M. H.). The Bible, the Rod, *etc.*

Gloucester, *Mass.* — *School Committee.* Annual Report . . . 1850–51. . . . Gloucester. 1851. 8° pp. 22.

Goldsbury (John). The Black-Board. — Exercises and Illustrations on the Black-Board; furnishing an easy and expeditious Method of giving Instruction. . . . Keene, N. H. 1847. 12°

Graves (*Mrs.* A. J.). Woman in America, *etc.* *See* Class III.

Great Britain — *Privy Council* — *Committee on Education.* Minutes of the Committee of Council on Education. — Correspondence, Tabulated Statements of Grants, etc.; and Reports by her Majesty's Inspectors of Schools. 1848–49–50. Vol. I.–II. Presented to both Houses of Parliament by Command of Her Majesty. 2 vols. London. 1850. 8°

See Shuttleworth (*Sir* J. K.). Public Education, *etc.*

[Greene (Samuel Stillman)]. *See* Association of Masters, *etc.*

[Hale (Joseph)]. *See* Association of Masters, *etc.*

Hall (*Rev.* Baynard R.). Teaching, a Science: the Teacher an Artist. . . . New-York. 1848. 12°

Hall (Samuel Read). The Instructor's Manual: or Lectures on School-Keeping. . . . Revised Ed. Boston. 1852. 18°

Hartford, *Conn.* High School. *See* Considerations and Facts, *etc.*

Hill (Frederic). National Education; its present State and Prospects. [Containing a view of the present state of Education in England, Wales, Scotland, Ireland, America, Prussia, and Spain.] . . . 2 vols. London. 1836. 12°

Hillard (George Stillman). Lecture on Public Instruction in Prussia. Read before the American Institute . . . . Philadelphia. 1836. 18°

Hints to Workmen. (Chambers's Miscel., X. no. 170.)

[HOWE (Mark Antony D'Wolf)], *D.D.* Review of the Reports of the Annual Visiting Committees, of the Public Schools of the City of Boston, 1845. [Signed "Scholiast."] Boston. 1846. 8° pp. 58.

See [FOWLE (W. B.)]. The Scholiast Schooled, *etc.*

[———] *See* COMMON SCHOOL Controversy, *etc.*

[HOWE (Samuel Gridley)], *M.D.* To the Citizens of Boston: The undersigned, authors of the Reports upon the Grammar and Writing Departments of the City Schools, for 1845, ... ask your attention ... . [Signed S. G. Howe, William Brigham, and J. I. T. Coolidge. March 31, 1846. With a brief statement by R. H. Neale, and a separate address by Theophilus Parsons.] [Boston. 1846.] 8° pp. 12. *No title-page.*

JOHNSON (Lorenzo D.). Memoria Technica: or the Art of abbreviating those Studies which give the greatest Labor to the Memory ... . To which is added, A Perpetual Almanac for Two Thousand Years of Past Time and Time to come. Adapted to the Use of Schools. ... 3d Ed., revised and improved. Boston. 1847. 8° (4.)

JOURNAL of Education, *American.* *See* AMERICAN, *etc.*

LAWRENCE, *Mass.* — *School Committee.* Fourth Annual Report ... for the Year 1850 - 51. Lawrence. 1851. 8° pp. 28.

LETTERS to a Young Student, *etc.* *See* [SMITH (A. D.)].

LOWELL — *School Committee.* The Thirteenth — Twenty-seventh Annual Report, being for the Year ending March 31, 1839 — the Year ending December 31, 1852. 15 vols. Lowell. 1839 - 53. 8°

LOWELL (*Mrs.* Anna Cabot [JACKSON]). Thoughts on the Education of Girls. Boston. 1853. 18°

LYNN — *School Committee.* Annual Report ... for the Year ending March, 1850. Lynn. 1850. 8° pp. 34.

LYON (William P.). Teachers' and Parents' Manual of Education: being a Plan for a uniform Course of Study for Schools and Academies ... with a Division of the Hours of the Day, and an appropriate Duty assigned to each. ... With a Synopsis of the College Course of Study in many [eleven] of our most respectable Colleges. ... New York. 1848. 18°

MAINE. An Act to provide for the Education of Youth. *See* Class IV. Part III.

MAINE — *Board of Education.* Fifth Report ... . [With the Fifth Annual Report of the Secretary of the Board, E. M. Thurston.] 1851. ... Augusta. 1851. 12°

MANAGEMENT of Infants. (CHAMBERS's Miscel., I. no. 6.)

[MANN (Horace)], *LL.D.* First — Twelfth Annual Report of the Secretary of the Board of Education. *See* MASSACHUSETTS — *Board of Education.*

See ASSOCIATION OF MASTERS, *etc.* Remarks on the Seventh Annual Report, *etc.*

[MANN (Horace)], *LL.D.* Reply to the "Remarks" of Thirty-one Boston Schoolmasters on the Seventh Annual Report of the Secretary of the Massachusetts Board of Education. ... Boston. 1844. 8°

See ASSOCIATION OF MASTERS, *etc.* Rejoinder, *etc.*

——— Answer to the "Rejoinder" of "Twenty-nine" Boston Schoolmasters, Part of the "Thirty-one" who published "Remarks" on the Seventh Annual Report of the Secretary of the Massachusetts Board of Education. ... Boston. 1845. 8°

——— Correspondence with M. H. Smith. *See* SMITH (M. H.). The Bible, the Rod, *etc.*

——— Sequel to the so called Correspondence between the Rev. M. H. Smith and Horace Mann, surreptitiously published by Mr. Smith; containing a Letter from Mr. Mann, suppressed by Mr. Smith, with the Reply therein promised. Boston. 1847. 8° pp. 56.

——— Letter to the Rev. Matthew Hale Smith, in Answer to his "Reply," or "Supplement." Boston. 1847. 8° pp. 22.

——— Lectures on Education. ... Boston. 1845. 12°

[———] The Massachusetts System of Common Schools; being an enlarged and revised Edition of the Tenth Annual Report of the First Secretary of the Massachusetts Board of Education. Boston. 1849. 8°

——— *Editor.* *See* COMMON SCHOOL Journal, *etc.*

[———] *See* COMMON SCHOOL Controversy, *etc.* 1844. 8°

MANSFIELD (*Prof.* Edward D.). American Education, its Principles and Elements. ... New York. 1851. 8°

MASSACHUSETTS. ... Report of the Committee on Education [by A. H. Everett], on so much of the Governor's Message as relates to the School Fund. [With an Outline of the Prussian System of Education.] [Boston. 1835.] 8° pp. 31. (House Doc., March, 1835, No. 54.)

——— ... Report by Committee on Education [James G. Carter, Chairman], relative to the Education of Children employed in Manufacturing Establishments. [Boston. 1836.] 8° pp. 14. (House Doc., March, 1836, No. 49.)

MASSACHUSETTS — *Board of Education.* ... First — Twelfth Annual Report of the B. of E., together with the First — Twelfth Annual Report of the Secretary of the Board [Horace Mann]. | Thirteenth — Sixteenth Annual Report ... together with the Thirteenth — Sixteenth Report of the Secretary of the Board [Barnas Sears]. 16 vols. Boston. 1838-53. 8°

Note. The First Report forms Senate Doc. No. 26, dated Feb. 1838; the Third Report, House Doc. No. 21, dated Jan. 1840; the Sixteenth, House Doc. No. 1. — Appended to Reports 10-16 are Statistical Tables of the School Returns, etc. The first Ten Reports will also be found in the "Common School Journal," Vol. I.-IX.

——— Report of the Secretary of the B. of E. [Horace Mann], on the Subject of School Houses, Supplementary to his First Annual Report. Boston. 1838. 8° pp. 64.

——— *See* COMMON School Controversy, *etc.*; — [MANN (H.)]. The Massachusetts System, *etc.*

MASSACHUSETTS — *State Normal School at West Newton*, formerly at *Lexington*. General Catalogue of the ... School .... July, 1850. Boston. 1850. 8° pp. 28.

MASSACHUSETTS TEACHERS' ASSOCIATION. The Massachusetts Teacher. Edited by a Committee of the M. T. A. Vol. I.–V. [Jan. 1848–Dec. 1852. — Monthly.] 5 vols. Boston. 1848–52. 8°

——— Transactions of the M. T. A. Edited by the Secretary [Charles J. Capen], under the Direction of the Committee of Publication. Vol. I. — 1845–1847. Boston. 1852. 12°

Containing *Lectures*, I. On the Claims of Teaching to the Rank of a distinct Profession. By ELBRIDGE SMITH. II. On the First Principles of School Government. By Rev. J. P. COWLES. III. On the Management of the School-Room. By ARIEL PARISH. IV. On Thorough Instruction. By JOSEPH HALE. V. On the Relation of Education to its Age. By SAMUEL W. BATES. VI. On the Relation of Common Schools to Higher Seminaries. By Rev. CHARLES HAMMOND. VII. On Teaching as a Profession. By NELSON WHEELER.

MAYHEW (Ira). Popular Education: for the Use of Parents and Teachers, and for Young Persons of both Sexes. ... Published in accordance with a Resolution of the Senate and House of Representatives of the State of Michigan. ... 2d Ed. New York. 1852. 12°

MECHANICS' Institutions. (CHAMBERS's Papers, *etc.* III. no. 23.)

MILTON (John). On Education. (Works, 1848. 8° III. 462–478.)

NECKER, *or* NECKER DE SAUSSURE (Albertine Andrienne [?] DE SAUSSURE), *Madame*. On Moral and Religious Education. *See* PHELPS (*Mrs.* A. H. L.). The Fireside Friend, *etc.*

Note. Quérard gives the name "Andrienne"; the Biographie Universelle has "Adrienne."

NEWTON (Edward A.). *See* COMMON SCHOOL Controversy, *etc.*

NEW YORK (*City of*) — *Board of Education.* The Fourth Annual Report of the B. of E. of the City and County of N. Y., of the Operations and Conditions of the Free Academy, in said City, January 1, 1853. New York. 1853. 8°

NEW YORK (*City of*) — *Free Academy.* Catalogue .... September, 1851. New York. 1851. 8° pp. 27.

——— *See* BENEDICT (E. C.). An Address, *etc.* 1850. 8°; — NEW YORK (*City of*) — *Board of Education.*

NORMAL School. *See* MASSACHUSETTS — *State Normal School.*

NORTHEND (Charles). The Teacher and the Parent; a Treatise upon Common-School Education; containing practical Suggestions to Teachers and Parents .... Boston. 1853. 12°

[NORTON (Charles Eliot)]. Dwellings and Schools for the Poor. *See* Class IV. Part II.

OHIO Journal (The) of Education. *See* OHIO STATE TEACHERS' ASSOCIATION.

OHIO STATE TEACHERS' ASSOCIATION. The Ohio Journal of Education.

Published monthly, under the Auspices of the O. S. T. A. Editors: A. D. Lord, Columbus. H. H. Barney, Cincinnati. J. C. Zachos, Dayton. M. F. Cowdery, Sandusky. I. W. Andrews, Marietta. Andrew Freese, Cleveland. Volume I. — [Jan. – Dec.] 1852. Columbus. 1852. 8°

PAGE (David P.). Theory and Practice of Teaching: or, The Motives and Methods of good School-Keeping. ... Syracuse. 1847. 12°

PALMER (Thomas H.). Prize Essay. — The Teacher's Manual: being an Exposition of an efficient and economical System of Education, suited to the Wants of a Free People. ... (COMMON SCHOOL Journal, II. 265, *et seqq.*)

PARSONS (*Prof.* Theophilus), *LL.D.* *See* HOWE (S. G.). To the Citizens of Boston, *etc.*

PENITENTIAL Tears. *See* [WITHINGTON (L.)].

PENNSYLVANIA — *Controllers of the Public Schools of the First School District of P., comprising the City and County of Philadelphia.* Twenty-ninth Annual Report ... for the Year ending June 30, 1847: with their Accounts. Philadelphia. 1847. 8°

PHELPS (*Mrs.* Almira HART LINCOLN). The Fireside Friend, or Female Student: being Advice to Young Ladies on the important Subject of Education. With an Appendix on Moral and Religious Education, from the French of Madame [Necker] de Saussure. ... Boston. 1840. 12° (SCHOOL Libr., Vol. XVIII.)

PHILADELPHIA — *Controllers of the Public Schools.* *See* PENNSYLVANIA — *Controllers*, etc.

POTTER (Alonzo), *D.D.*, *Bp. of Pennsylvania.* Observations on Reading. — Note on the Pleasures and Advantages of Literature and Moral Science. *See* BROUGHAM (H.). Discourses, *etc.*

POTTER (Alonzo), *D.D.*, *Bp.*, *and* EMERSON (George Barrell). The School and the Schoolmaster. A Manual for the Use of Teachers, Employers, Trustees, Inspectors, &c., &c., of Common Schools. In Two Parts. Part I. [The School: its Objects, Relations, and Uses.] By A. P. ... . Part II. [The Schoolmaster.] By G. B. E. Boston. 1843. 12°

Note. Each Part has also a distinct title-page. See that of Part II. under EMERSON (G. B.).

PURSUIT of Knowledge under Difficulties, *etc.* *See* Class XXIV. Part I.

PYCROFT (James). A Course of English Reading, *etc.* *See* Class XXIX.

RHODE ISLAND. School Laws. *See* Class IV. Part III.

RHODE ISLAND — *Commissioner of Public Schools.* Report and Documents relating to the Public Schools of R. I., for 1848. By Henry Barnard, Commissioner ... . Published by Order of the General Assembly. Providence. 1849. 8°

Note. The Report, of but two pages, is followed by the "Journal of the Rhode Island Institute of Instruction, for 1848. ... Vol. III.," which constitutes the "Documents" referred to. — Mr. Barnard's earlier Reports are contained in the preceding vols. of this Journal. To Vol. III. is prefixed an Index to the whole work.

RHODE ISLAND INSTITUTE OF INSTRUCTION. Journal .... For 1845-6 — 1847. Edited by Henry Barnard, Commissioner of Public Schools. Vol. I.-II. [Nov. 15, 1845 — Dec. 25, 1847. — Irregular.] 2 vols. Providence. 1846-47. 8°

Vol. III. *See* RHODE ISLAND — *Commissioner of Public Schools.* Report, *etc.* 1849. 8° *Note.*

ROXBURY, *Mass.* — *School Committee.* ... The Annual Report .... 1848. ... Roxbury. 1848. 8° pp. 45. (City Doc., No. 10.)

——— ... Report of the Examination of the Public Schools ... for the Year 1849-1851. ... 3 vols. Roxbury. 1849-51. 8° (City Doc., No. 6, 8, 12.)

——— ... Report ... for the Year 1853. ... Roxbury. 1853. 8° pp. 30. (City Doc., No. 7.)

[RUSSELL (William)]. *Editor. See* AMERICAN Journal of Education.

SALEM, *Mass.* — *School Committee.* Annual Report ... for the Municipal Year, 1845-6. Salem. 1846. 8°

——— Annual Report .... February ..... 1848 — February ..... 1853. 6 vols. Salem. 1848-53. 8°

——— Regulations for the Superintendence, Government, and Instruction of the Public Schools in the City of Salem. Adopted, 1847. Salem. 1847. 8° pp. 29.

SAUSSURE (Albertine Andrienne [?] DE), afterwards *Madame* NECKER. *See* NECKER.

SCHMIDT (*Prof.* H. I.), *D.D.* Education. ... Part II. A Plan of Culture and Instruction, based on Christian Principles, *etc. See* Class XXIX.

SCHOLIAST, *pseudon. See* [HOWE (Mark Antony D'Wolf)].

SCHOLIAST (The) Schooled. *See* [FOWLE (W. B.)].

SCHOOLMASTER (The). *See* SOCIETY FOR THE DIFFUSION OF USEFUL KNOWLEDGE.

SCHOOLS of Industry. (CHAMBERS'S Miscel., VII. no. 125.)

[SEARS (Barnas)], *D.D.* Thirteenth — Sixteenth Annual Report of the Secretary of the Board of Education. *See* MASSACHUSETTS — *Board of Education.*

SEDGWICK (*Prof.* Adam). Discourse on Classical, Metaphysical, Moral, and Natural Studies. *See* BROUGHAM (H.). Discourses, *etc.*

[SHEPARD (William A.)]. *See* ASSOCIATION OF MASTERS, *etc.*

SHUTTLEWORTH (*Sir* James Kay), *Bart.* Public Education as affected by the Minutes of the Committee of Privy Council from 1846 to 1852; with Suggestions as to future Policy. London. 1853. 8°

See GREAT BRITAIN — *Privy Council* — *Committee on Education.*

SILJESTRÖM (P. A.). The Educational Institutions of the United States, their Character and Organization. Translated from the Swedish of P. A. S. ... by Frederica Rowan. London. 1853. 12°

[SMITH (Asa D.)], *D.D.* Letters to a Young Student in the First Stage of a Liberal Education. Boston. 1832. 18°

SMITH (*Rev.* Matthew Hale). The Bible, the Rod, and Religion, in Common Schools. — The Ark of God on a New Cart: a Sermon, by Rev. M. Hale Smith. — A Review of the Sermon, by Wm. B. Fowle. ... . — Strictures on the Sectarian Character of the Common School Journal, by a member of the Mass. Board of Education. [A deceptive title given by Mr. Smith to some remarks by the Rev. Heman Humphrey, D.D.] — Correspondence between the Hon. Horace Mann, Sec. of the Board of Education, and Rev. Matthew Hale Smith. Boston. 1847. Large 12° (6.) pp. 59.

See MANN (H.). Sequel to the so called Correspondence, *etc.*

SOCIETY FOR THE DIFFUSION OF USEFUL KNOWLEDGE. ... The Schoolmaster: Essays on Practical Education, selected from the Works of Ascham, Milton, Locke, and Butler; from the Quarterly Journal of Education; and from Lectures delivered before the American Institute of Instruction. ... 2 vols. London. 1836. 12°

Vol. I. Analytical Account of ASCHAM's "Schoolmaster," with a Biographical Notice of Roger Ascham, and WOLSEY's Letter to the Masters of Ipswich School. — Of Education. By JOHN MILTON. — Analysis of "Some Thoughts concerning Education." By JOHN LOCKE. — Bishop BUTLER's Sermon on Charity Schools. — Introductory Discourse, delivered before the Amer. Inst. of Instruction. By FRANCIS WAYLAND. — Of Moral Education. By J. DE SAINTEVILLE. — Early Education. By MRS. BARWELL. — On the Importance of Physical Education. By J. C. WARREN, M. D. — On the Discipline of Large Boarding Schools. By G. LONG.

Vol. II. On teaching Reading. By CHARLES BAKER. — On the Spelling of Words, and a Rational Method of teaching their Meaning. By G. F. THAYER. — On Teaching by Pictures. By G. LONG. — On teaching Arithmetic. By A. DE MORGAN. — On the Method of teaching Fractional Arithmetic. By A. DE M. — On the Method of teaching the Elements of Geometry. By A. DE M. — On Mathematical Instruction. By A. DE M. — On Geographical and Statistical Knowledge. By A. VIEUSSEUX. — On the Study of Natural Philosophy. By A. DE MORGAN.

STOW (David). The Training System of Education, for the Moral and Intellectual Elevation of Youth, especially in Large Towns and Manufacturing Villages. ... 7th Ed., enlarged. Edinburgh. 1847. 16° (8.)

STOWE (*Prof.* Calvin Ellis), *D.D.* Report on Elementary Public Instruction in Europe, made to the Thirty-sixth General Assembly of the State of Ohio, Dec. 19, 1837. Reprinted by Order of the House of Representatives of the Legislature of Massachusetts, March 29, 1838. Boston. 1838. 8° pp. 68. (House Doc. No. 64.)

TAPPAN (Henry S.), *D. D.* University Education. New York. 1851. 12°

TAYLOR (John Orville). The District School. ... New-York. 1834. 12°

[THURSTON (Elisha Madison)]. Fifth Annual Report, *etc.* *See* MAINE — *Board of Education.* Fifth Report, *etc.*

TODD (*Rev.* John). The Student's Manual: designed, by specific Directions, to aid in forming and strengthening the Intellectual and Moral Character and Habits of the Student. ... 13th Ed. Northampton. 1845. 16°

VERPLANCK (Gulian Crommelin). On the Importance of Scientific Knowledge to the Manufacturer and Practical Mechanic. — The Influence of Moral Causes on Opinion, Science and Literature. *See* BROUGHAM (H.). Discourses, *etc.*

WAYLAND (Francis), *D.D.* Thoughts on the present Collegiate System in the United States. Boston. 1842. 16°

WEST NEWTON, *State Normal School at.* *See* MASSACHUSETTS — *State Normal School*, etc.

WINES (E. C.). How shall I govern my School? Addressed to Young Teachers; and also adapted to assist Parents in Family Government. ... Philadelphia. 1838. 12°

[WITHINGTON (*Rev.* Leonard)]. Penitential Tears; or a Cry from the Dust, by "the Thirty-one," prostrated and pulverized by the Hand of Horace Mann, Secretary, &c. ... Boston. 1845. 8° pp. 59.

WOBURN, *Mass.* — *School Committee.* Annual Report ... . Presented ... April 7, 1845. Woburn. 1845. 8° pp. 16.

——— Annual Report ... for the School Year 1850 – '51 — 1852 – 3. ... 3 vols. Woburn. 1851 – 53. 8°

WOODBRIDGE (William Channing). *Editor.* *See* AMERICAN Annals of Education, *etc.* Vol. I. – VII.; — AMERICAN Journal of Education ... . New Series, *etc.*

WORCESTER, *Mass.* ... Rules of the School Committee, and Regulations of the Public Schools of the City of W. ... Worcester. [1851.] 8° pp. 32. (City Doc., No. 5.)

WORCESTER, *Mass.* — *School Committee.* Report ... for the Year 1843. [By Wm. N. Green.] Worcester. [1844.] 8° pp. 12.

——— Report ... for ... 1844. [By Samuel F. Haven.] Worcester. 1845. 8° pp. 13.

——— Report ... submitted at the annual April Meeting, 1846. [By Geo. P. Smith, and Fred. W. Gale.] Worcester. 1846. 8° pp. 12.

——— Town of Worcester. Report of the Town School Committee. [By Warren Lazell. — Submitted, April, 1847.] ... *See* Class IV. Part I. WORCESTER, *Mass.*

——— Report ... for the School Year ending April, 1848. [By Samuel F. Haven.] Worcester. 1848. 8° pp. 19.

——— *See* Class IV. Part I. WORCESTER, *Mass.* City Document No. 1 – 7.

MATHEMATICAL SCIENCE.

(Classes VI. — IX.)

CLASS VI. GENERAL WORKS ON MATHEMATICS.

Note. For the *History* of Mathematics, see Class XXVIII.

Comte (Auguste). The Philosophy of Mathematics; translated from the Cours de Philosophie Positive of A. C., by W. M. Gillespie .... New York. 1851. 8°

Davies (*Prof.* Charles), *LL.D.* The Logic and Utility of Mathematics, with the best Methods of Instruction explained and illustrated. New York. 1850. 8°

Davies (*Prof.* Thomas Stephens). Solutions of the principal Questions of Dr. Hutton's Course of Mathematics: forming a general Key to that Work .... London. 1840. 8°

Francœur (*Prof.* Louis Benjamin). A complete Course of Pure Mathematics. Translated from the French by R. Blakelock .... 2 vols. Cambridge [Eng.]. 1830. 8°

Hickie (James). A Key to Rutherford's Edition of Hutton's Course of Mathematics, as adapted to the Course of Instruction now pursued in the Royal Military Academy, Woolwich .... London. 1849. 8°

Hutton (*Prof.* Charles), *LL.D.* A Course of Mathematics. ... Composed for the Use of the Royal Military Academy. ... Continued and amended by Olinthus Gregory, LL.D. .... 12th Ed., with considerable Alterations and Additions, by Thomas Stephens Davies .... 2 vols. London. 1841-43. 8°

See Davies (T. S.). Solutions, *etc.*

——— A Course of Mathematics, composed for the Use of the Royal Military Academy. ... A new and carefully corrected Ed., entirely re-modelled .... By William Rutherford .... London. 1846. 8° pp. vii., 895.

See Hickie (J.) A Key, *etc.*

Rutherford (William). *See* Hutton (C.). A Course, *etc.* 1846. 8°

CLASS VII. ARITHMETIC.

Adams (Daniel), *M.D.* Adams's New Arithmetic — revised Ed. — Arithmetic, in which the Principles of operating by Numbers are analytically explained and synthetically applied. ... Keene, N. H. [1848?] 12°

Adams (Frederic Augustus). Arithmetic, in Two Parts. Part First, Advanced Lessons in Mental Arithmetic. Part Second, Rules and

Examples for Practice in Written Arithmetic. ... 3d Ed., corrected and enlarged. Lowell. 1847. 12°

——— *The same.* 11th Thousand. Lowell. 1848. 12°

BARTRUM (Joseph Plura). Arithmetic in the Ancient Order, fully, yet familiarly, demonstrated ... . Prepared for Superior Schools ... . Boston. 1837. 12°

CHASE (Pliny Earle). The Common-School Arithmetic, designed ... particularly for those who are desirous of acquiring a thorough Knowledge of Practical Mathematics. ... Worcester, Mass. 1848. 12° (3 copies, one dated 1850.)

——— Key to the Common-School Arithmetic. ... Worcester, Mass. [1848?] 12° pp. 31.

See STONE (A. P.). A Key, *etc.*

——— The Elements of Arithmetic ... . In which Decimal and Integral Arithmetic are combined, and taught inductively, on the System of Pestalozzi. Part Second. Philadelphia. 1847. 12° (2 copies, one dated 1848.)

——— *See* MANN (H.) *and* CHASE (P. E.). Arithmetic, *etc.*

COLBURN (Dana P.). The Decimal System of Numbers; illustrated and practically applied, by a Series of Systematic and Progressive Exercises. ... Boston. 1852. 12°

COLBURN (Warren). Colburn's First Lessons.—Intellectual Arithmetic, upon the Inductive Method of Instruction. [With Part II., the Key.] ... New Ed., revised and improved. Boston. N. D. 18°

——— Arithmetic upon the Inductive Method of Instruction: being a Sequel to Intellectual Arithmetic. ... Stereotyped at ... Boston ... . Philadelphia. 1830. 12°

DAVIES (*Prof.* Charles), *LL.D.* Grammar of Arithmetic; or, An Analysis of the Language of Figures and Science of Numbers. ... New York. 1850. 18°

——— The University Arithmetic ... . New York. 1847. 12°

DE MORGAN (*Prof.* Augustus). An Essay on Probabilities, and on their Application to Life Contingencies and Insurance Offices. London. 8° (LARDNER's Cab. Cycl., **110.**)

DODD (*Prof.* James B.). High School Arithmetic; containing the Elementary and the Higher Principles and Applications of the Science, with the most useful Abbreviated Methods of Calculation; Practical Mensuration; and Appendices on Exchange, and Mathematical Probabilities; with Applications of the latter to Life Annuities and Life Insurance. ... New-York. 1852. 16°

EMERSON (Frederick). Emerson's Third Part.—The North American Arithmetic. Part Third, for Advanced Scholars. ... Boston. 1845. 12°

——— *The same.* New Ed.—enlarged. Boston. 1853. 12°

——— Key to the North American Arithmetic, Part Second and Part Third. ... Boston. 1845. 12° pp. 72.

Greenleaf (Benjamin). A Key to the Introduction to the National Arithmetic .... Boston. 1845. 12°

——— The National Arithmetic, on the Inductive System; combining the Analytic and Synthetic Methods, together with the Cancelling System; forming a complete Mercantile Arithmetic. ... New stereotype Ed., revised, enlarged, and much improved. Boston. 1847. 12°

——— *The same.* [With an Appendix on Weights and Measures.] Boston. 1853. 12°

——— A Key to the National Arithmetic .... Boston. 1853. 12°

Haddon (James). Rudimentary Arithmetic. ... London: John Weale. 1849. 12°

Hill (*Rev.* Thomas). An Elementary Treatise on Arithmetic, designed as an Introduction to Peirce's Course of Pure Mathematics, and as a Sequel to the Arithmetics used in the High Schools of New England. Boston. 1845. 12° pp. vi., 85. +

Lacroix (*Prof.* Silvestre François). An Elementary Treatise on Arithmetic, taken principally from the Arithmetic of S. F. Lacroix, and translated into English with ... Alterations and Additions [by Prof. John Farrar] .... Cambridge, N. E. 1818. 8°

Lardner (Dionysius), *LL.D.* A Treatise on Arithmetic, Theoretical and Practical. London. 8° (Lardner's Cab. Cycl., **100.**)

Leach (Daniel) *and* Swan (Robert). An Elementary Intellectual Arithmetic, containing numerous original Contractions in Multiplication. Boston. 1853. 16°

Leach (Daniel) *and* Swan (William D.). A Theoretical and Practical Arithmetic; designed for Common Schools and Academies. Philadelphia. 1851. 12° or 8° (6. and 8.)

Mann (Horace), *LL.D. and* Chase (Pliny Earle). Arithmetic, practically applied, for Advanced Pupils, and for Private Reference, designed as a Sequel to any of the ordinary Text-Books on the Subject. Philadelphia. 1850. 16° (8.)

Morgan (*Prof.* Augustus de). *See* De Morgan.

Peacock (George), *D.D.* Arithmetic. (Encycl. Metrop., I. 369–524.)

Perkins (George R.). Higher Arithmetic ...; in which some entirely New Principles are developed, and many Concise and Easy Rules given, which have never before appeared in any Arithmetic: with an Appendix. Stereotyped Ed., revised and improved. Hartford. 1849. 12°

Robinson (James). ... The American Arithmetic .... Boston. 1847. 12°

Russell (James S.). The Rational Arithmetic .... To which is appended, A Key .... Lowell. 1846. 12°

Stone (A. P.). A Key to Chase's Common School Arithmetic, with Explanations and Remarks .... Worcester. 1853. 12° pp. 96.

THOMSON (James Bates). Day and Thomson's Series. — Higher Arithmetic ; or the Science and Application of Numbers ; combining the Analytic and Synthetic Modes of Instruction. ... New York. 1848. 12°

Vogdes (William). The First Part of the United States Arithmetic. ... Philadelphia. 1847. 12°

——— The United States Arithmetic. ... Philadelphia. 1847. 12°

——— Key to the United States Arithmetic. ... Philadelphia. 1847. 12° pp. 48.

WALSH (Michael). The Mercantile Arithmetic, adapted to the Commerce of the United States ... : with an Appendix, containing Practical Systems of Mensuration, Gauging, and Book-Keeping. A new Ed., stereotyped, revised, and enlarged. Boston. 1831. 12°

Note. The Parts relating to Mensuration, etc., and to Book-Keeping, have each a distinct title-page.

CLASS VIII. ALGEBRA ; THE HIGHER CALCULUS.

ALSOP (Samuel). An Elementary Treatise on Algebra .... Philadelphia. 1847. 12° (2 copies.)

——— Key to an Elementary Treatise on Algebra. Philadelphia. 1847. 12°

BAILEY (Ebenezer). First Lessons in Algebra .... 18th improved stereotype Ed. Boston. 1843. 12°

——— A Key to the First Lessons in Algebra .... Boston. 1844. 12° pp. 84.

BARLOW (*Prof.* Peter). Theory of Numbers. (ENCYCL. Metrop., I. 641 - 671.)

BÉZOUT (Etienne). First Principles of the Differential and Integral Calculus ... taken chiefly from the Mathematics of B., and translated from the French for the Use of the Students of the University at Cambridge, New England. 2d Ed. Boston. 1836. 8°

BOURDON (*Prof.* Louis Pierre Marie). Elements of Algebra : translated from the French of M. Bourdon [by Lieut. Edward C. Ross]. Revised and ... [abridged] by Charles Davies, LL.D. ... Revised Ed. Philadelphia. 1843. 8°

CLARK (*Rev.* Davis W.). Elements of Algebra : embracing also the Theory and Application of Logarithms ; together with an Appendix, containing Infinite Series, the general Theory of Equations, and the most approved Methods of resolving the Higher Equations. ... New-York. 1843. 8°

COLBURN (Warren). An Introduction to Algebra, upon the Inductive Method of Instruction. ... Boston. 1844. 12°

DAVIES (*Prof.* Charles), *LL.D.* A Key, containing the Statements and Solutions of Questions in Davies' Elementary Algebra .... New York. 1846. 12° pp. 99.

DAVIES (*Prof.* Charles), *LL.D.* *See* BOURDON (L. P. M.). Elements, *etc.*

DAY (Jeremiah), *LL.D.* An Introduction to Algebra, being the First Part of a Course of Mathematics, adapted to the Method of Instruction in the American Colleges. ... 45th Ed. New Haven. 1842. 8°

——— *The same.* 47th Ed. New Haven. 1843. 8°

——— *The same.* 62d Ed. New Haven. 1848. 8°

——— *The same.* A new Ed. With Additions and Alterations by the Author, and Professor [Anthony D.] Stanley of Yale College. New Haven. 1852. 12°

——— A Key to Day's Algebra. New Haven. 1853. 12°

DE MORGAN (*Prof.* Augustus). Calculus of Functions. (ENCYCL. Metrop., II. 305 – 392.)

——— An Essay on Probabilities, *etc.* *See* Class VII.

——— Theory of Probabilities. (ENCYCL. Metrop., II. 393 – 490.)

DOCHARTY (*Prof.* Gerardus Beekman), *LL.D.* The Institutes of Algebra. Being the First Part of a Course of Mathematics, ... for the Use of Schools ... and Colleges. ... New York. 1852. 12°

GREENLEAF (Benjamin). A Practical Treatise on Algebra, designed for the Use of Students in High Schools and Academies. Boston. 1852. 12°

——— *The same.* Improved stereotype Ed. Boston. 1853. 12°

HACKLEY (*Prof.* Charles W.), *D.D.* School Algebra; containing the latest Improvements. ... New York. 1847. 8°

——— A Treatise on Algebra, containing the latest Improvements. Adapted to the Use of Schools and Colleges. ... New York. 1846. 8°

HADDON (James). Elements of Algebra. ... London: John Weale. 1850. 12°

HALL (*Prof.* Thomas Grainger). Calculus of Variations (ENCYCL. Metrop., II. 209 – 226), and of Finite Differences (*Ibid.* pp. 227 – 304).

LARDNER (Dionysius), *LL.D.* Algebra. (ENCYCL. Metrop., I. 524 – 631.)

LEVY (*Prof.* Arnaud). Differential and Integral Calculus. (ENCYCL. Metrop., I. 771 – 843, and II. 1 – 208.)

LOOMIS (*Prof.* Elias). A Treatise on Algebra. ... New York. 1846. 8°

MORGAN (*Prof.* Augustus DE). *See* DE MORGAN.

MOSELEY (*Prof.* Henry). Definite Integrals. (ENCYCL. Metrop., II. 491 – 544.)

PEIRCE (*Prof.* Benjamin), *LL.D.* An Elementary Treatise on Algebra: to which are added Exponential Equations and Logarithms. ... 6th Ed. Boston. 1851. 12°

——— An Elementary Treatise on Curves, Functions, and Forces. Volume First; containing Analytic Geometry and the Differential Calculus. ... New Ed. | Volume Second; containing Calculus of Imaginary Quantities, Residual Calculus, and Integral Calculus. ...

2 vols. [Vol. I.,] Boston and Cambridge. 1852. [Vol. II.,] Boston. 1846. 12°

PERKINS (George R.). The Elements of Algebra, designed for the Use of Common Schools .... Utica. 1848. 12°

——— A Treatise on Algebra, embracing ... all the Higher Parts usually taught in Colleges ; containing, moreover, the New Method of Cubic and Higher Equations, as well as the Development and Application of the more recently discovered Theorem of Sturm. ... Utica. 1842. 8°

——— *The same.* 2d Ed., revised, enlarged, and improved. Utica. 1847. 8°

ROBINSON (Horatio N.). An Elementary Treatise on Algebra. ... 5th Ed. Cincinnati. 1852. 12° (8. 4.)

——— University Ed. — A Theoretical and Practical Treatise on Algebra ; in which the Excellencies of the Demonstrative Methods of the French, are combined with the more Practical Operations of the English ; and Concise Solutions pointed out and particularly inculcated. ... 15th Ed. Cincinnati. 1852. 8° or 12° (8. 4. and 6.)

SHERWIN (Thomas). The Common School Algebra. ... Boston. 1847. 12°

——— An Elementary Treatise on Algebra, for the Use of Students in High Schools and Colleges. ... 3d Ed. Boston. 1849. 12°

——— *The same.* 5th Ed. Boston. 1850. 12°

——— A Key to the Elementary Treatise on Algebra. ... Boston. 1846. 12° pp. 56. (2 copies, one dated 1848.)

SMITH (*Prof.* Francis H.). An Elementary Treatise on Algebra : prepared for the Use of the Cadets of the Virginia Military Institute .... Philadelphia. 1850. 12°

SMYTH (*Prof.* William). Elements of Algebra .... 4th Ed. Brunswick. 1843. 12°

——— A Treatise on Algebra, for the Use of Schools and Colleges. ... Portland. 1852. 8° or 12° (8. and 6.)

WILLIAMS (John D.). An Elementary Treatise on Algebra .... With attempts to simplify ... particularly the Solution of Cubic Equations and of the Higher Orders. ... To which is added an Appendix, on the Application of Algebra to Geometry. ... Boston. 1840. 8° or 12° (8. and 6.) pp. v., 605. +

YOUNG (*Prof.* John Radford). An Elementary Treatise on Algebra ... with attempts to simplify ... particularly the Demonstration of the Binomial Theorem ... ; the Solution of Equations of the Higher Orders ; the Summation of Infinite Series, &c. ... 1st American Ed., with Additions and Improvements : by Samuel Ward, Junior. Philadelphia. 1832. 8°

CLASS IX. GEOMETRY AND TRIGONOMETRY; PRACTICAL MATHEMATICS, PARTICULARLY SURVEYING AND NAVIGATION.

Note. For *Mechanics* and *Astronomy*, see Class XI. Parts II. and III.

AINSLIE (John). A Treatise on Land Surveying. A new and enlarged Ed., embracing Railway, Military, Marine, and Geodetical Surveying, by Wm. Galbraith. Edinburgh and London. 1849. 8° and Plates, 4°

AIRY (*Prof.* George Biddell). Trigonometry. (ENCYCL. Metrop., I. 672 – 708.)

BARLOW (*Prof.* Peter). Geometry. (ENCYCL. Metrop., I. 304 – 368.)

BIOT (Jean Baptiste). An Elementary Treatise on Analytical Geometry: translated from the French of J. B. B., for the Use of the Cadets of the Virginia Military Institute .... By Francis H. Smith .... New-York & London. 1840. 8°

CROSBY (*Prof.* Alpheus). First Lessons in Geometry, upon the Model of Colburn's First Lessons in Arithmetic. ... With an Introduction, by Stephen Chase .... Boston. 1847. 16° or 12° (8. and 6.)

DAVIES (*Prof.* Charles), *LL.D.* Elements of Analytical Geometry .... 2d Ed. Revised and corrected. Hartford. 1839. 12° (6.)

——— Elements of Descriptive Geometry, with their Application to Spherical Trigonometry, Spherical Projections, and Warped Surfaces. ... New York. 1847. 8°

——— Elements of Surveying, and Navigation; with a Description of the Instruments and the necessary Tables. ... Revised Ed. New York. 1850. 8°

DAVIES (*Prof.* Thomas Stephens). Original Researches in Spherical Geometry. *See* YOUNG (J. R.). Elements, *etc.*

EUCLIDES. ... Elements of Geometry: containing the First Six Books of Euclid, with a Supplement on the Quadrature of the Circle, and the Geometry of Solids: to which are added, Elements of Plane and Spherical Trigonometry. By John Playfair .... From the last London Ed., enlarged. New York. 1847. 8°

FARRAR (*Prof.* John). An Elementary Treatise on the Application of Trigonometry to Orthographic and Stereographic Projection, Dialling, Mensuration of Heights and Distances, Navigation, Nautical Astronomy, Surveying and Levelling; together with Logarithmic and other Tables; designed for the Use of the Students of the University at Cambridge, New England. ... 2d Ed. Boston. 1828. 8°

GUMMERE (John). A Treatise on Surveying ...: to which is prefixed a ... System of Plane Trigonometry. ... 14th Ed., carefully revised, and enlarged .... Philadelphia. 1846. 8° (2 copies.)

HACKLEY (*Prof.* Charles W.), *D.D.* Elementary Course of Geometry. ... New York. 1847. 12°

——— A Treatise on Trigonometry, Plane and Spherical, with its

Application to Navigation and Surveying, Nautical and Practical Astronomy and Geodesy, with Logarithmic, Trigonometrical and Nautical Tables. ... 3d Ed. New York. 1852. 8° pp. xix., 372, 238.

HAMILTON (*Rev.* Henry Parr). Analytical Geometry. (ENCYCL. Metrop., I. 709 – 735.)

——— Conic Sections. (ENCYCL. Metrop., I. 736 – 770.)

HANN (James). The Elements of Plane Trigonometry. ... London: John Weale. 1849. 12°

INTRODUCTION (An) to Geometry, *etc.* *See* [LOWELL (*Mrs.* A. C. [J.])].

INTRODUCTION (An) to the present Practice of Surveying and Levelling .... By a Civil Engineer of many Years' Experience in the Profession. London. 1846. 8°

LARDNER (Dionysius), *LL.D.* Geometrical Analysis. (ENCYCL. Metrop., I. 632 – 640.)

——— A Treatise on Geometry, and its Application to the Arts. London. 8° (LARDNER's Cab. Cycl., **101.**)

LEGENDRE (Adrien Marie). ... Elements of Geometry .... Translated from the French, for the Use of the Students of the University at Cambridge, New England, by John Farrar .... New Ed., improved and enlarged. Boston. 1838. 8°

——— Elements of Geometry and Trigonometry. Translated from the French of A. M. L., by David Brewster, LL.D. Revised ... by Charles Davies .... New York. 1848. 8° (3 copies, one dated 1850.)

——— Elements of Geometry and Trigonometry, from the Works of A. M. L. Revised and adapted to the Course of Mathematical Instruction in the United States, by Charles Davies, LL.D. .... New-York. 1852. 8° (3 copies.)

Note. Essentially different from the preceding.

——— *See* THOMSON (J. B.) Elements of Geometry, *etc.*

LOOMIS (*Prof.* Elias). Elements of Geometry and Conic Sections. ... New York. 1847. 8°

[LOWELL (*Mrs.* Anna Cabot [JACKSON])]. An Introduction to Geometry and the Science of Form. Prepared from the most approved Prussian Text-Books. Boston. 1843. 12°

[———]. *The same.* Stereotype Ed., carefully revised. Boston. 1846. 12°

MATHEMATICAL Tables: Difference of Latitude and Departure: Logarithms, from 1 to 10,000; and Artificial Sines, Tangents, and Secants. Stereotype Ed. .... Philadelphia. 1846. 8° (Appended to GUMMERE's Surveying.)

NAVIGATION. *See* [WROTTESLEY (J.)].

NESBIT (Anthony). A Treatise on Practical Mensuration, in Ten Parts .... 13th Ed., enlarged, and greatly improved. ... London. 1845. 12°

PEIRCE (*Prof.* Benjamin), *LL.D.* An Elementary Treatise on Curves, Functions, and Forces. Volume First; containing Analytic Geometry, *etc.* *See* Class VIII.

——— An Elementary Treatise on Plane and Solid Geometry. ... Stereotype Ed. Boston. 1847. 12° (2 copies, one dated 1851.)

——— An Elementary Treatise on Plane & Spherical Trigonometry, with their Applications to Navigation, Surveying, Heights and Distances, and Spherical Astronomy, and particularly adapted to explaining the Construction of Bowditch's Navigator, and the Nautical Almanac. ... 3d Ed., with Additions. Boston. 1845. 12°

——— *The same.* New Ed., revised, with Additions. Boston and Cambridge. 1852. Large 12° (6.)

PERKINS (George R.). Elements of Geometry, with Practical Applications. ... Hartford. 1849. 12°

PLAYFAIR (*Prof.* John). *See* EUCLIDES. ... Elements of Geometry, *etc.* 1847. 8°

ROBINSON (Horatio N.). Elements of Geometry, Plane and Spherical Trigonometry, and Conic Sections. ... 4th Ed. Cincinnati. 1851. 8° or 12° (8. and 8. 4.)

——— A Treatise on Surveying and Navigation: uniting the Theoretical, the Practical, and the Educational Features of these Subjects. ... Cincinnati. 1852. 12° (8. 4.)

SCRIBNER (J. M.). Scribner's Engineers' and Mechanics' Companion, *etc.* *See* Class XIV. Part III.

SIMMS (Frederick W.). A Treatise on the principal Mathematical Instruments employed in Surveying, Levelling, & Astronomy: explaining their Construction, Adjustments and Use. ... 2d American Ed., from the 2d (improved and enlarged) London Ed. Revised, and with Additions, by J. H. Alexander. Baltimore. [1844?] 8°

STANLEY (*Prof.* Anthony Dumond). Tables of Logarithms of Numbers, and of Logarithmic Lines, Tangents, and Secants, to Seven Places of Decimals; together with other Tables of frequent Use in the Study of Mathematics, and in Practical Calculations. ... New Haven. 1847. 8°

THOMSON (James Bates). Elements of Geometry: on the Basis of Dr. Brewster's Legendre. To which is added a Book on Proportion; with Notes and Illustrations ... . New Haven. 1844. 12°

VOGDES (William). An Elementary Treatise on Mensuration and Practical Geometry; together with numerous Problems of Practical Importance in Mechanics. ... Philadelphia. 1847. 12°

WHITLOCK (*Prof.* George Clinton). Elements of Geometry, Theoretical and Practical: containing a full Explanation of the Construction and Use of Tables, and a New System of Surveying. ... New York. 1849. 8°

WILSON (*Rev.* Richard). A System of Plane and Spherical Trigonometry; to which is added a Treatise on Logarithms. ... Cambridge [Eng.]. 1831. 8°

[WROTTESLEY (John)], *Baron.* Navigation. [London. 1828.] 8° pp. 33. (LIBR. of Useful Knowl., Nat. Phil., III.)

Young (*Prof.* John Radford). Elements of Plane and Spherical Trigonometry, with its Applications to ... Navigation and Nautical Astronomy; with the Logarithmic and Trigonometrical Tables. By J. R. Young .... To which are added some original Researches in Spherical Geometry; by T. S. Davies .... Revised and corrected by J. D. Williams .... A new Ed. Philadelphia. 1848. 8°

——— Mathematical Tables; comprehending the Logarithms of all Numbers from 1 to 36,000; also the Natural and Logarithmic Sines and Tangents; computed to Seven Places of Decimals ....; with several other Tables .... Revised and corrected by J. D. Williams .... Philadelphia. 1848. 8° (Appended to Young's Trigonometry.)

PHYSICAL SCIENCE.

(Classes X. — XIII.)

CLASS X. GENERAL WORKS ON THE PHYSICAL SCIENCES.

Note. For the *History* of the Physical Sciences, see Class XXVIII.

Annual of Scientific Discovery, *etc.* *See* Class XXVIII.

Chambers (William *and* Robert). ... Treasury of Knowledge. In Three Parts. I. Elementary Lessons in Common Things. II. Practical Lessons on Common Objects. III. Introduction to the Sciences. Edited by D. M. Reese, M. D. .... New-York. 1853. 12° (Chambers's Educational Course, No. 1.)

Duncan (Henry), *D.D.* Sacred Philosophy of the Seasons. *See* Class II. Part I.

[Goodrich (Samuel Griswold)]. A Glance at the Physical Sciences; or the Wonders of Nature, in Earth, Air, and Sky: by the Author of Peter Parley's Tales. Boston. 1849. 16° or 18° (8. and 6.) (Cabinet Libr., **13.**)

Hunt (Robert). The Poetry of Science, or Studies of the Physical Phenomena of Nature. ... London. 1848. 8°

Lardner (Dionysius), *LL.D.* Popular Lectures on Science and Art, *etc.* *See* Class XI. Part I.

Library of Useful Knowledge. *See* [Society for the Diffusion of Useful Knowledge].

Parley (Peter), *pseudon.* *See* [Goodrich (Samuel Griswold)].

Scientific Tracts, designed for Instruction and Entertainment, and adapted to Schools, Lyceums, and Families. Conducted by Jerome V. C. Smith, M.D. Volume III. [Semi-monthly.] Boston. 1833. 12°

Continued under the title :—

SCIENTIFIC Tracts and Family Lyceum. ... Conducted by Jerome V. C. Smith, M.D. Vol. I.... New Series. | Vol. IV.—New Series. 2 vols. Boston. 1834-35. 16°

SMITH (Jerome Van Crowninshield), *M.D. Editor. See* SCIENTIFIC Tracts, *etc.*

[SOCIETY FOR THE DIFFUSION OF USEFUL KNOWLEDGE]. *Library of Useful Knowledge.* Natural Philosophy.

I. Objects, Advantages, and Pleasures of Science. [By Henry, Lord Brougham.] Mechanics. [Three treatises, by Dionysius Lardner, LL.D.] Hydrostatics. [By Lord Brougham.] Hydraulics. [By Prof. John (?) Millington.] Pneumatics. [By Dr. Lardner.] Heat. [By Mr. Ogg.] Optics. [By Sir David Brewster.] Double Refraction and Polarisation of Light. [By the same.] With an Explanation of Scientific Terms, and an Index. [By David Booth.]

II. Popular Introductions to Natural Philosophy. [By Mrs. Jane Marcet.] Newton's Optics. [By Dr. Lardner.] Description of Optical Instruments. [By Andrew Pritchard.] The Thermometer and Pyrometer. [By Prof. Thomas Stewart Traill, M.D.] Electricity. [By Peter Mark Roget, M.D.] Galvanism. [By the same.] Magnetism. [By the same.] Electro-Magnetism. [By the same.] With an Explanation of Scientific Terms, and an Index. [By David Booth.]

III. Astronomy. [By Sir Benjamin Heath Malkin.] History of Astronomy. [By Richard Wellesley Rothman.] Mathematical Geography. [By Edward Lloyd.] Physical Geography [by H. J. Lloyd], and Navigation [by John, Lord Wrottesley]. With an Explanation of Scientific Terms, and an Index. [By David Booth.]

IV. Chemistry. [By Prof. John Frederic Daniell.] Botany. [By Prof. John Lindley.] Animal Physiology. [By Thomas Southwood Smith, M.D.] Animal Mechanics. [By Sir Charles Bell.] With an Analytical Index. ...

4 vols. London. 1829-32-34-38. 8°

Note. The several treatises in these volumes are paged independently, and were at first published separately.

SOMERVILLE (Mary). On the Connection of the Physical Sciences. From the 7th London Ed. New York. 1846. 12° or 16° (6. and 8.) (Harper's New Miscel., XIV.)

YOUNG (*Prof.* Thomas), *M.D.* A Course of Lectures on Natural Philosophy, *etc. See* Class XI. Part I.

CLASS XI. NATURAL PHILOSOPHY.

PART I. GENERAL WORKS.

BIRD (Golding). Elements of Natural Philosophy; being an Experimental Introduction to the Study of the Physical Sciences. ... With Three Hundred and Seventy-two Illustrations. From the revised and enlarged 3d London Ed. Philadelphia. 1848. 12°

BREWSTER (*Sir* David), *LL.D.* Letters on Natural Magic .... New York. N. D. 18° (HARPER'S Fam. Libr., **50.**)

CHAMBERS (William *and* Robert). ... Elements of Natural Philosophy. In Three Parts. I. Laws of Matter and Motion. II. Mechanics. III. Hydrostatics, Hydraulics, and Pneumatics. Edited by D. M. Reese, M.D. .... New-York. 1849. 12° (Chambers's Educational Course, No. 3.)

COMSTOCK (John L.), *M.D.* A System of Natural Philosophy .... Designed for the Use of Schools and Academies. ... Stereotyped from the 53d Ed. New-York. 1843. 12°

——— *The same.* [A new stereotype Ed., copyrighted 1844.] New-York. 1845. 12°

DRAPER (*Prof.* John William), *M.D.* A Text-Book on Natural Philosophy. For the Use of Schools and Colleges. ... With nearly Four Hundred Illustrations. 3d Ed. New York. 1849. 12°

EULER (Leonhard). Letters of Euler on different Subjects in Natural Philosophy, addressed to a German Princess. [Translated by Henry Hunter, D.D.] With Notes, and a Life of Euler, by David Brewster .... Containing a Glossary .... With additional Notes, by John Griscom .... 2 vols. New York. [1834?] 18° (HARPER'S Fam. Libr., **55, 56.**)

GRAY (Alonzo). Elements of Natural Philosophy. Designed as a Text-Book for Academies, High-Schools, and Colleges. ... Illustrated by Three Hundred and Sixty Wood-Cuts. New York. 1850. 12°

GRUND (Francis J.) Elements of Natural Philosophy, with Questions for Review; ... for the Use of Schools. ... 7th Ed., stereotyped. Boston. 1841. 12°

HERSCHEL (*Sir* John Frederick William), *Bart.* A Preliminary Discourse on the Study of Natural Philosophy. London. 8° (LARDNER'S Cab. Cycl., **98.**)

HIGGINS (W. Mullinger). The Experimental Philosopher. ... London. 1838. 8°

HUNT (Robert). Elementary Physics, an Introduction to the Study of Natural Philosophy. ... London. 1851. 16° (8.)

JOHNSON (*Prof.* Walter Rogers). A System of Natural Philosophy, designed for the Use of Schools and Academies, on the Basis of the Book of Science by Mr. J. M. Moffat. ... 8th Ed. Philadelphia. 1846. 12° (2 copies, one dated 1847.)

JOHNSTON (*Prof.* John), *LL.D.* A Manual of Natural Philosophy ... designed for Use as a Text-Book in High Schools and Academies. Philadelphia. 1848. 12°

——— *The same.* A new and revised Ed., illustrated with Three Hundred and Twenty Engravings. Philadelphia. 1852. 12°

JOYCE (*Rev.* Jeremiah). Scientific Dialogues for the Instruction & Entertainment of Young People; in which the First Principles of Natural and Experimental Philosophy are fully explained & illustrated. A new and enlarged Ed., with Questions ... and other Additions, by William Pinnock .... London. 1846. 8°

Lardner (Dionysius), *LL.D.* Hand-Books of Natural Philosophy and Astronomy. . . . First Course. Mechanics — Hydrostatics — Hydraulics — Pneumatics — Sound — Optics. Illustrated by upwards of Four Hundred Engravings on Wood. Philadelphia. 1851. 12° pp. 749.

Note. This vol. is also divided into three Parts, with independent title-pages and paging; — I. Mechanics. II. Hydrostatics, Hydraulics, Pneumatics, and Sound. III. Optics.

——— *The same.* Second Course. Heat — Magnetism — Common Electricity — Voltaic Electricity. Illustrated by upwards of Two Hundred Engravings on Wood. Philadelphia. 1853. 12°

——— Popular Lectures on Science and Art, delivered in the principal Cities and Towns of the United States . . . . 2 vols. New York. 1846. 8°

Library of Useful Knowledge. *See* Society for the Diffusion, *etc.*

List (C.). Outlines of Natural Philosophy. ... Philadelphia. 1846. 18°

[Marcet (*Mrs.* Jane [Haldimand])]. Popular Introductions to Natural Philosophy. [London. 183–?] 8° pp. c. (Libr. of Useful Knowl., Nat. Phil., II.)

Moffatt (John M.). The Book of Science. *See* Johnson (W. R.). A System, *etc.*

Mueller (Johann), *Prof. of Physics in the Univ. of Freiburg.* Principles of Physics and Meteorology. ... [Translated by E. C. Otté.] 1st American Ed., revised and illustrated with 538 Engravings on Wood, and Two colored Plates. Philadelphia. 1848. 8° pp. xii., 25 – 635.

Note. Complete.

Natural Magic. (Chambers's Miscel., V. no. 82.)

Olmsted (*Prof.* Denison), *LL.D.* A Compendium of Natural Philosophy ... To which is now added A Supplement containing Instructions to young Experimenters, with a copious List of Experiments, accompanied by minute Directions for performing them. ... Stereotype Ed. New Haven. 1847. 12°

Note. The Supplement has a distinct title-page, dated 1844.

——— An Introduction to Natural Philosophy; designed as a Text Book, for the Use of the Students in Yale College. ... Vol. I. — Mechanics and Hydrostatics. ... | Vol. II. — Pneumatics, Acoustics, Electricity, Magnetism, and Optics. ... 4th Ed. 2 vols. New York. 1840. 8°

Note. Appended to Vol. II. are "Outlines of Professor Olmsted's Lectures on Meteorology," pp. 1 – 12.

Parker (Richard Green). A School Compendium of Natural and Experimental Philosophy . . . . With a Description of the Steam and Locomotive Engines. ... 18th Ed., with Additions and Improvements. New York. 1848. 12°

Phelps (*Mrs.* Almira Hart Lincoln). Natural Philosophy, for Schools . . . . New Ed., revised and corrected. New York. 1846. 12°

POPULAR Introductions to Natural Philosophy. *See* [MARCET (*Mrs.* J. [H.])].

POWELL (*Prof.* Baden). The History of Natural Philosophy. *See* Class XXVIII.

ROBINSON (Horatio N.). Elements of Natural Philosophy, with some of their Results and Applications. ... 4th Ed. Cincinnati. 1851. 12° or 8° (6. and 8.)

SOCIETY FOR THE DIFFUSION OF USEFUL KNOWLEDGE. *Library of Useful Knowledge.* Natural Philosophy. *See* Class X.

TOMLINSON (Charles). Introduction to the Study of Natural Philosophy .... London: John Weale. 1848. 12°

YOUNG (*Prof.* Thomas), *M.D.* A Course of Lectures on Natural Philosophy and the Mechanical Arts. ... A new Ed., with References and Notes, by the Rev. P. Kelland .... Illustrated by numerous Engravings on Copper. ... Volume I. — Text. | Volume II. — Plates. 2 vols. London. 1845. 8°

Note. Copious and valuable bibliographical references are appended to each Lecture. — Two of the Lectures treat of Vegetation and Animal Life.

PART II. MECHANICS; OR, LAWS OF MOTION AND EQUILIBRIUM; INCLUDING HYDROSTATICS, PNEUMATICS, ETC.

BARLOW (*Prof.* Peter). Mechanics. (ENCYCL. Metrop., III. 1 – 160.) Hydrodynamics. (*Ibid.*, pp. 161 – 296.) Pneumatics. (*Ibid.*, pp. 297 – 392.)

[BROUGHAM (Henry)], *Baron Brougham and Vaux.* Hydrostatics. [London. 182–.] 8° pp. 32. (LIBR. of Useful Knowl., Nat. Phil., I.)

CHAMBERLAIN (Nathan B. *and* Daniel). A Catalogue of Pneumatic Instruments manufactured and sold by N. B. & D. C.; with Experiments illustrated by numerous Engravings and Notes. Boston. 1844. 8° pp. 56.

Note. To this is appended "Hydrostatic and Hydraulic Apparatus," pp. 1 – 7, with only a head-title.

——— A Price Catalogue of Pneumatic Apparatus manufactured and sold by N. B. & D. C. .... Boston. 1844. 8° pp. xiv. (Bound with the preceding.)

EWBANK (Thomas). A Descriptive and Historical Account of Hydraulic and other Machines for raising Water, *etc.* *See* Class XXVIII.

HYDRAULICS. *See* [MILLINGTON (J. ?)].

HYDROSTATICS. *See* [BROUGHAM (H.)].

JAMIESON (Alexander), *LL.D.* Mechanics for Practical Men. ... Treatises on the Composition and Resolution of Forces; the Centre of Gravity; and the Mechanical Powers. Illustrated by Examples and Diagrams. ... 4th Ed. London. 1845. 8°

JAMIESON (Alexander), *LL.D.* Mechanics of Fluids for Practical Men, comprising Hydrostatics, Descriptive and Constructive: the whole illustrated by numerous Examples and appropriate Diagrams. ... London. 1837. 8°

KATER (*Capt.* Henry) *and* LARDNER (Dionysius), *LL.D.* A Treatise on Mechanics. London. 8° (LARDNER'S Cab. Cycl., **102.**)

[LARDNER (Dionysius)], *LL.D.* Mechanics. [Three Treatises, paged independently: — I. On Mechanical Agents, or Prime Movers. II. Elements of Machinery. III. Friction, and Rigidity of Cordage. — London. 182–.] 8° pp. 32, 64, 32. (LIBR. of Useful Knowl., Nat. Phil., I.)

[———] Pneumatics. [London. 182–.] 8° pp. 32. (LIBR. of Useful Knowl., Nat. Phil., I.)

——— A Rudimentary Treatise on the Steam Engine: for the Use of Beginners. ... London: John Weale. 1848. 12° (2 copies.)

——— The Steam Engine explained and illustrated; with an Account of its Invention and Progressive Improvement, and its Application to Navigation and Railways; including also a Memoir of Watt. ... 7th Ed., illustrated by Engravings on Wood. London. N. D. 8°

——— A Treatise on Hydrostatics and Pneumatics. London. 8° (LARDNER'S Cab. Cycl., **103.**)

——— *See* KATER (H.) *and* LARDNER (D.).

MECHANICS. *See* [LARDNER (D.)].

[MILLINGTON (*Prof.* John ?)]. Hydraulics. [London. 182–.] 8° pp. 32. (LIBR. of Useful Knowl., Nat. Phil., I.)

MOSELEY (*Prof.* Henry). Illustrations of Mechanics. ... Revised by James Renwick, LL.D. ... . New-York. 1844. 18° (HARPER'S Fam. Libr., **180.**)

PNEUMATICS. *See* [LARDNER (D.)].

TOMLINSON (Charles). Pneumatics; for the Use of Beginners. London: John Weale. 1848. 12°

——— Rudimentary Mechanics ... . London: John Weale. 1849. 12°

WEISBACH (*Prof.* Julius). Principles of the Mechanics of Machinery and Engineering. ... [Translated by Prof. L. Gordon.] 1st American Ed. Edited by Walter R. Johnson ... . Illustrated with One Thousand Engravings on Wood. Vol. I. Theoretical Mechanics. | ... Vol. II. Applied Mechanics. 2 vols. Philadelphia. 1848–49. Large 12° (6.)

Note. The title of Vol. II. reads "... *Eight Hundred and Thirteen* Engravings," etc. The actual number is eight hundred and sixty-five.

YOUNG (*Prof.* John Radford). The Elements of Mechanics, comprehending Statics and Dynamics, with a copious Collection of Mechanical Problems. With Plates. ... London. 1832. 12°

PART III. ASTRONOMY AND MATHEMATICAL GEOGRAPHY.

AIRY (*Prof.* George Biddell). Figure of the Earth. (ENCYCL. Metrop., V. 165 – *240.) Tides and Waves. (*Ibid.* pp. 241* – 396.*)

AMERICAN Almanac. *See* Class XXII. Part I.

ARAGO (*Prof.* Dominique François Jean). Popular Lectures on Astronomy; delivered at the Royal Observatory of Paris .... With extensive Additions and Corrections, by Dionysius Lardner, LL.D. .... New-York. 1845. 8° pp. 96. (Bound with LARDNER'S "Popular Lectures," *etc.* 1846. 8° Vol. I.)

Note. This work is based on an imperfect report of Arago's Lectures, published without the sanction of the author.

ASTRONOMY. *See* [MALKIN (*Sir* B. H.)].

BARLOW (*Prof.* Peter). Astronomy. (ENCYCL. Metrop., III. 485 – 606.)

BRADFORD (Duncan). The Wonders of the Heavens, being a Popular View of Astronomy .... Illustrated by numerous Maps and Engravings. ... Boston. 1837. 4°

COFFIN (James H.). Solar and Lunar Eclipses familiarly illustrated and explained, with the Method of calculating them according to the Theory of Astronomy, as taught in New England Colleges. ... New York. 1845. 8° pp. 83. +

Note. Thirty-one Astronomical Tables are appended, without paging.

COMPENDIUM (A) of Astronomy ... intended to accompany a Series of Diagrams ... exhibited by the improved Phantasmagoria Lantern. [London. N. D.] 18°? pp. 24.

DICK (Thomas), *LL.D.* Celestial Scenery; or, The Wonders of the Planetary System displayed. Illustrating the Perfections of Deity and a Plurality of Worlds. ... New-York. N. D. 18° (HARPER'S Fam. Libr., **83.**)

——— The Practical Astronomer, comprising ... a particular Account of the Earl of Rosse's large Telescopes .... Illustrated with One Hundred Engravings. New-York. 1846. 12° or 16° (6. and 8.) (Harper's New Miscel., V.)

——— The Sidereal Heavens and other Subjects connected with Astronomy, as illustrative of the Character of the Deity, and of an Infinity of Worlds. ... New-York. N. D. 18° (HARPER'S Fam. Libr., **99.**)

GUY (Joseph). Guy's Elements of Astronomy, and an Abridgment of Keith's New Treatise on the Use of the Globes. New American Ed., with Additions and Improvements, and an Explanation of the Astronomical Part of the American Almanac. 30th Ed. Philadelphia. 1845. 18° (2 copies, one dated 1847.)

Note. The treatise of Keith is paged independently, with a half-title.

HERSCHEL (*Sir* John Frederick William), *Bart.* Outlines of Astronomy .... London. 1849. 8° pp. xiv., 661. +

——— Physical Astronomy. (ENCYCL. Metrop., III. 647 – 734.)

HERSCHEL (*Sir* John Frederick William), *Bart.* A Treatise on Astronomy. London. 8° (LARDNER'S Cab. Cycl., **104.**)

HUGHES (*Prof.* William). A Manual of Mathematical Geography; comprehending an Inquiry into the Construction of Maps, with Rules for the Formation of Map-Projections. 2d Ed. London. 1852. 16°

KATER (*Capt.* Henry). Nautical Astronomy. (ENCYCL. Metrop., III. 607 – 646.)

KEITH (Thomas). A New Treatise on the Use of the Globes, *etc.* *See* GUY (J.).

KENDALL (E. Otis). Uranography; or, A Description of the Heavens; designed for Academies and Schools; accompanied by an Atlas of the Heavens .... Philadelphia. 1844. 18° or 12° (6. and 12.) Atlas, 1845. 4°

[LLOYD (Edward)]. Mathematical Geography. [London. 183 – ?] 8° pp. 32. (LIBR. of Useful Knowl., Nat. Phil., III.)

LONDON RELIGIOUS TRACT SOCIETY. *See* RELIGIOUS TRACT SOCIETY

LOOMIS (*Prof.* Elias). The Recent Progress of Astronomy; especially in the United States. ... New York. 1850. 12°

M'INTIRE (James), *M.D.* A new Treatise on Astronomy, and the Use of the Globes, in Two Parts. ... For the Use of High Schools and Academies. ... New-York. 1850. 12°

[MALKIN (*Sir* Benjamin Heath)]. Astronomy. [London. 1830 – 34.] 8° (LIBR. of Useful Knowl., Nat. Phil., III.)

MASON (Ebenezer Porter). Introduction to Practical Astronomy, designed as a Supplement to Olmsted's Astronomy; containing special Rules for the Adjustment and Use of Astronomical Instruments, together with the Calculation of Eclipses and Occultations, and the Methods of finding the Latitude and Longitude. New York. 1843. 8° (Appended to OLMSTED'S Introduction to Astronomy, 1843. 8°)

MATHEMATICAL Geography. *See* [LLOYD (E.)].

MATTISON (*Prof.* Hiram). An Elementary Astronomy, for Academies and Schools. Illustrated by numerous original Diagrams .... 5th Ed. 12th Thousand. New York. 1849. 18° or 12° (6.)

MITCHEL (*Prof.* Ormsby McKnight). The Planetary and Stellar Worlds: a Popular Exposition of the Great Discoveries and Theories of Modern Astronomy. In a Series of Ten Lectures. ... New York. 1848. 12°

NICHOL (*Prof.* J. P.), *LL.D.* The Phenomena and Order of the Solar System. ... From the last Edinburgh Ed. Illustrated with Plates. New-York. 1843. 12°

——— Thoughts on some important Points relating to the System of the World. ... 1st American Ed., revised and enlarged. Boston and Cambridge. 1848. 12°

——— Views of the Architecture of the Heavens. ... Republished from the last London and Edinburgh Editions: to which has [*sic*] been added Notes, a Glossary, &c. by the American Publishers. 2d Ed. New-York. 1842. 12°

NORTON (*Prof.* William Augustus). An Elementary Treatise on Astronomy: in Four Parts. ... With Solar, Lunar, and other Astronomical Tables. Designed for Use as a Text-Book in Colleges and the Higher Academies. ... Stereotype Ed. Corrected, improved, and enlarged. New York. 1845. 8°

OLMSTED (*Prof.* Denison), *LL.D.* A Compendium of Astronomy .... Adapted to the Use of Schools and Academies .... 2d Ed. ... New York. 1841. 12°

——— An Introduction to Astronomy; designed as a Text Book for the Students of Yale College. 3d Ed. ... New York. 1843. 8°

See MASON (E. P.). Introduction, *etc.*

——— Letters on Astronomy, addressed to a Lady: in which the Elements of the Science are familiarly explained in Connection with its Literary History. With numerous Engravings. ... Boston. 1842. 12° (SCHOOL Libr., Vol. XX.)

——— *The same.* New York. 1847. 12°

RECENT Discoveries in Astronomy. (CHAMBERS's Papers, *etc.* III. no. 21.)

RELIGIOUS TRACT SOCIETY, *London.* The Solar System. Part II. ... London: the Religious Tract Society. Philadelphia: American Sunday-School Union. [1846.] 18°

ROBINSON (Horatio N.). A Treatise on Astronomy, Descriptive, Theoretical, and Physical .... Albany. 1849. 8° or 12° (8. and 6.)

——— A Treatise on Astronomy, Descriptive, Physical, and Practical. ... Albany. 1850. 8° or 12° (8. and 6.)

SMITH (Asa). Smith's Illustrated Astronomy .... New-York. 1848. 4° pp. v., 68.

SOLAR System (The). *See* RELIGIOUS TRACT SOCIETY.

WONDERS of the Telescope. (CHAMBERS's Miscel., X. no. 175.)

PART IV. LAWS OF SOUND, LIGHT, AND HEAT; OR, ACOUSTICS, OPTICS, AND "THERMOTICS."

BACHE (*Prof.* Alexander Dallas). *See* BREWSTER (*Sir* D.). A Treatise on Optics, *etc.* 1844. 12°

BARLOW (*Prof.* Peter). Optics. (ENCYCL. Metrop., III. 393 – 484.)

[BREWSTER (*Sir* David)]. On the Double Refraction and Polarisation of Light. [London. 182 – .] 8° pp. 64. (LIBR. of Useful Knowl., Nat. Phil., I.)

[———] Optics. [London. 182 – .] 8° pp. 68. (LIBR. of Useful Knowl., Nat. Phil., I.)

——— A Treatise on Optics. London. 8° (LARDNER's Cab. Cycl., **105.**)

——— A Treatise on Optics. ... A new Ed. With an Appendix,

containing an Elementary View of the Application of Analysis to Reflexion and Refraction, by A. D. Bache .... Philadelphia. 1844. 12°

Note. The Appendix is paged independently.

DOUBLE Refraction (On the) and Polarisation of Light. *See* [BREWSTER (*Sir* D.)].

HEAT. *See* [OGG (——)].

HERSCHEL (*Sir* John Frederick William), *Bart.* Light. (ENCYCL. Metrop., IV. 341 – 586.)

——— Sound. (ENCYCL. Metrop., IV. 747 – 824.)

[LARDNER (Dionysius)], *LL.D.* A Popular Account of Newton's Optics. [London. 183 – ?] 8° pp. 64. (LIBR. of Useful Knowl., Nat. Phil., II.)

——— A Treatise on Heat. London. 8° (LARDNER'S Cab. Cycl., **106.**)

LUNN (*Rev.* Francis). Heat. (ENCYCL. Metrop., IV. 225 – 340.)

MICROSCOPE (The) and its Marvels. (CHAMBERS'S Papers, *etc.* VI. no. 41.)

NEWTON'S Optics. *See* [LARDNER (D.)].

[OGG (——)]. Heat. [London. 182 – .] 8° pp. 64. (LIBR. of Useful Knowl., Nat. Phil., I.)

OPTICAL Instruments. *See* [PRITCHARD (A.)].

OPTICS. *See* [BREWSTER (*Sir* D.)].

PEIRCE (*Prof.* Benjamin), *LL.D.* An Elementary Treatise on Sound; being the Second Volume of a Course of Natural Philosophy, designed for the Use of High Schools and Colleges. Compiled by B. P. .... Boston. 1836. 8°

[PRITCHARD (Andrew)]. Optical Instruments. [London. 183 – ?] 8° pp. 60. (LIBR. of Useful Knowl., Nat. Phil., II.)

SCIENCE of the Sunbeam. (CHAMBERS'S Papers, *etc.* IV. no. 31.)

THERMOMETER (The) and Pyrometer. *See* [TRAILL (T. S.)].

[TRAILL (*Prof.* Thomas Stewart)], *M.D.* The Thermometer and Pyrometer. [London. 183 – ?] 8° pp. 64. (LIBR. of Useful Knowl., Nat. Phil., II.)

WONDERS of the Microscope. (CHAMBERS'S Miscel., IX. no. 150.)

WONDERS of the Telescope. (CHAMBERS'S Miscel., X. no. 175.)

PART V. MAGNETISM AND ELECTRICITY.

BAIN (Alexander). *See* REID (D. B.) *and* BAIN (A.). ... Elements, *etc.*

BARLOW (*Prof.* Peter). Magnetism. — Electro-Magnetism. (ENCYCL. Metrop., III. 735 – 847, and IV. 1 – 40.)

DAVIS (Daniel), *Jr.* A Manual of Magnetism, including Galvanism, Magnetism, Electro-Magnetism, Electro-Dynamics, Magneto-Electricity, and Thermo-Electricity. [Principally prepared by John Bacon, Jr., M.D., and William F. Channing, M.D.] With 180 original Illustrations. 2d Ed. Boston: Daniel Davis, Jr. 1847. 12°

Note. With the half-title: — "Davis's Manual of Magnetism."

[———] ? The Medical Application of Electricity, *etc.* *See* Class XIII. Part V. § 2.

ELECTRICITY. *See* [ROGET (P. M.)].

ELECTRO-MAGNETISM. *See* [ROGET (P. M.)].

GALVANISM. *See* [ROGET (P. M.)].

HARRIS (*Sir* William Snow). Rudimentary Electricity .... London: John Weale. 1848. 12°

LARDNER (Dionysius), *LL.D.*, *and* WALKER (Charles V.) A Manual of Electricity, Magnetism, and Meteorology. 2 vols. London. 8° (LARDNER's Cab. Cycl., **108, 109.**)

LOVERING (*Prof.* Joseph). Elements of Electricity, Magnetism, and Electro-Dynamics ... for the Use of the Students of Harvard University; being the Second Part of a Course of Natural Philosophy, by John Farrar, LL.D. and the First Part of a New Course of Physics, by Joseph Lovering .... Boston. 1842. 8°

LUNN (*Rev.* Francis). Electricity. (ENCYCL. Metrop., IV. 41 – 172.)

MAGNETISM. *See* [ROGET (P. M.)].

REID (David Boswell), *M.D.*, *and* BAIN (Alexander). ... Elements of Chemistry and Electricity. *See* Class XII.

[ROGET (Peter Mark)], *M.D.* Electricity. [London. 183 – ?] 8° pp. 64. (LIBR. of Useful Knowl., Nat. Phil., II.)

[———] Electro-Magnetism. [London. 183 – ?] 8° pp. 100. (*Ibid.*)

[———] Galvanism. [London. 183 – ?] 8° pp. 32. (*Ibid.*)

——— Galvanism. (ENCYCL. Metrop., IV. 173 – 224.)

[———] Magnetism. [London. 183 – ?] 8° pp. 96. (LIBR. of Useful Knowl., Nat. Phil., II.)

WALKER (Charles V.). *See* LARDNER (D.) *and* WALKER (C. V.).

PART VI. METEOROLOGY.

BROCKLESBY (*Prof.* John). Elements of Meteorology, with Questions for Examination, designed for Schools and Academies. ... With Engravings. 3d revised and stereotype Ed. ... New York. 1849. 12°

HARVEY (George). Meteorology. (ENCYCL. Metrop., V. 1 – *174.)

LARDNER (Dionysius), *LL.D.*, *and* WALKER (Charles V.). A Manual of Electricity ... and Meteorology. *See* Part V.

LAW (The) of Storms. (CHAMBERS's Papers, *etc.* VII. no. 53.)

MUELLER (Johann), *Prof. of Physics in the Univ. of Freiburg.* Principles of Physics and Meteorology. *See* Part I.

CLASS XII. CHEMISTRY.

Alchemy and the Alchemists. (Chambers's Papers, *etc.* IX. no. 66.)

Booth (*Prof.* James C.). The Encyclopædia of Chemistry, Practical and Theoretical: embracing its Application to the Arts, Metallurgy, Mineralogy, Geology, Medicine, and Pharmacy. By James C. Booth .... Assisted by Campbell Morfit .... Philadelphia. 1850. 8° or large 12° (4. and 6.) pp. 4, 974.

Campbell (Dugald). A Practical Text-Book of Inorganic Chemistry, with Qualitative and Quantitative Analysis. ... London. 1849. 8° or 16° (8.)

Chemistry. *See* [Daniell (J. F.)].

[Daniell (*Prof.* John Frederic)]. Chemistry. [London. 1829-31.] 8° (Libr. of Useful Knowl., Nat. Phil., IV.)

——— An Introduction to the Study of Chemical Philosophy: being a preparatory View of the Forces which concur to the Production of Chemical Phenomena. ... The 2d Ed., revised and enlarged. London. 1843. 8° pp. xvi., 764.

Donovan (Michael). A Treatise on Chemistry. London. 8° (Lardner's Cab. Cycl., **107.**)

Draper (*Prof.* John William), *M.D.* A Text-Book of Chemistry, for the Use of Schools and Colleges. With nearly Three Hundred Illustrations. New York. 1846. 12°

Gray (Alonzo). Elements of Chemistry .... 7th Ed., revised and enlarged. New York. 1843. 12°

Griffiths (*Prof.* Thomas). Chemistry of the Four Seasons ... Philadelphia. 1846. 8°

Grund (Francis J.). Elements of Chemistry .... For the Use of Schools. Stereotype Ed. Boston. 1841. 12°

Introduction (An) to Practical Organic Chemistry. ... Philadelphia. 1846. 24° (8. 4.) pp. 66. (Small Books, *etc.* I. no. 4.)

Kane (*Prof.* Robert), *M.D.* Elements of Chemistry, including the ... Applications of the Science to Medicine and Pharmacy, and to the Arts. ... With Additions and Corrections ... by John William Draper .... New-York. 1846. 8° pp. xii., 9-704.

Lunn (*Rev.* Francis). Chemistry. (Encycl. Metrop., IV. 587-*762.)

Morfit (Campbell). Chemical and Pharmaceutic Manipulations .... By C. M. ... assisted by Alexander Muckle, ... With Four Hundred and Twenty-three Illustrations. Philadelphia. 1849. 8°

Reid (David Boswell), *M. D. and* Bain (Alexander). ... Elements of Chemistry and Electricity. In Two Parts. Part I. By D. B. R. .... Part II. By A. B. .... Edited by D. M. Reese, M.D. .... New-York. 1851. 12° (Chambers's Educational Course, No. 4.)

Science of the Sunbeam. (Chambers's Papers, *etc.* IV. no. 31.)

STOECKHARDT (*Prof.* Julius Adolf). The Principles of Chemistry, illustrated by simple Experiments. ... Translated by C. H. Peirce, M.D. 8th American, from the 5th German Ed. Cambridge. 1851. 12° pp. xix., 681.

TURNER (Edward), *M.D.* Elements of Chemistry, including the actual State and prevalent Doctrines of the Science. ... 8th Ed. Edited by Baron Liebig ... and William Gregory ... . Part I. — Inorganic Chemistry. | Part II. — Organic Chemistry. 2 pts. London. 1847. 8° pp. xvi., 1394.

WILL (*Prof.* Heinrich). Outlines of the Course of Qualitative Analysis followed in the Giessen Laboratory. ... With a Preface by Baron Liebig. Boston. 1847. 12°

CLASS XIII. NATURAL HISTORY.

PART I. GENERAL WORKS; PHYSICAL GEOGRAPHY.

BUCKE (Charles). On the Beauties, Harmonies, and Sublimities of Nature; with Notes, Commentaries, and Illustrations. ... Selected and revised by the Rev. William P. Page. New-York. 1846. 18° (HARPER'S Fam. Libr., **145.**)

DAY (John Quinby). Outlines of Physical Geography: designed as a Companion to the Common School Geography, and for the Use of Grammar and High Schools. Boston. 1846. 12°

FROST (John). The Class Book of Nature; comprising Lessons on the Universe, the Three Kingdoms of Nature, and the Form and Structure of the Human Body. With Questions ... . Edited by J. F. 10th Ed. Hartford. 1846. 12°

Note. Originally published, in substance, by the Society for promoting Christian Knowledge.

[GOODRICH (Samuel Griswold)]. The World and its Inhabitants. By the Author of Peter Parley's Tales. Boston. 1849. 16° or 18° (8. and 6.) (CABINET Libr., **20.**)

GUYOT (*Prof.* Arnold). The Earth and Man: Lectures on Comparative Physical Geography, in its Relation to the History of Mankind. Translated from the French, by C. C. Felton ... . 2d Ed., revised. Boston. 1850. 12°

HIGGINS (W. Mullinger). The Earth: its Physical Condition and most remarkable Phenomena. ... New-York. 1846. 18° (HARPER'S Fam. Libr., **78.**)

HUMBOLDT (Friedrich Heinrich Alexander, *Baron* VON). Aspects of Nature, in different Lands and different Climates; with Scientific Elucidations. By A. von H. Translated by Mrs. Sabine. Philadelphia. 1849. 12°

JOHNSTON (Alexander Keith). The Physical Atlas a Series of Maps & Illustrations of the Geographical Distribution of Natural Phenomena embracing I Geology. II Hydrography. III Meteorology. IV Natural History. By A. K. J. ... with the Co-operation of Men eminent in the different Departments of Science. Edinburgh. 1849. fol.

[LLOYD (H. J.)]. Physical Geography. [London. 183–?] 8° pp. 64. (LIBR. of Useful Knowl., Nat. Phil., III.)

MICROSCOPE (The) and its Marvels. (CHAMBERS's Papers, *etc.* VI. no. 41.)

MUDIE (Robert). A Popular Guide to the Observation of Nature .... New York. 1847. 18° (HARPER's Fam. Libr., **57.**)

PARLEY (Peter), *pseudon.* *See* [GOODRICH (Samuel Griswold)].

PHYSICAL Geography. *See* [LLOYD (H. J.)].

[SOCIETY FOR PROMOTING CHRISTIAN KNOWLEDGE]. The Class Book of Nature, *etc.* *See* FROST (J.).

SWAINSON (William). A Preliminary Discourse on the Study of Natural History. London. 8° (LARDNER's Cab. Cycl., **111.**)

VESTIGES of the Natural History of Creation. 3d Ed., from the 3d London Ed., greatly amended by the Author. To which is appended an Article from the North British Review. New York. 1845. 12°

WHITE (*Rev.* Gilbert). The Natural History of Selborne. ... New-York. 1847. 18° (HARPER's Fam. Libr., **147.**)

WONDERS (The) of the Microscope. (CHAMBERS's Miscel., IX. no. 150.)

PART II. MINERALOGY AND GEOLOGY.

ANSTED (*Prof.* David Thomas). The Ancient World; or, Picturesque Sketches of Creation. ... Philadelphia. 1847. 8° or 16° (8.)

BROOKE (Henry James). Crystallography. — Mineralogy. (ENCYCL. Metrop., VI. 425–528.)

DANA (James Dwight). A System of Mineralogy, comprising the most recent Discoveries: with numerous Wood Cuts and four Copper Plates. ... 2d Ed. New York and London. 1844. 8° pp. 633.

FOSTER (J. W.) *and* WHITNEY (J. D.). Report on the Geology and Topography of a Portion of the Lake Superior Land District, in the State of Michigan. *See* Class XXII. Part III.

[GOODRICH (Samuel Griswold)]. The Wonders of Geology, by the Author of Peter Parley's Tales. ... Boston. 1849. 16° or 18° (8. and 6.) (CABINET Libr., **14.**)

HALL (James). Palæontology of New-York. Vol. I. containing Descriptions of the Organic Remains of the Lower Division of the New-York System. (Equivalent of the Lower Silurian Rocks of Europe.) Albany. 1847. 4° (Forming Part VI. Vol. I. of the "Natural History of New York.")

HITCHCOCK (*Prof.* Edward), *LL.D.* Elementary Geology. ... 8th Ed., revised, enlarged, and adapted to the present Advanced State of the Science. With an Introductory Notice, by John Pye Smith .... New York. 1847. 12°

——— Final Report on the Geology of Massachusetts: Vol. I. containing I. Economical Geology. II. Scenographical Geology. | Vol. II. containing III. Scientific Geology. IV. Elementary Geology. With an appended Catalogue of the Specimens of Rocks and Minerals in the State Collection. ... [With 55 Plates.] 2 vols. Northampton. 1841. 4°

LEE (*Prof.* Charles A.), *M.D.* The Elements of Geology, for Popular Use; containing a Description of the Geological Formations and Mineral Resources of the United States. ... New-York. [1846 ?] 18° (HARPER's Fam. Libr., **178.**)

LOOMIS (*Prof.* Justin Ralph). The Elements of Geology ... . With numerous Illustrations. Boston. 1852. 12°

LYELL (*Sir* Charles). Elements of Geology. ... 1st American, from the 1st London Ed. Philadelphia. 1839. 12°

——— A Manual of Elementary Geology: or, The Ancient Changes of the Earth and its Inhabitants as illustrated by Geological Monuments. ... 3d and entirely revised Ed. Illustrated with more than Five Hundred Woodcuts. London. 1851. 8°

——— Principles of Geology; or, The Modern Changes of the Earth and its Inhabitants considered as illustrative of Geology. ... 7th Ed., entirely revised. ... London. 1847. 8° pp. xvi., 810. +

MANTELL (Gideon Algernon), *LL.D.* The Medals of Creation; or, First Lessons in Geology, and in the Study of Organic Remains. ... Vol. I. containing Fossil Vegetables, Infusoria, Zoophytes, Echinoderms, and Mollusca. | Vol. II. containing Fossil Cephalopoda, Crustacea, Insects, Fishes, Reptiles, Birds, and Mammalia, with Notes of Geological Excursions. 2 vols. London. 1844. 16° or 8° (8.)

Note. The two vols. are paged continuously.

——— The Wonders of Geology ... . [Edited by Prof. Benjamin Silliman, with an Introduction.] First American from the 3d London Ed. 2 vols. Newhaven, Conn. [Printed in London.] 1839. 16°

MILLER (Hugh). The Foot-prints of the Creator: or, The Asterolepis of Stromness. ... From the 3d London Ed. With a Memoir of the Author, by Louis Agassiz. Boston. 1850. 12°

——— The Old Red Sandstone; or, New Walks in an Old Field. ... With numerous Engravings. From the 4th London Ed. Boston. 1851. 12°

PAGE (David). ... Elements of Geology. Edited by D. M. Reese, M.D. ... . New-York. 1851. 12° (Chambers's Educational Course, No. 7.)

PARLEY (Peter), *pseudon.* *See* [GOODRICH (Samuel Griswold)].

PHILLIPS (*Prof.* John). A Treatise on Geology. 2 vols. London. 8° (LARDNER's Cab. Cycl., **124, 125.**)

PHILLIPS (*Prof.* John), *and* DAUBENY (*Prof.* Charles Giles Bridle), *M.D.* Geology. (ENCYCL. Metrop., VI. 529 – 808.)

PORTLOCK (*Lieut.-Col.* Joseph Ellison). A Rudimentary Treatise on Geology ... . London: John Weale. 1849. 12°

RICHARDSON (G. F.) Geology for Beginners; comprising a familiar Explanation of Geology, and its Associate Sciences, Mineralogy, Physical Geology, Fossil Conchology, Fossil Botany, and Palæontology. ... 3d Ed., enlarged. London. 1848. 12° pp. xx., 624.

ROMANCE (The) of Geology. (CHAMBERS's Miscel., I. no. 18.)

SMITH (John Pye), *D.D.* On the Relation between the Holy Scriptures and some Parts of Geological Science. ... New-York. 1840. 12°

TREASURES of the Earth. — I. Mineral. — II. Metallic. (CHAMBERS's Miscel., VIII. no. 130, and IX. no. 155.)

PART III. BOTANY.

BIGELOW (*Prof.* Jacob), *M.D.* Florula Bostoniensis. A Collection of Plants of Boston and its Vicinity, with ... Descriptions ... . 3d Ed. enlarged, and containing a Glossary of Botanical Terms. Boston. 1840. 12°

CURIOSITIES of Vegetation. (CHAMBERS's Miscel., III. no. 58.)

EDWARDS (Thomas) *and* DON (George). Botany. (ENCYCL. Metrop., VII. 1-108.)

HAMILTON (G.), *M.D.* ... Elements of Vegetable and Animal Physiology. In Two Parts. Edited by D. M. Reese ... . New-York. 1851. 12° (Chambers's Educational Course, No. 5.)

HENSLOW (*Prof.* John Stevens). The Principles of Descriptive and Physiological Botany. London. 8° (LARDNER's Cab. Cycl., **123.**)

INTRODUCTION (An) to Vegetable Physiology ... . Philadelphia. 1846. 24° (8. 4.) (SMALL Books, *etc.* III. no. 9.)

LINDLEY (*Prof.* John), *LL.D.* ... Botany. In Four Parts. 1. Structural Botany. 2. Physiology. 3. Systematic Botany. 4. Descriptive Botany. ... London. 1838. 8° (LIBR. of Useful Knowl., Nat. Phil., IV.)

VEGETABLE Substances used for the Food of Man. [Originally published by the Society for the Diffusion of Useful Knowledge. — With omissions.] New-York. 1846. 18° (HARPER's Fam. Libr., **169.**)

PART IV. ZOÖLOGY.

AGASSIZ (*Prof.* Louis) *and* GOULD (Augustus Addison), *M.D.* Principles of Zoölogy: touching the Structure, Development, Distribution, and Natural Arrangement of the Races of Animals, living and extinct; with numerous Illustrations. For the Use of Schools and Colleges. Part I. Comparative Physiology. Boston. 1848. 12°

ANECDOTES of Ants. (CHAMBERS's Miscel., V. no. 88.)

ANECDOTES of the Cat. (CHAMBERS's Miscel., III. no. 55.)

ANECDOTES of Dogs. (CHAMBERS's Miscel., I. no. 15.)

ANECDOTES of Elephants. (CHAMBERS's Miscel., IV. no. 61.)

ANECDOTES of the Horse. (CHAMBERS's Miscel., III. no. 41.)

ANECDOTES of Serpents. (CHAMBERS's Miscel., V. no. 80.)

ANECDOTES of Spiders. (CHAMBERS's Miscel., VI. no. 100.)

ANIMAL Instincts and Intelligence. (CHAMBERS's Papers, *etc.* XI. no. 82.)

ANIMAL Mechanics. *See* [BELL (*Sir* C.)].

ANIMAL Physiology. *See* [SMITH (T. S.)].

[BELL (*Sir* Charles)]. Animal Mechanics. [London. 1828–29.] 8° pp. 63. (LIBR. of Useful Knowl., Nat. Phil., IV.)

BIRDS, Natural History of. *See* [RENNIE (J.)].

CARPENTER (William Benjamin), *M.D.* Animal Physiology. ... A new Ed., carefully revised. London. 1851. 8°

CHAMBERS (William *and* Robert). Elements of Zoology; or, Natural History of Animals. From the last Edinburgh Ed. Chambers' Educational Course. Revised and improved by D. M. Reese, M.D. ... . 3d American Ed. New York. 1849. 12°

——— ... Elements of Zoology ... . Edited by D. M. Reese ... . New-York. 1853. 12° (Chambers's Educational Course, No. 6.)

ELEPHANT. *See* NATURAL History. The Elephant.

[GOODRICH (Samuel Griswold)]. Illustrative Anecdotes of the Animal Kingdom: by the Author of Peter Parley's Tales. Boston. 1849. 16° or 18° (8. and 6.) (CABINET Libr., **15.**)

HAMILTON (G.), *M.D.* ... Elements of Vegetable and Animal Physiology. *See* Part III.

HAPPY Families of Animals. (CHAMBERS's Miscel., I. no. 3, pp. 14–16.)

[HARRIS (Thaddeus William)], *M.D.* ... A Report on the Insects of Massachusetts, injurious to Vegetation. Published agreeably to an Order of the Legislature, by the Commissioners on the Zoological and Botanical Survey of the State. Cambridge. 1841. 8°

INSECTS, The Natural History of. *See* [RENNIE (J.) *and* WESTWOOD (J. O.)].

JARDINE (*Sir* William), *Bart.* The Naturalist's Library. Edited by Sir W. J. ... . 40 vols. Edinburgh. [1836–43?] 16°

Vol. I.—XIV. Ornithology.

Vol. I.—IV. Birds of Great Britain and Ireland.—Part I.—IV. By the Editor.
Vol. V. Sun-Birds. By the Editor.
Vol. VI. VII. Humming Birds.—Part I. II. By the Editor.
Vol. VIII. Game Birds. By the Editor.
Vol. IX. Pigeons. By Prideaux John Selby ... .
Vol. X. Parrots. By Prideaux John Selby ... .
Vol. XI. XII. Birds of Western Africa—Part I. II. By W. Swainson ... .
Vol. XIII. Flycatchers. By W. Swainson ... .
Vol. XIV. Gallinaceous Birds. By the Editor.

Vol. XV.—XXVII. Mammalia.

Vol. XV. Introduction to Mammalia. By Lieut.-Col. Charles Hamilton Smith ... .
Vol. XVI. Lions, Tigers, &c., &c. By the Editor.

Vol. XVII. British Quadrupeds, by W. Macgillivray ....
Vol. XVIII. XIX. Dogs. — Vol. I. II. By Lieut.-Col. Charles Hamilton Smith ....
Vol. XX. Horses. By Lieut.-Col. Charles Hamilton Smith ....
Vol. XXI. Deer, Antelopes, Camels, &c. By the Editor.
Vol. XXII. Goats, Sheep, Oxen, &c. By the Editor.
Vol. XXIII. Thick-skinned Quadrupeds. By the Editor.
Vol. XXIV. Marsupialia or Pouched Animals. By G. R. Waterhouse ....
Vol. XXV. Amphibious Carnivora. By Robert Hamilton ....
Vol. XXVI. Whales, etc. By Robert Hamilton ....
Vol. XXVII. Monkeys. By the Editor.

Vol. XXVIII. — XXXIV. Entomology.

Vol. XXVIII. Introduction to Entomology. By James Duncan ....
Vol. XXIX. British Butterflies. By James Duncan ....
Vol. XXX. British Moths, Sphinxes, etc. By James Duncan ....
Vol. XXXI. Foreign Butterflies. By James Duncan ....
Vol. XXXII. Exotic Moths. By James Duncan ....
Vol. XXXIII. Beetles. By James Duncan ....
Vol. XXXIV. Bees. ...

Vol. XXXV. — XL. Ichthyology.

Vol. XXXV. Fishes, particularly their Structure and Economical Uses. By J. S. Bushnan, M.D. ....
Vol. XXXVI. XXXVII. British Fishes. — Part I. II. By R. Hamilton ....
Vol. XXXVIII. Fishes of the Perch Family. By the Editor.
Vol. XXXIX. XL. Fishes of British Guiana. — Part I. II. By R. H. Schomburgk, Esq.

KIRBY (*Rev.* William) *and* SPENCE (William). An Introduction to Entomology; or, Elements of the Natural History of Insects: comprising an Account of Noxious and Useful Insects, of their Metamorphoses, Food, Stratagems, Habitations, Societies, Motions, Noises, Hybernation, Instinct, etc. etc. With Plates. ... From the 6th London Ed., which was corrected and considerably enlarged. Philadelphia. 1846. Large 12° (6.)

LIBRARY of Entertaining Knowledge. *See* SOCIETY, *etc.*

MASSACHUSETTS — *Commissioners on the Zoölogical and Botanical Survey of the State. See* [HARRIS (T. W.)]. A Report on the Insects, *etc.*

NATURAL History. The Elephant .... New-York. 1848. 18° (HARPER's Fam. Libr., **164.**)

NATURAL History of Birds. *See* [RENNIE (J.)].

NATURAL History (The) of Insects. *See* [RENNIE (J.) *and* WESTWOOD (J. O.)].

NATURAL History of Quadrupeds. ... New-York. 1840. 18° (HARPER's Fam. Libr., **104.**)

Note. This and the three preceding works are abridged from the volumes on Menageries, Birds, and Insects, in the "Library of Entertaining Knowledge," published by the Society for the Diffusion of Useful Knowledge. They are *all* ascribed to Prof. Rennie, in Harper's Illustrated Catalogue.

PEARLS and Pearl Fisheries. (CHAMBERS's Miscel., X. no. 167.)

[RENNIE (*Prof.* James)]. Natural History of Birds. Their Architecture, Habits, and Faculties. ... New-York. 1839. 18° (HARPER's Fam. Libr., **98.**)

[———] *See* NATURAL History of Quadrupeds. ... *Note.*

[RENNIE (*Prof.* James) *and* WESTWOOD (John Obadiah)]. The Natural History of Insects. ... First Series. [Vol. I.] | ... Vol. II. 2 vols. New-York. 1843–46. 18° (HARPER's Fam. Libr., **8, 74.**)

See NATURAL History of Quadrupeds. ... *Note.*

SELECT Poems on Birds. (CHAMBERS's Miscel., IX. no. 160.)

SELECT Poems on Insects. (CHAMBERS's Miscel., VIII. no. 143.)

SHUCKARD (William E.) *and* SWAINSON (William). On the History and Natural Arrangement of Insects. London. 8° (LARDNER's Cab. Cycl., **120.**)

[SMITH (Thomas Southwood)], *M.D.* Animal Physiology. [London. 1829–30.] 8° (LIBR. of Useful Knowl., Nat. Phil., IV.)

SOCIETY FOR THE DIFFUSION OF USEFUL KNOWLEDGE. *Library of Entertaining Knowledge. See* NATURAL History of Quadrupeds. ... *Note.*

SOUTH (John Flint). Zoology. (ENCYCL. Metrop., VII. 109–382*.)

SWAINSON (William). Animals in Menageries. London. 8° (LARDNER's Cab. Cycl., **114.**)

——— On the Habits and Instincts of Animals. London. 8° (LARDNER's Cab. Cycl., **121.**)

——— On the Natural History and Classification of Birds. 2 vols. London. 8° (LARDNER's Cab. Cycl., **115, 116.**)

——— On the Natural History and Classification of Fishes, Amphibians, and Reptiles. 2 vols. London. 8° (LARDNER's Cab. Cycl., **117, 118.**)

——— On the Natural History and Classification of Quadrupeds. London. 8° (LARDNER's Cab. Cycl., **113.**)

——— Taxidermy. With the Biography of Zoologists, and Notices of their Works. London. 8° (LARDNER's Cab. Cycl., **122.**)

——— A Treatise on the Geography and Classification of Animals. London. 8° (LARDNER's Cab. Cycl., **112.**)

——— A Treatise on Malacology; or, The Natural Classification of Shells and Shell-Fish. London. 8° (LARDNER's Cab. Cycl., **119.**)

——— *See* SHUCKARD (W. E.) *and* SWAINSON (W.).

[WESTWOOD (John Obadiah)]. *See* [RENNIE (J.) *and* WESTWOOD (J.O.)].

PART V. PHYSICAL HISTORY OF MAN; MEDICINE.

§ 1. *Physical History of Man, Anatomy, Physiology, Hygiene.*

[BARLOW (*Rev.* John)]. The Connection between Physiology and Intellectual Philosophy. 2d Ed., enlarged. Philadelphia. 1846. 24° (8. 4.) pp. 85. (SMALL Books, *etc.* I. no. 2.)

[BELL (*Sir* Charles)]. Animal Mechanics. *See* Part IV.

CARPENTER (William Benjamin), *M.D.* Elements of Physiology, including Physiological Anatomy, for the Use of the Medical Student. ... With One Hundred and Eighty Illustrations. Philadelphia. 1846. 8°

CLEANLINESS — Bathing — Ventilation. (CHAMBERS's Miscel., III. no. 51.)

COMBE (Andrew), *M.D.* The Principles of Physiology applied to the Preservation of Health, and to the Improvement of Physical and Mental Education. ... From the 7th Edinburgh Ed. New-York. 1848. 18° (HARPER's Fam. Libr., **71.**)

CUTTER (Calvin), *M.D.* First Book on Anatomy, Physiology, and Hygiene, for Grammar Schools and Families. With Eighty-three Engravings. ... Stereotype Ed. Boston. 1849. 12°

——— A Treatise on Anatomy, Physiology, and Hygiene: designed for Colleges, Academies, and Families. With One Hundred and Fifty Engravings. Stereotype Ed. Boston. 1849. 12°

GRISCOM (*Prof.* John H.) Animal Mechanism and Physiology ... . New-York. 1848. 18° (HARPER's Fam. Libr., **85.**)

JARVIS (Edward), *M.D.* Practical Physiology; for the Use of Schools and Families. Philadelphia. 1847. 12°

MANAGEMENT of Infants. (CHAMBERS's Miscel., I. no. 6.)

PRICHARD (James Cowles), *M.D.* The Natural History of Man; comprising Inquiries into the Modifying Influence of Physical and Moral Agencies on the different Tribes of the Human Family. ... 3d Ed., enlarged, with Fifty coloured and Five plain Illustrations engraved on Steel, and Ninety-seven Engravings on Wood. London. 1848. 8° pp. xvii., 677.

——— Six Ethnographical Maps with a Sheet of Letterpress. By J. C. P. ... . In Illustration of his Works: — "The Natural History of Man," and "Researches into the Physical History of Mankind." ... [London. 1843 ?] fol.

SANITARY Movement (The). (CHAMBERS's Papers, *etc.* II. no. 9.)

SMITH (Henry H.), *M.D.* Anatomical Atlas, illustrative of the Structure of the Human Body. By H. H. S. ... . Under the Supervision of Wm. E. Horner, *M.D.* ... . Philadelphia. 1847. 8°

[SMITH (Thomas Southwood)], *M.D.* Animal Physiology. *See* Part IV.

SOUTH (John Flint) *and* CLARK (F. Le Gros). Anatomy. (ENCYCL. Metrop., VII. 381–494.)

TICKNOR (Caleb), *M.D.* The Philosophy of Living; or, The Way to enjoy Life and its Comforts. ... New-York. 1846. 18° (HARPER's Fam. Libr., **77.**)

VOLUNTARY Distortions — Tight Lacing. (CHAMBERS's Miscel., V. no. 93.)

§ 2. *Pathology and Therapeutics, Surgery, Materia Medica.*

BARLOW (*Rev.* John). On Man's Power over himself to prevent or control Insanity. *See* Class I.

BOWMAN (William). Surgery. (ENCYCL. Metrop., VII. 824 – 880.)

[DAVIS (Daniel), *Jr.*] ? The Medical Application of Electricity; with Descriptions of Apparatus, and Instructions for its Use. 2d Ed. Boston: Daniel Davis, Jr. 1847. 12° pp. 24. (Bound with DAVIS's "Manual of Magnetism," *etc.*)

JOHNSON (George), *M.D.* Materia Medica. (ENCYCL. Metrop., VII. 494 – 526.)

LIFE at Græfenberg. (CHAMBERS's Papers, *etc.* VIII. nos. 59, 60.)

MORFIT (Campbell). Chemical and Pharmaceutical Manipulations. *See* Class XII.

SPECTRAL Illusions. (CHAMBERS's Miscel., IV. no. 70.)

WILLIAMS (Robert), *M.D.* Medicine. (ENCYCL. Metrop., VII. 527 – 823.)

THE ARTS.

CLASS XIV. THE ARTS.

PART I. GENERAL WORKS.

Note. For the *History* of the Arts, see Class XXVII.

ANTISELL (T.), *M.D.* ... Hand-Book of the Useful Arts; including Agriculture, Architecture, Domestic Economy, Engineering, Machinery, Manufactures, Mining, Photogenic and Telegraphic Art .... New-York. 1852. 12° pp. vii., 692. (PUTNAM's Home Cyclopedia, Vol. III.)

[GOODRICH (Samuel Griswold)]. Enterprise, Industry and Art of Man, as displayed in Fishing, Hunting, Commerce, Navigation, Mining, Agriculture and Manufactures. By the Author of Peter Parley's Tales. ... Boston. 1849. 16° or 18° (8. and 6.) (CABINET Libr., **18.**)

HAZEN (Edward). Popular Technology; or, Professions and Trades. ... 2 vols. New-York. 1846 – 41. 18° (HARPER's Fam. Libr., **149, 150.**)

PARLEY (Peter), *pseudon.* *See* [GOODRICH (Samuel Griswold)].

POTTER (Alonzo), *D.D.*, *Bp. of Pennsylvania.* The Principles of Science applied to the Domestic and Mechanic Arts, and to Manufactures and Agriculture: with Reflections on the Progress of the Arts, and their Influence on National Welfare. ... Boston. [1840 ?] 12° [School Libr., Vol. XXI.)

Ure (Andrew), *M.D.* A Dictionary of Arts, Manufactures, and Mines .... Illustrated with nearly Fifteen Hundred Engravings on Wood. 11th American, from the last London Ed. To which is appended, A Supplement of Recent Improvements to the Present Time. New York. 1847. 8° pp. **1340**, and Suppl., pp. **304**.

Note. The Supplement is paged independently, with the title: — "Recent Improvements in Arts, Manufactures, and Mines," etc.

Part II. Agriculture, Horticulture, Rural and Domestic Economy.

Beecher (Catherine Esther). A Treatise on Domestic Economy, for the Use of Young Ladies at Home, and at School. Revised Ed., with numerous Additions and illustrative Engravings. Boston. 1843. 12° (School Libr., Vol. XXVI.)

Buel (Jesse). The Farmer's Companion; or, Essays on the Principles and Practice of American Husbandry. With the Address prepared to be delivered before the Agricultural and Horticultural Societies of New-Haven County, Connecticut, and an Appendix, containing Tables .... By the late Honorable J. B. .... To which is prefixed, A Eulogy on ... Judge Buel. By Amos Dean, Esq. Boston. [1840 ?] 12° (School Libr., Vol. XVI.)

Domestic Flower-Culture. (Chambers's Miscel., II. no. **37**.)

Don (George). Horticulture. (Encycl. Metrop., VI. 87* – 186.*)

Donovan (Michael). A Treatise on Domestic Economy. Vol. I. containing Brewing, Distilling, Wine-Making, Baking, &c. | Vol. II. Human Food, Animal and Vegetable. 2 vols. London. 8° (Lardner's Cab. Cycl., **126, 127.**)

Russell (Michael), *Bp. of Glasgow.* Agriculture. (Encycl. Metrop., VI. 1 – 76.)

Spooner (William Charles). Veterinary Art. (Encycl. Metrop., VII. 881 – 913.)

Part III. Other Useful Arts.

Note. For *Surveying* and *Navigation*, see Class IX. For *Medicine*, see Class XIII. Part V.

Babbage (Charles). Introductory View of the Principles of Manufactures. (Encycl. Metrop., VIII. 1 – 84.)

Barlow (*Prof.* Peter). Manufactures. (Encycl. Metrop., VIII. 85 – 834.)

Bigelow (*Prof.* Jacob), *M.D.* The Useful Arts, considered in Connexion with the Applications of Science: with numerous Engravings. ... 2 vols. Boston. 1842. 12° (School Libr., Vol. XI. XII.)

——— *The same.* 2 vols. New York. 1847. 12°

BOSTON — *School Committee.* Reports and other Documents relating to the Ventilation of the School Houses of the City of B. ... Boston. 1848. 8° pp. 43.

——— *See* [BRYENT (W.) *and* HERMAN (L.)]. An Exposition, *etc.*

[BRYENT (Walter) *and* HERMAN (Leopold)]. An Exposition on heating and ventilating the School Houses of the City of Boston, in 1846 and 1847, together with important Information by a Scientific Gentleman, upon the Effects of Red Hot Iron upon Air, &c. Boston: Bryent and Herman. 1848. 8° pp. 24.

CRESY (Edward). An Encyclopædia of Civil Engineering, Historical, Theoretical, and Practical. ... Illustrated by upwards of Three Thousand Engravings on Wood ... . London. 1847. 8° pp. xii., 1655.

Note. Also with title-pages for the division of the work into two vols.

CURIOSITIES of Art. — II. Mechanics — Manufactures. (CHAMBERS's Miscel., VII. no. 113.)

EWBANK (Thomas). A Descriptive and Historical Account of Hydraulic and other Machines for raising Water, *etc.* *See* Class XXVIII.

HARVEY (George). Naval Architecture. (ENCYCL. Metrop., VI. 329-424.)

HOLLAND (John). A Treatise on the Progressive Improvement and Present State of the Manufactures in Metal. 3 vols. London. 8° (LARDNER's Cab. Cycl., **129-131.**)

MITCHELL (*Maj.* Charles C.) *and* PROCTER (*Col.* George). Fortification. (ENCYCL. Metrop., VI. 268-328.)

NICHOLSON (Peter). Carpentry. (ENCYCL. Metrop., VI. 229-267.)

PORTER (George Richardson). A Treatise on the Manufacture of Silk. London. 8° (LARDNER's Cab. Cycl., **128.**)

——— A Treatise on the Origin, Progressive Improvement, and Present State of the Manufactures of Porcelain and Glass. London. 8° (LARDNER's Cab. Cycl., **132.**)

SCRIBNER (J. M.). Scribner's Engineers' and Mechanics' Companion: comprising U. S. Weights and Measures; Mensuration of Superficies and Solids; Tables of Squares and Cubes, Square and Cube Roots; Circumference and Areas of Circles. The Mechanical Powers: Centers of Gravity, Gravitation of Bodies, Pendulums, Specific Gravity of Bodies, Strength, Weight and Crush of Materials, Water Wheels, Hydrostatics, Hydraulics, Statics, Centers of Percussion and Gyration, Friction, Heat, Tables of the Weight of Metals, Pipes, Scantling, and Interest. Steam and the Steam Engine. 2d Ed. — Revised, enlarged, and improved. ... New-York. 1846. 18° or 12° (6. and 12.)

SWAINSON (William). Taxidermy. *See* Class XIII. Part IV.

YOUNG (*Prof.* Thomas), *M.D.* A Course of Lectures on Natural Philosophy and the Mechanical Arts, *etc.* *See* Class XI. Part I.

Part IV. Gymnastics; Games and Sports.

Smith (Horatio). Festivals, Games, and Amusements, *etc.* *See* Class XXVII.

Part V. The Fine Arts, — Architecture, Drawing, Painting, Engraving, Sculpture, Music.

Note. For *Heraldry*, see Class XXIV. Part I. For *Æsthetics*, see Class I.

Barnard (Henry). School Architecture; or Contributions to the Improvement of School-Houses in the United States. ... 2d Ed. New York. 1848. 8°

Catalogue of Paintings, by Col. [John] Trumbull; including Eight Subjects of the American Revolution ... . (Trumbull's Autobiography, *etc.* 1841. 8° pp. 405 – 439.)

Clark (John). ... Elements of Drawing in Two Parts. Embracing Exercises for the Slate and Black-Board. Edited by D. M. Reese, M.D. ... . New-York. 1849. 12° (Chambers's Educational Course, No. 2.)

Curiosities of Art. — I. Architecture. (Chambers's Miscel., VI. no. 108.)

Fowle (William Bentley). An Introduction to Linear Drawing; translated from the French of M. Francœur; with Alterations and Additions ... . To which are added, The Elements of Linear Perspective; and Questions on the Whole. By W. B. F. ... . 3d Ed. Boston. 1830. 12° pp. vi., 86. +

Francœur (*Prof.* Louis Benjamin). *See* Fowle (W. B.). An Introduction, *etc.*

Gwilt (Joseph). Music. (Encycl. Metrop., V. 685 – 779.)

James (John Thomas), *Bp. of Calcutta, and* Lindsay (*Rev.* John). Painting. (Encycl. Metrop., V. 466 – [592*].)

Lindsay (*Rev.* John). Engraving. (Encycl. Metrop., V. 780 – 851.)

Narrien (*Prof.* John). Architecture. (Encycl. Metrop., V. 237 – 432.)

Peale (Rembrandt). Graphics, the Art of accurate Delineation ... . In Five Books ... with an Introduction ... . Philadelphia. [184 – .] 12°

Note. Pages i. – xii., with the title, are wanting.

Popular Cultivation of Music. (Chambers's Papers, I. no. 7.)

Recent Decorative Art. (Chambers's Papers, IX. no. 65.)

Ripley (George) *and* Taylor (Bayard). ... Hand-Book of Literature and the Fine Arts; comprising complete and accurate Definitions of all Terms employed in Belles-Lettres, Philosophy, Theology, Law, Mythology, Painting, Music, Sculpture, Architecture, and all kindred Arts. Compiled and arranged by G. R. and B. T. New-York. 1852. 12° pp. vi., 647. (Putnam's Home Cyclopedia, Vol. II.)

TAYLOR (Bayard). *See* RIPLEY (G.) *and* TAYLOR (B.).

WESTMACOTT (Richard), *Jr.* Sculpture. (ENCYCL. Metrop., V. 433–465.)

WOOD-ENGRAVING. (CHAMBERS'S Miscel., V. no. 85.)

LANGUAGE; WITH AN APPENDIX.

(Classes XV. — XVIII.)

CLASS XV. LANGUAGE.

PART I. GENERAL WORKS; WORKS RELATING TO SEVERAL LANGUAGES.

CLASSICAL Museum (The), a Journal of Philology, and of Ancient History and Literature. [Edited by Leonhard Schmitz, Ph. D.] Volume the First — Seventh. [June, 1843 — Dec. 1849.] 7 vols. London. 1844–50. 8°

Note. Discontinued.

GENERAL Principles (The) of Grammar. [With a treatise on English Grammar.] Philadelphia. 1847. 24° (8. 4.) (SMALL Books, *etc.* III. no. 12.)

PRIESTLEY (Joseph), *LL.D.* English Grammar; Lectures on the Theory of Language and Universal Grammar, *etc.* *See* Part II. § 2. A.

SACY (Antoine Isaac SILVESTRE, *Baron* DE). *See* SILVESTRE DE SACY.

SCHLEGEL (Karl Wilhelm Friedrich VON). The Philosophy of Life, and Philosophy of Language. *See* Class I.

SILVESTRE DE SACY (Antoine Isaac), *Baron.* Principles of General Grammar … . Translated and fitted for American Use by D. Fosdick, Jr. 2d American, from the 5th French Ed. Andover. 1837. 12°

STODDART (*Sir* John). Grammar. (ENCYCL. Metrop., I. 1–192.)

TRENCH (*Prof.* Richard Chenevix). On the Study of Words. … From the 2d London Ed., revised and enlarged. New York. 1852. 12°

WEBSTER (Noah), *LL.D.* An American Dictionary of the English Language; … to which is prefixed an Introductory Dissertation on the Origin, History, and Connection, of the Languages of Western Asia and Europe, *etc.* *See* Part II. § 2. B.

PART II. PARTICULAR LANGUAGES. (Arranged alphabetically.)

§ 1. *Anglo-Saxon.*

BOSWORTH (Joseph), *D.D.*, *Ph. D.* A Compendious Anglo-Saxon and English Dictionary. … London. 1852. 8°

KLIPSTEIN (Louis F.), *Ph. D.* Analecta Anglo-Saxonica. — Selections, in Prose and Verse, from the Anglo-Saxon Literature: with an Introductory Ethnological Essay, and Notes .... 2 vols. New York. 1849. 12°

——— A Grammar of the Anglo-Saxon Language .... 2d Ed. New York. 1848. 12°

§ 2. *English.*

A. Grammar, with General and Introductory Works.

AMERICAN SOCIETY FOR THE DIFFUSION OF USEFUL KNOWLEDGE. ... The English Spelling Book .... New-York. 1847. 12°

ARNOLD (*Rev.* Thomas Kerchever). An English Grammar for Classical Schools, with Questions, and a Course of Exercises; being a Practical Introduction to English Prose Composition. ... 3d Ed. London. 1843. 12°

BROWN (Goold). The Grammar of English Grammars, with an Introduction Historical and Critical .... New York. 1851. 8° pp. xix., 1028.

——— The Institutes of English Grammar .... Stereotype Ed., revised by the Author. New-York. [1832?] 12°

CHANDLER (Joseph R.). Chandler's Common School Grammar. — A Grammar of the English Language; adapted to the Schools of America. ... Philadelphia. 1847. 12° or 8° (6. and 8.)

CLARK (S. W.). The Science of the English Language. — A Practical Grammar; in which Words, Phrases, and Sentences are classified according to their Offices, and their Relation to each other, illustrated by a complete System of Diagrams. ... 2d Ed. New York. 1848. 12°

CRAIK (*Prof.* George Lillie). Outlines of the History of the English Language for the Use of the Junior Classes in Colleges and the Higher Classes in Schools. ... London. 1851. 16°

EVERETT (Erastus). A System of English Versification ...; illustrated by numerous Examples from the best Poets. ... New-York. 1848. 12°

FOWLE (William Bentley). The Common School Grammar, Part Second .... Boston. 1847. 12°

FOWLER (*Prof.* William Chauncey). English Grammar. — The English Language in its Elements and Forms. With a History of its Origin and Development. ... New York. 1850. 8° pp. xxiii., 17-675.

GENERAL Principles (The) of Grammar. [With a treatise on English Grammar.] *See* Part I.

GOLDSBURY (John). The Common School Grammar .... 6th Ed. Boston. 1845. 12° pp. 94.

——— A Sequel to the Common School Grammar. ... Boston. 1842. 12°

Greene (Samuel Stillman). Greene's Analysis. — A Treatise on the Structure of the English Language ; or the Analysis and Classification of Sentences and their component Parts ; with Illustrations and Exercises, adapted to the Use of Schools .... Philadelphia. 1848. 12°

Harrison (*Rev.* Matthew). The Rise, Progress, and Present Structure of the English Language. ... London. 1848. 12°

Hart (John S.), *LL.D.* English Grammar .... Philadelphia. 1845. 12°

Latham (Robert Gordon), *M.D.* An Elementary English Grammar, for the Use of Schools. ... Revised Ed. [by Prof. Francis J. Child]. Cambridge. 1852. 16°

——— The English Language. ... 2d Ed., revised and greatly enlarged. London. 1848. 8° pp. xl., 581.

——— *The same.* ... 3d Ed., revised and greatly enlarged. London. 1850. 8° pp. xlii., 609.

——— A Hand-Book of the English Language, for the Use of Students of the Universities and Higher Classes of Schools. ... London. 1851. 12°

——— History and Etymology of the English Language, for the Use of Classical Schools. London. 1849. 16° pp. iv., 96.

Lowth (Robert), *D.D.*, successively *Bp. of St. David's, Oxford,* and *London.* A short Introduction to English Grammar, with Critical Notes. ... 2d Cambridge, from the Author's last Ed. Cambridge [Mass.]. 1838. 18°

Mulligan (John). Exposition of the Grammatical Structure of the English Language ; being an Attempt to furnish an Improved Method of teaching Grammar. For the Use of Schools and Colleges. ... New-York. 1852. 8°

Murray (Lindley). An English Grammar ... illustrated by appropriate Exercises, and a Key to the Exercises. ... 5th American, from the last English Ed., corrected and much enlarged. 2 vols. (bound in one). New-York. 1823. 8°

New England Primer. *See* Class II. Part III.

Priestley (Joseph), *LL.D.* English Grammar ; Lectures on the Theory of Language and Universal Grammar ; and on Oratory and Criticism. ... With Notes and an Appendix, by John Towill Rutt. London. 1833. 8°

Quackenbos (G. P.). First Lessons in Composition, *etc.* *See* Class XVII.

Spalding (William). The History of English Literature ; with an Outline of the Origin and Growth of the English Language, *etc.* *See* Class XXIX.

Weld (Allen Hayden). Weld's English Grammar, Illustrated by Exercises in Composition, Analyzing and Parsing. ... 3d Ed. Portland. 1847. 12°

——— *The same.* 7th Ed. Portland. 1847. 12°

Welsford (Henry). On the Origin and Ramifications of the English

Language. Preceded by an Inquiry into the Primitive Seats, Early Migrations, and Final Settlements of the principal European Nations. ... London. 1845. 8°

WILSON (John). A Treatise on English Punctuation ... . With an Appendix, containing a List of Abbreviations, Hints on Proof-reading, etc. 2d Ed. of "Grammatical Punctuation," enlarged. Boston. 1850. 12°

B. Lexicography.

Note. Compare Class XXX.

BUTTER (Henry). Etymological Expositor. *See* SCHOLAR'S Companion.

DUBLIN, Richard, *Archbishop of.* *See* WHATELY.

GRAHAM (George Farquhar). English Synonymes classified and explained; with Practical Exercises, designed for Schools and Private Tuition. ... Edited, with an Introduction and illustrative Authorities, by Henry Reed ... . New York. 1847. 12°

HALLIWELL (James Orchard). A Dictionary of Archaic and Provincial Words, Obsolete Phrases, Proverbs, and Ancient Customs, from the Fourteenth Century. ... 2d Ed. 2 vols. London. 1852. 8°

Note. The two vols. are paged continuously.

LONDON Encyclopædia. *See* Class XXX.

Note. This work contains a Dictionary of the English Language, in which the use of words is illustrated by copious citations from approved writers.

LYND (*Prof.* James). The Class-Book of Etymology, designed to promote Precision in the Use, and facilitate the Acquisition of a Knowledge of the English Language. ... Revised Ed. Philadelphia. 1848. 12°

——— The First Book of Etymology ... . Revised Ed. Philadelphia. 1847. 12°

McELLIGOTT (James N.). Manual, Analytical and Synthetical of Orthography and Definition. ... New York. 1846. 8° ? (4.)

——— The Young Analyzer; being an easy Outline of the Course of Instruction in the English Language, presented in McElligott's Analytical Manual ... . New York. 1846. 8° ? (4.) pp. 54.

McMURTRIE (*Prof.* Henry), *M.D.* Lexicon Scientiarum. — A Dictionary of Terms used in the various Branches of Anatomy, Astronomy, Botany, Geology, Geometry, Hygiene, Mineralogy, Nat. Philosophy, Physiology, Zoology, &c. ... Philadelphia. 1847. 12°

OSWALD (John). An Etymological Dictionary of the English Language, on a Plan entirely New. ... Revised and improved ... by J. M. Keagy. Philadelphia. 1846. 12°

RICHARDSON (Charles). A new Dictionary of the English Language. 2 vols. London. 1838. 4°

——— *The same.* (ENCYCL. Metrop., Vol. XIV. — XXV.)

SCHOLAR'S Companion (The); containing Exercises in the Orthography, Derivation, and Classification of English Words. Arranged on the Basis of Butter's Etymological Expositor. A new Ed., enlarged and improved. Philadelphia. 1844. 12°

WALKER (John). A Rhyming, Spelling, and Pronouncing Dictionary of the English Language, in which I. The whole Language is arranged according to its Terminations .... To which ... is added an Index of [Perfect and] Allowable Rhymes .... A new and revised Ed. Philadelphia. 1852. 12° pp. 706.

WEBSTER (Noah), *LL.D.* An American Dictionary of the English Language; ... to which is prefixed an Introductory Dissertation on the Origin, History, and Connection, of the Languages of Western Asia and Europe, with an Explanation of the Principles on which Languages are formed. ... Revised and enlarged, by Chauncey A. Goodrich. With Pronouncing Vocabularies of Scripture, Classical, and Geographical Names [prepared under the direction of Prof. Noah Porter]. Springfield, Mass. 1848. 4° pp. lxxxiv., 1367. (2 copies, one dated 1850.)

[WHATELY (Richard)], *Abp. of Dublin.* A Selection of English Synonymes. 1st American Ed., from the 2d London Ed., revised and enlarged. Boston and Cambridge. 1852. 12°

WORCESTER (Joseph Emerson), *LL.D.* A Comprehensive Pronouncing and Explanatory Dictionary of the English Language; with Pronouncing Vocabularies of Classical, Scripture, and Modern Geographical Names. Carefully revised and enlarged. Boston. 1845. 12°

——— A Universal and Critical Dictionary of the English Language: to which are added Walker's Key to the Pronunciation of Classical and Scripture Proper Names, much enlarged and improved; and a Pronouncing Vocabulary of Modern Geographical Names. ... Boston. 1846. 8° pp. lxxvi., 956. (2 copies, one dated 1851.)

§ 3. *French.*

A. Grammar, with General and Introductory Works.

BOLMAR (Anthony). *See* LÉVIZAC (J. P. V. LECOUTZ, *Abbé* DE).

BUGARD (B. F.). French Practical Translator; or, Easy Method of learning to translate French into English. ... 5th Ed. Boston. 1841. 12°

COLLOT (*Prof.* A. G.). Progressive Pronouncing French Reader .... Philadelphia. 1844. 12° or 16° (12. and 8.)

CUBI I SOLER (Mariano). Le Traducteur François; or a Practical System for translating the French Language; to which are added Observations on the Modes generally pursued in learning Languages. ... 2d Ed., ... enlarged, and greatly improved. Boston. 1828. 12°

DUCREST DE SAINT-AUBIN (Stéphanie Félicité), *Countess de Genlis.* *See* GENLIS.

FENWICK DE PORQUET (Louis). *See* PORQUET.

FIVAS (Victor DE). An Introduction to the French Language: containing Fables ... &c. with a Dictionary .... From the 5th English Ed. New York. 1850. 12°

GENLIS (Stéphanie Félicité DUCREST DE SAINT-AUBIN, *Countess* DE). A Manual, containing Expressions most used in Travelling, *etc.* *See* POPPLETON (G. H.). New Elements, *etc.* 1835. 12°

GIRAULT (*Prof.* A. N.). Colloquial and Grammatical Exercises, intended to impart ... both a Theoretical and Practical Knowledge of the French Language. ... 2d Ed. Philadelphia. 1846. 18°

LÉVIZAC (Jean Pons Victor LECOUTZ, *Abbé* DE). A Theoretical and Practical Grammar of the French Language .... By M. de L. With numerous Corrections and Improvements ... a complete Treatise on the Genders of French Nouns ... also ... all the French Verbs .... By A. Bolmar .... 11th Ed. Philadelphia. 1844. 12°

Note. The part relating to the Verbs is paged independently, as an Appendix. It was also published separately.

LHOMOND (Charles François), *the Abbé.* Elements of French Grammar .... Translated from the French, with Notes and Exercises. [By Henry W. Longfellow.] 8th Ed. Boston. 1845. 12°

LITAIS DE GAUX (——). Théorie des Verbes, *etc.* *See* § 3. B. VERLAC (——). Dictionnaire, *etc.* 1845. 4°

[LONGFELLOW (*Prof.* Henry Wadsworth)]. *Translator*, etc. *See* LHOMOND (C. F.). Elements, *etc.*

OLLENDORFF (H. G.). A Key to the Exercises in Ollendorff's New Method of learning to read, write, and speak the French Language. Revised Ed. New York. 1846. 12°

PICOT (Charles). No. 1 of Charles Picot's Series of [French] School Books. First Lessons in French .... 2d improved Ed. Philadelphia. 1847. 12°

——— No. 2 .... The French Student's Assistant .... 2d improved Ed. Philadelphia. 1845. 12° pp. 48. (2 copies.)

——— No. 3 .... Interesting Narrations in French .... Philadelphia. 1845. 12°

——— No. 4 .... Historical Narrations in French .... Philadelphia. 1845. 12°

——— No. 5 .... Scientific Narrations, etc. in French .... Philadelphia. 1847. 12°

——— No. 6 .... Fleurs du Parnasse Français; or Elegant Extracts from the most approved Productions of the best French Poets .... Philadelphia. 1845. 12°

——— No. 7 .... Beauties of the French Drama ... comprising Athalie, a Tragedy of J. Racine; Le Cid, a Tragedy of P. Corneille; Mérope, a Tragedy of Voltaire; Le Misanthrope, a Comedy of Molière; followed by ... Extracts from the other Master-pieces of the same Authors, as well as those of the most eminent Dramatic

Writers of Modern Time; with Notes and Explanations .... Philadelphia. 1846. 12°

PINNEY (Norman). The First Book in French; or, A Practical Introduction to reading, writing, and speaking the French Language. ... Hartford. 1848. 18°

——— A Key to the First Book in French. ... Hartford. 1848. 18° pp. 55.

——— The Practical French Teacher; or a New Method of learning to read, write, and speak the French Language. ... Hartford. 1847. 12°

——— *The same.* [Improved Ed.] New York. 1849. 12°

——— The Progressive French Reader; ... with Notes and a Lexicon. ... New York. 1850. 12°

POPPLETON (G. H.). New Elements of Conversation, in English and French. ... By Professor G. [H.] P., at Paris: followed by the Manual of Idiotisms of Madame de Genlis. 4th American Ed. Revised ... by F. Sales .... Boston. 1835. 12°

Note. Also with the title:—"Nouveaux Élémens," etc.—The Manual of Madame de Genlis has an independent title-page.

PORQUET (Louis Fenwick DE). Parisian Phraseology .... From the 4th London Ed. Revised ... by F. Sales .... Boston. 1833. 12°

——— The Turning of English Idioms into French at Sight; or, Sequel to any Grammar Exercises. ... Revised ... by F. Sales .... Boston. 1833. 12°

——— Key to Sequel to any Grammar Exercises .... Revised ... by F. Sales .... Boston. 1834. 12°

B. Lexicography.

DOBSON (J.). *See* FLEMING (——) *and* TIBBINS (J.). A ... French and English Dictionary, *etc.*

FLEMING (*Prof.* ——) *and* TIBBINS (*Prof.* J.). A ... French and English and English and French Dictionary, on the Basis of the Royal Dictionary English and French and French and English: compiled from ... [the best sources]. ... With complete Tables of the Verbs on an entirely New Plan .... By Charles Picot .... The whole prepared, with the Addition ... of a very great Number of Terms in the Natural Sciences, Chemistry, Medicine etc. etc. ... by J. Dobson .... 3d Ed., revised and corrected. Philadelphia. 1846. 8° pp. 1376.

——— Royal Dictionary English and French and French and English; compiled from the ... [best sources]. Vol. I.—English and French. ... | Grand Dictionnaire Français-Anglais et Anglais-Français .... Tome II.—Français-Anglais. ... 2 vols. Paris. 1844–45. 4° pp. 10, 1234, and xi., 1104.

SPIERS (*Prof.* A.). General English and French Dictionary ... [from the best sources]. Work adopted by the University of France for

French Colleges. 3d Ed. Paris. 1849. 8° pp. 716. + (Bound with the following.)

Spiers (*Prof.* A.). General French and English Dictionary ... [from the best sources]. Paris. 1849. 8° pp. xi., 615.

Tibbins (*Prof.* J.). *See* Fleming (——) *and* Tibbins (J.).

Verlac (——). Dictionnaire Synoptique de tous les Verbes de la Langue Française ... entièrement conjugués ... par M. V. précédé d'une Théorie des Verbes et d'un Traité complet des Participes ... . Par M. Litais de Gaux ... . Paris. 1845. 4°

§ 4. *German.*

Adler (*Prof.* George J.). A Dictionary of the German and English Languages; indicating the Accentuation of every German Word, containing several hundred German Synonyms, together with a Classification and Alphabetical List of the Irregular Verbs, and a Dictionary of German Abbreviations. Compiled from the Works of Hilpert, Flügel, Grieb, Heyse, and others. In Two Parts: I. German and English.—II. English and German. ... 2d revised Ed. New-York. 8° 1849. pp. xvi., 848, 522.

[Follen (Charles Theodore Christian)]. German Reader for Beginners. Boston. 1831. 12°

Note. Also with the title:—"Deutsches Lesebuch," etc.

Grieb (Christoph Friedrich). A Dictionary of the English and German Languages. To which is added a Synopsis of English Words differently pronounced by different Orthoëpists. ... Vol. I. English and German. | Vol. II. German and English. 2 vols. Stuttgart. 1847. Large 8°

Note. Also with the title:—"Englisch-Deutsches ... Wörterbuch," etc.

§ 5. *Greek.*

A. Grammar, with General and Introductory Works.

Anthon (*Prof.* Charles), *LL.D.* A Grammar of the Greek Language, principally from the German of Kühner, with Selections from Matthiæ, Buttmann, Thiersch, and Rost. For the Use of Schools and Colleges. ... New-York. 1844. 12°

——— A Greek Reader, selected principally from the Work of Frederic Jacobs ... . With English Notes ... a Metrical Index to Homer and Anacreon, and a copious Lexicon. ... New-York. 1850. 12° pp. xiv., 614.

Arnold (*Rev.* Thomas Kerchever). First Greek Book; on the Plan of the First Latin Book. ... Carefully revised ... by Rev. J. A. Spencer ... . New-York. 1850. 12°

——— First Greek Lessons. ... Re-arranged and carefully corrected by Rev. J. A. Spencer, A.M. From the 3d London Ed. New-York. 1848. 12°

——— A Greek Grammar; intended as a sufficient Grammar of Reference for Schools and Colleges. ... 2d Ed. London. 1848. 8°

——— Practical Introduction to Greek Accidence. ... 2d Ed. London. 1842. 8°

——— Practical Introduction to Greek Construing. *See* SPENCER (J. A.). Greek Reading Book, *etc.*

——— A Practical Introduction to Greek Prose Composition .... Carefully revised and corrected by Rev. J. A. Spencer .... From the 5th London Ed. New-York. 1849. 12°

——— A Practical Introduction to Greek Prose Composition. Part II. (The Particles.) ... First American Ed., revised and improved [by J. A. Spencer]. New-York. 1852. 12°

BOS (Lambert). Bos' Greek Ellipses, abridged and translated into English from Professor Schæfer's Edition; with Notes. By the Rev. John Seager .... London. [1830?] 8°

BULLIONS (Peter), *D.D.* A Greek Reader, selected chiefly from Jacobs' Greek Reader, adapted to Bullions' Greek Grammar, with an Introduction on the Idioms of the Greek Language — Notes ... and an improved Lexicon. ... 2d Ed. New-York. 1846. 12°

——— The Principles of Greek Grammar ... for the Use of Schools and Colleges. Revised and improved. ... New-York. 1847. 12°

BUTTMANN (Philipp Karl). A Catalogue of Irregular Greek Verbs, with all the Tenses extant, their Formation, Meaning, and Usage. Translated and edited ... by the Rev. J. R. Fishlake .... 2d Ed. London. 1844. 8°

——— A Greek Grammar for the Use of High Schools and Universities. Translated from the German, with Additions, by Edward Robinson. 2d Ed. Andover. 1839. 8°

——— A Greek Grammar for the Use of High Schools and Universities. By Philip Buttmann. Revised and enlarged by his Son, Alexander Buttmann. Translated from the 18th German Ed., by Edward Robinson. New York. 1851. 8°

CARMICHAEL (Archibald Nisbet). Greek Verbs; their leading Formations, Defects, and Irregularities ... illustrated by copious and special Reference to the Classical Authors; with Observations ... on Peculiarities of Form, Meaning, Construction, and Quantity. ... London. 1841. 12°

CHAMPLIN (*Prof.* James Tift). A short and comprehensive Greek Grammar, with Materials for Oral Exercises, for Schools and Colleges. ... New York. 1852. 12°

COLTON (John Owen). A Greek Reader, consisting of New Selections and Notes; with References to the Grammar of E. A. Sophocles .... New Haven. 1839. 8°

CROSBY (*Prof.* Alpheus). A Grammar of the Greek Language. ... 6th Ed. Boston. 1850. 12°

——— Greek Lessons: consisting of Selections from Xenophon's Anabasis, with Directions for the Study of the Grammar, Notes, Exercises in Translation from English into Greek, and a Vocabulary .... Boston. 1850. 12°

Day (Alfred), *LL.D.* The Syntax of the Relative Pronoun, *etc.* *See* § 7. A.

Donaldson (John William), *D.D.* A complete Greek Grammar for the Use of Learners. ... London. 1848. 8°

——— Constructionis Græcæ Præcepta in Usum Scholarum concinnavit Joannes Gulielmus D. .... Londini. 1845. 12° pp. xi., 64.

——— The New Cratylus, or Contributions towards a more accurate Knowledge of the Greek Language. ... Cambridge. 1839. 8° pp. xii., 598.

Felton (*Prof.* Cornelius Conway), *LL.D.* A Greek Reader, for the Use of Schools; containing Selections in Prose and Poetry, with English Notes and a Lexicon. Adapted particularly to the Greek Grammar of E. A. Sophocles .... 5th Ed., revised. Hartford. 1849. 12°

Fisk (Benjamin Franklin). A Grammar of the Greek Language. ... 2d Ed. Boston. 1831. 12°

——— Greek Exercises. .... Adapted to the Author's Greek Grammar. ... Boston. 1831. 12°

——— A Key to the Exercises adapted to Fisk's Greek Grammar. ... Boston. 1831. 12° pp. 82.

Goettling (*Prof.* Karl Wilhelm). Elements of Greek Accentuation. Translated from the German of Dr. K. G., by a Member of the University of Oxford. London. 1831. 8°

Greek Primitives (The). *See* [Lancelot (C.)].

Hermann (*Prof.* Johann Gottfried Jacob). Hermann's Elements of the Doctrine of Metres, abridged and translated into English. By the Rev. John Seager .... London. [1830?] 8°

Jacobs (*Prof.* Friedrich Christian Wilhelm). Greek Reader. *See* Anthon (C.); — Bullions (P.).

Jelf (William Edward). A Grammar of the Greek Language, chiefly from the German of Raphael Kühner. ... Part I. Accidence. | [Part II.] Syntax. 2 pts. Oxford. 1845 – 42. 8°

Kendrick (*Prof.* Asahel C.) Greek Ollendorff; being a Progressive Exhibition of the Principles of Greek Grammar: designed for Beginners in Greek, and as a Book of Exercises for Academies and Colleges. ... New-York. 1851. 12°

——— An Introduction to the Greek Language .... Utica. 1841. 12°

Kuehner (Raphael). An Elementary Grammar of the Greek Language. ... Translated by John H. Millard .... London. 1844. 8°

——— An Elementary Grammar of the Greek Language, containing a Series of Greek and English Exercises for Translation, with the requisite Vocabularies, and an Appendix on the Homeric Verse and Dialect. ... From the German by Samuel H. Taylor .... Andover. 1846. 12°

——— Grammar of the Greek Language, for the Use of High Schools and Colleges. ... Translated from the German by B. B. Edwards ... and S. H. Taylor .... Andover. 1844. 8° pp. 604.

——— *See* Anthon (C.); — Jelf (W. E.).

[Lancelot (Claude)]. The Greek Primitives, of the Messieurs de Port-Royal. [That is, "Le Jardin des Racines Grecques," by C. L.] To which are added Rules for Derivation, or the Formation of Words; *selected principally from Buttmann's Greek Grammar.* Boston. 1831. 12°

M'Clintock (John), *D.D.* A Second Book in Greek; containing Syntax, with Reading Lessons in Prose; Prosody and the Dialects, with Reading Lessons in Verse, forming a sufficient Greek Reader. With a Vocabulary. ... New York. 1850. 12°

M'Clintock (John), *D.D., and* Crooks (George R.). A First Book in Greek; containing a full View of the Forms of Words, with Vocabularies and copious Exercises, on the Method of constant Imitation and Repetition. ... 3d Ed., with the Addition of brief Summaries of the Doctrine of the Verb, and of the Rules of Syntax. New York. 1850. 12°

Matthiae (August Heinrich). A copious Greek Grammar .... Translated from the German by Edward Valentine Blomfield .... 5th Ed., thoroughly revised, and greatly enlarged from the last Ed. of the Original, by John Kenrick, M.A. 2 vols. London. 1837. 8°

Note. The two vols. are paged continuously; pp. liv., 1199. The work is "revised and enlarged" from the *second* German edition; not the third, published in 1835.

Munk (Eduard). The Metres of the Greeks and Romans. *See* § 7. A.

Owen (John Jason), *D.D.* A Greek Reader ... adapted to Sophocles's and Kuhner's Grammars, with Notes and a Lexicon, for the Use of Schools .... New-York. 1852. 12°

Pennington (George James). An Essay on the Pronunciation of the Greek Language. ... London. 1844. 8°

Port-Royal, *Messieurs de.* The Greek Primitives. *See* [Lancelot (C.)].

Rost (*Prof.* Valentin Christian Friedrich). Greek Grammar, for the Use of Schools. Translated from the German .... London. 1829. 8°

Rudiments of the Greek Language. For the Use of the Edinburgh Academy. ... 6th Ed.: to which has been added a List of Greek Verbs, exhibiting the Cases which accompany each in its different Significations. Edinburgh. 1849. 12°

Schmitz (Leonhard), *Ph. D.* Elementary Grammar of the Greek Language .... Edinburgh. 1853. 8° or 16° (8.)

Sophocles (Evangelinus Apostolides). A Catalogue of Greek Verbs. For the Use of Colleges. ... Hartford. 1844. 12°

——— Greek Exercises, followed by an English and Greek Vocabulary, containing about Seven Thousand Three Hundred Words. ... [With the Key.] 3d Ed. Hartford. 1843. 12°

SOPHOCLES (Evangelinus Apostolides). A Greek Grammar, for the Use of Schools and Colleges. ... A new Ed. Hartford. 1850. 12°

——— Greek Lessons, adapted to the Author's Greek Grammar; for the Use of Beginners. ... Hartford. 1843. 18°

——— History of the Greek Alphabet, with Remarks on Greek Orthography and Pronunciation. ... Cambridge. 1848. 12°

SPENCER (*Rev.* Jesse A.). Greek Reading Book, for the Use of Schools: containing the Substance of the Practical Introduction to Greek Construing, and a Treatise on the Greek Particles, by Thomas Kerchever Arnold ... and also a copious Selection from Greek Authors, with English Notes ... and a Lexicon. ... New-York. 1848. 12° pp. 618.

SPITZNER (Ernst Franz Heinrich), *Ph.D.* Elements of Greek Prosody. Translated from the German ... by a Member of the University of Oxford. London. 1831. 8°

STUART (*Prof.* Moses). Practical Rules for Greek Accents and Quantity. From the German of P. Buttmann and F. Passow. ... Andover. 1829. 12°

THIERSCH (*Prof.* Friedrich). Greek Tables ... . To which is added an Essay on the Dialects, from Buttmann's Grammar. Translated by R. B. Patton ... . 2d Ed. revised and enlarged. New-York. 1830. 8° pp. 92.

VEITCH (*Rev.* William). Greek Verbs, Irregular and Defective; their Forms, Meaning, and Quantity: embracing all the Tenses used by the Greek Writers, with References to the Passages in which they are found. Edinburgh. 1848. 12°

B. Lexicography.

BUTTMANN (Philipp Karl). Lexilogus; or a Critical Examination of the Meaning and Etymology of numerous Greek Words and Passages, intended principally for Homer and Hesiod. ... Translated and edited ... by the Rev. J. R. Fishlake. ... . 2d Ed., revised. London. 1840. 8° pp. xvi., 597.

DONNEGAN (James), *M.D.* A new Greek and English Lexicon; principally on the Plan of the Greek and German Lexicon of Schneider ... . 1st American, from the 2d London Ed., revised and enlarged, by R. B. Patton. Boston. 1838. 8° pp. viii., 1413.

——— A new Greek and English Lexicon ... . 4th Ed., considerably enlarged, carefully revised, and materially improved throughout. London. 1846. 8° pp. viii., 4, 1743.

LIDDELL (Henry George) *and* SCOTT (Robert). A Greek-English Lexicon, based on the German Work of Francis Passow. ... With Corrections and Additions, and the Insertion ... of the Proper Names occurring in the principal Greek Authors, by Henry Drisler ... . New York. 1846. 8° pp. xxix., 1705.

PASSOW (Franz Ludwig Karl Friedrich). *See* LIDDELL (H. G.) *and* SCOTT (R.).

PICKERING (John), *LL.D.* A Comprehensive Lexicon of the Greek

Language, adapted to the Use of Colleges and Schools in the United States. ... Boston. 1847. 8° pp. xii., 1456.

PILLON (Alexandre). Handbook of Greek Synonymes, from the French of M. Alex. P. ... . Edited, with Notes, by the Rev. Thomas Kerchever Arnold ... . London. 1850. 12°

YONGE (C. D.). An English-Greek Lexicon. ... London. 1849. 4°

§ 6. *Italian.*

BACHI (Pietro). A Grammar of the Italian Language ... . A new Ed. revised and improved, with the Addition of Practical Exercises and numerous Illustrations, drawn from the Italian Classics. ... Boston. 1838. 12° pp. xxxiii., 568. +

GRAGLIA (C.). Italian Pocket Dictionary: in Two Parts: I. Italian and English: — II. English and Italian. Preceded by an Italian Grammar. First American, from the 14th London Ed., with Corrections and Additions. Boston. 1839. 16°

OLLENDORFF (H. G.). Ollendorff's New Method of learning to read, write, and speak the Italian Language ... . With Additions and Corrections by Felix Foresti, LL.D. ... . New-York. 1846. 12°

§ 7. *Latin.*

A. Grammar, with General and Introductory Works.

ADAM (Alexander), *LL.D.* Adam's Latin Grammar: with numerous Additions and Improvements ... . By C. D. Cleveland ... . Philadelphia. 1836. 12°

See FISK (A.).

ALLEN (Alexander). An Etymological Analysis of Latin Verbs. For the Use of Schools and Colleges. ... London. 1836. 16° (8.)

ANDREWS (*Prof.* Ethan Allen), *LL.D.* A First Latin Book; or Progressive Lessons in reading and writing Latin. ... 3d Ed. Boston. 1851. 12°

——— First Lessons in Latin; or an Introduction to Andrews and Stoddard's Latin Grammar. 6th Ed. Boston. 1844. 18°

——— The First Part of Jacobs and Döring's Latin Reader: adapted to Andrews and Stoddard's Latin Grammar. 7th Ed. Boston. 1843. 12°

——— Latin Exercises; adapted to Andrews and Stoddard's Latin Grammar. 6th Ed. Boston. 1844. 12°

——— A Key to Latin Exercises; adapted to Andrews and Stoddard's Latin Grammar. Boston. 1838. 12°

——— Lhomond's Viri Romæ, *etc.* *See* LHOMOND (C. F.).

[———] Questions upon Andrews and Stoddard's Latin Grammar. Boston. 1842. 18°

ANDREWS (*Prof.* Ethan Allen), *LL.D.*, *and* STODDARD (*Prof.* Solomon). A Grammar of the Latin Language; for the Use of Schools and Colleges. 11th Ed. Boston. 1845. 12°

——— *The same.* The 18th Ed., carefully revised and corrected, by E. A. Andrews, LL.D. Boston. 1850. 12° (2 copies, one dated 1852.)

ANTHON (*Prof.* Charles), *LL.D.* A System of Latin Versification, in a Series of Progressive Exercises, including Specimens of Translation from English and German Poetry into Latin Verse. For the Use of Schools and Colleges. ... New-York. 1845. 12°

——— Key to Anthon's Latin Versification. New-York. 1845. 12°

ARNOLD (*Rev.* Thomas Kerchever). First Latin Book. *See* HARKNESS (A.).

——— A First and Second Latin Book and Practical Grammar. ... Carefully revised and corrected by Rev. J. A. Spencer .... 11th Ed., revised. New York. 1850. 12°

Note. The two Parts have also independent title-pages, but are paged continuously.

——— Longer Latin Exercises, Part I. ... London. 1844. 8° pp. 96. +

——— A Practical Introduction to Latin Prose Composition: Part II. ... London. 1843. 8°

——— A Practical Introduction to Latin Prose Composition. [In two Parts.] ... Carefully revised and corrected by Rev. J. A. Spencer .... 8th American Ed. New-York. 1850. 12°

Note. Part II. has an independent title-page.

——— A Practical Introduction to Latin Verse Composition. ... London. 1842. 8°

BEARD (J. R.), *D.D.* Latin made easy; ... comprising a Grammar, Exercise Book, and Vocabulary. 2d Ed., revised and enlarged. London. 1846. 12°

BECK (*Prof.* Charles), *Ph. D.* Syntax of the Latin Language, chiefly from the German of C. G. Zumpt. ... 2d Ed. Boston. 1844. 12°

BULLIONS (Peter), *D.D.* The First Part of Jacobs' Latin Reader, adapted to Bullions' Latin Grammar; with an Introduction, on the Idioms of the Latin Language; an improved Vocabulary; and Exercises in Latin Prose Composition, on a new Plan. ... New-York. 1845. 12°

——— The Principles of Latin Grammar; ... for the Use of Colleges and Academies. ... New-York. 1843. 12°

CHAMPLIN (*Prof.* James Tift). Kühner's Latin Grammar; with Exercises, Latin Reader and Vocabularies. Translated and remodelled by J. T. C. .... Boston. 1850. 12°

CLEVELAND (*Prof.* Charles Dexter). *See* ADAM (A.). Adam's Latin Grammar, *etc.*

DAY (Alfred), *LL.D.* The Syntax of the Relative Pronoun and its

Cognates; copiously illustrated by Examples from the Latin and Greek Tongue. London. 1844. 8°

DONALDSON (John William), *D.D.* A complete Latin Grammar, for the Use of Learners . . . . London. 1852. 16° (8.)

——— Varronianus: a Critical and Historical Introduction to the Philological Study of the Latin Language. ... Cambridge [Eng.]. 1844. 8°

——— Varronianus: a Critical and Historical Introduction to the Ethnography of Ancient Italy and to the Philological Study of the Latin Language. ... 2d Ed., revised and considerably enlarged. London. 1852. 8°

ETON Latin Grammar. *See* WHITE (J. T.).

FISK (Allen). Adam's Latin Grammar; simplified, by means of an Introduction: ... with appropriate Exercises . . . . 2d Ed., revised and corrected. New-York. 1824. 8°

Note. Appended are "Questions," etc. paged independently.

GROTEFEND (Friedrich August Ludwig Adolph). Materials for Translation into Latin . . . . Translated from the German by the Rev. H. H. Arnold, B. A. and edited (with Notes and Excursuses from Grotefend) by the Rev. T. K. Arnold . . . . London. 1842. 8°

HARKNESS (Albert). Arnold's First Latin Book; remodelled and rewritten, and adapted to the Ollendorff Method of Instruction. ... New-York. 1851. 12°

——— Second Latin Book; comprising a Historical Latin Reader, with Notes ...; and an Exercise-Book, developing a complete Analytical Syntax . . . . New-York. 1853. 12°

HARRISON (*Prof.* Gessner), *M.D.* An Exposition of some of the Laws of the Latin Grammar. ... New York. 1852. 12°

JACOBS (*Prof.* Friedrich Christian Wilhelm) *and* DOERING (Friedrich Wilhelm). Latin Reader. *See* ANDREWS (E. A.); — BULLIONS (P.).

KENNEDY (Benjamin Hall), *D.D.* An Elementary Grammar of the Latin Language, for the Use of Schools. ... 5th Ed. London. 1849. 12°

KENRICK (*Rev.* John). Exercises on Latin Syntax; adapted to Zumpt's Grammar. To which are added Extracts from the Writings of Muretus. ... 2d Ed. London. 1831. 8°

——— A Key to Exercises on Latin Syntax, adapted to Zumpt's Grammar. ... To which are added Extracts from ... Muretus. The 2d Ed. London. 1830. 8°

KEY (Thomas Hewitt). A Latin Grammar on the System of Crude Forms. ... London. 1846. 12°

KREBS (*Prof.* Johann Philipp). Guide for writing Latin: consisting of Rules and Examples for Practice. ... From the German, by Samuel H. Taylor . . . . Andover. 1843. 12°

——— *The same.* 2d Ed. [With alterations and additions.] Andover. 1845. 12°

KUEHNER (Raphael). Kühner's Latin Grammar. *See* CHAMPLIN (J. T.).

Lhomond (Charles François), *the Abbé.* Lhomond's Viri Romæ; adapted to Andrews and Stoddard's Latin Grammar, and to Andrews' First Latin Book. By E. A. Andrews, LL.D. 5th Ed. Boston. 1851. 12°

M'Clintock (John), *D.D.* A Second Book in Latin; containing Syntax, and Reading Lessons in Prose, forming a sufficient Latin Reader. With Imitative Exercises and a Vocabulary. ... New York. 1853. 12°

M'Clintock (John), *D.D., and* Crooks (George R.). A First Book in Latin; containing Grammar, Exercises, and Vocabularies, on the Method of constant Imitation and Repetition. ... 7th Ed. New York. 1850. 12° (2 copies.)

Madvig (*Prof.* Johan Nicolai). A Latin Grammar for the Use of Schools .... Translated from the Original German, with the Sanction and Cooperation of the Author, by the Rev. George Woods .... 2d Ed., with an Index of Authors. Oxford. 1851. 8°

Munk (Eduard). The Metres of the Greeks and Romans. A Manual for Schools and Private Study. Translated from the German. By Charles Beck and C. C. Felton. Boston. 1844. 12°

Schmitz (Leonhard), *Ph. D.* ... Elementary Latin Grammar and Exercises. Philadelphia. 1852. 18° (6.) (Schmitz and Zumpt's Classical Series.)

——— ... Grammar of the Latin Language. ... Philadelphia. 1849. 12° or 16° (12. and 8.) (Schmitz and Zumpt's Classical Series.)

Sears (Barnas), *D.D.* The Ciceronian; or, The Prussian Method of teaching the Elements of the Latin Language. Adapted to the Use of American Schools. Boston. 1844. 18°

Viri Romæ. *See* Lhomond (C. F.).

Willard (Samuel), *D.D.* An Introduction to the Latin Language. ... Boston. 1835. 12°

White (*Rev.* John T.). A Latin Grammar, containing: Part I. The Eton Grammar, revised and corrected; Part II. A Second or Larger Grammar, in English .... London. 1852. 12°

Zumpt (*Prof.* Carl Gottlob [*Lat.* Timotheus]). A Grammar of the Latin Language. From the Ninth Ed. of the Original, adapted to the Use of English Students. By Leonhard Schmitz .... Corrected and enlarged, by Charles Anthon .... 3d Ed. New-York. 1846. 12° pp. xx., 594.

——— A School Grammar of the Latin Language. ... Translated, and adapted to the Use of the High School of Edinburgh, by Leonhard Schmitz .... Corrected and enlarged, by Charles Anthon, LL.D. .... New York. 1847. 12°

——— Syntax, *etc.* *See* Beck (C.); — Kenrick (J.). Exercises, *etc.*

B. Lexicography.

Andrews (*Prof.* Ethan Allen), *LL.D.* A Copious and Critical Latin-English Lexicon, founded on the larger Latin-German Lexicon of

Dr. William Freund: with Additions and Corrections from the Lexicons of Gesner, Facciolati, Scheller, Georges, etc. [Edited] By E. A. Andrews. [Translated from the German by William W. Turner and R. D. C. Robbins; the Preface translated by Theodore D. Woolsey.] New York. 1851. 8° pp. xxvi., 1663.

ANTHON (*Prof.* Charles), *LL.D.* A Latin-English and English-Latin Dictionary, for the Use of Schools. Chiefly from the Lexicons of Freund, Georges, and Kaltschmidt. ... New York. 1852. 12° pp. viii., 1260. +

——— *Editor*, etc. *See* RIDDLE (J. E.) *and* ARNOLD (T. K.).

ARNOLD (*Rev.* Thomas Kerchever). *See* RIDDLE (J. E.) *and* ARNOLD (T. K.).

DOEDERLEIN (Johann Christoph Wilhelm Ludwig). Döderlein's Hand-Book of Latin Synonymes. Translated from the German, by the Rev. H. H. Arnold, B. A. London. 1841. 8°

FACCIOLATI (Jacopo). *See* FORCELLINI (E.).

FORCELLINI (Egidio). Totius Latinitatis Lexicon Consilio et Cura Jacobi Facciolati Opera et Studio Ægidii Forcellini ... lucubratum edidit Anglicam Interpretationem in Locum Italicæ substituit Appendicem Patavinam Lexico passim intertexuit pauca de suo ... huc atque illuc sparsit Auctarium denique et Horatii Tursellini de Particulis Latinæ Orationis Libellum etiam Gerrardi Siglarium Romanum et Gesneri Indicem Etymologicum adjecit Jacobus Bailey .... 2 vol. Londini. 1828. 4°

Note. Also with the half-title: — "The Universal Latin Lexicon of Facciolatus and Forcellinus," etc. — The appended works of Tursellinus (Torsellini), Gerrard, and Gesner are each paged separately.

FREUND (Wilhelm). A Copious and Critical Latin-English Lexicon. *See* ANDREWS (E. A.); — RIDDLE (J. E.).

GERRARD (John). Siglarium Romanum; sive Explicatio Notarum ac Literarum quæ hactenus reperiri potuerunt, in Marmoribus, Lapidibus, Nummis, Auctoribus, aliisque Romanorum Veterum Reliquiis .... Ex Editione Johannis Gerrard, Lond. 1792. (Appended to FORCELLINI (E.). ... Lexicon, *etc.* 1828. 4° Vol. II.)

GESNER (Johann Matthias). Latinitatis Index Etymologicus. (Appended to FORCELLINI (E.). ... Lexicon, *etc.* 1828. 4° Vol. II.)

KALTSCHMIDT (Jacob Heinrich). ... A School Dictionary of the Latin Language In Two Parts I. Latin-English | II. English-Latin 2 pts. Philadelphia. 1851. 18° or 16° (6. and 8.) (Schmitz and Zumpt's Classical Series.)

LEVERETT (Frederick Percival). A new and copious Lexicon of the Latin Language; compiled chiefly from the Magnum Totius Latinitatis Lexicon of Facciolati and Forcellini, and the German Works of Scheller and Luenemann. Edited by F. P. L. [assisted by H. W. Torrey, W. Pirscher, and T. G. Bradford]. Boston. 1842. 8° pp. iv., 1004.

See [TORREY (H. W.)]. An English-Latin Lexicon, *etc.*

RAMSHORN (*Prof.* Johann Gottlob Ludwig). Dictionary of Latin

Synonymes, for the Use of Schools and Private Students, with a complete Index. By Lewis R. From the German, by Francis Lieber. Boston. 1839. 12°

RICH (Anthony), *Jr.* The Illustrated Companion to the Latin Dictionary, and Greek Lexicon: forming a Glossary of all the Words representing visible Objects connected with the Arts, Manufactures, and everyday Life of the Greeks and Romans, with Representations of nearly Two Thousand Objects from the Antique. ... London. 1849. 8° pp. xi., 754.

RIDDLE (*Rev.* Joseph Esmond). A Copious and Critical Latin-English Lexicon; founded on the German-Latin Dictionaries of Dr. William Freund. ... London. 1849. 4° pp. viii., 1400.

RIDDLE (*Rev.* Joseph Esmond) *and* ARNOLD (*Rev.* Thomas Kerchever). A Copious and Critical English-Latin Lexicon, founded on the German-Latin Dictionary of Dr. Charles Ernest Georges. ... First American Ed., carefully revised, and containing a Copious Dictionary of Proper Names ... by Charles Anthon ... . New York. 1849. 8° pp. viii., 754. +

ROBERTSON (William). A Dictionary of Latin Phrases ... . A new Ed., with considerable Additions ... and Corrections. London. 1829. 12° pp. iv., 888.

[TORREY (Henry Warren)]. An English-Latin Lexicon, prepared to accompany Leverett's Latin-English Lexicon. Boston. 1842. 8° (Bound with Leverett.)

TORSELLINI (Orazio). ... De Particulis Latinæ Orationis Libellus ... post Curas Jacobi Thomasii et Jo. Conradi Schwarzii denuo recognitus et auctus. Ex Editione in Germania quinta ... Anglica Interpretatione (vice Germanicæ) instruendum curavit Jacobus Bailey. (Appended to FORCELLINI (E.). ... Lexicon, *etc.* 1828. 4° Vol. II.)

TURSELLINUS (Horatius). *See* TORSELLINI (O.).

§ 8. *Scottish.*

JAMIESON (John), *D.D.* A Dictionary of the Scottish Language. ... Abridged ... by John Johnstone ... . [With a Memoir of the Author.] Edinburgh. 1846. 8° pp. xvi., 775.

§ 9. *Spanish.*

OLLENDORFF (H. G.). New Method, *etc.* *See* VELAZQUEZ DE LA CADENA (M.) *and* SIMONNÉ (T.).

VELAZQUEZ DE LA CADENA (*Prof.* Mariano). Seoane's Neuman and Baretti — by Velazquez. A Pronouncing Dictionary of the Spanish and English Languages: ... upon the Basis of Seoane's Edition of Neuman and Baretti, and from the English Dictionaries of Webster, Worcester and Walker: with the Addition of more than Eight Thousand Words, Idioms, and Familiar Phrases, the Irregularities of all the Verbs, and a Grammatical Synopsis of both Languages. In Two

Parts. I. Spanish-English. — II. English-Spanish. ... 2 pts. New-York. 1852. 8° pp. xvi., 675, and xvi., 604.

Note. Part II. has an independent title-page.

VELAZQUEZ DE LA CADENA (*Prof.* Mariano) *and* SIMONNÉ (*Prof.* T.). Ollendorff's New Method of learning to read, write, and speak: [*sic*] the Spanish Language: with an Appendix, containing a ... Recapitulation of the Rules .... New-York. 1851. 12°

APPENDIX TO "LANGUAGE."

CLASS XVI. ANCIENT GREEK AND LATIN AUTHORS, WITH SPECIAL ILLUSTRATIVE WORKS.

PART I. INTRODUCTION TO THE STUDY OF THE CLASSICS; CLASSICAL DICTIONARIES; PHILOLOGICAL CRITICISM ON SEVERAL CLASSIC AUTHORS.

Note. For Greek and Roman *Antiquities*, see Class XXVII.

ANTHON (*Prof.* Charles), *LL.D.* A Classical Dictionary: containing an Account of the principal Proper Names mentioned in Ancient Authors .... [By C. A.] Together with an Account of Coins, Weights, and Measures, with Tabular Values of the same. [By Abraham B. Conger.] ... New-York. 1841. 8° pp. viii., 1423.

——— *Editor*, etc. *See* SMITH (W.). A new Classical Dictionary, *etc.*

BAIRD (James S. S.). The Classical Manual: an Epitome of Ancient Geography, Greek and Roman Mythology, Antiquities, and Chronology. Chiefly intended for the Use of Schools, ... Philadelphia. 1852. 18° (6.)

CLASSICAL Manual (A), being a Mythological, Historical, and Geographical Commentary on Pope's Homer, and Dryden's Æneid of Virgil: with a copious Index [adapting it for use as a Classical Dictionary]. London. 1833. 8° pp. vi., 697. +

CLASSICAL Studies. *See* SEARS (B.).

COLERIDGE (Henry Nelson). Introductions to the Study of the Greek Classic Poets. *See* Class XXIX.

ESCHENBURG (*Prof.* Johann Joachim). Manual of Classical Literature. From the German of J. J. E. .... With Additions. Embracing Treatises on ... I. Classical Geography and Topography. II. Classical Chronology. III. Greek and Roman Mythology. IV. Greek Antiquities. V. Roman Antiquities. VI. Archæology of Greek Literature. VII. Archæology of Roman Literature. VIII. Archæology of Art. IX. History of Greek Literature. X. History of Roman Literature. By N. W. Fiske .... 4th Ed..... 6th Thousand. Philadelphia. 1843. 8° pp. xxviii., 690.

See FISKE (N. W.). Supplemental Plates, *etc.*

FISKE (*Prof.* Nathan Welby). Supplemental Plates to the Manual of Classical Literature. ... Philadelphia. 1843. 8° pp. vii., *and* 32 *Plates.*

——— *Translator*, etc. *See* ESCHENBURG (J. J.). Manual, *etc.*

LEMPRIERE (John). Lempriere's Classical Dictionary .... Abridged from the best English Editions. Hartford. 1850. 12° or 18° (12. and 6.) (12 copies.)

SEARS (Barnas), *D.D.* Classical Studies: Essays on Ancient Literature and Art. With the Biography and Correspondence of eminent Philologists. By Barnas Sears, ... B. B. Edwards, ... C. C. Felton, ... Boston. 1843. 12°

SMITH (William), *LL.D.* A new Classical Dictionary of Greek and Roman Biography, Mythology, and Geography, partly based upon the Dictionary of Greek and Roman Biography and Mythology. ... Revised, with numerous Corrections and Additions, by Charles Anthon, LL.D. .... New York. 1851. 8° pp. xv., 1039.

Note. Chronological Tables of Greek and Roman History, and of Greek and Roman Measures, Weights, and Money, are appended.

PART II. ANCIENT GREEK AUTHORS, WITH PARTICULAR LEXICONS, INDEXES, AND COMMENTARIES.

ÆSCHYLUS. The Agamemnon of Æ. [*Gr.*], with Notes. By C. C. Felton .... Boston. 1847. 12°

——— Agamemnon, and the Choëphoræ. Translated by Robert Potter. (BRITISH Poets, L. 5 – 136.)

——— The Prometheus of Æ. [*Gr.*], with Notes .... By T. D. Woolsey .... 3d Ed., revised. Boston. 1841. 12°

LINWOOD (*Rev.* William). A Lexicon to Æschylus containing a Critical Explanation of the more Difficult Passages in the Seven Tragedies. ... 2d Ed. London. 1847. 8°

ARISTOPHANES. The Comedies of A. [The Acharnians, the Knights, or the Demagogues, the Clouds, the Wasps, and the Dicast turned Gentleman [the concluding Part of the Wasps]. Translated, with a Preliminary Discourse,] By T. Mitchell .... (BRITISH Poets, XLIII., XLIV. 1 – 145.)

Note. The Clouds is translated by Richard Cumberland.

——— The Birds of A. [*Gr.*] With Notes, and a Metrical Table. By C. C. Felton .... Cambridge. 1849. 12° or 8° (6. and 4.)

——— The Clouds of A. [*Gr.*] With Notes. By C. C. Felton .... New and revised Ed. Cambridge. 1848. 12°

ARISTOTELES. Aristotelis Ethica Nicomachea. [*Gr.*] Ex Recensione Bekkeri. Oxonii. 1845. 16°

BION. *See* BRIGGS (T.). Poetæ Bucolici, *etc.*

BRIGGS (Thomas). Poetæ Bucolici Græci sive Theocriti Bionis et Moschi quæ supersunt. Cum Notis Variorum et suis edidit T. B. ... [*Gr.* and *Lat.*] Cantabrigiæ. 1821. 8° pp. vi., 339, 418.

COLUTHUS. The Rape of Helen, translated by Sir Edward Sherburne. (BRITISH Poets, V. 313–324.)

DEMOSTHENES. The I. II. III. Philippics of D. [*Gr.*] With Historical Introductions and Critical and Explanatory Notes. By M. J. Smead, Ph.D. . . . . Boston and Cambridge. 1851. 12°

EURIPIDES. The Hecuba, Medea, Phœnissæ, and Orestes, of E., literally translated into English from the Text of G. Dindorf, with Porson's Various Readings. To which are added Critical Notes . . . . London. 1846. 12°

Note. Each play is paged independently.

——— The Bacchæ, and Iphigenia in Aulis. Translated by Robert Potter. (BRITISH Poets, L. 289–442.)

——— Phœnissæ. *See* Class XX. GASCOIGNE (G.) *and* KINWELMARSH (F.). Iocasta, *etc.*

HERODOTUS. . . . H., from the Text of Schweighæuser: with English Notes. Edited by C. S. Wheeler . . . . Vol. I. 2d Ed. | Vol. II. 2 vols. Boston. 1843–42. 12°

——— H., translated from the Greek, with Notes and Life of the Author. By the Rev. William Beloe. A new Ed., corrected and revised. Philadelphia. 1839. 8°

ANALYSIS (An) and Summary of Herodotus. With a Synchronistical Table of principal Events; Tables of Weights, Measures, Money, and Distances; an Outline of the History and Geography; and the Dates completed from Gaisford, Baehr, etc. Oxford. 1848. 8°

CARY (Henry). A Lexicon to Herodotus, Greek and English, adapted to the Text of Gaisford and Baehr. [Mostly taken from Schweighæuser.] Oxford. 1843. 8°

GAISFORD (*Prof.* Thomas). Adnotationes Wesselingii, Valckenaerii, Larcheri, Schweighaeuseri aliorumque in Herodoti Historiarum Libros IX. Edidit T. G. . . . . 2 tom. Lipsiae. 1826. 8°

Note. Also with the title:—". . . Herodoti . . . Historiarum Libri IX. . . . [edited by] Thomas Gaisford . . . . Tom. III.—IV."

LARCHER (Pierre Henri). . . . Historical and Critical Comments on the History of Herodotus, with a Chronological Table. From the French of P. H. L. . . . . New Ed., with Corrections and Additions, by William Desborough Cooley. . . . 2 vols. London. 1844. 8°

[LONG (George)]. A Summary of Herodotus [by G. L.], and a copious Index [by Henry H. Davis]. London. 1829. 12°

Note. Also with the title:—"Herodotus. Summary and Index. Vol. III." The Summary and Index are each paged independently.

NIEBUHR (Barthold Georg). A Dissertation on the Geography of Herodotus, *etc. See* Class XXII. Part II.

TURNER (Dawson William). Notes on Herodotus, original and selected from the best Commentators. . . . Oxford. 1848. 8°

HOMERUS. Homeri Ilias, Græce et Latine. Annotationes . . . scripsit atque edidit Samuel Clarke, S.T.P. Ed. undecima. . . . 2 vol. Londini. 1790. 8°

Note. The title-page and preface of Vol. II. are wanting.

——— . . . The Iliad of Homer, from the Text of Wolf. With English Notes [and Flaxman's Illustrations]. By C. C. Felton . . . . New and revised Ed. Boston. 1847. Large 12° (6.)

HOMERUS. ... The Iliad of Homer, according to the Text of Wolf; with Notes .... By John J. Owen, D.D. .... New-York. 1851. 12° pp. 740.

——— The First Six Books of Homer's Iliad [*Gr.*], with English Notes ..., a Metrical Index, and Homeric Glossary. By Charles Anthon, LL.D. .... New York. 1847. 12° pp. viii., 897.

——— The First Three Books of Homer's Iliad, according to the Ordinary Text, and also with the Restoration of the Digamma, to which are appended English Notes ..., a Metrical Index, and Homeric Glossary. By Charles Anthon .... New-York. 1844. 12°

——— The Iliad, translated by Alexander Pope. (BRITISH Poets, Vols. XL., XLI.)

——— The First Book of the Iliad, translated by Thomas Tickell. (BRITISH Poets, XVII. 125 – 149.)

——— ... The Odyssey of Homer, according to the Text of Wolf; with Notes: for the Use of Schools and Colleges. ... By John J. Owen .... New-York. 1845. 12°

——— The Odyssey, translated by Alexander Pope. (BRITISH Poets, Vol. XLII.)

——— Batrachomuomachia: or, The Battle of the Frogs and Mice. Translated by Thomas Parnell. (BRITISH Poets, XIII. 93 – 112.)

BUTTMANN (Philipp Karl). Lexilogus. *See* Class XV. Part II. § 5. B.

CLASSICAL Manual (A), being a Mythological, Historical, and Geographical Commentary on Pope's Homer and Dryden's Æneid of Virgil. *See* Part I.

CRUSIUS (Gottlieb Christian). A Complete Greek and English Lexicon of the Poems of Homer and the Homeridæ. ... From the German of G. Ch. C.: translated, with Corrections and Additions, by Henry Smith .... Hartford. 1844. 8°

OWGAN (Henry). Miscellanea Homerica; being a Compilation of original and selected Articles on those Points of Greek Literature which are auxiliary ... to the Critical Study of Homer. ... Dublin. 1840. 8°

ISOCRATES. The Panegyricus of I., from the Text of Bremi. With English Notes. By C. C. Felton .... Cambridge. 1847. 12° or 8° (6. and 4.)

MOSCHUS. *See* BRIGGS (T.). Poetæ Bucolici, *etc.*

PINDARUS. Pindaric Odes, [including the Second Olympic, and First Nemæan Ode of Pindar, translated] by Abraham Cowley. (BRITISH Poets, VI. 95 – 110.)

——— The First Nemæan Ode, translated by Sir William Jones. (BRITISH Poets, XXXV. 113 – 117.)

PLUTARCHUS. Plutarch's Lives, translated from the Original Greek: with Notes, Critical and Historical: and a Life of Plutarch. By John Langhorne, D.D. and William Langhorne, A.M. A new Ed., carefully revised and corrected. New-York. 1839. 8° pp. xx., 748.

SOPHOCLES. Œdipus Tyrannus, and Antigone. Translated by Thomas Franklin. (BRITISH Poets, L. 137 – 287.)

THEOCRITUS. *See* BRIGGS (T.). Poetæ Bucolici, *etc.*

THUCYDIDES. ... The History of the Peloponnesian War, by Thucydides [*Gr.*] : illustrated by Maps, taken entirely from actual Surveys; with Notes, chiefly Historical and Geographical, by Thomas Arnold, D.D. ... . 2d Ed. 3 vols. Oxford. 1840–42. 8°

——— The History of the Peloponnesian War, by T.; according to the Text of L. Dindorf; with Notes ... . [The First Three Books.] By John J. Owen ... . New-York. 1848. 12° pp. x., 683. +

——— The History of T., newly translated into English ... with very copious Annotations, Exegetical, Philological, Historical, and Geographical; almost entirely Original ... . Prefixed, is an entirely new Life of T.: with a Memoir on the State of Greece ... at the Commencement of the Peloponnesian War. By the Rev. S. T. Bloomfield ... . 3 vols. London. 1829. 8° *With six Maps.*

——— History of the Peloponnesian War, translated from the Greek of T. By William Smith ... . A new Ed., ... revised. Philadelphia. 1836. 8° or 12° (4. and 6.)

XENOPHON. The Anabasis of X. [*Gr.*], with English Notes ... a Map ... and a Plan of the Battle of Cunaxa. By Charles Anthon, LL.D. ... . New York. 1850. 12° pp. xxii., 632. +

——— Grammar School Classics. — The Anabasis of X.: based upon the Text of Bornemann; with Notes, original and selected, and Three Maps ... . By the Rev. J. F. Macmichael ... . 3d Ed., revised and corrected. London. 1850. 8°

——— The Cyropædia of X.; chiefly from the Text of L. Dindorf: with Notes ... Examination Questions, and ... Indices. By E. H. Barker ... . [London.] 1831. 12°

——— ... The Cyropædia of X., according to the Text of L. Dindorf; with Notes: for the Use of Schools and Colleges. By John J. Owen ... . New-York. 1848. 12°

——— Xenophon's Memorabilia of Socrates [*Gr.*], with English Notes ..., the Prolegomena of Kühner, Wiggers' Life of Socrates, etc. By Charles Anthon, LL.D. ... . New York. 1848. 12°

AINSWORTH (William F.). Travels in the Track of the Ten Thousand Greeks, *etc.* *See* Class XXIII.

PART III. ANCIENT LATIN AUTHORS, WITH PARTICULAR LEXICONS, INDEXES, AND COMMENTARIES.

AUSONIUS (Decimus Magnus). Opera. (WALKER's Corpus Poet. Lat., pp. 1060–1124.)

AVIANUS (Flavius). Fabulæ. *See* PHÆDRUS. Phædri, Aviani ... Fabulæ, *etc.*

CÆSAR (Caius Julius). ... De Bellis Gallico et Civili Pompeiano, nec non A. Hirtii, aliorumque, de Bellis Alexandrino, Africano, et Hispaniensi, Commentarii. Recensuit et accuravit Joannes Carey, LL.D. Londini. 1822. 24°

——— ... Opera Omnia. — ... The Text revised ... with Notes ...

by James Prendeville .... The 3d Ed., augmented ...: with a copious Historical and Geographical Index; revised by George B. Wheeler .... Dublin. 1846. 12°

CÆSAR (Caius Julius). ... Commentariorum de Bello Civili Libri III. Grammatisch, kritisch und historisch erklärt von M. Christian Gottlob Herzog .... Leipzig. 1834. 8°

——— ... Commentariorum de Bello Gallico Libri VIII. Grammatisch und historisch erklärt von M. Christian Gottlob Herzog .... 2te, durchaus verbesserte mit einer Charte von Gallia Antiqua von Reichard vermehrte Auflage. Leipzig. 1831. 8° pp. xliv., 746.

——— ... Commentarii de Bello Gallico. [With Notes, etc. by L. Schmitz.] Philadelphia. 1847. 18° or 24° (6. and 8. 4.) (Schmitz and Zumpt's Classical Series.)

——— ... Commentaries on the Gallic War. With English Notes ... a Lexicon, Indexes, etc. By Rev. J. A. Spencer .... New York. 1848. 12°

——— Cæsar's Commentaries on the Gallic War; and the First Book of the Greek Paraphrase; with English Notes ... Plans of Battles, Sieges, etc., and Historical, Geographical, and Archæological Indexes. By Charles Anthon .... New-York. 1849. 12°

——— ... Commentaries on the Gallic War; with a Dictionary and Notes. By Prof. E. A. Andrews. 4th Ed. Boston. 1850. 12°

——— Grammar School Classics. — C. Julii Caesaris Commentarii de Bello Gallico. With Notes, by George Long. London. 1853. 8° or 16°

——— The First Six Books of Cæsar's Commentaries on the Gallic War, adapted to Bullions' Latin Grammar; with an Introduction, on the Idioms of the Latin Language; ... Notes; and an Index of Proper Names, etc. By Rev. Peter Bullions, D.D. .... New-York. 1845. 12°

CALPURNIUS SICULUS (Titus ?). Bucolicon Liber. (WALKER's Corpus Poet. Lat., pp. 1051 – 1060.)

CATO (Dionysius). Disticha de Moribus, ad Filium. *See* PHÆDRUS. Phaedri, Aviani ... Fabulæ, *etc.*

CATULLUS (Caius *or* Quintus Valerius). Carmina. (WALKER's Corpus Poet. Lat., pp. 1 – 20.)

CICERO (Marcus Tullius). Selections from Cicero [*Lat.*], with English Notes. Part I. Selections from the Orations: containing the Fourth Book of the Impeachment of Verres: the Four Speeches against Catiline: the Speech for the Poet Archias. | Part II. Selections from the Epistles. Edited ... by Thomas Kerchever Arnold .... 2 pts. London. 1847 – 49. 12°

——— Cicero's Cato Major; with a double Translation: for the Use of Students on the Hamiltonian System. London. 1827. 8°

——— The Life [by C. Middleton] and Letters [translated by W. Melmoth and W. Heberden] of M. T. C. *See* Class XXIV. Part II.

——— ... De Officiis Libri Tres. Accedunt in Usum Juventutis Notæ quædam Anglice scriptæ. Ex Editione postrema et emendatissima Valpiana. Philadelphia. 1833. 18° (6.)

——— ... De Officiis Libri Tres. With English Notes, chiefly selected and translated from the Editions of Zumpt and Bonnell, by Thomas A. Thacher ... . New York. 1850. 12°

——— ... Orationes. With a Commentary by George Long. Vol. I. Verrinarum Libri Septem. London. 1851. 8°

Note. Also with the title: — "Bibliotheca Classica. Edited by George Long ... and the Rev. A. J. Macleane ... . Vol. I. M. Tullii Ciceronis Orationes," etc.

——— ... Select Orations of C. [Cat., Arch., Marcell., Manil., Mur.] With English Notes ... and Historical, Geographical, and Legal Indexes. By Charles Anthon, LL.D. ... . A new Ed., with Improvements. New-York. 1841. 12°

——— Orationes quædam selectæ [Cat., Manil., Marcell., Lig., Deiot., Arch., 2d Phil.], Notis illustratæ. In Usum Academiæ Exoniensis. [Edited by Charles Folsom.] Editio stereotypa, Tabulis Analyticis instructa. Bostoniæ. 1848. 12°

——— ... Orationes selectae XII. [4th Ver., Manil., Cat., Sul., Lig., Deiot., 1st and 14th Phil., Arch. — With Notes, by J. Richter.] Philadelphia. 1850. 16° or 24° (8. and 12.) (Schmitz and Zumpt's Classical Series.)

——— Select Orations of M. T. C. [Cat., Arch., Marcell., Lig., Deiot., Manil., Mil.], with English Notes ... . By Rev. Peter Bullions, D.D. ... . New-York. 1851. 12°

——— ... Oratio pro T. Annio Milone: chiefly from the Text of Orelle [Orelli?]. With English Explanatory Notes, &c. &c. By D. B. Hickie, LL.D. ... . Cambridge. 1842. 8°

——— The Tusculan Disputations, Book First; the Dream of Scipio; and Extracts from the Dialogues on Old Age and Friendship. With English Notes, by Thomas Chase ... . Cambridge. 1851. 16°

——— *See* Class XV. Part II. § 7. A. SEARS (B.). The Ciceronian, *etc.*

CLAUDIANUS (Claudius). Opera. (WALKER's Corpus Poet. Lat., pp. 1125 – 1203.)

——— Description of the Phœnix, translated by Thomas Tickell. (BRITISH Poets, XVII. 151 – 155.)

CORNELIUS NEPOS. *See* NEPOS.

CURTIUS RUFUS (Quintus). ... De Gestis Alexandri Magni, Regis Macedonum, Libri qui supersunt VIII. [With Notes, etc. by C. G. Zumpt.] Philadelphia. 1849. 16° or 24° (8. and 12.) (Schmitz and Zumpt's Classical Series.)

FLACCUS (Caius Valerius). Argonauticon Libri VIII. (WALKER's Corpus Poet. Lat., pp. 1007 – 1050.)

HIRTIUS (Aulus). De Bello Alexandrino. De Bello Africano. *See* CÆSAR (C. J.). De Bellis Gallico et Civili, *etc.* 1822. 24°

HORATIUS FLACCUS (Quintus). The Works of Horace, with English Notes ... by Charles Anthon ... . A new Ed., with Corrections and Improvements. New-York. 1844. 12°

——— The Works of Horace: with English Notes. ... By J. L. Lincoln ... . New-York. [1851.] 12° pp. xxxviii., 575.

——— Opera. (WALKER's Corpus Poet. Lat., pp. 523 – 585.)

——— Eclogæ Horatianæ. — Pars I. Carmina prope omnia continens. Addita est Interpretatio, quam ex Adnotationibus Mitscherlichii, Doeringii, Orellii, Dillenburgii, aliorum excerpsit Thomas Kerchever Arnold ... . Ed. altera. | Pars II. Sermones prope omnes continens. Addita est familiaris Interpretatio Orellii. Edidit T. K. A. ... . 2 partes. Londini. 1848 – 43. 12°

——— ... Eclogae ex Q. Horatii Flacci Poematibus. [With Notes, etc. by C. G. Zumpt and A. W. Zumpt.] Philadelphia. 1852. 18° or 16° (6. and 8.) (Schmitz and Zumpt's Classical Series.)

——— The Odes of Horace, translated by John Scriven. ... London. 1843. 16° (8.)

JUSTINUS. Justini Historiæ Phillippicæ: cum Versione Anglica, ad Verbum, quantum fieri potuit, facta. ... By John Clarke ... . The 9th Ed. Glocester. 1790. 8°

JUVENALIS (Decimus Junius). Satirarum Libri V. (WALKER's Corpus Poet. Lat., pp. 672 – 701.)

LIVIUS (Titus). ... Historiarum Liber Primus et Selecta quædam Capita. Curavit Notulisque instruxit Carolus Folsom ... . Ed. stereotypa. Bostoniæ. 1838. 12°

——— ... Selections from the first Five Books, together with the Twenty-First and Twenty-Second Books entire. Chiefly from the Text of Alschefski. With English Notes for Schools and Colleges. By J. L. Lincoln ... . With an accompanying Plan of Rome, and a Map of the Passage of Hannibal. New York. 1847. 12°

——— ... Historiarum Libri I, II, XXI, XXII. Philadelphia. 1851. 18° or 16° (12. 6. and 8.) (Schmitz and Zumpt's Classical Series.)

——— The History of Rome. Translated from the Original, with Notes and Illustrations, by George Baker ... . A new Ed., carefully corrected and revised. ... 2 vols. Philadelphia. 1844. 8° or 12° (4. and 6.)

LUCANUS (Marcus Annæus). Pharsaliæ Libri X. (WALKER's Corpus Poet. Lat., pp. 604 – 665.)

LUCRETIUS CARUS (Titus). De Rerum Natura Libri VI. (WALKER's Corpus Poet. Lat., pp. 21 – 80.)

MARTIALIS (Marcus Valerius). De Spectaculis Liber; Epigrammatum Libri XIV.; Quædam Martiali afficta. (WALKER's Corpus Poet. Lat., pp. 702 – 797.)

NEPOS (Cornelius). C. N.: with Answered Questions, and Imitative Exercises. Part I. [Miltiades — Datames.] By the Rev. Thomas Kerchever Arnold ... . Revised and corrected by E. A. Johnson ... . New York. 1846. 12°

——— C. N.: with Answered Questions, and Imitative Exercises. By the Rev. Thomas Kerchever Arnold .... Carefully revised, with Notes by E. A. Johnson .... A new Ed., enlarged .... New-York. 1848. 12°

——— ... Liber de Excellentibus Ducibus exterarum Gentium cum Vitis Catonis et Attici. [With Notes, etc. by L. Schmitz ?] Philadelphia. 1853. 18° (6.) (Schmitz and Zumpt's Classical Series.)

OVIDIUS NASO (Publius). Opera. (WALKER's Corpus Poet. Lat., pp. 240 - 522.)

——— ... Excerpta ex P. Ovidii Nasonis Carminibus. [With Notes, etc. by M. Isler.] Philadelphia. 1851. 18° or 16° (6. and 8.) (Schmitz and Zumpt's Classical Series.)

——— The Metamorphoses of P. O. N.; ... with English Notes, Historical, Mythological, and Critical, and illustrated by Pictorial Embellishments: with a Clavis .... By Nathan Covington Brooks .... Philadelphia. 1848. 8°

——— Translations from the Metamorphoses, Books II. III. IV. by Joseph Addison. (BRITISH Poets, XIV. 110 - 179.)

PERSIUS FLACCUS (Aulus). Satirarum Liber. (WALKER's Corpus Poet. Lat., pp. 666 - 671.)

——— The Satires ... translated into English Verse. By William Gifford, Esq. (BRITISH Poets, XLIV. 377 - 494.)

PHÆDRUS. Fabularum Libri V; cum Appendice. (WALKER's Corpus Poet. Lat., pp. 586 - 603.)

——— Phædri, Aviani, aliorumque Veterum Fabulæ; P. Syri Sententiæ; Catonis Disticha Moralia, et Symposii Ænigmata. Recensuit et accuravit Joannes Carey. Londini. 1823. 24°

PROPERTIUS (Sextus Aurelius). Elegiarum Libri IV. (WALKER's Corpus Poet. Lat., pp. 208 - 239.)

QUINTUS CURTIUS RUFUS. *See* CURTIUS RUFUS.

SALLUSTIUS (Caius Crispus). Sallust's Jugurthine War and Conspiracy of Catiline, with an English Commentary, and Geographical and Historical Indexes. By Charles Anthon .... 9th Ed., corrected and enlarged. New-York. 1842. 12°

——— Sallust's History of the War against Jugurtha, and of the Conspiracy of Catiline: with a Dictionary and Notes. By Prof. E. A. Andrews. Philadelphia. 1845. 12°

——— ... De Bello Catilinario et Jugurthino. [With Notes, etc. by C. G. Zumpt.] Philadelphia. 1848. 18° or 24° (6. and 8. 4.) (Schmitz and Zumpt's Classical Series.)

SICULUS (Titus ? Calpurnius). *See* CALPURNIUS SICULUS.

SILIUS ITALICUS (Caius). Punicorum Libri XVII. (WALKER's Corpus Poet. Lat., pp. 915 - 1006.)

STATIUS (Publius Papinius). Opera. (WALKER's Corpus Poet. Lat., pp. 799 - 914.)

——— The Thebais, Book I. translated by Alexander Pope. (BRITISH Poets, XX. 164 - 190.)

SULPICIA. Satira. (WALKER's Corpus Poet. Lat., p. 798.)

SYMPOSIUS (Cælius Firmianus). Ænigmata. *See* PHÆDRUS. Phædri, Aviani ... Fabulæ, *etc.*

SYRUS (Publius). Sententiæ. *See* PHÆDRUS. Phædri, Aviani ... Fabulæ, *etc.*

TACITUS (Caius Cornelius). The Works of Cornelius Tacitus; with an Essay on his Life and Genius, Notes, Supplements, &c. By Arthur Murphy .... A new Ed. with the Author's last Corrections. Philadelphia. 1840. 8° pp. xviii., 742.

——— The Germania and Agricola of C. C. T. [*Lat.*], with Notes for Colleges. By W. S. Tyler .... New York and London. 1847. 12°

TERENTIUS AFER (Publius). Select Comedies of Terence [The Andrian, The Brothers, and Phormio], translated by George Colman. ... (BRITISH Poets, XLIV. 147-376.)

TIBULLUS (Albius). Carminum Libri IV. (WALKER's Corpus Poet. Lat., pp. 192-207.)

VALERIUS FLACCUS (Caius). *See* FLACCUS.

VIRGILIUS MARO (Publius). Pvblivs Virgilivs Maro Varietate Lectionis et perpetva Adnotatione illustratvs a Christ. Gottl. Heyne Editio qvarta Cvravit Ge. Phil. Eberard. Wagner Volvmen Primvm Bvcolica et Georgica | Volvmen Secvndvm Aeneidis Libri I—VI | Volvmen Tertivm Aeneidis Libri VII—XII et Index Notarvm qvibvs avcta est nova Editio | Volvmen Qvartvm Carmina Minora Qvaestiones Virgilianae [by Wagner] et Notitia Literaria | Volvmen Qvintvm 5 vol. Lipsiae. 1830-32-33-32-31. 8°

——— ... Bucolica, Georgica, et Æneis.—Virgil; with English Notes, prepared for the Use of Classical Schools and Colleges. By Francis Bowen .... Stereotype Ed. Boston. 1843. 8° or 12° (8. and 6.) pp. 600.

——— ... P. Virgilii Maronis Carmina. [With Notes, etc. by L. Schmitz ?] Philadelphia. 1848. 18° or 24° (6. and 8. 4.) (Schmitz and Zumpt's Classical Series.)

——— The Bucolics, Georgics, and Aeneid of Virgil: with English Notes, a Life of Virgil, and Remarks upon Scanning, by Edward Moore, M.A. Boston. 1849. 12°

——— ... Opera ad optimorum Librorum Fidem edidit perpetua et aliorum et sua Adnotatione illustravit Dissertationem de Virgilii Vita et Carminibus atque Indicem Rerum locupletissimum adiecit Albertus Forbiger. Pars I.-III. Editio tertia correcta et aucta. 3 partes. Lipsiæ. 1852. 8°

——— Opera. (WALKER's Corpus Poet. Lat., pp. 81-191; see also pp. 1204-1209.)

——— The Bucolics and Georgics of Virgil [*Lat.*]; with Notes, Exercises, Terms of Husbandry, and a Flora Virgiliana, by Thomas Keightley .... London. 1847. 12°

——— The Eclogues and Georgics of Virgil. With English Notes ... and a Metrical Index. By Charles Anthon .... New-York. 1847. 12°

——— ... Æneis. In Usum studiosæ Juventutis accurate recensuit J. Edwards .... Londini. 1841. 16°

——— The Æneid of Virgil, with English Notes ... a Metrical Clavis, and an Historical, Geographical, and Mythological Index. By Charles Anthon .... New-York. 1850. 12° pp. xiii., 942.

——— The Destruction of Troy. Translated by John Denham. (British Poets, VI. 315 – 334.)

——— Translation from the Fourth Georgic. By Joseph Addison. (British Poets, XIV. 184 – 196.)

Classical Manual (A), being a Mythological, Historical, and Geographical Commentary on Pope's Homer, and Dryden's Æneid of Virgil. *See* Part I.

Edwards (J.). Quæstiones Virgilianæ; or, Notes and Questions on the first Six and the Ninth Books of the Æneid: adapted to the Middle Forms in Schools. London. 1841. 16° (Bound with Edwards's edition of the "Æneis.")

Walker (William Sidney). Corpus Poetarum Latinorum. Edidit Gulielmus Sidney Walker .... Londini. 1849. 8° pp. vi., 1209.

CLASS XVII. RHETORIC AND LITERARY CRITICISM.

Note. For the *History of Literature*, see Class XXIX.

Blair (*Prof.* Hugh), *D.D.* Lectures on Rhetoric and Belles Lettres. ... With a Memoir of the Author's Life. To which are added, Copious Questions; and an Analysis of each Lecture, by Abraham Mills .... Stereotype University ... Ed. Philadelphia. 1844. 8°

Note. The volume contains no "Memoir of the Author's Life."

Boyd (*Rev.* James Robert). Elements of Rhetoric and Literary Criticism .... Including, also, a succinct History of the English Language, and of British and American Literature .... On the Basis of the recent Works of Alexander Reid and Robert Connel; with large Additions .... New-York. 1844. 18°

——— *The same.* 7th Ed. New York. 1851. 18°

Campbell (George), *D.D.* The Philosophy of Rhetoric. ... A new Ed., with the Author's last Additions and Corrections. New-York. 1841. 8°

Getty (John A.). The Art of Rhetoric, *etc.* *See* Class XVIII.

Home (Henry), *Lord Kames.* Elements of Criticism .... With Analyses, and [bad] Translations of Ancient and Foreign Illustrations. Edited by Abraham Mills .... New Ed. New-York. 1838. 12°

Hudson (*Rev.* Henry Norman). Lectures on Shakspeare. ... 2d Ed. New York. 1848. 12°

Hughes (John). Poetry. (Encycl. Metrop., V. 651 – 684.)

KAMES, Henry, *Lord.* *See* HOME.

NEWMAN (*Prof.* Samuel Phillips). A Practical System of Rhetoric, or the Principles and Rules of Style, inferred from Examples of Writing. ... 3d Ed., enlarged and improved. Boston. 1832. 12°

——— *The same.* To which is added a Historical Dissertation on English Style. ... 30th Ed. New York. 1849. 12°

PARKER (Richard Green). Aids to English Composition .... 5th Ed. New York. 1848. 12°

——— Progressive Exercises in English Composition. ... New stereotype Ed. ... enlarged and improved, from the 55th Ed. Boston. 1849. 12°

QUACKENBOS (G. P.). First Lessons in Composition, in which the Principles of the Art are developed in connection with the Principles of Grammar; embracing full Directions on ... Punctuation; with copious Exercises. ... New-York. 1852. 12°

WALKER (John). The Teacher's Assistant in English Composition .... To which are added, Hints for correcting and improving Juvenile Composition. ... Boston. 1810. 12°

WHATELY (Richard), *Abp. of Dublin.* Rhetoric. (ENCYCL. Metrop., I. 241 - 303.)

——— Elements of Rhetoric. Comprising the Substance of the Article in the Encyclopædia Metropolitana with Additions, &c. ... Boston. 1845. 12°

CLASS XVIII. ELOCUTION AND ORATORY; WITH ORATIONS AND SPEECHES.

PART I. ELOCUTION AND ORATORY.

BRONSON (C. P.), *M.D.* Elocution; or Mental and Vocal Philosophy .... 24th Ed. — 25th Thousand. Louisville. [1845?] 8°

DAY (*Prof.* Henry Noble). The Art of Elocution, exemplified in a Systematic Course of Exercises. ... New Haven. 1844. 12°

DWYER (John Hanbury). An Essay on Elocution: with elucidatory Passages from various Authors. To which are added Remarks on reading Prose and Verse, with Suggestions to Instructors of the Art. 6th Ed., with Additions. Albany. 1846. 12°

GETTY (John A.). The Art of Rhetoric: or, The Elements of Oratory. ... Methodically arranged from the Ancient and Modern Rhetorical Writers .... By John Holmes .... To which is added Quintilian's Course of an Ancient Roman Education; from the Pupil's first Elements, to his Entrance into the School of Oratory. A new ... Ed., in Two Books. Entirely remodeled .... By J. A. G. .... Philadelphia. 1849. 12°

GOLDSBURY (John) *and* RUSSELL (William). The American Common-School Reader and Speaker: being a Selection of Pieces in Prose and Verse, with Rules for Reading and Speaking. ... Boston. [1844 ?] 12°

HOLMES (John). The Art of Rhetoric, *etc.* *See* GETTY (J. A.).

HOWS (*Prof.* John W. S.). The Shakspearian Reader, *etc.* *See* Class XX. SHAKESPEARE (W.).

MAGLATHLIN (Henry Bartlett). The Practical Elocutionist ... . Boston. 1849. 12° pp. 58. (3 copies.)

MANDEVILLE (*Prof.* Henry), *D.D.* An Introduction to the Author's "Course of Reading," and "Elements of Reading and Oratory." Part First. ... New York. 1848. 12°

——— *The same.* Part Second. New York. 1848. 12°

——— Course of Reading for Common Schools and the Lower Classes of Academies, on the Plan of the Author's "Elements of Reading and Oratory." New York. 1846. 12° (2 copies.)

——— The Elements of Reading and Oratory. ... A new revised Ed. New York. 1849. 12°

——— ... The Second Reader. New-York. 1849. 12°

MARSHALL (Edward Carrington). The Book of Oratory: a new Collection of Extracts in Prose, Poetry, and Dialogue ... . For the Use of Colleges, Academies, and Schools. ... New York. 1851. 12°

MAURY (Jean Siffrein), *Cardinal.* The Principles of Eloquence. [Translated, with Notes, by John Neal Lake.] With an Introduction, etc., by A. Potter, D.D. ... . New-York. [1841 ?] 18° (HARPER's Fam. Libr., **184.**)

MURDOCH (James E.) *and* RUSSELL (William). Orthophony: or Vocal Culture in Elocution; a Manual of Elementary Exercises, adapted to Dr. Rush's "Philosophy of the Human Voice," and designed as an Introduction to Russell's "American Elocutionist." ... With an Appendix containing Directions for the Cultivation of Pure Tone, by G. J. Webb ... . Boston. 1845. 12°

PORTER (*Prof.* Ebenezer), *D.D.* Lectures on Eloquence and Style. ... Revised for Publication by Rev. Lyman Matthews ... . Andover. 1836. 8°

——— The Rhetorical Reader; consisting of Instructions for regulating the Voice, with a Rhetorical Notation, illustrating Inflection, Emphasis, and Modulation; and a Course of Rhetorical Exercises. ... 200th Ed., with an Appendix. New York. [Copyrighted in 1835.] 12°

RUSSELL (Anna U. *and* William). The Young Ladies' Elocutionary Reader; containing a Selection of Reading Lessons, by Anna U. Russell: with Introductory Rules and Exercises in Elocution, adapted to Female Readers, by William Russell ... . Boston. 1845. 12° (2 copies, one dated 1846.)

RUSSELL (Francis T.). The Juvenile Speaker; comprising Elementary Rules and Exercises in Declamation, with a Selection of Pieces for Practice. ... New York. 1850. 12°

RUSSELL (William). The University Speaker: a Collection of Pieces designed for College Exercises in Declamation and Recitation. With Suggestions on the appropriate Elocution of particular Passages. ... Boston and Cambridge. 1852. 12°

——— *See* GOLDSBURY (J.) *and* RUSSELL (W.); — MURDOCH (J. E.) *and* RUSSELL (W.); — RUSSELL (A. U. *and* W.).

SARGENT (Epes). The Standard Speaker; containing Exercises ... for Declamation ... newly translated or compiled from celebrated Orators, Authors, and Popular Debaters, Ancient and Modern. A Treatise on Oratory and Elocution. Notes Explanatory and Biographical. Philadelphia. 1852. 8°

SCOTT (William). Lessons in Elocution, or, A Selection of Pieces ... for the Improvement of Youth in Reading & Speaking. To which are prefixed, Elements of Gesture. Leicester. 1817. 12°

VANDENHOFF (G.). The Art of Elocution: or, Logical and Musical Reading and Declamation. With an Appendix, containing a copious Practice in Oratorical, Poetical, and Dramatic Reading and Recitation; the whole forming a complete Speaker .... 5th Ed. New-York. 1849. 12°

WARE (*Prof.* Henry), *Jr.*, *D.D.* Hints on Extemporaneous Preaching. (Works, II. 347 – 412.)

ZACHOS (J. C.). The New American Speaker: a Collection of Oratorical and Dramatical Pieces, Soliloquies and Dialogues, with an original Introductory Essay on the Elements of Elocution. ... New York. 1852. 12° (8. 4.)

PART II. ORATIONS AND SPEECHES.

BETHUNE (George W.), *D.D.* Orations and Occasional Discourses. New-York. 1850. 12°

EVERETT (Edward). Orations and Speeches, on various Occasions. Boston. 1836. 8° pp. 637.

——— Orations and Speeches on various Occasions. Vol. I. 2d Ed. | Vol. II. 2 vols. Boston. 1850. 8°

GOODRICH (*Prof.* Chauncey Allen). Select British Eloquence; embracing the best Speeches entire, of the most Eminent Orators of Great Britain for the last Two Centuries; with Sketches of their Lives ..., and Notes .... New York. 1853. 8° pp. vii., 947.

WEBSTER (Daniel). The Works of D. W. *See* Class IV. Part I.

WORKS OF IMAGINATION AND FANCY, WIT AND HUMOR.

(Classes XIX. — XXI.)

CLASS XIX. POETRY.

Note. In references under this Class, "British Poets" denotes Sanford and Walsh's Collection. For *Ancient Greek and Latin Authors*, see Class XVI. Parts II. and III.

Addison (Joseph). Select Poems. (British Poets, XIV. 1 - 228.)

Aikin (John), *M.D.* Select Works of the British Poets, in a Chronological Series from Ben Jonson to Beattie. With Biographical and Critical Notices. 10th Ed. Philadelphia. 1843. 8° pp. viii., 807.

——— *The same*, from Falconer to Sir Walter Scott. With Biographical and Critical Notices. Designed as a Continuation of Dr. Aikin's British Poets. By John Frost, A. M. Philadelphia. 1838. 8° pp. 732.

——— *The same*, from Southey to Croly : with Biographical and Critical Notices [mostly copied from Mrs. S. C. Hall's "Book of Gems"]. Designed as a Continuation of Dr. Aikin's British Poets. [Edited by John Frost.] Philadelphia. 1843. 8° pp. 760.

Note. Each of these volumes has also an engraved title-page, differing from the above.

Akenside (Mark), *M.D.* Select Poems. (British Poets, XXVIII. 1 - 207.)

Alexander (William), 1*st Earl of Stirling.* Select Poems. (British Poets, IV. 297 - 325.)

Armstrong (John), *M.D.* Select Poems. (British Poets, XXXI. 119 - 230.)

Bachelor (The Old). *See* Old Bachelor.

Bailey (Philip James). Festus A Poem ... 1st American Ed. Boston. 1845. 16°

Bampfylde (John). Select Poems. (British Poets, XXXVII. 271 - 275.)

Beattie (James), *LL.D.* Poetical Works. *See* Milton (J.). The Poetical Works of Milton, Young, *etc.*

——— Select Poems. (British Poets, XXXII. 1 - 101.)

Beaumont (*Sir* John), *Bart.* Select Poems. (British Poets, V. 57 - 87.)

Bishop (*Rev.* Samuel). Select Poems. (British Poets, XXXVII. 263 - 269.)

Blacklock (Thomas), *D.D.* Select Poems. (British Poets, XXXV. 243 - 310.)

BLACKMORE (*Sir* Richard). Select Poems. (BRITISH Poets, XV. 241–428.)

BLACKSTONE (*Sir* William). The Lawyer's Farewell to his Muse. (BRITISH Poets, XXXVII. 213–216.)

BLAIR (*Rev.* Robert). Select Poems. (BRITISH Poets, XXI. 305–333.)

BOURNE (Vincent). Latin Poems, with Translations by William Cowper. (BRITISH Poets, XXXVI. 290–302.)

BOYSE (Samuel). Select Poems. (BRITISH Poets, XXXI. 327–373.)

BRITISH Poets. *See* AIKIN (J.); — SANFORD (E.) *and* WALSH (R.).

BROME (Alexander). Select Poems. (BRITISH Poets, V. 252–271.)

BROWNE (William). Select Poems. (BRITISH Poets, V. 351–417.)

BRUCE (Michael). Lochleven, &c. (BRITISH Poets, XXXVII. 323–347.)

BRYANT (William Cullen). Selections from the American Poets. New-York. 1848. 18° (HARPER'S Fam. Libr., **111.**)

BUCKINGHAM, John, 1*st Duke of.* *See* SHEFFIELD.

BURNS (Robert). Poems. (BRITISH Poets, XXXVIII., XXXIX. 1–165.)

BUTLER (Samuel). Poetical Works. (BRITISH Poets, IX., X. 1–174.)

CAMOENS *or* CAMÕES (Luis DE). The Lusiad; or the Discovery of India. . . . Translated . . . by William Julius Mickle. (BRITISH Poets, Vol. XLVII.)

CAMPBELL (Thomas). Poetical Works. *See* ROGERS (S.). The Poetical Works of Rogers, Campbell, *etc.*

CAREW (Thomas). Select Poems. (BRITISH Poets, IV. 373–406.)

CARTWRIGHT (*Rev.* William). Select Poems. (BRITISH Poets, V. 241–252.)

CARY (*Rev.* Henry Francis). *Translator*, etc. *See* DANTE ALIGHIERI.

CAWTHORN (James). Select Poems. (BRITISH Poets, XXIV. 301–356.)

CHATTERTON (Thomas). Select Poems. (BRITISH Poets, XXIX. 113–286.)

CHAUCER (Geoffrey). Select Poems. (BRITISH Poets, I. 1–216.)

CHEVY Chase. The Beggar's Daughter of Bethnal Green. (CHAMBERS'S Miscel., I. no. 21.)

CHILD (The) of Elle, and other Ballads. (CHAMBERS'S Miscel., VI. no. 111.)

CHURCHILL (Charles). Select Poems. (BRITISH Poets, XXVII. 1–162.)

COLERIDGE (Samuel Taylor). The Ancient Mariner, and other Poems. (CHAMBERS'S Miscel., III. no. 59.)

COLLINS (William). Poetical Works. (BRITISH Poets, XXIII. 333–402.)

——— *The same.* *See* MILTON (J.). The Poetical Works of Milton, Young, *etc.*

COLMAN (George). *Translator.* *See* Class XVI. Part III. TERENTIUS AFER (P.). Select Comedies, *etc.*

COLTON (George Hooker). Tecumseh; or, The West Thirty Years since. A Poem. ... New-York. 1842. 12°

CONGREVE (William). Select Poems. (BRITISH Poets, XIV. 361 – 383.)

COOPER (John Gilbert). Select Poems. (BRITISH Poets, XXVIII. 209 – 286.)

CORBET (Richard), successively *Bp. of Oxford* and *Norwich*. Select Poems. (BRITISH Poets, IV. 327 – 371.)

COTTON (*Capt.* Charles). Select Poems. (BRITISH Poets, V. 213 – 239.)

COTTON (Nathaniel), *M.D.* Select Poems. (BRITISH Poets, XXXV. 311 – 396.)

COWLEY (Abraham). Select Poems. (BRITISH Poets, VI. 1 – 155.)

COWPER (William). The Task, Table Talk, and other Poems of W. C. With Critical Observations of various Authors on his Genius and Character, and Notes ... by James Robert Boyd .... New York. 1853. 12°

——— Select Poems. (BRITISH Poets, XXXVI., XXXVII. 1 – 187.)

——— Select Poetical Pieces of C. (CHAMBERS's Miscel., VI. no. 103.)

COWPER (William) *and* THOMSON (James). The Works of Cowper and Thomson, including many Letters and Poems never before published in this Country, with a new ... Memoir of the Life of Thomson .... Philadelphia. 1837. 8°

CRABBE (George). The Poetical Works of Crabbe, Heber, and Pollok .... Philadelphia. 1839. 8°

——— Poems — The Village, The Library, Phœbe Dawson, Dream of the Condemned Felon, Trades. (CHAMBERS's Miscel., V. no. 86.)

CRASHAW (Richard). Select Poems. (BRITISH Poets, V. 189 – 212.)

CUNNINGHAM (John). Select Poems. (BRITISH Poets, XXXII. 259 – 342.)

DANIEL (Samuel). Select Poems. (BRITISH Poets, II. 281 – 320.)

DANTE ALIGHIERI. The Vision; or, Hell, Purgatory, and Paradise, of D. A. Translated by the Rev. Henry Francis Cary. [With a Life of Dante.] (BRITISH Poets, Vols. XLV., XLVI.)

DAVENANT (*Sir* William). Select Poems. (BRITISH Poets, V. 125 – 161.)

DAVIES (*Sir* John). Select Poems. (BRITISH Poets, IV. 1 – 132.)

DENHAM (John). Poetical Works. (BRITISH Poets, VI. 251 – 334.)

DILLON (Wentworth), *4th Earl of Roscommon.* Select Poems. (BRITISH Poets, X. 217 – 257.)

DODSLEY (Robert). Select Poems. (BRITISH Poets, XXVI. 187 – 273.)

DONNE (John), *D.D.* Select Poems. (BRITISH Poets, IV. 133 – 195.)

DORSET, Charles, *6th Earl of.* *See* SACKVILLE.

DRAYTON (Michael). Select Poems. (BRITISH Poets, II. 321 – 391.)

DRUMMOND (William). Select Poems. (BRITISH Poets, V. 1 – 55.)

DRYDEN (John). Poetical Works. (BRITISH Poets, Vols. XI., XII.)

DUKE (Richard). Select Poems. (BRITISH Poets, XIII. 309 – 326.)

DYER (John). Poetical Works. (BRITISH Poets, XIX. 257 – 390.)

EVERETT (Alexander Hill). Poems. (Appended to his "Essays," 1845. 12° — *See* Class XXXI.)

FALCONER (William). Select Poems. (BRITISH Poets, XXVII. 163 – 268.)

FENTON (Elijah). Select Poems. (BRITISH Poets, XIV. 385 – 411.)

FERGUSSON (Robert). The Farmer's Ingle. (BRITISH Poets, XXXVII. 203 – 208.)

FLETCHER (Giles *and* Phineas). Poems. (BRITISH Poets, V. 89 – 110.)

FRANCKLIN (Thomas). *Translator.* *See* Class XVI. Part II. SOPHOCLES. Œdipus Tyrannus, *etc.*

FROST (John). Select Works of the British Poets, *etc.* *See* AIKIN (J.).

GARTH (*Sir* Samuel), *M.D.* Select Poems. (BRITISH Poets, XIV. 229 – 324.)

GASCOIGNE (*Capt.* George). Select Poems. (BRITISH Poets, I. 365 – 378.)

GAY (John). Poetical Works. (BRITISH Poets, Vol. XVI.)

GIFFORD (William). *Translator.* *See* Class XVI. Part III. PERSIUS FLACCUS (A.). The Satires, *etc.*

GLOVER (Richard). Select Poems. (BRITISH Poets, XXXIII. 1 – 322.)

GLYNN (Richard), *M.D.* The Day of Judgment. (BRITISH Poets, XXXVII. 385 – 396.)

GOLDSMITH (Oliver), *M.D.* Poems, Plays and Essays. *See* Class XXXI.

——— Select Poems. (BRITISH Poets, XXX. 1 – 100.)

GOWER (John). Select Poems. (BRITISH Poets, I. 217 – 255.)

GRAHAM (George Farquhar). Studies from the English Poets : a Reading-Book for the Higher Classes in Schools, or for Home Teaching. ... London. 1852. 12°

GRAINGER (James), *M.D.* Select Poems. (BRITISH Poets, XXVII. 269 – 373.)

GRANVILLE, *or* GREENVILLE (George), *Baron Lansdowne.* Select Poems. (BRITISH Poets, XVII. 157 – 203.)

GRAY (Thomas). Letters and Poems. *See* MILTON (J.). The Poetical Works of Milton, Young, *etc.*

——— Select Poems. (BRITISH Poets, XXIX. 1 – 111.)

GREEN (Matthew). Poetical Works. (BRITISH Poets, XVII. 235 – 282.)

GRISWOLD (Rufus Wilmot). The Poets and Poetry of America. With an Historical Introduction. ... 8th Ed., revised and enlarged, with Illustrations. Philadelphia. 1847. 8°

HABINGTON (William). Select Poems. (BRITISH Poets, V. 163 – 174.)

HALIFAX, Charles, 1*st Earl of.* *See* MONTAGUE.

HALL (Joseph), *D.D.*, successively *Bp. of Exeter* and *Norwich.* Select Poems. (BRITISH Poets, IV. 197 – 296.)

[HALLECK (Fitz-Greene)]. Selections from the British Poets. ... 2 vols. New-York. [1840?] 18° (HARPER's Fam. Libr., **112, 113.**)

Note. With the half-title: — "Selections ... . By Fitz-Greene Halleck."

HAMMOND (James). Poetical Works. (BRITISH Poets, XVII. 283 – 318.)

HART (John S.), *LL.D.* Class Book of Poetry: consisting of Selections from distinguished English and American Poets, from Chaucer to the Present Day. ... With Biographical and Critical Remarks. ... Philadelphia. 1845. 12°

HARTE (*Rev.* Walter). Select Poems. (BRITISH Poets, XXIX. 321 – 391.)

HEBER (Reginald), *D.D. Bp. of Calcutta.* Poetical Works. *See* CRABBE (G.). The Poetical Works of Crabbe, Heber, *etc.*

HEIR of Linne, and other Ballads. (CHAMBERS's Miscel., IV. no. 77.)

HEMANS (*Mrs.* Felicia Dorothea [BROWNE]). The Poetical Works ... . New Ed. with a Critical Preface, and a Biographical Memoir. Philadelphia. 1841. 8°

HERMIT (The) of Warkworth, and other Ballads. (CHAMBERS's Miscel., II. no. 39.)

HERRICK (Robert). Select Poems. (BRITISH Poets, V. 325 – 335.)

HOWARD (Henry), *Earl of Surrey.* Select Poems. (BRITISH Poets, I. 337 – 364.)

HUGHES (John). Select Poems. (BRITISH Poets, XIV. 325 – 338.)

HUNT (*Rev.* John Higgs). *Translator.* *See* TASSO (T.). ... Jerusalem Delivered, *etc.*

JAGO (*Rev.* Richard). Select Poems. (BRITISH Poets, XXXVII. 219 – 228.)

JENYNS (Soame). Select Poems. (BRITISH Poets, XXXII. 343 – 387.)

JOHNSON (Benjamin). *See* JONSON.

JOHNSON (Samuel), *LL.D.* Select Poems. (BRITISH Poets, XXXI. 1 – 118.)

JONES (*Sir* William). Select Poems. (BRITISH Poets, XXXV. 1 – 242.)

JONSON, *or* JOHNSON (Ben). Select Poems. (BRITISH Poets, III. 215 – 385.)

KING (William), *LL.D.* Select Poems. (BRITISH Poets, XIII. 327 – 356.)

LAMB (Charles). Poetical Works. *See* ROGERS (S.). The Poetical Works of Rogers, Campbell, *etc.*

LANGHORNE (John), *D.D.* Select Poems. (BRITISH Poets, XXX. 101 – 270.)

LANSDOWNE, George, *Baron.* *See* GRANVILLE.

LLOYD (Robert). Chit-Chat. (BRITISH Poets, XXXVII. 191 – 199.)

LOGAN (*Rev.* John). Select Poems. (BRITISH Poets, XXXVII. 241 – 252.)

LONGFELLOW (*Prof.* Henry Wadsworth). Poems. ... A new Ed. 2 vols. Boston. 1853. 16°

LOVELL (Robert). Sonnets. (BRITISH Poets, XXXVII. 291 – 295.)

LOVIBOND (Edward). Select Poems. (BRITISH Poets, XXXVII. 297 – 321.)

LYTTELTON (*Sir* George), 1*st Lord Lyttelton, Baron of Frankley.* Select Poems. (BRITISH Poets, XXXI. 253 – 325.

MACAULAY (Thomas Babington). Pompeii. — The Battle of Ivry. (MACAULAY's Essays, 1842, *etc.* 12° Vol. I. — *See* Class XXXI.)

——— Lays of Ancient Rome. (*Ibid.*, Vol. IV.)

[MACNEILL (Hector)]. The History of Will and Jean. (CHAMBERS's Miscel., IV. no. 68.)

——— Select Poems. (BRITISH Poets, XXXIX. 213 – 399.)

MALLET [*originally* MALLOCH] (David). Select Poems. (BRITISH Poets, XXVI. 275 – 331.)

MICKLE (William Julius). Select Poems. (BRITISH Poets, XXXIV. 1 – 178.)

——— *Translator. See* CAMOENS (L. DE). The Lusiad, *etc.*

MILTON (John). The Poetical Works of J. M.: with a Life of the Author; Preliminary Dissertations on each Poem; Notes Critical and Explanatory; an Index to the Subjects of Paradise Lost; and a Verbal Index to all the Poems. Edited by Charles Dexter Cleveland. ... Philadelphia. 1853. 12° pp. 688.

——— The Poetical Works of Milton, Young, Gray, Beattie, and Collins. ... Philadelphia. 1836. 8°

——— Poetical Works. (BRITISH Poets, Vols. VII., VIII.)

——— The Paradise Lost. With Notes Explanatory and Critical. Edited by Rev. James Robert Boyd .... New York. 1850. 12° or 8° (12. and 8.) (2 copies, one dated 1852.)

MITCHELL (Thomas). *Translator. See* Class XVI. Part II. ARISTOPHANES. The Comedies, *etc.*

MONTAGUE (Charles), 1*st Earl of Halifax.* Select Poems. (BRITISH Poets, XIII. 367 – 378.)

MONTGOMERY (James). Poetical Works. *See* ROGERS (S.). The Poetical Works of Rogers, Campbell, *etc.*

MOORE (Edward). Select Poems. (BRITISH Poets, XXIII. 403 – 431.)

NEALE (Edmund), *afterwards* SMITH. *See* SMITH.

NUGENT (Robert Craggs), *Earl Nugent and Viscount Clare.* Select Poems. (BRITISH Poets, XXXVII. 252 – 262.)

OLD Bachelor (The). (BRITISH Poets, XXXVII. 397 – 402.)

OTWAY (Thomas). Select Poems. (BRITISH Poets, X. 253 – 286).

PARNELL (Thomas), *D.D.* Poetical Works. (BRITISH Poets, XIII. 1 – 116.)

PATTISON (William). Select Poems. (BRITISH Poets, XIV. 413 – 432.)

PERCY (Thomas), *Bp. of Dromore.* Reliques of Ancient English Poetry: consisting of Old Heroic Ballads, Songs, and other Pieces of our Earlier Poets; together with some few of later Date. ... New Ed. 3 vols. London. 1847. 8° or 16° (8.)

PHILIPS (John). Poetical Works. (BRITISH Poets, XIII. 117 – 222.)

PITT (Christopher). Select Poems. (BRITISH Poets, XXI. 335 – 416.)

POETICAL Selections. (CHAMBERS'S Miscel., X. no. 168.)

POLLOK (Robert). The Course of Time. *See* CRABBE (G.). The Poetical Works of Crabbe, Heber, *etc.*

POMFRET (John). Select Poems. (BRITISH Poets, X. 287 – 390.)

POPE (Alexander). The Poetical Works of A. P. New Ed. London. 1847. 12°

Note. Also with an engraved title-page: — "The Poems," etc.

——— Poetical Works. (BRITISH Poets, XX., XXI. 1 – 304.)

——— *Translator.* *See* Class XVI. Part II. HOMERUS. The Iliad, *etc.*; — *also*, The Odyssey, *etc.*

PORTEUS (Beilby), successively *Bp. of Chester* and *London.* Death, a Poem. (BRITISH Poets, XXXVII. 371 – 383.)

POTTER (Robert). *Translator.* *See* Class XVI. Part II. ÆSCHYLUS. Agamemnon, *etc.*; — *also*, EURIPIDES. The Bacchæ, *etc.*

PRIOR (Matthew). Select Poems. (BRITISH Poets, XV. 1 – 240.)

RALEIGH (*Sir* Walter). Select Poems. (BRITISH Poets, V. 111 – 123.)

RAMSAY (Allan). Select Poems. (BRITISH Poets, XXVI. 333 – 437.)

RICHARDSON (William). Ode to a Singing Bird. (BRITISH Poets, XXXVII. 209 – 211.)

[ROBBINS (*Rev.* Chandler)]. The Social Hymn-Book; consisting of Psalms and Hymns for Social Worship and Private Devotion. [Edited by the Rev. C. R.] Boston. 1843. 18°

ROBERTS (William Hayward), *D.D.* Select Poems. (BRITISH Poets, XXXVII. 349 – 369.)

ROCHESTER, John, 2*d Earl of.* *See* WILMOT.

ROGERS (Samuel). The Poetical Works of Rogers, Campbell, J. Montgomery, Lamb, and Kirke White. ... Philadelphia. 1839. 8°

ROSCOMMON, Wentworth, 4*th Earl of.* *See* DILLON.

ROWE (Nicholas). Select Poems. (BRITISH Poets, XIII. 379 – 412.)

RUSSELL (Thomas). Sonnets. (BRITISH Poets, XXXVII. 277 – 295.)

SACKVILLE (Charles), 6*th Earl of Dorset.* Select Poems. (BRITISH Poets, XIII. 223 – 234.)

SANFORD (Ezekiel) *and* WALSH (Robert), *Jr.* The Works of the British Poets, with Lives of the Authors. ... [Vols. I. – XVII., edited by Ezekiel Sanford; Vols. XVIII. – L., by Robert Walsh, Jr.] 50 vols. Philadelphia. 1819 – 23. 24°

Note. Also with an engraved title-page: — "First American Edition of the British Poets," etc.

SAVAGE (Richard). Poetical Works. (BRITISH Poets, XIX. 1 – 256.)

SCHOOL Hymn-Book (The); for Normal, High, and Grammar Schools. Boston. 1850. 18°

SCOTT (John). Select Poems. (BRITISH Poets, XXXII. 103 – 255.)

Scott (*Sir* Walter), *Bart.* The Poetical Works of Sir W. S., with a Sketch of his Life, by J. W. Lake. ... Philadelphia. 1839. 8°

——— Select Poetical Pieces. (Chambers's Miscel., V. no. 95.)

Select Poems of the Domestic Affections — The Cotter's Saturday Night [by Burns], &c. (Chambers's Miscel., I. no. 11.)

Select Poems of Kindness to Animals. (Chambers's Miscel., II. no. 30.)

Select Poems on Birds. (Chambers's Miscel., IX. no. 160.)

Select Poems on Insects. (Chambers's Miscel., VIII. no. 143.)

Select Poems on Love for Flowers. (Chambers's Miscel., III. no. 49.)

Selections from American Poetry. (Chambers's Miscel., VII. no. 119.)

Selections from the Elizabethan Poets. (Chambers's Miscel., IX. no. 151.)

Selections from French and German Poetry. (Chambers's Miscel., VIII. no. 135.)

Shakespeare (William). Select Poems. (British Poets, III. 1 - 213.)

Shaw (Cuthbert). Select Poems. (British Poets, XXXI. 231 - 252.)

Sheffield (John), 1*st Duke of Buckingham.* Select Poems. (British Poets, XIV. 339 - 360.)

Shenstone (William). Poetical Works. (British Poets, XXIV. 1 - 300.)

Sherburne (*Sir* Edward). Select Poems. (British Poets, V. 273 - 324.)

Skelton (John). Select Poems. (British Poets, I. 257 - 282.)

Smart (Christopher). Select Poems. (British Poets, XXX. 271 - 353.)

Smith [*originally* Neale] (Edmund). Select Poems. (British Poets, XIII. 281 - 308.)

Smollett (Tobias), *M.D.* Select Poems. (British Poets, XXXIII. 323 - 386.)

Social Hymn-Book (The). *See* [Robbins (C.)].

Somervile (William). Select Poems. (British Poets, XVII. 319 - 420.)

Songs of Home and Fatherland. (Chambers's Miscel., X. no. 177.)

Spenser (Edmund). Select Poems. (British Poets, II. 1 - 280.)

Sprat (Thomas), *Bp. of Rochester.* Select Poems. (British Poets, XIII. 357 - 365.)

Stepney (George). Select Poems. (British Poets, XIII. 235 - 256.)

Stirling, William, 1*st Earl of.* *See* Alexander.

Suckling (*Sir* John). Select Poems. (British Poets, V. 175 - 188.)

Surrey, Henry, *Earl of.* *See* Howard.

Swift (Jonathan), *D.D.*, *Dean of St. Patrick's.* Select Poems. (British Poets, Vol. XVIII.)

Tasso (Torquato). ... Jerusalem Delivered, an Heroic Poem. ... Translated by the Reverend J. H. Hunt .... (British Poets, Vols. XLVIII., XLIX.)

Thompson (William). Select Poems. (British Poets, XXVIII. 287 - 391.)

THOMSON (James). Works. *See* COWPER (W.). The Works of Cowper and Thomson, *etc.*

——— Poetical Works. (BRITISH Poets, Vol. XXII.)

——— The Seasons. By J. T. With Critical Observations of various Authors on his Genius and Character; and Notes ... by James Robert Boyd .... New York. 1852. 12°

TICKELL (Thomas). Poetical Works. (BRITISH Poets, XVII. 1 – 155.)

VIDA (Marco Girólamo), *Bp. of Alba.* Art of Poetry, in Three Books. Translated from the Latin, by Christopher Pitt. (BRITISH Poets, XXI. 341 – 416.)

WALLER (Edmund). Select Poems. (BRITISH Poets, VI. 157 – 250.)

WALSH (William). Select Poems. (BRITISH Poets, XIII. 257 – 279.)

WARE (*Prof.* Henry), *Jr.*, *D.D.* Poems. (Works, I. 201 – 370.)

WARTON (Joseph). Select Poems. (BRITISH Poets, XXXIV. 179 – 237.)

WARTON (Thomas). Select Poems. (BRITISH Poets, XXXIV. 239 – 400.)

WATTS (Isaac), *D.D.* Select Poems. (BRITISH Poets, XXIII. 1 – 332.)

WHITE (Henry Kirke). Poetical Works. *See* ROGERS (S.). The Poetical Works of Rogers, Campbell, *etc.*

WHITEHEAD (William). Variety; a Tale for Married People. (BRITISH Poets, XXXVII. 229 – 240.)

WILL and Jean. *See* [MACNEILL (H.)].

WILMOT (John), *2d Earl of Rochester.* Select Poems. (BRITISH Poets, X. 175 – 215.)

WITHER (George). Select Poems. (BRITISH Poets, V. 337 – 350.)

WYAT (*Sir* Thomas). Select Poems. (BRITISH Poets, I. 283 – 335.)

YALDEN (Thomas), *D.D.* Select Poems. (BRITISH Poets, XVII. 205 – 234.)

YOUNG (Edward), *D.D.* Poetical Works. (BRITISH Poets, XXV., XXVI. 1 – 185.)

——— *The same.* *See* MILTON (J.). The Poetical Works of Milton, Young, *etc.*

——— Night Thoughts on Life, Death, and Immortality. With a Memoir of the Author, a Critical View of his Writings, and Explanatory Notes. By James Robert Boyd .... New York. 1852. 12°

CLASS XX. DRAMATIC LITERATURE.

Note. For *Ancient Greek and Latin Authors*, see Class XVI. Parts II. and III.

[CHILD (*Prof.* Francis James)]. *Editor*, etc. *See* FOUR Old Plays.

COLLOT (A. G.). Chefs-d'Œuvre Dramatiques de la Langue Française, mis en Ordre progressif, et annotés .... New York. 1847. 12°

CORNEILLE (Pierre). Le Cid. *See* Class XV. Part II. § 3. A. PICOT (C.). No. 7 .... Beauties, *etc.*

FOUR Old Plays Three Interludes: Thersytes Jack Jugler and Heywoods Pardoner and Frere: and Jocasta a Tragedy by Gascoigne and Kinwelmarsh With an Introduction and Notes [by Prof. Francis J. Child] Cambridge. 1848. 12°

GASCOIGNE (George) *and* KINWELMARSH (Francis). Iocasta: a Tragedie [viz. the Phœnissæ] vvritten in Greke by Euripides, translated [with great alterations] and digested into Acte by George Gascoygne, and Francis Kinvvelmershe .... 1566. *See* FOUR Old Plays, *etc.*

GOLDSMITH (Oliver). Poems, Plays and Essays. *See* Class XXXI.

HERTZ (Henrik). King René's Daughter: a Danish Lyrical Drama. Translated by Theodore Martin. Boston. 1850. 12° pp. 75. +

HEYWOOD (John). A Mery Playe betwene the Pardoner and the Frere the Curate and Neybour Pratte. [From the Ed. of 1533.] *See* FOUR Old Plays, *etc.*

JACK Jugler. A new Enterlued for Chyldren to playe, named Jacke Jugeler, both wytte, and very playsent. Newly imprented. .... *See* FOUR Old Plays, *etc.*

LONGFELLOW (*Prof.* Henry Wadsworth). The Golden Legend. Boston. 1853. 16°

MOLIÈRE (Jean Baptiste POQUELIN DE). Le Misanthrope. *See* Class XV. Part II. § 3. A. PICOT (C.). No. 7 .... Beauties, *etc.*

PICOT (Charles). Beauties of the French Drama. *See* Class XV. Part II. § 3. A.

RACINE (Jean). Athalie. *See* Class XV. Part II. § 3. A. PICOT (C.). No. 7 .... Beauties, *etc.*

SCHILLER (Johann Christoph Friedrich VON). The Works of Frederick S. [Vol. II.] Historical and Dramatic. History of the Revolt of the Netherlands, continued — Trials of Counts Egmont and Horn. Wallenstein and Wilhelm Tell, Historical Dramas. Translated from the German [Wallenstein's Camp, by James Churchill; The Piccolomini, and Death of Wallenstein, by S. T. Coleridge, with additions to his version; W. Tell, by Theodore Martin].

The Works .... [Vol. III.] Historical Dramas, etc. Don Carlos. — Mary Stuart. — The Maid of Orleans. — The Bride of Messina. [With an Essay on the Use of the Chorus in Tragedy.] Translated from the German [Don C., by R. D. Boylan; M. S., by Joseph Mellish, with additions to his version; The Maid of O., by Anna Swanwick; The Bride of M., by A. Lodge].

The Works .... [Vol. IV.] Early Dramas and Romances. The Robbers, Fiesco, Love and Intrigue, Demetrius, The Ghost-Seer, and The Sport of Destiny. Translated from the German, chiefly by Henry G. Bohn.

3 vols. London. 1847 – 47 – 49. 8° (BOHN's Stand. Libr.)

SHAKESPEARE (William). The Dramatic Works of William Shakspeare; with a Life of the Poet, and Notes, original and selected. 7 vols. Boston. 1849. 8°

——— Selections from S. (CHAMBERS's Miscel., VII. no. 127.)

——— The Shakspearian Reader: a Collection of the most approved Plays of Shakspeare; carefully revised [and *altered*] with ... Notes, and a Memoir of the Author. Prepared expressly for the Use of Classes, and the Family Reading Circle. By John W. S. Hows .... New-York. 1849. 12°

SHERIDAN (Richard Brinsley). The Dramatic Works of the Right Honorable Richard Brinsley Sheridan. With a Memoir of his Life, by G. G. S. London. 1848. 8° (BOHN's Stand. Libr.)

THERSYTES. A new Enterlude called Thersytes Thys Enterlude Folowynge dothe Declare howe that the greatest boesters are not the greatest doers. ... *See* FOUR Old Plays, *etc.*

VOLTAIRE (François Marie AROUET DE). Mérope. *See* Class XV. Part II. § 3. A. PICOT (C.). No. 7 .... Beauties, *etc.*

CLASS XXI. PROSE FICTION; WORKS OF WIT AND HUMOR.

Note. Some of the stories placed in this Class are *substantially* true. Where these relate to persons whose real names are given, they are also entered under Class XXIV. If several tales form one Tract, they appear, for the most part, only under the title of the first.

ABBY's Year in Lowell. *See* HALL (*Mrs.* A. M. [F.], *wife of* S. C.). There is no Hurry, *etc.*

BECKER (*Prof.* Wilhelm Adolph). Charicles. *See* Class XXVII.

——— Gallus. *See* Class XXVII.

[BERTHOUD (Samuel Henri)]. *See* SISTER (The) of Rembrandt.

BLACK Gondola (The) — a Venetian Tale. (CHAMBERS's Papers, *etc.* VIII. no. 61.)

BLACK Pocket-Book (The) — a Tale. (CHAMBERS's Papers, *etc.* IV. no. 27.)

BONIFACE SAINTINE (Xavier). *See* SAINTINE.

CHRISTMAS Holiday (The). Be Just before you are Generous. (CHAMBERS's Miscel., VIII. no. 134.)

CRAYON (Geoffrey), Gent^{n}., *pseudon.* *See* [IRVING (Washington)].

CROWE (*Mrs.* Catharine [STEVENS]). The Two Beggar Boys. — The Widow's Son. [By Mrs. Stone.] (CHAMBERS's Miscel., I. no. 10.)

DESERTERS (The). (CHAMBERS's Miscel., IX. no. 147.)

EDMUND Atherton — a Tale of Circumstantial Evidence. (CHAMBERS's Papers, *etc.* II. no. 11.)

GOLDMAKERS' Village. *See* [ZSCHOKKE (J. *H.* D.)].

GRACE Ayton. (CHAMBERS's Repos., II. no. 14.)

HALF-CASTE (The) — a Tale. (CHAMBERS's Papers, *etc.* XII. no. 94.)

HALL (*Mrs.* Anna Maria [FIELDING], *wife of* S. C.). "Do you think I'd inform?" The Schoolmaster's Dream. (CHAMBERS's Miscel., VIII. no. 129.)

HALL (*Mrs.* Anna Maria [FIELDING], *wife of* S. C.). It 's only a Drop. (CHAMBERS's Miscel., III. no. 56.)

——— There is no Hurry! — a Tale of Life Assurance. Abby's Year in Lowell, — a Tale of Self-Denial. [From the "Lowell Offering."] (CHAMBERS's Miscel., VII. no. 118.)

——— Time Enough: an Irish Tale. — My Native Bay: a Poem. [By "R. C."; Robert Chambers?] (CHAMBERS's Miscel., I. no. 5.)

HALL (*Mrs.* S. C.). *See* HALL (*Mrs.* A. M. [F.], *wife of* S. C.).

HARRIETTE; or, The Rash Reply — a Tale. (CHAMBERS's Papers, *etc.* X. no. 75.)

HEIRESS (The) of the Vaughans. *See* TOWER of Fontenay, *etc.*

HELEN Gray. (CHAMBERS's Repos., I. no. 3.)

HERMANN — a Tale. (CHAMBERS's Papers, *etc.* VI. no. 43.)

HOARE (*Mrs.* ——). Jim Cronin, an Irish Tale. (CHAMBERS's Miscel., X. no. 176.)

IRIARTE (Tomas DE). Fábulas Literarias . . . . Nueva Ed., añadidas las Variantes de otras Ediciones, y Nueve Fábulas Póstumas del mismo Autor. [Edited by Charles Folsom.] Cambrigia. 1830. 18°

IRVING (Washington). The Alhambra. Author's revised Ed. New-York. 1851. 12° (Works, Vol. XV.)

[———] Bracebridge Hall, or the Humorists. A Medley. By Geoffrey Crayon, Gent^{n}. . . . Author's revised Ed. . . . New-York. 1849. 12° (Works, Vol. VI.)

[———] Chronicle of the Conquest of Granada. *See* Class XXVII. Part IV. § 1. B. *Spain and Portugal.*

——— The Crayon Miscellany. Author's revised Ed. . . . New-York. 1849. 12° (Works, Vol. IX.)

[———] A History of New-York, from the Beginning of the World to the End of the Dutch Dynasty . . . . By Diedrich Knickerbocker. . . . The Author's revised Ed. . . . New-York. 1849. 12° (Works, Vol. I.)

[———] The Sketch Book of Geoffrey Crayon, Gent^{n}. . . . The Author's revised Ed. New-York. 1852. 12° (Works, Vol. II.)

[———] Tales of a Traveller. By Geoffrey Crayon, Gent^{n}. . . . Author's revised Ed. . . . New-York. 1849. 12° (Works, Vol. VII.)

IVORY Mine (The) — a Tale of the Frozen Sea. (CHAMBERS's Papers, *etc.* II. no. 14.)

JOHNSON (Samuel), *LL.D.* Rasselas, and other Tales. (Works, 1837. 8° Vol. I.)

JOURNAL of a Poor Vicar. — Blanche Raymond: a Parisian Story. (CHAMBERS's Miscel., I. no. 17.)

KNICKERBOCKER (Diedrich), *pseudon.* *See* [IRVING (Washington)].

LAST of the Ruthvens (The). (CHAMBERS's Papers, *etc.* V. no. 35.)

[LEE (*Mrs.* Hannah F. [SAWYER])]. The Three Ways of Living — Living within the Means, Living up to the Means, Living beyond the Means. (CHAMBERS's Miscel., VI. no. 110.)

LEON Gondy : a Legend of Ghent. (CHAMBERS's Repos., II. no. 11.)

LIFE in an Indiaman. (CHAMBERS's Papers, *etc.* VII. no. 52.)

Note. Perhaps not fictitious.

LONE Star (The) — a Tale. (CHAMBERS's Papers, *etc.* VI. no. 46.)

LONGFELLOW (*Prof.* Henry Wadsworth). Hyperion, a Romance. ... 12th Ed. Boston. 1853. 16°

——— Kavanagh, a Tale. ... Boston. 1853. 16°

LOST Laird (The) — a Tale of '45. (CHAMBERS's Papers, *etc.* IX. no. 67.)

LOST Letter (The) — The Somnambule. (CHAMBERS's Papers, *etc.* VII. no. 51.)

[MACNEILL (Hector)]. *See* SCOTTISH Adventurers.

MAGIC Flute (The). *See* [SMIDT (H.)].

MARFREDA ; or, The Icelanders. (CHAMBERS's Papers, *etc.* XII. no. 91.)

MAURICE and Genevieve. (CHAMBERS's Miscel., I. no. 13.)

MINA Block ; the Face-Model. (CHAMBERS's Repos., I. no. 6.)

MRS. MACCLARTY : Scenes from the "Cottagers of Glenburnie." (CHAMBERS's Miscel., III. no. 46.)

MORAL Tales from the French — The Little Gipsy Girl. The Two Brothers. Victor Dacheux. (CHAMBERS's Miscel., X. no. 165.)

PASSION and Principle. [From the French.] (CHAMBERS's Miscel., III. no. 43.)

PICCIOLA. *See* [SAINTINE (X. B.)].

POOR Joe [Berr]. The Kidnapped Boy. (CHAMBERS's Miscel., IX. no. 145.)

PRESENT (A) to Apprentices — George Macqueen : a Story. Friendly Hints to Young People. James Wallace : a Story. (CHAMBERS's Miscel., IX. no. 148.)

QUEEN (The) of Spades — Antonio Melidori. (CHAMBERS's Papers, *etc.* V. no. 38.)

QUINTIN Matsys, the Blacksmith of Antwerp. (CHAMBERS's Miscel., VII. no. 126.)

REALIZED Wishes — a Tale. (CHAMBERS's Papers, *etc.* XI. no. 83.)

[SAINTINE (Xavier BONIFACE)]. Picciola, or the Prison-Flower. [Abridged from Saintine.] (CHAMBERS's Miscel., I. no. 7.)

ST. JUST (*Lady* Marjory), *pseudon.* Lady Marjory St. Just — an Autobiography. (CHAMBERS's Papers, *etc.* IV. no. 30.)

SANTILLIAN's Choice — a Tale. (CHAMBERS's Papers, *etc.* VII. no. 54.)

SCOTTISH Adventurers (The). [Abridged from a work by Hector Macneill.] (CHAMBERS's Miscel., IV. no. 74.)

SCOTTISH Traditionary Stories. (CHAMBERS's Miscel., V. no. 83.)

SCULPTOR (The) of the Black Forest. (CHAMBERS's Miscel., V. no. 94.)

SIGISMUND Temple — a Tale. (CHAMBERS's Papers, *etc.* IX. no. 70.)

SISTER (The) of Rembrandt. [Extended from the French of Berthoud.] (CHAMBERS's Miscel., III. no. 54.)

[SMIDT (Heinrich)]. The Magic Flute: a Moral Tale from the German. Why the Sea is Salt, or, The Adventures of Silly Nicholas. (CHAMBERS's Miscel., IX. no. 156.)

SPECULATOR (The) — a Tale of Mammon-Worship. (CHAMBERS's Papers, *etc.* III. no. 19.)

STAEL-HOLSTEIN (Anne Louise Germaine [NECKER], *Baroness* DE). Corinne, ou l'Italie .... Nouvelle Éd., revue et corrigée. Boston. 1846. 12°

STORIES of Aims and Ends. (CHAMBERS's Miscel., VIII. no. 138.)

STORY of Catherine of Russia. (CHAMBERS's Miscel., V. no. 84.)

STORY of Jacquard. (CHAMBERS's Miscel., IX. no. 158.)

STORY of Richard Falconer. — Byron's Narrative. (CHAMBERS's Miscel., II. no. 33.)

STORY (The) of Valentine Duval. (CHAMBERS's Miscel., IV. no. 67.)

STORY of Walter Ruysdael, the Watchmaker. (CHAMBERS's Miscel., I. no. 20.)

SUNKEN Rock (The). A Tale of the Mediterranean. (CHAMBERS's Papers, *etc.* I. no. 6.)

TEMPTATION (The) — a Tale. (CHAMBERS's Papers, *etc.* X. no. 78.)

THREE Ways of Living. *See* [LEE (*Mrs.* H. F. [S.])].

TINTORETTO (The). (CHAMBERS's Miscel., IV. no. 72.)

TOULMIN (Camilla). A Story of the Factories. (CHAMBERS's Miscel., V. no. 79.)

TOWER of Fontenay; and The Heiress of the Vaughans. (CHAMBERS's Papers, *etc.* XI. no. 86.)

TRADITIONARY Tales of Tweeddale — The Maid of Neidpath, Burnet of Castlehill, Helen Symington, Neil Maclaren, The First Earl of Traquair, Allan Scott, The Border Widow. (CHAMBERS's Miscel., V. no. 90.)

VALERIE Duclos .... (CHAMBERS's Papers, *etc.* I. no. 3.)

VILLAGE Mayor (The). *See* [ZSCHOKKE (J. *H.* D.)].

WHITE Swallow (The) — an Indian Tale. (CHAMBERS's Papers, *etc.* III. no. 22.)

WOMEN's Trials in Humble Life — Story of Peggy Dickson. ... Of Isbel Lucas. ... Of Nell Forsyth. Jerry Guttridge: a Tale of the Early American Settlements. [Abridged from the Knickerbocker Magazine for May, 1839.] (CHAMBERS's Miscel., X. no. 162.)

[ZSCHOKKE (Johann Heinrich Daniel)]. The Goldmakers' Village. [From the German of Z., with some alterations.] (CHAMBERS's Miscel., II. no. 34.)

[———] The Village Mayor [from the German of Z.], The Story of Fritz, The Bird-Catcher and his Canary [" from Pratt's Gleanings"]. (CHAMBERS's Miscel., VI. no. 101.)

HISTORY OF MAN, IN HIS HIGHER RELATIONS.

(Classes XXII. — XXIX.)

Note. For the *Physical* History of Man, see Class XIII. Part V.

CLASS XXII. CIVIL GEOGRAPHY, TOPOGRAPHY, AND STATISTICS.

Note. For *Mathematical* Geography, see Class XI. Part III.; for *Physical* Geography, Class XIII. Part I.

PART I. GENERAL WORKS.

AMERICAN Almanac (The) and Repository of Useful Knowledge for the Year 1830 .... 3d Ed. Vol. I. | 1831. 2d Ed. | 1832. | 1833. 2d Ed. | 1834-1853. 24 vols. Boston. [1831-52?] 12°

Note. The vols. for 1830 and 1833 are dated 1839. — The vol. for 1830 was edited by Jared Sparks. From 1831 to 1842 the work was conducted by Joseph E. Worcester; from 1843 to 1847 by Francis Bowen, since which time it has been under the editorial charge of George P. Sanger. Francis E. Parker was associated with Mr. Sanger for one or two years.

The vols. for 1839 and 1849 contain General Indexes to the vols. for 1830-39 and 1840-49, respectively.

BRADFORD (Thomas Gamaliel) *and* GOODRICH (Samuel Griswold). A Universal, Illustrated Atlas, exhibiting a Geographical, Statistical, and Historical View of the World. Boston. 1846. Large 4° (2.)

BRUUN (Malthe Conrad). *See* MALTE-BRUN (C.).

CALLICOT (T. Carey). ... Hand-Book of Universal Geography; being a Gazetteer of the World. ... New York. 1853. 12° pp. iv., 856. (PUTNAM's Home Cyclopedia, Vol. V.)

[GOODRICH (Samuel Griswold)]. Manners and Customs of the Principal Nations of the Globe. By the Author of Peter Parley's Tales. Boston. 1849. 16° or 18° (8. and 6.) (CABINET Libr., **19.**)

——— A National Geography, for Schools; illustrated by 220 Engravings, and 33 Maps; with a Globe Map, on a new Plan .... New York. 1846. 4°

[———] The World and its Inhabitants. *See* Class XIII. Part I.

HOUZÉ (A.). ... Atlas Universel Historique et Géographique composé de Cent Une Cartes donnant les différentes Divisions et Modifications territoriales des diverses Nations aux principales Époques de leur Histoire, avec une Notice sur tous les Faits importants, et l'Indication des Lieux ou ils se sont passés .... Adopté par le Conseil de l'Université [of France] pour être placé dans les Bibliothèques des Lycées et Colléges. Paris. [1849?] 4°

McCULLOCH (John Ramsey). M'Culloch's Universal Gazetteer. — A

Dictionary, Geographical, Statistical, and Historical, of the various Countries, Places, and principal Natural Objects in the World. ... In which the Articles relating to the United States have been greatly multiplied and extended ... . By Daniel Haskel ... . Illustrated with Seven large Maps. ... 2 vols. New-York. 1843 – 44. 8°

MALTE-BRUN (Conrad) [*Danish*, BRUUN (Malthe Conrad)]. A System of Universal Geography ... . With Additions and Corrections, by James G. Percival. ... With a complete Atlas, and a Series of ... Engravings. 3 vols. Boston. 1834. 4°

MITCHELL (S. Augustus). An Accompaniment to Mitchell's Map of the World, on Mercator's Projection; containing an Index to the various Countries, Cities, Towns, Islands, &c., represented on the Map ...: also, a General Description of the Five Great Divisions of the Globe, ... with their several Empires, Kingdoms, States, Territories, &c. Philadelphia. 1847. 8°

Note. With a large colored Map representing the Flags of the principal nations of the world.

MURRAY (Hugh). The Encyclopædia of Geography ... . By Hugh Murray ... assisted in Astronomy, &c. by Prof. Wallace, Geology, &c. by Prof. Jameson, Botany, &c. by Professor Hooker, Zoology, &c. by W. Swainson, Esq. Illustrated by Eighty-two Maps, and about Eleven Hundred other Engravings on Wood ... together with a new Map of the United States. Revised, with Additions, by Thomas G. Bradford. ... 3 vols. Philadelphia. 1845 – 45 – 43. [Stereotyped 1836.] 8°

PARKER (Richard Green). ... Questions in Geography, adapted for the Use of Morse's, ... or any other respectable Collection of Maps ... . To which is added, A concise Description of the Terrestrial Globe. ... 2d Ed. New York. 1847. 12° pp. 65.

PARLEY (Peter), *pseudon.* *See* [GOODRICH (Samuel Griswold)].

WOODBRIDGE (William Channing). System of Modern Geography, on the Principles of Comparison and Classification. ... Accompanied by an Atlas ... . Improved Ed. Hartford. 1845. 12°

——— Problems on the Globes, *etc.* *See* Part II. WILLARD (*Mrs.* E. [H.]) Ancient Geography, *etc.*

WORCESTER (Joseph Emerson), *LL.D.* Elements of Geography, Modern and Ancient, with a Modern and Ancient Atlas. Revised and improved Ed. Boston. 1842. 12°

Note. The "Elements of Ancient Geography" is paged independently; pp. 74.

PART II. ANCIENT AND MEDIÆVAL GEOGRAPHY.

AINSWORTH (William Francis). Travels in the Track of the Ten Thousand Greeks, *etc.* *See* Class XXIII.

ANTHON (*Prof.* Charles), *LL.D.* A System of Ancient and Mediæval Geography. ... New York. 1850. 8° pp. viii., 769.

ARNOLD (*Rev.* Thomas Kerchever). A First Classical Atlas. Intended as a Companion to the "Historiæ Antiquæ Epitome." Edited by the Rev. T. K. A. ... . [15 Maps.] London. [1849 ?] 12°

ATLAS Classica being a Collection of Maps of the Countries mentioned by the Ancient Authors both Sacred & Profane with their various Subdivisions at different Periods. [53 Maps.] Published by H. S. Tanner. Philadelphia. N. D. 4°

BUTLER (Samuel), *D.D.* An Atlas of Antient Geography. [21 Maps.] ... Philadelphia. 1849. 8°

——— Geographia Classica: or the Application of Antient Geography to the Classics. ... 2d American, from the 9th London Ed., with Questions on the Maps, by John Frost. Philadelphia. 1831. 8°

COLEMAN (*Prof.* Lyman), *D.D.* An Historical Geography of the Bible. Illustrated by [7] Maps .... New Ed., with Additions. Philadelphia. 1851. 8° or 16° (8.)

FINDLAY (Alexander G.). A Classical Atlas, to illustrate Ancient Geography; comprised in Twenty-five Maps .... With an Index of the Ancient and Modern Names. London. 1847. 8°

GELL (*Sir* William). The Topography of Rome and its Vicinity. ... A new Ed., revised and enlarged, by Edward Herbert Bunbury .... London. 1846. 8°

Note. Accompanied by a large Map of "Rome & its Environs, from a Trigonometrical Survey. By Sir William Gell," etc., dated Sept. 1834.

HAZLITT (William). The Classical Gazetteer: a Dictionary of Ancient Geography, Sacred and Profane. ... London. 1851. 8°

JENKS (William), *D.D.* The Explanatory Bible Atlas and Scripture Gazetteer. *See* Class II. Part III.

KIEPERT (Heinrich). Topographisch-historischer Atlas von Hellas und den Hellenischen Colonien in 24 Blättern unter Mitwirkung des Professors Carl Ritter .... Berlin. 1846. fol.

——— Supplementheft zum Atlas von Hellas und den Hellenischen Colonien .... Enthaltend neue Ausgaben der Blätter IV. V. XV. XX., nebst Erläuterungen und Berichtigungen zur ersten Ausgabe des Atlas. Berlin. 1851. fol.

KUTSCHEIT (Johannes Valerius). Hand-Atlas der alten Geschichte und Geographie für den Schul- und Privatgebrauch in zehn illuminirten Karten. Berlin. 1843. fol.

MITCHELL (S. Augustus). Mitchell's Ancient Geography .... Together with an Ancient Atlas .... Philadelphia. 1845. 12° Atlas, 4°

NIEBUHR (Barthold Georg). A Dissertation on the Geography of Herodotus, with a Map. Researches into the History of the Scythians, Getæ, and Sarmatians. Translated from the German of B. G. N. Oxford. 1830. 8° pp. ii., 86.

PUETZ (Wilhelm). Manual of Ancient Geography and History. *See* Class XXV. Part II. § 1.

——— Handbook of Mediæval Geography and History. *See* Class XXV. Part III.

SMITH (William), *LL.D.* A Dictionary of Greek and Roman Geography. By various Writers. Edited by W. S. .... Illustrated by numerous Engravings on Wood. [Part I. — VI. Abacaenum — Cyrrhestica.] 6 pts. London. Jan. 1, 1852 — April 1, 1853. 8°

SPRUNER (Karl VON). Atlas Antiquus. Delineavit Dr. C. de Spruner. XXVII Tabulas Coloribus illustratas et alias LXIV Tabellas in Margine illarum inclusas continens. ... [With a sheet of letter-press.] Gothae. 1850. fol.

TANNER (H. S.). *See* ATLAS Classica, *etc.* N. D. 4°

WILLARD (*Mrs.* Emma [HART]). Ancient Geography, as connected with Chronology; and preparatory to Ancient History. Accompanied by an Ancient Atlas .... Revised Ed. Also, Problems on the Globes, and Rules for constructing Maps. By W. C. Woodbridge. Hartford. 1845. 12° pp. 96.

——— Another copy. (Appended to WOODBRIDGE's Modern Geography, 1845. 12°)

WORCESTER (Joseph Emerson), *LL.D.* Elements of Ancient Classical and Scripture Geography. *See* Part I.

PART III. MODERN GEOGRAPHY OF PARTICULAR COUNTRIES.

ACCOUNT of the Highlands. (CHAMBERS's Miscel., VIII. no. 141.)

ADAMS (George). The Massachusetts Register for the Year 1853, containing a Business Directory of the State, with a Variety of Useful Information. Serial Number, LXXXVII. Boston. 1853. 8°

AMERICAN Almanac. *See* Part I.

AUSTRALIA and its Gold Regions. (CHAMBERS's Repos., I. no. 2.)

AUSTRALIA and Van Diemen's Land. (CHAMBERS's Papers, *etc.* VI. no. 45.)

[BARROW (*Sir* John)], *Bart.* A Description of Pitcairn's Island and its Inhabitants. With an authentic Account of the Mutiny of the Ship Bounty, and of the subsequent Fortunes of the Mutineers. New-York. N. D. 18° (HARPER's Fam. Libr., **31.**)

BLACK's County Atlas of Scotland, with the Parochial Divisions, including Seven Historical Maps, Topographical Descriptions, and an Index to all the Parishes, shewing the Presbytery, Synod, and County in which they are situated, with the Post Town and Population of each. [39 Maps.] Edinburgh: Adam and Charles Black. 1848. 4° pp. 46. +

BORNEO. *See* RAJAH BROOKE and Borneo.

CALIFORNIA. (CHAMBERS's Papers, *etc.* IV. no. 26.)

CLARKE (Benjamin). The British Gazetteer, Political, Commercial, Ecclesiastical, and Historical .... Illustrated by a full Set of County Maps, with all the Railways accurately laid down .... 3 vols. London. [Stereotyped and printed at Glasgow.] 1852. Large 8° (4.)

COTTON Metropolis (The) [i. e. Manchester, Eng.]. (CHAMBERS's Repos., I. no. 1.)

DAVIS (*Sir* John Francis). The Chinese: a General Description of the

Empire of China and its Inhabitants. ... 2 vols. New-York. 1848. 18° (HARPER's Fam. Libr., **80, 81.**)

DESCRIPTION (A) of Pitcairn's Island, *etc.* *See* [BARROW (*Sir* J.)].

DESERTS (The) of Africa. (CHAMBERS's Papers, *etc.* IX. no. 69.)

EDINBURGH. *See* STRANGER's Visit.

FOSTER (J. W.) *and* WHITNEY (J. D.). Report on the Geology and Topography of a Portion of the Lake Superior Land District, in the State of Michigan. ... In Two Parts. Part I. Copper Lands. Washington. 1840. 8° (31st Congr., 1st Sess. Ho. of Reps. Ex. Doc. No. 69.)

GREENLAND. *See* HISTORICAL and Descriptive Account, *etc.*

HIGHLANDS. *See* ACCOUNT.

HINTON (John Howard). The History and Topography of the United States. *See* Class XXV. Part IV. § 4. B. *a.* *United States.*

HISTORICAL (An) and Descriptive Account of Iceland, Greenland, and the Faroe Islands. New-York. 1846. 18°

ICELAND. *See* HISTORICAL and Descriptive Account, *etc.*

ISTHMUS (The) of Panama. (CHAMBERS's Papers, *etc.* VII. no. 55.)

ISTHMUS (The) of Suez. (CHAMBERS's Papers, *etc.* XI. no. 81.)

JAPAN. *See* MANNERS and Customs, *etc.*

JEWISH Life in Central Europe. (CHAMBERS's Papers, *etc.* V. no. 39.)

JOHNSTON (William). England as it is, Political, Social, and Industrial, in the Middle of the Nineteenth Century. ... 2 vols. London. 1851. 12°

MACGREGOR (John). The Progress of America, from the Discovery by Columbus to the Year 1846. ... Vol. I. Historical and Statistical. | Vol. II. Geographical and Statistical. 2 vols. London. 1847. Large 8° pp. xii., 1520, and viii., 1334, 84.

[MANCHESTER, *Eng.*]. *See* COTTON Metropolis.

MANNERS and Customs of the Japanese, in the Nineteenth Century. From the Accounts of recent Dutch Residents in Japan, and from the German Work of Dr. Ph. Fr. von Siebold. New-York. 1848. 18° (HARPER's Fam. Libr., **132.**)

MASSACHUSETTS Register. *See* ADAMS (G.).

MITCHELL (S. Augustus). An Accompaniment to Mitchell's Reference and Distance Map of the United States: containing an Index of the various Counties ... Towns, etc. and an Index of the Rivers; together with a Geographical Description of every State and Territory in the Union; also an accurate Synopsis of the Population in the Year 1840 ... Statistical Aggregates, Accounts of Rail Roads and Canals, Colleges, &c. and a Synopsis of the New Postage Law. Philadelphia. 1848. 8°

Note. The "Geographical Description," etc. is paged independently, with the title: — "A General View of the United States," etc., dated 1846; so also the "Synopsis," etc., with the title: — "An accurate Synopsis of the Sixth Census of the United States," etc., dated 1848.

MURRAY (Hugh). An Historical and Descriptive Account of British

America; comprehending ... also an Account of the Manners and Present State of the Aboriginal Tribes. ... 2 vols. New-York. 1848. 18° (HARPER's Fam. Libr., **101, 102.**)

MURRAY's Official Handbook. *See* Class IV. Part I. [REDGRAVE (S.)].

NEW ZEALAND. (CHAMBERS's Papers, *etc.* XI. no. 85.)

PANAMA. *See* ISTHMUS.

PITCAIRN's ISLAND. *See* DESCRIPTION.

PITS (The) and the Pitmen [in England]. (CHAMBERS's Repos., II. no. 12.)

PROGRESS (The) of America. (CHAMBERS's Papers, *etc.* XII. no. 95.)

RAJAH BROOKE and Borneo. (CHAMBERS's Papers, *etc.* V. no. 34.)

RHINE (The). (CHAMBERS's Repos., I. no. 5.)

RUSSELL (Michael), *D.D.*, *Bp. of Glasgow.* ... View of Ancient and Modern Egypt; with an Outline of its Natural History .... New-York. 1846. 18° (HARPER's Fam. Libr., **23.**)

——— Polynesia. *See* Class XXV. Part IV. § 5.

SIAM and the Siamese. (CHAMBERS's Papers, *etc.* X. no. 79.)

SIBERIA and the Russian Penal Settlements. (CHAMBERS's Papers, *etc.* X. no. 74.)

SLAVERY in America. (CHAMBERS's Miscel., II. 27.)

STRANGER's Visit (The) to Edinburgh. (CHAMBERS's Miscel., VII. no. 121.)

SUEZ. *See* ISTHMUS.

UNGEWITTER (Francis H.), *LL.D.* Europe, Past and Present: a comprehensive Manual of European Geography and History; with separate Descriptions and Statistics of each State, and a copious Index .... New York. 1850. 12° pp. x., 671.

WARE (*Rev.* William). Sketches of European Capitals. [Being Lectures on Ancient Rome, St. Peter's and the Vatican, Florence, Naples, the Italians of Middle Italy, and London.] ... Boston. 1851. 12°

CLASS XXIII. VOYAGES AND TRAVELS.

AFRICAN Discovery. (CHAMBERS's Miscel., VIII. no. 142.)

AINSWORTH (William Francis). Travels in the Track of the Ten Thousand Greeks; being a Geographical and Descriptive Account of the Expedition of Cyrus and of the Retreat of the Ten Thousand Greeks, as related by Xenophon. London. 1844. 12°

ALLEN (Paul). History of the Expedition under the Command of Captains Lewis and Clarke, to the Sources of the Missouri, thence across the Rocky Mountains, and down the River Columbia to the Pacific Ocean: performed during the Years 1804, 1805, 1806 .... Revised and abridged, ... with an Introduction and Notes, by Archibald

M'Vickar. ... 2 vols. New-York. 1847. 18° (HARPER's Fam. Libr., **154, 155.**)

AMERICA. *See* PRE-COLUMBIAN Discovery, *etc.*

ANTARCTIC Explorations. (CHAMBERS's Papers, *etc.* V. no. 37.)

ARCTIC Explorations. (CHAMBERS's Papers, *etc.* III. no. 17.)

[AUSTRALIA]. *See* LIFE in the Bush.

[BLIGH (*Capt.* William)]. Narrative of the Mutiny of the Bounty. [Abridged.] (CHAMBERS's Miscel., VII. no. 122.)

[BUIST (*Dr.* ——)]. Overland Journey to India. (CHAMBERS's Miscel., X. no. 164.)

CAPE COLONY. *See* FOUR Months.

CIRCUMNAVIGATION of the Globe. *See* HISTORICAL Account, *etc.*

[DANA (Richard Henry)], *Jr.* Two Years before the Mast. A Personal Narrative of Life at Sea. ... New-York. 18° [1840 ?] (HARPER's Fam. Libr., **106.**)

DISCOVERY and Adventure, *etc.* *See* MURRAY (H.).

[ENGELHARDT (G.)]. Narrative of an Expedition to the Polar Sea, *etc.* *See* WRANGEL (F. VON).

EXCURSION to the Oregon. [Chiefly from a work by J. K. Townsend, published at Philadelphia in 1839.] (CHAMBERS's Miscel., III. no. 45.)

FOUR Months in Cape Colony. (CHAMBERS's Miscel., X. no. 173.)

FRÉMONT (*Lt.-Col.* John Charles). Report of the Exploring Expedition to the Rocky Mountains in the Year 1842, and to Oregon and North California in the Years 1843 - '44. ... Printed by Order of the Senate of the United States. Washington. 1845. 8° pp. 693. (Sen. Doc. 174.)

GOETHE (Johann Wolfgang VON). The Auto-biography of G. ... The Concluding Books. Also Letters from Switzerland, and Travels in Italy. Translated by the Rev. A. J. W. Morrison, M.A. London. 1849. 8° (BOHN's Stand. Libr.)

GRÆFENBERG. *See* LIFE at Græfenberg.

HISTORICAL Account (An) of the Circumnavigation of the Globe, and of the Progress of Discovery in the Pacific Ocean, from the Voyage of Magellan to the Death of Cook. ... New-York. N. D. 18° (HARPER's Fam. Libr., **82.**)

HUMBOLDT (Friedrich Heinrich Alexander, *Baron* VON). Travels. *See* MACGILLIVRAY (W.).

INDIA. Overland Journey to India. *See* [BUIST (*Dr.* ——)].

JAMESON (*Prof.* Robert). Narrative of Discovery, *etc.* *See* MURRAY (H.).

LANDER (Richard *and* John). Journal of an Expedition to explore the Course and Termination of the Niger ... . 2 vols. New-York. 1846. 18° (HARPER's Fam. Libr., **35, 36.**)

LAYARD (Austen Henry). Nineveh and its Remains: with an Account of a Visit to the Chaldæan Christians of Kurdistan, and the Yezidis, or Devil-Worshippers ; and an Inquiry into the Manners and Arts of the Ancient Assyrians. ... 2 vols. New-York. 1849. 8°

LESLIE (*Sir* John). Narrative of Discovery, *etc.* *See* MURRAY (H.).

LIFE (The) and Travels of Mungo Park ; with the Account of his Death from the Journal of Isaaco, the Substance of later Discoveries relative to his lamented Fate, and the Termination of the Niger. New York. 1847. 18° (HARPER's Fam. Libr., **105.**)

LIFE at Græfenberg. ... [By a Lady.] (CHAMBERS's Papers, *etc.* VIII. nos. 59, 60.)

LIFE in the Bush [Australia]. (CHAMBERS's Miscel., I. no. 8.)

LONGFELLOW (*Prof.* Henry Wadsworth). Outre-Mer, a Pilgrimage beyond the Sea. ... 5th Ed. Boston. 1852. 16°

MACGILLIVRAY (William). The Travels and Researches of Alexander von Humboldt ; being a condensed Narrative of his Journeys in the Equinoctial Regions of America, and in Asiatic Russia : — together with Analyses of his more important Investigations. ... New York. N. D. 18° (HARPER's Fam. Libr., **54.**)

[MACLAREN (Duncan)]. A Visit to Madeira and Teneriffe. (CHAMBERS's Miscel., IV. no. 64.)

MADEIRA. *See* [MACLAREN (D.)].

MEDUSA. *See* SHIPWRECK.

MORGAN (*Lady* Sidney [OWENSON]). Italy. ... 2 vols. New-York. 1821. 8°

MURRAY (Hugh). Narrative of Discovery and Adventure in Africa, from the Earliest Ages to the Present Time : with Illustrations of the Geology, Mineralogy, and Zoology. By Professor Jameson, James Wilson, ... and Hugh Murray ... . New York. 1846. 18° (HARPER's Fam. Libr., **16.**)

Note. Also with the title : — "Discovery and Adventure in Africa."

——— ... Narrative of Discovery and Adventure in the Polar Seas and Regions : with Illustrations of their Climate, Geology, and Natural History ; and an Account of the Whale-Fishery. By Professor Leslie, Professor Jameson, and Hugh Murray ... . [The Narrative by H. M.] New-York. 1839. 18° (HARPER's Fam. Libr., **14.**)

Note. Also with the title : — "Discovery and Adventure in the Polar Seas and Regions."

MUTINY. Narrative of the Mutiny of the Bounty. *See* [BLIGH (W.)].

OCEAN Routes. (CHAMBERS's Papers, *etc.* VIII. no. 57.)

OREGON. *See* EXCURSION.

OVERLAND Journey to India. *See* [BUIST (*Dr.* ——)].

PARK (Mungo). The Life and Travels of M. P., *etc.* *See* LIFE.

PARRY (*Sir* William Edward). Three Voyages for the Discovery of a Northwest Passage from the Atlantic to the Pacific, and Narrative of an Attempt to reach the North Pole. ... 2 vols. New-York. [1840 ?] 18° (HARPER's Fam. Libr., **107, 108.**)

POLO (Marco). The Travels of Marco Polo, greatly amended and enlarged from valuable early Manuscripts recently published .... With copious Notes .... By Hugh Murray .... New-York. 1845. 18° (HARPER's Fam. Libr., **173.**)

PRE-COLUMBIAN Discovery of America. (CHAMBERS's Papers, *etc.* VI. no. 42.)

SHETLAND. *See* VISIT.

SHIPWRECK of the Medusa. (CHAMBERS's Miscel., V. no. 92.)

Two Years before the Mast. *See* [DANA (R. H.)], *Jr.*

TYTLER (Patrick Fraser). Historical View of the Progress of Discovery on the more Northern Coasts of America, from the Earliest Period to the Present Time. ... With Descriptive Sketches of the Natural History of the North American Regions. By James Wilson .... To which is added an Appendix, containing Remarks on a late Memoir of Sebastian Cabot, with a Vindication of Richard Hakluyt. ... New-York. 1846. 18° (HARPER's Fam. Libr., **53.**)

VESUVIUS. *See* VISIT.

VISIT (A) to Madeira. *See* [MACLAREN (D.)].

VISIT (A) to Shetland. (CHAMBERS's Miscel., IV. no. 75.)

VISIT (A) to Vesuvius, Pompeii, and Herculaneum. (CHAMBERS's Miscel., II. no. 28.)

VOYAGES round the World from the Death of Captain Cook to the Present Time .... New-York. 1844. 18° (HARPER's Fam. Libr., **172.**)

WRANGEL (Ferdinand VON). Narrative of an Expedition to the Polar Sea, in the Years 1820, 1821, 1822, and 1823. Commanded by ... Admiral Wrangell .... [Drawn up in German from the papers of the Baron von Wrangel, by G. Engelhardt. Translated by Lieut. Col. Edward Sabine.] New-York. [1841 ?] 18° (HARPER's Fam. Libr., **148.**)

CLASS XXIV. BIOGRAPHY.

PART I. COLLECTIVE BIOGRAPHY, GENEALOGY, AND HERALDRY; TALES OF REAL LIFE.

Note. An asterisk is prefixed to the titles of works which are *analyzed* under Part II.

AMERICAN Adventure by Land and Sea. Being Remarkable Instances of Enterprise and Fortitude among Americans: Shipwrecks, Adventures at Home and Abroad, Indian Captivities, &c. ... 2 vols. New-York. 1847. 18° (HARPER's Fam. Libr., **174, 175.**)

ANECDOTES of the Deaf, Dumb, and Blind. (CHAMBERS's Miscel., III. no. 52.)

ANECDOTES of the Early Painters — Cimabue and Giotto, Leonardo da Vinci, Michael-Angelo Buonarotti, Raffaelle d'Urbino, Albert Durer

[Dürer], Corregio [Correggio], Hans Holbein, Titian Vecelli, Salvator Rosa, Velasquez — Murillo. (CHAMBERS's Miscel., IX. no. 154.)

ANECDOTES of Shoemakers [*viz.* James Lackington, Thomas Holcroft, William Gifford, Noah Worcester, and John Pounds]. (CHAMBERS's Miscel., VII. no. 115.)

ANNALS of the Poor — Female Industry and Intrepidity — Catherine of Liverpool, Lizzy M'Callum, Nanny Wilson, Mrs. Reston, Hannah Muir, The Soldier's Widow. (CHAMBERS's Miscel., II. no. 26.)

ASTRONOMERS. *See* EMINENT Astronomers.

*BELKNAP (Jeremy), *D.D.* American Biography. With Additions and Notes, by F. M. Hubbard. ... 3 vols. New-York. 1846 – 46 – 44. 18° (HARPER's Fam. Libr., **161 – 163.**)

*BELL (Robert). Lives of the most Eminent English Poets. 2 vols. London. 8° (LARDNER's Cab. Cycl., **93, 94.**)

Note. In Vol. II. pp. 91 – 224 may be found sketches of *forty-seven* "minor English poets"; and, pp. 227 – 231, an enumeration of *twenty-six* others. No references are made to this part of the work in the present Catalogue.

——— *See* DUNHAM (S. A.); — SOUTHEY (R.) *and* BELL (R.).

BONAPARTE Family (The). (CHAMBERS's Papers, *etc.* I. no. 1.)

——— *See* COURT (The) and Camp of Bonaparte.

BOURBON Family (The). (CHAMBERS's Papers, *etc.* IV. no. 25.)

BREWSTER (*Sir* David), *LL.D.* *See* SHELLEY (*Mrs.* M. W. [G.]).

*BROUGHAM (Henry), *Baron Brougham and Vaux.* Historical Sketches of Statesmen who flourished in the Time of George III. To which is [*sic*] added, Remarks on Party, and an Appendix. First Series. ... 2 vols. Philadelphia. 1839. 12°

*——— *The same.* Second Series. ... 2 vols. Philadelphia. 1839. 12°

*——— Lives of Men of Letters and Science, who flourished in the Time of George III. ... Philadelphia. 1845. 12°

BUCKINGHAM (Joseph TINKER). Specimens of [American] Newspaper Literature: with Personal Memoirs, *etc.* *See* Class XXIX.

CASES of Circumstantial Evidence — William Shaw, The French Refugee [Jaques Du Moulin], Brunell's Case, Lady Mazel, The Young Sailmaker, Thomas Geddely's Case, Bradford the Innkeeper, The Lyons Courier, Cases in America. (CHAMBERS's Miscel., II. no. 32.)

CHILDREN of the Wilds — Peter the Wild Boy, Mademoiselle Leblanc, Victor, the Savage of Aveyron, Caspar Hauser. (CHAMBERS's Miscel., III. no. 48.)

CIRCUMSTANTIAL Evidence. *See* CASES, *etc.*

COURT (The) and Camp of Bonaparte [or, Sketches of his Family, Ministers, Marshals, and Generals]. New York. 1848. 18° (HARPER's Fam. Libr., **29.**)

COURTENAY (Thomas Peregrine). Lives of British Statesmen. *See* FORSTER (J.). Lives, *etc.*

[CRAIK (*Prof.* George Lillie)]. Pursuit of Knowledge under Difficulties; its Pleasures and Rewards. Illustrated by Memoirs of Eminent Men. [Reprinted, with some omissions and alterations, from the edition published by the Society for the Diffusion of Useful Knowledge, in the Library of Entertaining Knowledge.] ... 2 vols. New-York. 1847-40. 18° (HARPER's Fam. Libr., **94, 95.**)

——— The Pursuit of Knowledge under Difficulties. Illustrated by Anecdotes. (With Portraits.) Revised Ed., with a Preface and Notes by Francis Wayland, D.D. ... 2 vols. Boston. 1840-44. 12° (SCHOOL Libr., Vol. XIV., XV.)

CROWE (Eyre Evans). *See* JAMES (G. P. R.) *and* CROWE (E. E.).

*CUNNINGHAM (Allan). ... The Lives of the most Eminent British Painters and Sculptors. ... 5 vols. New-York. 1846-44-44. [Vol. IV. and V., N. D.] 18° (HARPER's Fam. Libr., **17-19, 66, 67.**)

CURIOSITIES of Criminal Law. (CHAMBERS's Repos., II. no. 10.)

DAVENPORT (R. A.). Perilous Adventures; or, Remarkable Instances of Courage, Perseverance, and Suffering. ... New-York. 1844. 18° (HARPER's Fam. Libr., **159.**)

DEAF, Dumb, and Blind, Anecdotes of the. *See* ANECDOTES.

DISTINGUISHED Men of Modern Times. *See* [SOCIETY FOR THE DIFFUSION OF USEFUL KNOWLEDGE]. *Library of Entertaining Knowledge.*

*DUNHAM (S. A.), *LL.D.* Lives of the British Dramatists. By Dr. Dunham, Robert Bell, and others. 2 vols. London. 8° (LARDNER's Cab. Cycl., **96, 97.**)

*DUNHAM (S. A.), *LL.D., and* BELL (Robert). The Early Writers of Great Britain. London. 8° (LARDNER's Cab. Cycl., **95.**)

EMINENT Astronomers — Copernicus, Tycho Brahe, Galileo, Kepler, Newton, Huygens, Halley, Ferguson, Sir William Herschel. (CHAMBERS's Miscel., X. no. 169.)

FEMALE Industry and Intrepidity. *See* ANNALS of the Poor.

FÉNELON (François DE SALIGNAC DE LA MOTHE), *Abp. of Cambrai.* Lives of the Ancient Philosophers [*viz.* Anacharsis, Anaxagoras, Antisthenes, Aristippus, Aristotle, Bias, Bion, Chilo, Cleobulus, Crates, Democritus, Diogenes, Empedocles, Epimenides, Epicurus, Heraclitus, Periander, Pittacus, Plato, Pyrrho, Pythagoras, Socrates, Solon, Thales, Xenocrates, and Zeno]; translated from the French of Fenelon, with Notes, and a Life of the Author. By the Rev. John Cormack. New-York. 1842. 18° (HARPER's Fam. Libr., **140.**)

*FORSTER (John). Lives of the most Eminent British Statesmen. (Vol. II. III. IV. VI. and VII. by Forster; Vol. I. by Sir James Mackintosh; Vol. V. by T. P. Courtenay.) 7 vols. London. 8° (LARDNER's Cab. Cycl., **76-82.**)

GEORGIAN Era (The): Memoirs of the most Eminent Persons, who have flourished in Great Britain, from the Accession of George the First to the Demise of George the Fourth. ... [Arranged in classes, chronologically.] 4 vols. London. 1832-34. 8°

Note. Vol. IV. contains a General Index.

*GLEIG (*Rev.* George Robert). Lives of the most Eminent British Military Commanders. 3 vols. London. 8° (LARDNER'S Cab. Cycl., **67-69.**)

GODWIN (Parke). ... Hand-Book of Universal Biography. New-York. 1852. 12° pp. vi., 821. (PUTNAM'S Home Cyclopedia, Vol. IV.)

[GOODRICH (Samuel Griswold)]. Lives of Benefactors; by the Author of Peter Parley's Tales. [*Viz.* Arkwright, Bowditch, Copernicus, Davy, Franklin, Fulton, Galileo, Guttenberg, Hargraves, Henry, Herschel, Howard, Huber, Jay, Jenner, Kosciusko, La Fayette, Linnæus, Oberlin, William Tell, Washington, Whitney.] Boston. 1849. 16° or 18° (8. and 6.) (CABINET Libr., **4.**)

[———] Lives of Celebrated American Indians ... . [*Viz.* Acamapitzin, Tupac Amaru, Atahualpa, Black Hawk, Brant, Huayna Capac, Mango Capac, Mayta Capac, Caupolican, Cofachiqui, Logan, Donna Marina, Montezuma I., Montezuma II., Philip, Pocahontas, Pontiac, Quetzalcoatl, Red Jacket, Shongmunecuthe, or the Ietan, Tascaluza, Tecumseh, Vitachuco, Xolotl, Ychoalay.] Boston. 1849. 16° or 18° (8. and 6.) (CABINET Libr., **5.**)

[———] Lives of Celebrated Women ... . [*Viz.* Mrs. Adams, Mrs. Barbauld, Lucretia and Maria Davidson, Elizabeth, Queen of England, Madame de Genlis, Isabella of Spain, Joan of Arc, Josephine, Marie Antoinette, Mary Queen of Scots, Hannah More, Madame Roland, Madame de Sévigné, Madame de Stael, Lady Hester Stanhope, Mrs. Washington.] Boston. 1849. 16° or 18° (8. and 6.) (CABINET Libr., **6.**)

GORTON (John). A General Biographical Dictionary. ... A new Ed. To which is added a Supplementary Volume completing the Work to the present Time. ... 4 vols. London. 1851. 8°

Note. A Catalogue of Works relating to Biography and Literary History, and a Chronological Table, are appended to the fourth volume.

GRISWOLD (Rufus Wilmot). The Poets and Poetry of America, *etc.* *See* Class XIX.

——— The Prose Writers of America, *etc.* *See* Class XXXI.

*HERBERT (Henry William). The Captains of the Old World [*viz.* Miltiades, Themistocles, Pausanias, Xenophon, Epaminondas, Alexander, Hannibal]; as compared with the great Modern Strategists, their Campaigns, Characters and Conduct, from the Persian, to the Punic Wars. New York. 1851. 12°

IMPOSTORS. *See* RELIGIOUS Impostors.

INTELLIGENT Negroes. (CHAMBERS'S Miscel., IV. no. 63.)

IRVING (Washington). Mahomet and his Successors. 2 vols. New-York. 1850. 12° (Works, Vol. XII., XIII.)

*JAMES (George Payne Rainsford) *and* CROWE (Eyre Evans). Lives of the most Eminent Foreign Statesmen. 5 vols. London. 8° (LARDNER's Cab. Cycl., **83 - 87.**)

*JAMESON (*Mrs.* Anna [MURPHY]). Memoirs of Celebrated Female Sovereigns. ... 2 vols. New York. 1848. 18° (HARPER's Fam. Libr., **33, 34.**)

JOHNSON (Samuel), *LL.D.* Lives of Eminent Persons. — Ascham, Barretier, Blake, Boerhaave, Browne, Burman, Cave, Cheynel, Sir Francis Drake, [Frederick II.] King of Prussia, Morin, Father Paul Sarpi, Sydenham. (Works, 1837. 8° II. 305 - 384.)

——— Lives of the English Poets. — Addison, Akenside, Blackmore, Broome, Butler, Collins, Congreve, Cowley, Denham, Dorset [Sackville], Dryden, Duke, Dyer, Fenton, Garth, Gay, Granville, Gray, Halifax [Montague], Hammond, Hughes, King, Lyttelton, Mallet, Milton, Otway, Parnell, A. Philips, J. Philips, Pitt, Pomfret, Pope, Prior, Rochester [Wilmot], Roscommon [Dillon], Rowe, Savage, Sheffield, Shenstone, Smith, Somervile, Sprat, Stepney, Swift, Thomson, Tickell, Waller, Walsh, Watts, West, Yalden, Young. (Works, 1837. 8° II. 3 - 304.)

LIBRARY of Entertaining Knowledge. *See* SOCIETY, *etc.*

LIBRARY of Useful Knowledge. *See* SOCIETY, *etc.*

*LIVES of Eminent Individuals, celebrated in American History. ... Vol. I. containing Lives of John Stark, David Brainerd, Robert Fulton, and John Smith. | Vol. II. containing Lives of Ethan Allen, Sebastian Cabot, Henry Hudson, Joseph Warren, Israel Putnam, and David Rittenhouse. | Vol. III. containing Lives of William Pinkney, Sir Henry Vane, Anthony Wayne, William Ellery, and Richard Montgomery. 3 vols. Boston. 1839. 12° (SCHOOL Libr., Vol. IV. - VI.)

LODGE (Edmund). Portraits of Illustrious Personages of Great Britain. With Biographical and Historical Memoirs of their Lives and Actions. ... 8 vols. 1849 - 50. 8° (Bohn's Illustrated Library.)

MACKINTOSH (*Sir* James). Lives of British Statesmen. *See* FORSTER (J.). Lives, *etc.*

[MALDEN (H.)]. *Author ?* *See* SOCIETY, *etc.* *Library of Entertaining Knowledge.* Distinguished Men, *etc.*

MEN (The) of the Time or Sketches of Living Notables ... . New-York. 1852. 12°

MONTGOMERY (James). *See* SHELLEY (*Mrs.* M. W. [G.]). Lives, *etc.*

MONTYON Prizes (The) — Pauline Copain, Jean Vigier, Henriette Garden, Jeanne Jugan, Pierre Bécard, Eustache, Alexandre Martin, Pierre Guillot and Louis Brune, The Three Brothers Conté. (CHAMBERS's Miscel., VI. no. 107.)

Note. These prizes are awarded for acts of virtue and heroism in humble life.

NEGROES, Intelligent. (CHAMBERS's Miscel., IV. no. 63.)

PAINTERS. *See* ANECDOTES of the Early Painters, *etc.*

PARLEY (Peter), *pseudon.* *See* [GOODRICH (Samuel Griswold)].

PLUTARCHUS. Plutarch's Lives, translated ... with Notes .... By John Langhorne, D.D. and William Langhorne, A.M. [Containing Lives of Agesilaus, Agis, Alcibiades, Alexander, Antony, Aratus, Aristides, Artaxerxes, Brutus, Julius Cæsar, Camillus, Cato the Censor, Cato the Younger, Cicero, Cimon, Cleomenes, Coriolanus, Crassus, Demetrius, Demosthenes, Dion, Eumenes, Fabius Maximus, T. Q. Flaminius [Flamininus], Galba, Caius Gracchus, Tiberius Gracchus, Lucullus, Lycurgus, Lysander, Marcellus, Marius, Nicias, Numa, Otho, Paulus Æmilius, Pelopidas, Pericles, Philopœmen, Phocion, Pompey, Publicola, Pyrrhus, Romulus, Sertorius, Solon, Sylla, Themistocles, Theseus, Timoleon.] *See* Class XVI. Part II.

PORT-ROYALISTS, The. (STEPHEN (*Sir* J.). ... Essays, pp. 248–313.)

PURSUIT of Knowledge under Difficulties. *See* [CRAIK (G. L.)].

RANKE (*Prof.* Franz Leopold). The History of the Popes, *etc.* *See* Class XXVI.

RELIGIOUS Impostors [*viz.* Thomas Munzer, John Bockholt, or John of Leyden, Richard Brothers, Ann Lee, Jemima Wilkinson, Joanna Southcott, Robert Matthews, John Nicolls Thoms, Joseph Smith]. (CHAMBERS's Miscel., I. no. **14.**)

*ROSCOE (Henry). Lives of Eminent British Lawyers. London. 8° (LARDNER's Cab. Cycl., **75.**)

*ST. JOHN (James Augustus). The Lives of Celebrated Travellers. ... 3 vols. New York. 1847. 18° (HARPER's Fam. Libr., **38–40.**)

*SHELLEY (*Mrs.* Mary Wollstonecraft [GODWIN]). Lives of the most Eminent Literary and Scientific Men of France. By Mrs. Shelley, and others. 2 vols. London. 8° (LARDNER's Cab. Cycl., **91, 92.**)

*——— Lives of the most Eminent Literary and Scientific Men of Italy, Spain, and Portugal. By Mrs. Shelley, Sir David Brewster, James Montgomery, and others. 3 vols. London. 8° (LARDNER's Cab. Cycl., **88–90.**)

SHOEMAKERS. *See* ANECDOTES of Shoemakers.

SMITH (William), *LL.D.* Dictionary of Greek and Roman Biography and Mythology. Edited by W. S. .... Illustrated by numerous Engravings on Wood. ... 3 vols. London. 1844–46–49. 8°

*[SOCIETY FOR THE DIFFUSION OF USEFUL KNOWLEDGE]. *Library of Entertaining Knowledge.* Distinguished Men of Modern Times. [Selected from a work ascribed to H. Malden, published by the "Society," etc.] ... 2 vols. New York. [1840 ?] 18° (HARPER's Fam. Libr., **123, 124.**)

——— *L. of E. K.* Pursuit of Knowledge under Difficulties. *See* [CRAIK (G. L.)].

*——— *Library of Useful Knowledge.* Lives of Eminent Persons; consisting of Galileo [by John Eliot Drinkwater Bethune], Kepler [by J. E. D. Bethune], Newton [by Jean Baptiste Biot, translated by Howard Elphinstone], Mahomet [by John Arthur Roebuck], Wolsey [by Mrs. Anthony Todd Thomson], Sir E. Coke [by Ed. Plunkett

Burke], Lord Somers [by David Jardine], Caxton [by — Stephenson], Blake [by John Gorton], Adam Smith [by Wm. Draper], [Carsten] Niebuhr [by Mrs. Sarah Austin], Sir C. Wren [by Henry Bellenden Ker], and Michael Angelo [Buonarroti, by Thomas Roscoe]. ... London. [1833?] 8°

Note. These Lives are all paged independently, and were originally published separately.

*SOUTHEY (Robert) *and* BELL (Robert). Lives of the British Admirals. With an Introductory View of the Naval History of England. (Vol. V. by Robert Bell.) 5 vols. London. 8° (LARDNER's Cab. Cycl., **70 – 74.**)

*SPARKS (Jared). The Library of American Biography. Conducted by Jared Sparks. 10 vols. New York. [Stereotyped and printed at Cambridge.] 1839 – 45. 16° or 12° (8. and 6.)

Note. Vols. I. II. and VIII. have only one set of signatures (8.).

*——— *The same.* Second Series. 15 vols. Boston. 1844 – 48. 16°

Note. The last volume of each series contains a General Index.

*STRICKLAND (Agnes). Lives of the Queens of England, from the Norman Conquest; with Anecdotes of their Courts, now first published from Official Records and other Authentic Documents ... . New Ed., with Corrections and Additions. ... 12 vols. (bound in 6). Philadelphia. 1848. 12°

SULLIVAN (William), *LL.D.* The Public Men of the Revolution. Including Events from the Peace of 1783 to the Peace of 1815. In a Series of Letters. ... With a Biographical Sketch of the Author, and additional Notes and References by his Son, John T. S. Sullivan. ... Philadelphia. 1847. 8°

SWAINSON (William). A Bibliography of Zoology; with Biographical Sketches, *etc.* *See* Class XIII. Part IV. SWAINSON (W.). Taxidermy, *etc.*

TALE (A) of Norfolk Island. (CHAMBERS's Miscel., I. no. 2.)

*THACKERAY (William Makepeace). The English Humourists of the Eighteenth Century [Swift, Congreve, Addison, Steele, Prior, Gay, Pope, Hogarth, Smollett, Fielding, Sterne, and Goldsmith]. A Series of [six] Lectures. [With an additional Lecture on "Charity and Humour."] ... New York. 1853. 12°

THACHER (Benjamin Bussey). Indian Biography; or, An Historical Account of those Individuals who have been distinguished among the North American Natives as Orators, Warriors, Statesmen, and other Remarkable Characters. ... 2 vols. New York. 1848. 18° (HARPER's Fam. Libr., **45, 46.**)

PART II. INDIVIDUAL BIOGRAPHY.

Note. Sketches of the lives of Authors, not referred to here, may often be found prefixed to their Works. For other sources of biographical information, see Classes XXIX. and XXX. The Penny Cyclopædia and the Encyclopædia Americana deserve special mention.

ABBOT (*Rev.* John Emery). Sketch of his Life and Character. (WARE's Works, II. 1 – 24.)

ABERCROMBY (*Sir* Ralph), *Bart.* Life, by G. R. Gleig. (LARDNER's Cab. Cycl., **69**, pp. 197 – 250.)

ADDISON (Joseph). Life and Writings. (MACAULAY's Essays, V. 82 – 183.)

——— Life. (SPECTATOR. Selections, *etc.* 1840. 18° I. ix. – xxvi.)

——— Life and Writings. (THACKERAY's English Humourists.)

ADELICIA *of Louvaine, Second Queen of Henry I.* Life. (STRICKLAND's Queens of England, I. 119 – 141.)

AKENSIDE (Mark). Life, by Robert Bell. (LARDNER's Cab. Cycl., **94**, pp. 364 – 370.)

ALBERONI (Giulio), *Cardinal.* Life, by G. P. R. James. (LARDNER's Cab. Cycl., **86**, pp. 130 – 267.)

[ALCOTT (William A.)]. Confessions of a Schoolmaster. Andover. 1839. 18°

ALDROVANDI (Ulisse). Memoir. (JARDINE's Nat. Libr., XVII. 17 – 58.)

ALEXANDER *the Great, King of Macedon.* History . . . . By Jacob Abbott. With Engravings. New York. [1848 ?] 16°

——— Campaigns and Character. (HERBERT's Captains, *etc.* pp. 265 – 334. — *See* Part I.)

——— The Life and Actions of A. . . . . By Rev. J. Williams . . . . New-York. 1843. 18° (HARPER's Fam. Libr., **7.**)

——— Cæsar and Alexander : an Historical Comparison. *See* Class XXV. Part III. SCHLEGEL (K. W. *F.* VON). A Course of Lectures, *etc.*

ALFIERI (Vittorio). Life. (LARDNER's Cab. Cycl., **89**, pp. 247 – 302.)

ALFRED *the Great, King of England.* History . . . . By Jacob Abbott. With Engravings. New York. [1849.] 16°

——— Life. — English Civilization in the Ninth Century. (LARDNER's Cab. Cycl., **95**, pp. 60 – 124.)

ALLAN (David). Life. (CUNNINGHAM's Lives of Brit. Painters, *etc.* V. 25 – 47.)

ALLEN (*Brig.-Gen.* Ethan). Life of E. A.; by Jared Sparks. (SPARKS's Amer. Biogr., I. 227 – 356 ; — SCHOOL Libr., V. 1 – 83.)

AMBOISE (Georges D'), *Cardinal.* Life, by Eyre Evans Crowe. (LARDNER's Cab. Cycl., **83**, pp. 1 – 24.)

ANDRAYNE (Alexandre), Story of. (CHAMBERS's Miscel., VI. no. 99.

ANDRÉ (*Maj.* John). Arnold and André. (CHAMBERS's Repos., II. no. 15.)

ANGELO (Michael). *See* BUONARROTI (Michel Angelo).

ANGHIERA (Pietro Martire D'), *or* PETER MARTYR. (IRVING's Life of Columbus, *etc.* III. 423 - 428.)

ANNE, *Queen of Great Britain and Ireland.* Life. (STRICKLAND's Queens of England, XI. 223 - 286, XII.)

——— Memoir. (JAMESON's Memoirs of Celebrated Female Sovereigns, II. 82 - 125.)

ANNE BOLEYN, *Second Queen of Henry VIII.* Life. (STRICKLAND's Queens of England, IV. 122 - 215.)

ANNE *of Bohemia, surnamed* the Good, *First Queen of Richard II.* Life. (STRICKLAND's Queens of England, II. 206 - 222.)

ANNE *of Cleves, Fourth Queen of Henry VIII.* Life. (STRICKLAND's Queens of England, IV. 236 - 278.)

ANNE *of Denmark, Consort of James I.* Life. (STRICKLAND's Queens of England, VII. 233 - 363.)

ANNE *of Warwick, Queen of Richard III.* Life. (STRICKLAND's Queens of England, III. 242 - 253.)

APOLLONIUS TYANÆUS. Life. — Miracles. By the Rev. J. H. Newman. (ENCYCL. Metrop., X. 619 - 644.)

APPLETON (Jesse), *D.D.* Memoir, by Prof. A. S. Packard. (Works, 1837. 8° I. 9 - 82.)

AQUINAS (*Saint* Thomas). *See* THOMAS AQUINAS.

ARBLAY (Frances [BURNEY], *Madame* D'). Life. (MACAULAY's Essays, V. 9 - 81.)

ARC (Jeanne D'), *or* JOAN OF ARC, *Maid of Orleans.* (CHAMBERS's Miscel., II. no. 25.)

ARCHIMEDES. Life, by William Whewell. (ENCYCL. Metrop., IX. 686 - 694.)

ARGAL (*Sir* Samuel) *and* Sir George YEARDLEY. Lives. (BELKNAP's Amer. Biogr., II. 148 - 173.)

ARIOSTO (Lodovico). Life. (LARDNER's Cab. Cycl., **88**, pp. 196 - 255.)

ARISTOTELES. Life, by the Rev. Joseph Williams Blakesley. (ENCYCL. Metrop., X. 90* - 129*.)

——— Memoir. (JARDINE's Nat. Libr., XIV. 17 - 112.)

ARNOLD (*Maj.-Gen.* Benedict). Arnold and André. (CHAMBERS's Repos., II. no. 15.)

——— The Life and Treason of B. A. By Jared Sparks. New-York. 1844. 16° or 12° (8. and 6.) (SPARKS's Amer. Biogr., Vol. III.)

ARNOLD (Thomas), *D.D.* The Life and Correspondence of T. A. . . . . By Arthur Penrhyn Stanley . . . . 2d American Ed., reprinted entire from the last London Ed. Two volumes complete in one. New-York. 1846. 8°

ASHBURTON, John, 1*st Baron*. *See* DUNNING.

AZARA (Felix DE). Memoir. (JARDINE's Nat. Libr., XIX. 17 - 76.)

BACON (Francis), *Baron Verulam, and Viscount St. Albans*. Memoir. (DISTINGUISHED Men of Mod. Times, I. 152 - 164.)

——— Life. (MACAULAY's Essays, II. 286 - 402.)

BACON (John). Life. (CUNNINGHAM's Lives of Brit. Painters and Sculptors, III. 174 - 213.)

BACON (Nathaniel). A Memoir of N. B.; by William Ware. (SPARKS's Amer. Biogr., 2d Ser., III. 239 - 306.)

BALBOA (Vasco Nuñez DE). Sketch of his Life. (IRVING's Life of Columbus, *etc.* III. 138 - 246.)

[BALL (Charles)]. Life of a Negro Slave. [Abridged from his own Narrative published at New York in 1832.] (CHAMBERS's Miscel., IX. no. 149.)

BALTIMORE, George, *Baron*. *See* CALVERT.

BANKS (*Sir* Joseph), *Bart*. Memoir. (JARDINE's Nat. Libr., XXXVIII. 17 - 48.)

BANKS (Thomas). Life. (CUNNINGHAM's Lives of Brit. Painters and Sculptors, III. 74 - 107.)

BARCLAY (John), *M.D.* Memoir. (JARDINE's Nat. Libr., XXIV. 17 - 44.)

BARÈRE DE VIEUZAC (Bertrand). Life. (MACAULAY's Essays, V. 183 - 287.)

BARNEVELDT (Johan VAN OLDEN). *See* OLDEN-BARNEVELDT.

BARRÈRE DE VIEUZAC (Bertrand). *See* BARÈRE DE VIEUZAC.

BARRY (James). Life. (CUNNINGHAM's Lives of Brit. Painters, *etc.* II. 54 - 123.)

BATUTA (Ibn). *See* IBN BATUTA.

BAXTER (Richard). Life and Times. (STEPHEN's Essays, pp. 150 - 196.)

BEAUMONT (Francis) *and* John FLETCHER. Lives, *etc.* (LARDNER's Cab. Cycl., **96**, pp. 203 - 251.)

BEAUMONT (*Sir* George Howland), *Bart.* Life. (CUNNINGHAM's Lives of Brit. Painters, *etc.* V. 117 - 133.)

BECKNER (Volney). Heroism. (CHAMBERS's Miscel., I. no. 12, pp. 11 - 13.)

BEHN (*Mrs.* Aphara [JOHNSON]). Life. (LARDNER's Cab. Cycl., **97**, pp. 146 - 154.)

BELISARIUS. The Life of B. By [Philip Henry Stanhope] Lord Mahon. Philadelphia. 1832. 12°

BELL (John). Life. (ST. JOHN's Lives of Cel. Travellers, II. 125 - 163.)

BELZONI (Giovanni). Life. (ST. JOHN's Lives of Cel. Travellers, III. 327 - 345.)

BERENGARIA *of Navarre, Queen of Richard I.* (STRICKLAND's Queens of England, II. 9 - 27.)

BERNARDIN DE ST. PIERRE (Jacques Henri). *See* ST. PIERRE.

BERNI (Francesco). Life. (LARDNER's Cab. Cycl., **88**, pp. 188 - 195.)

BERNIER (François). Life. (ST. JOHN's Lives of Cel. Travellers, I. 205 - 233.)

BÉTHUNE (Maximilien DE), *Duke de Sully*. *See* SULLY.

BEWICK (Thomas). Memoir. (JARDINE's Nat. Libr., X. 17 - 51.)

BIARNE, BIORN, *or* BIRON. Life. (BELKNAP's Amer. Biogr., I. 77 - 128.)

BIRD (Edward). Life. (CUNNINGHAM's Lives of Brit. Painters, *etc.* II. 208 - 222.)

BIRON. *See* BIARNE.

BLACK (Joseph). Life. (BROUGHAM's Lives of Men of Letters and Science, *etc.* pp. 194 - 208.)

BLACKSTONE (*Sir* William), *LL.D.* Life, by Henry Roscoe. (LARDNER's Cab. Cycl., **75**, pp. 240 - 257.)

BLAKE (Robert), *Admiral.* Life. [By John Gorton.] *See* Part I. SOCIETY, *etc.* ... Lives, *etc.*

BLAKE (William). Life. (CUNNINGHAM's Lives of Brit. Painters, *etc.* II. 124 - 155.)

BOCCACCIO (Giovanni). Life. (LARDNER's Cab. Cycl., **88**, pp. 116 - 150.)

——— *See* PETRARCA (F.). Life ... . By Thomas Campbell, *etc.*

BOILEAU DESPRÉAUX (Nicolas). Life. (LARDNER's Cab. Cycl., **91**, pp. 259 - 295.)

BOJARDO (Matteo Maria). Life. (LARDNER's Cab. Cycl., **88**, pp. 181 - 187.)

BOLINGBROKE, Henry, *Viscount*. *See* ST. JOHN.

BONAPARTE (Napoleon). *See* NAPOLEON I.

BONAROTA *or* BONARROTI (Michel Angelo). *See* BUONARROTI.

BONINGTON (Richard Parkes). Life. (CUNNINGHAM's Lives of Brit. Painters, *etc.* IV. 245 - 258.)

BONNEVILLE (*Lieut.-Col.* Benjamin L. E.) The Adventures of Captain B., U. S. A., in the Rocky Mountains and the Far West. Digested from his Journal and illustrated from various other Sources. By Washington Irving. Author's revised Ed. [With a Map.] ... New-York. 1851. 12° (IRVING's Works, Vol. X.)

BOONE (Daniel). Lives of Daniel Boone [by John M. Peck] and Benjamin Lincoln. Boston. 1847. 16° (SPARKS's Amer. Biogr., 2d Ser., Vol. XIII.)

BOSCAN ALMOGAVER (Mosen Juan). Life. (LARDNER's Cab. Cycl., **90**, pp. 21 - 35.)

BOSSUET (Jacques Benigne), successively *Bp. of Condom* and *Meaux*. Memoir. (DISTINGUISHED Men of Mod. Times, II. 19 - 32.)

BRADFORD (William). Life. (BELKNAP's Amer. Biogr., III. 7 - 52.)

BRAHE (Tycho [*Danish*, Tyge]). Life. *See* GALILEI (G.). The Martyrs of Science, *etc.*

Brainerd (David). Life of D. B., Missionary to the Indians; by William B. O. Peabody. (Sparks's Amer. Biogr., VIII. 257 – 373; — School Libr., IV. 77 – 151.)

Brewster (William). Life. (Belknap's Amer. Biogr., III. 53 – 69.)

Brooke (*Sir* James). Rajah B. and Borneo. (Chambers's Papers, *etc.* V. no. 34.)

Brougham (Henry), *Baron Brougham and Vaux.* Lord B. (Chambers's Papers, *etc.* XI. no. 88.)

Brown (Charles Brockden). Life of C. B. B.; by William H. Prescott. (Sparks's Amer. Biogr., I. 117 – 180.)

Bruce (James). The Life and Adventures of Bruce, the African Traveller. By Major Sir Francis B. Head. ... From the last London Ed. New-York. 1846. 18° (Harper's Fam. Libr., **128.**)

——— Memoir. (Jardine's Nat. Libr., XI. 17 – 84.)

——— Life. (St. John's Lives of Cel. Travellers, II. 233 – 301.)

Bruce (Robert). *See* Wallace (W.).

Buckingham (Joseph Tinker). Personal Memoirs and Recollections of Editorial Life. By J. T. B. ... 2 vols. Boston. 1852. 16°

Buel (Jesse), *Judge.* Eulogy, by Amos Dean. (School Libr., XVI. v. – xxiv.)

Buffon (George Louis Leclerc, *Count* de). *Éloge*, by P. L. Courier. (Jardine's Nat. Libr., XXVII. 37 – 59.)

——— Memoir. (Distinguished Men of Mod. Times, II. 149 – 158.)

——— Memoir. (Jardine's Nat. Libr., XXVII. 17 – 34.)

Buonaparte (Napoleon). *See* Napoleon I.

Buonarroti (Michel Angelo *or* Michelagnolo). Life. [By Thomas Roscoe.] *See* Part I. Society, *etc.* ... Lives, *etc.*

Burckhardt (John Lewis). Life and Travels. (Chambers's Miscel., VIII. no. 133.)

——— Memoir. (Jardine's Nat. Libr., XI. 17 – 126.)

——— Life. (St. John's Lives of Cel. Travellers, III. 168 – 218.)

Burke (Edmund). Sketch. (Brougham's "Hist. Sketches of Statesmen," *etc.* 1st Ser., I. 159 – 189.)

——— Memoir. (Distinguished Men of Mod. Times, II. 195 – 208.)

Burleigh, William, *Baron.* *See* Cecil.

Burnet (James). Life. (Cunningham's Lives of Brit. Painters, *etc.* V. 261 – 269.)

Burney (Frances), afterwards *Madame* d'Arblay. *See* Arblay.

Butler (Samuel). Life, by Robert Bell. (Lardner's Cab. Cycl., **93,** pp. 264 – 304.)

Byron (George Gordon Noel), 6*th Baron.* ... The Life of Lord B. By John Galt, Esq. New-York. 1845. 18° (Harper's Fam. Libr., **9.**)

——— Character and Writings. (Legaré's Writings, II. 356 – 448.)

CABOT (Sebastian). Life of S. C.; by Charles Hayward, Jr. (SPARKS's Amer. Biogr., IX. 89 - 162; — SCHOOL Libr., V. 85 - 134.)

CÆSAR (Caius Julius). History .... By Jacob Abbott. With Engravings. New York. [1849?] 16°

——— Life of J. C. .... 2d Ed. New-York. 1846. 18° (Monthly Series of Useful Reading, No. I.)

——— Cæsar and Alexander: an Historical Comparison. *See* Class XXV. Part III. SCHLEGEL (K. W. *F.* VON). A Course of Lectures, *etc.*

CALDERON DE LA BARCA (Pedro). Life. (LARDNER's Cab. Cycl., **90**, pp. 278 - 287.)

CALVERT (George) and Cecilius CALVERT, *Lords Baltimore;* also Leonard CALVERT. (BELKNAP's Amer. Biogr., III. 206 - 224.)

CALVERT (Leonard), 1*st Gov. of Maryland.* Lives of Leonard Calvert [by George W. Burnap], Samuel Ward, and Thomas Posey. Boston. 1846. 16° (SPARKS's Amer. Biogr., 2d Ser., Vol. IX.)

CAMOENS *or* CAMÕES (Luis DE). Life. (LARDNER's Cab. Cycl., **90**, pp. 295 - 333.)

CAMPBELL (Thomas). (CHAMBERS's Papers, *etc.* III. no. 24.)

CAMPER (Pieter). Memoir. (JARDINE's Nat. Libr., XXI. 17 - 82.)

CANNING (George). Sketch. (BROUGHAM's "Hist. Sketches of Statesmen," *etc.* 1st Ser., II. 91 - 101.)

CANOVA (Antonio). Life and Works. (A. H. EVERETT's Essays, pp. 234 - 282.)

CARITAT (Marie Jean Antoine DE), *Marquis de Condorcet.* *See* CONDORCET.

CARNOT (Lazare Nicolas Marguerite). Sketch. (BROUGHAM's "Hist. Sketches of Statesmen," *etc.* 2d Ser., II. 111 - 138.)

CARROLL (Charles), *of Carrollton.* Sketch. (BROUGHAM's "Hist. Sketches of Statesmen," *etc.* 2d Ser., II. 33 - 38.)

CARTIER (Jacques). (BELKNAP's Amer. Biogr., I. 230 - 257.)

CARVALHO E MELLO (Sebastião José), *Count of Oeiras, Marquis of Pombal.* *See* POMBAL.

CARVER (John). Life. (BELKNAP's Amer. Biogr., II. 295 - 333.)

CASAS (Bartolomé DE LAS), *Bp. of Chiapa.* Life. (IRVING's Life of Columbus, *etc.* III. 415 - 423.)

CASTLEREAGH, Robert, 2*d Viscount.* *See* STEWART.

CATHARINE *of Braganza, Consort of Charles II.* Life. (STRICKLAND's Queens of England, VIII. 199 - 352.)

CATHERINE I. *Empress of Russia.* Story of C. of R. (CHAMBERS's Miscel., V. no. 84.)

CATHERINE II. *Empress of Russia.* Sketch. (BROUGHAM's "Hist. Sketches of Statesmen," *etc.* 1st Ser., II. 189 - 200.)

——— Memoir. (JAMESON's Memoirs of Cel. Female Sovereigns, II. 198 - 248.)

CATHERINE *of Valois*. *See* KATHERINE *of Valois*.

CAVENDISH (Henry). Life. (BROUGHAM'S Lives of Men of Letters and Science, *etc.* pp. 250 – 259.)

CAVENDISH (Thomas). Life, by Robert Southey. (LARDNER'S Cab. Cycl., **72**, pp. 243 – 282.)

——— Life and Voyages. *See* DRAKE (*Sir* F.). ... Lives, *etc.*

CAXTON (William). Life of W. C., with an Account of the Invention of Printing, and of the Modes and Materials used for transmitting Knowledge before that took place. ... [By —— Stephenson.] *See* Part I. SOCIETY, *etc.* ... Lives, *etc.*

CECIL (Robert), 1*st Earl of Salisbury*. Life, by Thomas P. Courtenay. (LARDNER'S Cab. Cycl., **80**, pp. 1 – 197.)

CECIL (William), *Baron Burleigh*. Life. (LARDNER'S Cab. Cycl., **76**, pp. 241 – 352.)

CELLINI (Benvenuto). Memoirs of B. C. ... written by himself; containing a variety of Information respecting the Arts, and the History of the Sixteenth Century. Now first collated with the new Text of Giuseppe Molini, and corrected and enlarged from the last Milan Ed., with Notes ... of G. P. Carpani. Translated by Thomas Roscoe. ... London. 1847. 8° (BOHN'S Stand. Libr.)

CENTLIVRE (*Mrs.* Susanna [FREEMAN]). Life. (LARDNER'S Cab. Cycl., **97**, pp. 308 – 320.)

CERVANTES SAAVEDRA (Miguel DE). Memoir. (DISTINGUISHED Men of Mod. Times, I. 113 – 124.)

——— Life. (LARDNER'S Cab. Cycl., **90**, pp. 120 – 188.)

CHAMANS (Marie DE), *Count de Lavalette*. *See* LAVALETTE.

CHAMPLAIN (Samuel). *See* MONTS (P. DU GUAST, *Sieur* DE).

CHANNING (William Ellery), *D.D.* Memoir of W. E. C., with Extracts from his Correspondence and Manuscripts. [By William Henry Channing.] ... 5th Ed. 3 vols. Boston. 1851. 12°

CHARDIN (*Sir* John). Life. (ST. JOHN'S Lives of Cel. Travellers, I. 233 – 270.)

CHARLEMAGNE. The History of C. By G. P. R. James ... . New York. N. D. 18° (HARPER'S Fam. Libr., **60**.)

CHARLES I. *King of England*. History ... . By Jacob Abbott. With Engravings. New York. [1848 ?] 16°

CHARLES II. *King of England*. History ... . By Jacob Abbott. With Engravings. New York. [1849 ?] 16°

CHARLES V. *Emperor of Germany*. The History ... . By William Robertson. *See* Class XXV. Part IV. § 1. B. *Austria*.

CHATHAM, William, 1*st Earl of*. *See* PITT.

CHAUCER (Geoffrey). Memoir. (DISTINGUISHED Men of Mod. Times, I. 38 – 50.)

——— Life. (LARDNER'S Cab. Cycl., **95**, pp. 125 – 172.)

CHIABRERA (Gabbriello). Life. (LARDNER'S Cab. Cycl., **89**, pp. 163 – 168.)

CHOISEUL *or* CHOISEUL-STAINVILLE (Étienne François, *Duke* DE). Life, by G. P. R. James. (LARDNER's Cab. Cycl., **87**, pp. 217 – 239.)

CHOISEUL-GOUFFIER (Marie Gabriel Florens Auguste, *Count* DE). Life. (ST. JOHN's Lives of Cel. Travellers, III. 154 – 167.)

CHRISTINA, *Queen of Sweden.* Memoir. (JAMESON's Memoirs of Cel. Female Sovereigns, II. 5 – 82.)

CHURCHILL (John), 1*st Duke of Marlborough.* Memoirs of the Duke of Marlborough, with his Original Correspondence .... By William Coxe .... A new Ed., revised by John Wade .... 3 vols. London. 1847 – 48. 8° (BOHN's Stand. Libr.)

——— Life, by G. R. Gleig. (LARDNER's Cab. Cycl., **67**, pp. 318 – 359, and **68**, pp. 1 – 227.)

CIBBER (Caius Gabriel). Life. (CUNNINGHAM's Lives of Brit. Painters and Sculptors, III. 19 – 30.)

CIBBER (Colley). Life. (LARDNER's Cab. Cycl., **97**, pp. 276 – 307.)

CICERO (Marcus Tullius). The Life of M. T. C. By J. F. Hollings .... London. 1839. 16°

——— The Life and Letters of M. T. C. — The Life of C. By Dr. [Conyers] Middleton. Cicero's Letters to several of his Friends. Translated by Wm. Melmoth. Cicero's Letters to Atticus. Translated by Dr. [Wm.] Heberden. London. 1840. 8° pp. xxiii., 829.

Note. Also with an engraved title-page, dated 1839.

——— Life. By the Rev. J. H. Newman. (ENCYCL. Metrop., X. 279 – 294.)

CLARKE (Edward Daniel). Life. (ST. JOHN's Lives of Cel. Travellers, III. 238 – 261.)

CLEOPATRA, *Queen of Egypt.* History .... By Jacob Abbott. With Engravings. New York. [1851 ?] 16°

——— Memoir. (JAMESON's Memoirs of Cel. Female Sovereigns, I. 31 – 57.)

CLIFFORD (George), 3*d Earl of Cumberland.* Life, by Robert Southey. (LARDNER's Cab. Cycl., **72**, pp. 1 – 66.)

CLINTON (Dewitt). Life of D. C. By James Renwick, LL.D. .... New-York. [1840 ?] 18° (HARPER's Fam. Libr., **125**.)

CLIVE (Robert), *Lord Clive, Baron of Plassey.* Life, by G. R. Gleig. (LARDNER's Cab. Cycl., **69**, pp. 1 – 114.)

——— Life. (MACAULAY's Essays, III. 84 – 166.)

COKE (*Sir* Edward). Life. [By Ed. Plunkett Burke.] *See* Part I. SOCIETY, *etc.* ... Lives, *etc.*

——— Memoir. (DISTINGUISHED Men of Mod. Times, I. 176 – 191.)

——— Life, by Henry Roscoe. (LARDNER's Cab. Cycl., **75**, pp. 1 – 43.)

COLBERT (Jean Baptiste), Contrôleur-Général *of Finance under Louis XIV.* Story of Colbert. (CHAMBERS's Miscel., I. no. 3, pp. 1 – 14.)

——— Life, by G. P. R. James. (LARDNER's Cab. Cycl., **85**, pp. 108 – 219.)

COLBURN (Warren). *See* Class XXIX. EDSON (T.). An Address, *etc.*

COLOMBO (Cristoforo). Life. (BELKNAP'S Amer. Biogr., I. 156 – 229.)

——— Life of Columbus. (CHAMBERS'S Miscel., VI. no. 96.

——— The Life and Voyages of Christopher Columbus; to which are added those of his Companions. By Washington Irving. ... Author's revised Ed. [Vol. II. and III. each with a Chart.] 3 vols. New-York. 1848 – 49. 12° (IRVING'S Works, Vol. III. – V.)

——— The Life and Voyages of Christopher Columbus. By Washington Irving. (Abridged by the same.) Including the Author's Visit to Palos. With a Portrait, Map, and other Illustrations. Boston. 1839. 12° (SCHOOL Libr., Vol. I.)

COLUMBA, *Saint.* Life. — The Introduction of Christianity and Civilization into North Britain. (LARDNER'S Cab. Cycl., **95**, pp. 1 – 59.)

COLUMBUS (Christopher). *See* COLOMBO.

COLONNA (Vittoria). Life. (LARDNER'S Cab. Cycl., **89**, pp. 75 – 81.)

CONDORCET (Marie Jean Antoine DE CARITAT, *Marquis* DE). Life. (LARDNER'S Cab. Cycl., **92**, pp. 175 – 194.)

CONFESSIONS of a Schoolmaster. *See* [ALCOTT (W. A.)].

CONFUCIUS *or* KOONG-FOO-TSE. (CHAMBERS'S Papers, *etc.* X. no. 77.)

CONGREVE (William). Life. (LARDNER'S Cab. Cycl., **97**, pp. 232 – 251.)

——— Life and Writings. (THACKERAY'S English Humourists.)

COOK (*Capt.* James). Life of Captain Cook. (CHAMBERS'S Miscel., III. no. 40.)

COPERNICUS, CÖPERNIK, *or* ZEPERNIK (Nicolaus). Memoir. (DISTINGUISHED Men of Mod. Times, I. 61 – 74.)

COPLEY (John Singleton). Life. (CUNNINGHAM'S Lives of Brit. Painters, *etc.* IV. 138 – 157.)

CORNEILLE (Pierre). Life. (LARDNER'S Cab. Cycl., **91**, pp. 40 – 62.)

CORNWALLIS (Charles), 1*st Marquis Cornwallis.* Life, by G. R. Gleig. (LARDNER'S Cab. Cycl., **69**, pp. 115 – 196.)

CORTÉS *or* CORTEZ (Hernando *or* Fernando). Memoir. (DISTINGUISHED Men of Mod. Times, I. 74 – 89.)

——— Life, by William H. Prescott. (In PRESCOTT'S Hist. of the Conquest of Mexico. *See* Class XXV. Part IV. § 4. B. *a. Mexico.*)

COSWAY (Richard). Life. (CUNNINGHAM'S Lives of Brit. Painters, *etc.* V. 9 – 24.)

COWLEY (Abraham). Life, by Robert Bell. (LARDNER'S Cab. Cycl., **93**, pp. 38 – 90.)

COWLEY (*Mrs.* Hannah [PARKHOUSE]). Life. (LARDNER'S Cab. Cycl., **97**, pp. 366 – 385.)

COWPER (William). Memoir. (DISTINGUISHED Men of Mod. Times, II. 221 – 233.)

CRANMER (Thomas), *Abp. of Canterbury.* Life. (LARDNER'S Cab. Cycl., **76**, pp. 184 – 240.)

CROMWELL (Oliver). Oliver Cromwell's Letters and Speeches: with Elucidations. By Thomas Carlyle. ... 2 vols. in 4 pts. New-York. 1845. 12° (Wiley and Putnam's Library of Choice Reading.)

——— Cromwell and his Contemporaries. (CHAMBERS's Papers, *etc.* VIII. no. 58.)

——— Life, by John Forster. (LARDNER's Cab. Cycl., **81, 82.**)

——— Life, by G. R. Gleig [with particular reference to his military achievements]. (LARDNER's Cab. Cycl., **67,** pp. 199 - 317.)

——— The Life of O. C. By J. T. Headley .... New York. 1848. 12°

——— ... Life of O. C. By the Rev. M. Russell, LL.D. .... 2 vols. New-York. 1846. 18° (HARPER's Fam. Libr., **62, 63.**)

CUMBERLAND, George, 3*d Earl of.* *See* CLIFFORD.

CUMBERLAND (Richard). Life. (LARDNER's Cab. Cycl., **97,** pp. 340 - 365.)

CURRAN (John Philpot), Note on. (BROUGHAM's "Hist. Sketches of Statesmen," *etc.* 2d Ser., II. 27 - 30.)

CUSHMAN (Robert). Life, by John Davis. (BELKNAP's Amer. Biogr., III. 70 - 84.)

CUVIER (George Léopold Chrétien Frédéric Dagobert), *Baron.* Memoir. (DISTINGUISHED Men of Mod. Times, II. 287 - 302.)

——— Memoir. (JARDINE's Nat. Libr., XVI. 17 - 58.)

CYRUS *the Elder, King of Persia.* History .... By Jacob Abbott. With Engravings. New York. [1850.] 16°

DAMER (*Mrs.* Anne Seymour [CONWAY]). Life. (CUNNINGHAM's Lives of Brit. Painters and Sculptors, III. 214 - 236.)

DAMPIER (William). Life and Voyages. *See* DRAKE (*Sir* F.). ... Lives, *etc.*

DANA (Richard Henry), *Jr.* Two Years before the Mast. *See* Class XXIII.

DANBY, Thomas, 1*st Earl of.* *See* OSBORNE.

DANTE ALIGHIERI. Memoir. (DISTINGUISHED Men of Mod. Times, I. 9 - 24.)

——— Life [by James Montgomery]. (LARDNER's Cab. Cycl., **88,** pp. 1 - 60.)

D'ARBLAY (Frances [BURNEY]), *Madame.* *See* ARBLAY.

DARIUS I. *King of Persia.* History .... By Jacob Abbott. With Engravings. New York. [1850 ?] 16°

DARLING (Grace), the Heroine. (CHAMBERS's Miscel., I. no. 12, pp. 1 - 11.)

DAVENANT (William). Life, with an Account of the Stage in the Seventeenth Century. (LARDNER's Cab. Cycl., **97,** pp. 70 - 122.)

DAVIDSON (Lucretia Maria). A Memoir of L. M. D.; by [Catharine M. Sedgwick] the Author of Redwood, *etc.* (SPARKS's Amer. Biogr., VII. 219 - 294.)

DAVIE (William Richardson), *Gov. of North Carolina.* Lives of W. R. D. [by Fordyce M. Hubbard] and Samuel Kirkland. Boston. 1848. 16° (SPARKS's Amer. Biogr., 2d Ser., Vol. XV.)

DAVY (*Sir* Humphry). Life. (BROUGHAM's Lives of Men of Letters and Science, *etc.* pp. 260 – 269.)

DECATUR (*Com.* Stephen). Life of S. D., a Commodore in the Navy of the United States. By Alexander Slidell Mackenzie, U. S. N. ... Boston. 1846. 16° (SPARKS's Amer. Biogr., 2d Ser., Vol. XI.)

DEFOE (Daniel). (CHAMBERS's Papers, *etc.* VII. no. 56.)

——— Memoir. (DISTINGUISHED Men of Mod. Times, II. 87 – 100.)

DE LA TUDE (Henri MASERS). *See* MASERS DE LA TUDE.

DELAWARE *or* DELAWARR, Thomas, *3d Baron. See* WEST.

DE L'ÉPÉE (Charles Michel), *the Abbé. See* L'ÉPÉE.

DELLA VALLE (Pietro). *See* VALLE.

DEMOSTHENES. Demosthenes, the Man, the Statesman and the Orator. (LEGARÉ's Writings, I. 443 – 501.)

DENON (Dominique Vivant), *Baron.* Life. (ST. JOHN's Lives of Cel. Travellers, III. 345 – 356.)

DERWENTWATER, James, *3d and last Earl of. See* RADCLIFFE.

DESCARTES (René). Memoir. (DISTINGUISHED Men of Mod. Times, I. 248 – 255.)

DE VERE (*Sir* Francis); being a Specimen of the Military Commanders in the Elizabethan Age. Life, by G. R. Gleig. (LARDNER's Cab. Cycl., **67**, pp. 124 – 198.)

DEVEREUX (Robert), *2d Earl of Essex.* Life, by Robert Southey. (LARDNER's Cab. Cycl., **73**, pp. 1 – 208.)

[DIEZ (Juan Martinez)], *the Empecinado.* The Guerilla: a Story of the Peninsular War. (CHAMBERS's Miscel., X. no. 171.)

DRAKE (*Sir* Francis). ... Lives and Voyages of Drake, Cavendish, and Dampier; including an Introductory View of the Earlier Discoveries in the South Sea, and the History of the Bucaniers. With Portraits on Steel. New-York. 1846. 18° (HARPER's Fam. Libr., **30.**)

——— *See* HAWKINS (*Sir* J.).

DRAYTON (Michael). Life, by Robert Bell. (LARDNER's Cab. Cycl., **93**, pp. 1 – 37.)

DRURY (Dru). Memoir. (JARDINE's Nat. Libr., XV. 17 – 71.)

DRURY (Robert). Adventures. [Abridged from his Autobiography.] (CHAMBERS's Miscel., V. no. 81.)

DRYDEN (John). Life, by Robert Bell. (LARDNER's Cab. Cycl., **94**, pp. 1 – 88.)

DUBOIS (Guillaume), *Cardinal.* Life, by G. P. R. James. (LARDNER's Cab. Cycl., **86**, pp. 64 – 129.)

DUNDAS (Henry), 1*st Viscount Melville.* (BROUGHAM's "Hist. Sketches of Statesmen," *etc.* 1st Ser., II. 31 – 38.)

DUNNING (John), *1st Baron Ashburton.* Life, by Henry Roscoe. (LARDNER's Cab. Cycl., **75**, pp. 287 - 306.)

DU PLESSIS (Armand Jean), *Cardinal de Richelieu. See* RICHELIEU.

DUVAL (Valentin JAMERAY). The Story of Valentine Duval. (CHAMBERS's Miscel., IV. no. 67.)

DWIGHT (Timothy), *D.D., LL.D.* Life of T. D., President of Yale College; by William B. Sprague. (SPARKS's Amer. Biogr., 2d Ser., IV. 223 - 364.)

EATON (*Gen.* William). Life of W. E.; by Cornelius C. Felton. (SPARKS's Amer. Biogr., IX. 163 - 358.)

EDWARDS (*Rev.* Jonathan), *the Elder.* Lives of Jonathan Edwards [by Samuel Miller] and David Brainerd. New York. 1839. 16° (SPARKS's Amer. Biogr., Vol. VIII.)

EFFINGHAM, Charles, *2d Baron Howard of. See* HOWARD.

ELDON, John, *1st Earl of. See* SCOTT.

ELEANOR *of Provence, surnamed* la Belle, *Queen of Henry III.* Life. (STRICKLAND's Queens of England, II. 46 - 87.)

ELEANORA *of Aquitaine, Queen of Henry II.* Life. (STRICKLAND's Queens of England, I. 166 - 203.)

ELEANORA *of Castile, surnamed* the Faithful, *First Queen of Edward I.* Life. (STRICKLAND's Queens of England, II. 88 - 108.)

ELIOT (*Rev.* John). Life of J. E., the Apostle to the Indians. By Convers Francis. New-York. 1844. 16° or 12° (8. and 6.) (SPARKS's Amer. Biogr., Vol. V.)

——— Life, by John Forster. (LARDNER's Cab. Cycl., **77**, pp. 1 - 177.)

ELIZABETH, *Queen of England and Ireland.* History .... By Jacob Abbott. With Engravings. New York. [1849?] 16°

——— Conduct towards Mary, Queen of Scots. (BROUGHAM's "Hist. Sketches of Statesmen," *etc.* 1st Ser., II. 210 - 216.)

——— Memoir. (JAMESON's Memoirs of Cel. Female Sovereigns, I. 213 - 245.)

——— Life. (STRICKLAND's Queens of England, Vol. VI., VII. 5 - 232.)

ELIZABETH *of York, surnamed* the Good, *Queen of Henry VII.* Life. (STRICKLAND's Queens of England, IV. 17 - 62.)

ELIZABETH WOODVILLE, *Queen of Edward IV.* Life. (STRICKLAND's Queens of England, III. 205 - 241.)

ELLERY (William). Life of W. E.; by Edward T. Channing. (SPARKS's Amer. Biogr., VI. 85 - 159; — SCHOOL Libr., VI. 305 - 353.)

ELLIOTT (Ebenezer). (CHAMBERS's Papers, *etc.* I. no. 8.)

EPAMINONDAS. Campaigns and Character. (HERBERT's Captains, *etc.* pp. 226 - 264. — *See* Part I.)

ERASMUS (Desiderius). Memoir. (DISTINGUISHED Men of Mod. Times, I. 50 - 61.)

ERCILLA (Alonso DE). Life. (LARDNER's Cab. Cycl., **90**, pp. 103 - 119.)

ERSKINE (Thomas), *Lord.* Sketch. (BROUGHAM'S "Hist. Sketches of Statesmen," *etc.* 1st Ser., II. 41 - 49.)

—— Life, by Henry Roscoe. (LARDNER'S Cab. Cycl., **75**, pp. 329 - 391.)

ESPINEL (Vicente) and Estéban Manuel de VILLÉGAS. Lives. (LARDNER'S Cab. Cycl., **90**, pp. 238 - 242.)

ESSEX, Robert, *2d Earl of.* *See* DEVEREUX.

ETTRICK Shepherd (The). *See* [HOGG (James)].

EULER (Leonhard). Memoir. (DISTINGUISHED Men of Mod. Times, II. 141 - 148.)

FARQUHAR (George). Life. (LARDNER'S Cab. Cycl., **97**, pp. 252-275.)

FAYETTE (Marie Paul Joseph Roch Ives Gilbert DE MOTIER, *Marquis* DE LA). *See* LAFAYETTE.

FÉNELON (François DE SALIGNAC DE LA MOTHE). (CHAMBERS'S Papers, *etc.* IV. no. 28.)

—— Remarks on the Character and Writings of Fenelon. (CHANNING'S Works, I. 167 - 215.)

—— Memoir. (DISTINGUISHED Men of Mod. Times, II. 45 - 56.)

—— Life. (LARDNER'S Cab. Cycl., **91**, pp. 329 - 373.)

FERDINAND V. *of Castile and* II. *of Aragon.* *See* PRESCOTT'S "Hist. of the Reign of Ferdinand," *etc.* Class XXV. Part IV. § 1. B. *Spain.*

FICHTE (Johann Gottlieb). Fichte — a Biography. (CHAMBERS'S Papers, *etc.* IX. no. 72.)

FIELDING (Henry). Life and Writings. (THACKERAY'S English Humourists.)

FILICAJA (Vincenzo DA). Life. (LARDNER'S Cab. Cycl., **89**, pp. 180 - 184.)

FITCH (John). Life of J. F.; by Charles Whittlesey. (SPARKS'S Amer. Biogr., 2d Ser., VI. 81 - 166.)

FLAXMAN (John). Life. (CUNNINGHAM'S Lives of Brit. Painters and Sculptors, III. 237 - 315.)

FLETCHER (John). Life. *See* BEAUMONT (F.).

FLEURY (André Hercule, *Cardinal* DE). Life, by G. P. R. James. (LARDNER'S Cab. Cycl., **87**, pp. 1 - 68.)

FLORIDA BLANCA (José [Francisco Antonio ?] MOÑINO, *Count* DE). Life, by G. P. R. James. (LARDNER'S Cab. Cycl., **87**, pp. 157 - 216.)

FOE (Daniel DE). *See* DEFOE.

FONTAINE (Jean DE LA). *See* LA FONTAINE.

FORD (John). Life. (LARDNER'S Cab. Cycl., **96**, pp. 295 - 321.)

FORSTER (George). Life. (ST. JOHN'S Lives of Cel. Travellers, II. 198 - 232.)

FOSCOLO (Niccolò Ugo). Life. (LARDNER'S Cab. Cycl., **89**, pp. 353 - 394.)

FOX (Charles James). Sketch. (BROUGHAM'S "Hist. Sketches of Statesmen," *etc.* 1st Ser., I. 193 - 207.)

——— Memoir. (DISTINGUISHED Men of Mod. Times, II. 248 - 263.)

FRANCIS (*Sir* Philip). Sketch. (BROUGHAM'S "Hist. Sketches of Statesmen," *etc.* 2d Ser., I. 113 - 129.)

FRANKLIN (Benjamin), *LL.D.* Sketch. (BROUGHAM'S "Hist. Sketches of Statesmen," *etc.* 1st Ser., II. 129 - 133.)

——— Memoirs of B. F.; written by himself, *etc.* *See* Class XXXI.

——— The Life of B. F.; containing the Autobiography, with Notes and a Continuation. By Jared Sparks. . . . . Boston. 1848. 8° pp. xv., 612. +

Note. Also with an engraved title-page, dated 1844.

FREDERICK II. *King of Prussia.* Sketch. (BROUGHAM'S "Hist. Sketches of Statesmen," *etc.* 1st Ser., II. 137 - 158.)

——— The Life of F. . . . . By [George James Weldore Agar Ellis] Lord Dover. . . . 2 vols. New York. 1848. 18° (HARPER'S Fam. Libr., **41, 42.**)

——— Life. (MACAULAY'S Essays, IV. 217 - 306.)

FRENCH Prisoner. Story of a French Prisoner of War in England. (CHAMBERS'S Miscel., VII. no. 116.)

FROBISHER *or* FORBISHER (*Sir* Martin). Life, by Robert Bell. (LARDNER'S Cab. Cycl., **74,** pp. 1 - 38.)

FROUDE (*Rev.* Richard Hurrell). *See* WHITEFIELD (G.).

FUCA (Juan DE). *See* VALERIANOS (Apostolos).

FULTON (Robert). Lives of Robert Fulton [by James Renwick], Joseph Warren, Henry Hudson, and Father Marquette. New-York. 1845. 16° or 12° (8. and 6.) (SPARKS'S Amer. Biogr., Vol. X.)

——— Life of R. F.; by James Renwick. (SCHOOL Libr., IV. 153 - 209.)

FUSELI [*originally* FUESSLI] (Henry). Life. (CUNNINGHAM'S Lives of Brit. Painters, *etc.* II. 223 - 273.)

GAINSBOROUGH (Thomas). Life. (CUNNINGHAM'S Lives of Brit. Painters, *etc.* I. 282 - 305.

GALILEI (Galileo). Life. [By J. E. Drinkwater Bethune.] *See* Part I. SOCIETY, *etc.* . . . Lives, *etc.*

——— The Martyrs of Science; or, The Lives of Galileo, Tycho Brahe, and Kepler. By Sir David Brewster . . . . New-York. 1847. 18° (HARPER'S Fam. Libr., **130.**)

——— Memoir. (DISTINGUISHED Men of Mod. Times, I. 206 - 217.)

——— Life. (LARDNER'S Cab. Cycl., **89,** pp. 1 - 62.)

GALLISON (John). Memoir. (CHANNING'S Works, V. 343 - 360.)

GARCILASSO DE LA VEGA. Life. (LARDNER'S Cab. Cycl., **90,** pp. 36 - 57.)

GAY (John). Life and Writings. (THACKERAY'S English Humourists.)

GEER (Carl, *Baron* DE). Memoir. (JARDINE'S Nat. Libr., XXVIII. 59 - 66.)

GEORGE III. *King of Great Britain and Ireland.* Sketch. (BROUGHAM'S "Hist. Sketches of Statesmen," *etc.* 1st Ser., I. 19 - 28.)

GEORGE IV. *King of Great Britain, etc.* Sketch of George IV. with Sir John Leach and others. (BROUGHAM'S "Hist. Sketches of Statesmen," *etc.* 2d Ser., I. 13 - 66.)

——— Life and Times of ... George the Fourth. With Anecdotes of Distinguished Persons of the last Fifty Years. By the Rev. George Croly. New York. N. D. 18° (HARPER'S Fam. Libr., **15.**)

GESNER (Conrad). Memoir. (JARDINE'S Nat. Libr., XX. 17 - 58.)

GIBBON (Edward). Memoirs, by himself. *See* Class XXXI.

GIBBONS (Grinling). Life. (CUNNINGHAM'S Lives of Brit. Painters and Sculptors, III. 5 - 18.)

GIBBS (*Sir* Vickary), *Lord Chief Justice.* Sketch. (BROUGHAM'S "Hist. Sketches of Statesmen," *etc.* 1st Ser., I. 139 - 148.)

GILBERT (Bartholomew). *See* GOSNOLD (B.).

GILBERT (Humphrey). Life. (BELKNAP'S Amer. Biogr., I. 272 - 288.)

GIRON (Pedro TELLEZ Y), *Duke of Ossuña.* *See* OSSUÑA.

GOETHE (Johann Wolfgang VON). The Auto-biography of G. Truth and Poetry: from my own Life. Translated from the German, by John Oxenford, Esq. [Vol. I.] Thirteen Books. | Vol. II. ... The Concluding Books. Also Letters from Switzerland, and Travels in Italy. Translated by the Rev. A. J. W. Morrison, M.A. 2 vols. London. 1848 - 49. 8° (BOHN'S Stand. Libr.)

GOLDONI (Carlo). Life. (LARDNER'S Cab. Cycl., **89**, pp. 213 - 246.)

GOLDSMITH (Oliver). The Life and Adventures of O. G. A Biography: in Four Books. By John Forster. ... . London. 1848. 8° (4.) pp. xvii., 704. +

——— Oliver Goldsmith: a Biography. By Washington Irving. New-York. 1849. 12° (IRVING'S Works, Vol. XI.)

——— The Life of O. G., with Selections from his Writings. By Washington Irving. *See* Class XXXI.

——— Life and Writings. (THACKERAY'S English Humourists.)

GONDI (Jean François Paul DE), *Cardinal de Retz.* *See* RETZ.

GONGORA Y ARGOTE (Luis DE). Life. (LARDNER'S Cab. Cycl., **90**, pp. 243 - 254.)

GORGES (Ferdinando) and John MASON. Lives. (BELKNAP'S Amer. Biogr., II. 47 - 95.)

GORTON (Samuel). Life of S. G., one of the First Settlers of Warwick, in Rhode Island; by John M. Mackie. (SPARKS'S Amer. Biogr., 2d Ser., V. 315 - 411.)

GOSNOLD (Bartholomew), Martin PRING, Bartholomew GILBERT, and George WEYMOUTH. Lives. (BELKNAP'S Amer. Biogr., II. 206 - 253.)

GRAHAME (James). Memoir, by Josiah Quincy. (Prefixed to GRAHAME'S Hist. of the U. S. 1848. 8° pp. v. - xxviii.)

GRANT (*Sir* William). Sketch. (BROUGHAM'S "Hist. Sketches of Statesmen," *etc.* 1st Ser., I. 151 - 156.)

GRANVELLE (Antoine PERRENOT), *Cardinal*, and MAURICE, *Elector of*

Saxony. Lives, by Eyre Evans Crowe. (LARDNER's Cab. Cycl., **83**, pp. 99 - 155.)

GRATTAN (Henry). Sketch. (BROUGHAM's "Hist. Sketches of Statesmen," *etc.* 1st Ser., II. 71 - 78.)

GREENE (*Maj.-Gen.* Nathanael). Life of N. G., Major-General in the Army of the Revolution. By his Grandson, George W. Greene .... Boston. 1846. 16° (SPARKS's Amer. Biogr., 2d Ser., Vol. X.)

GRENVILLE *or* GREENVILLE (*Sir* Richard). Life, by Robert Southey. (LARDNER's Cab. Cycl., **72**, pp. 328 - 339.)

——— *See* RALEIGH (*Sir* W.).

GRENVILLE (William Wyndham), *Lord.* Sketch. (BROUGHAM's "Hist. Sketches of Statesmen," *etc.* 1st Ser., II. 63 - 67.)

GROTIUS (Hugo) [*Dutch*, GROOT (Huig DE)]. Memoir. (DISTINGUISHED Men of Mod. Times, I. 231 - 247.)

GUARINI (Giovanni Battista). Life. (LARDNER's Cab. Cycl., **89**, pp. 82 - 95.)

GUICCIARDINI (Francesco). Life. (LARDNER's Cab. Cycl., **89**, pp. 63 - 74.)

GUILFORD *or* GUILDFORD, Francis, 1*st Earl of.* *See* NORTH.

GUILFORD *or* GUILDFORD, Frederick, 2*d Earl of.* *See* NORTH.

GUSTAVUS II. ADOLPHUS, *King of Sweden.* Memoir. (DISTINGUISHED Men of Mod. Times, I. 192 - 205.)

GUSTAVUS III. *King of Sweden.* Sketch. (BROUGHAM's "Hist. Sketches of Statesmen," *etc.* 1st Ser., II. 161 - 172.)

GUZMAN (Gaspar DE), *Count Duke Olivarez.* *See* OLIVAREZ.

HADRIANUS (Publius Ælius), *Emperor of Rome.* Life, by Maj. A. S. H. Mountain. (ENCYCL. Metrop., X. 664 - 676.)

HALE (*Sir* Matthew). Memoir. (DISTINGUISHED Men of Mod. Times, I. 308 - 324.)

——— Life, by Henry Roscoe. (LARDNER's Cab. Cycl., **75**, pp. 59 - 83.)

HALLER (Albrecht, *Baron* VON). Memoir. (JARDINE's Nat. Libr., XIII. 17 - 63.)

HAMILTON (Alexander). *See* JAY (J.).

HAMPDEN (John). Memoir. (DISTINGUISHED Men of Mod. Times, I. 218 - 231.)

——— Life, by John Forster. (LARDNER's Cab. Cycl., **78**, pp. 306 - 380.)

——— Life. (MACAULAY's Essays, II. 52 - 102.)

HANDEL (George Frederic), Memoir of. (DISTINGUISHED Men of Mod. Times, II. 100 - 113.)

HANNIBAL, *the Carthaginian.* History .... By Jacob Abbott. With Engravings. New York. [1849 ?] 16°

——— Campaigns and Character. (HERBERT's Captains, *etc.* pp. 335 - 364.)

HANWAY (Jonas). Life. (ST. JOHN'S Lives of Cel. Travellers, II. 301 - 319.)

HARLOW (George Henry). Life. (CUNNINGHAM'S Lives of Brit. Painters, *etc.* IV. 229 - 245.)

HARO (Luis DE). Life, by G. P. R. James. (LARDNER'S Cab. Cycl., **86**, pp. 1 - 63.)

HARRO HARRING (Paul). Biographical Sketch. (A. H. EVERETT'S Essays, 2d Ser., pp. 1 - 94.)

HARVEY (William). Memoir. (DISTINGUISHED Men of Mod. Times, I. 255 - 267.)

HASSELQUIST (Fredrik). Life. (ST. JOHN'S Lives of Cel. Travellers, II. 52 - 72.)

HASTINGS (Warren). Life. (MACAULAY'S Essays, IV. 81 - 216.)

HAWKINS (*Sir* John) and Sir Francis DRAKE. Lives, by Robert Southey. (LARDNER'S Cab. Cycl., **72**, pp. 67 - 242.)

HAWKINS (*Sir* Richard). Life, by Robert Southey. (LARDNER'S Cab. Cycl., **72**, pp. 283 - 327.)

HEBER (Reginald), *Bp. of Calcutta.* Life. (ST. JOHN'S Lives of Cel. Travellers, III. 356 - 386.)

HENRIETTA MARIA, *Consort of Charles I.* Life. (STRICKLAND'S Queens of England, VIII. 5 - 198.)

HENRY IV. *King of France.* Life. (CHAMBERS'S Miscel., V. no. 78.)

HENRY (Patrick). Life, by Alexander H. Everett. (SPARKS'S Amer. Biogr., 2d Ser., I. 207 - 398.)

HEROINE of Siberia (The). *See* [LOPOULOFF (Prascovie)].

HERRERA (Fernando). Life, with Notices of Saa de Miranda, Jorge de Montemayor, Cristoval Castillejo, and the Early Dramatists. (LARDNER'S Cab. Cycl., **90**, pp. 83 - 102.)

HEYNE (Christian Gottlob). Heyne — a Biography. (CHAMBERS'S Papers, *etc.* VI. no. 48.)

HEYWOOD (John). Life, with the Origin and Early History of the English Stage [including notices of John Skelton, John Rastall, John Bale, and Nicholas Udall]. (LARDNER'S Cab. Cycl., **95**, pp. 173 - 311.)

HOGARTH (William). Life. (CUNNINGHAM'S Lives of Brit. Painters, *etc.* I. 57 - 170.)

——— Life and Works. (THACKERAY'S English Humourists.)

[HOGG (James)]. The Ettrick Shepherd. (CHAMBERS'S Miscel., VII. no. 123.)

HOJEDA *or* OJEDA (Alonso DE). Life, by Washington Irving. (IRVING'S Life of Columbus, *etc.* III. 17 - 33, and 51 - 101.)

HOPPNER (John). Life. (CUNNINGHAM'S Lives of Brit. Painters, *etc.* IV. 203 - 214.)

HORATIUS FLACCUS (Quintus). Life. By the Rev. Henry Thomson. (ENCYCL. Metrop., X. 383 - 416.)

HORNE (John), afterwards TOOKE. *See* TOOKE.

HORNER (Francis). Mr. Horner — Lord King — Mr. Ricardo. (BROUGHAM's "Hist. Sketches of Statesmen," *etc.* 2d Ser., II. 7 - 27.)

HOWARD (Charles), *2d Baron Howard of Effingham, and 1st Earl of Nottingham.* Life, by Robert Southey. (LARDNER's Cab. Cycl., **71**, pp. 278 - 371.)

HOWARD (John). Life. (CHAMBERS's Miscel., VII. no. 112.)

HUBER (François). Memoir. (JARDINE's Nat. Libr., XXXIV. 17 - 25.)

HUDSON (Henry). Life of H. H., by Henry R. Cleveland. (SPARKS's Amer. Biogr., X. 185 - 261 ; — SCHOOL Libr., V. 135 - 182.)

HUMBOLDT (Friedrich Heinrich Alexander, *Baron* VON). Memoir. (JARDINE's Nat. Libr., XXXVII. 17 - 39.)

HUME (David). Life. (BROUGHAM's Lives of Men of Letters and Science, *etc.* pp. 121 - 156.)

HUNTER (John). Memoir. (JARDINE's Nat. Libr., XXII. 17 - 83.)

HUTCHINSON (Anne). Life of Anne Hutchinson ; with a Sketch of the Antinomian Controversy in Massachusetts ; by George E. Ellis. (SPARKS's Amer. Biogr., 2d Ser., VI. 167 - 376.)

HUTCHINSON (*Col.* John). Memoirs of the Life of Colonel Hutchinson ... by his Widow Lucy .... From the original Manuscript by the Rev. Julius Hutchinson. To which is prefixed the Life of Mrs. Hutchinson, written by herself. 7th Ed. To which is now first added, An Account of the Siege of Lathom House, defended by the Countess of Derby against Sir Thomas Fairfax. London. 1848. 8° (BOHN's Stand. Libr.)

HUTTON (William). Life. (CHAMBERS's Miscel., IV. no. 69.)

IBN BATUTA. Life. (ST. JOHN's Lives of Cel. Travellers, I. 69 - 109.)

IGNACIO [*Lat.* IGNATIUS] DE LOYOLA, *Saint.* Memoir. (DISTINGUISHED Men of Mod. Times, I. 89 - 102.)

——— Ignatius Loyola and his Associates. (STEPHEN (*Sir* J.). ... Essays, pp. 314 - 385.)

IRON MASK. *See* [MATTHIOLI (G.)], *Count.*

ISABELLA *of Angoulême, Queen of King John.* Life. (STRICKLAND's Queens of England, II. 28 - 45.)

ISABELLA *of Castile.* Memoir. (JAMESON's Memoirs of Cel. Female Sovereigns, I. 112 - 171.)

——— *See* PRESCOTT's "History of the Reign of Ferdinand and Isabella," Class XXV. Part IV. § 1. B. *Spain.*

ISABELLA *of France, surnamed* the Fair, *Queen of Edward II.* Life. (STRICKLAND's Queens of England, II. 122 - 172.)

ISABELLA *of Valois, surnamed* the Little Queen, *Second Queen of Richard II.* Life. (STRICKLAND's Queens of England, III. 9 - 37.)

JACKSON (John). Life. (CUNNINGHAM's Lives of Brit. Painters, *etc.* V. 229 - 249.)

JACQUARD (Joseph Marie). Story of Jacquard. (CHAMBERS's Miscel., IX. no. 158.)

JAMESONE (George). Life. (CUNNINGHAM'S Lives of Brit. Painters, *etc.* IV. 7 - 33.)

JANE SEYMOUR, *Third Queen of Henry VIII.* Life. (STRICKLAND'S Queens of England, IV. 216 - 235.)

JAY (John). Lives of John Jay [by Henry B. Renwick] and Alexander Hamilton [by James Renwick, LL.D.]. New-York. 1845. 18° (HARPER'S Fam. Libr., **129.**)

JEFFREY (Francis). (CHAMBERS'S Papers, *etc.* II. no. 16.)

JEFFREYS, JEFFERYS, *or* JEFFERIES (George), *Baron Jeffreys.* Life, by Henry Roscoe. (LARDNER'S Cab. Cycl., **75,** pp. 113 - 139.)

JENKINSON (Robert Banks), *2d Baron Hawkesbury, and 2d Earl of Liverpool.* (BROUGHAM'S "Hist. Sketches of Statesmen," *etc.* 2d Ser., I. 165 - 177.)

JENNER (Edward), *M.D.* Memoir. (DISTINGUISHED Men of Mod. Times, II. 273 - 287.)

JERVIS (John), 1*st Viscount and Earl St. Vincent.* Lord St. Vincent — Lord Nelson. (BROUGHAM'S "Hist. Sketches of Statesmen," *etc.* 2d Ser., I. 197 - 212.)

JESUS CHRIST, *the Saviour of the World.* The Gospel History of our Lord's Life & Ministry, as recorded by the Evangelists, with thirteen hundred Notes; accompanied by a Series of Questions, Practical Lessons, and Geographical Exercises; chronologically arranged, and illustrated by several Maps . . . . By R. Mimpriss . . . . 2d Ed., enlarged. London. [1842.] 16°

JOAN OF ARC. *See* ARC (Jeanne D').

JOANNA I. *Queen of Naples.* Memoir. (JAMESON'S Memoirs of Cel. Female Sovereigns, I. 65 - 95.)

JOANNA II. *Queen of Naples.* Memoir. (JAMESON'S Memoirs of Cel. Female Sovereigns, I. 95 - 112.)

JOANNA *of Navarre, Queen of Henry IV.* Life. (STRICKLAND'S Queens of England, III. 38 - 82.)

JOHN SOBIESKI, *King of Poland.* Memoir. (DISTINGUISHED Men of Mod. Times, II. 5 - 19.)

JOHNSON (Benjamin). *See* JONSON.

JOHNSON (Samuel), *LL.D.* The Life of S. J. . . . including a Journal of a Tour to the Hebrides, by James Boswell, Esq. A new Ed. With numerous Additions and Notes, by John Wilson Croker . . . . 2 vols. New-York. 1837. 8°

——— The Life [by Arthur Murphy] and Writings of S. J. . . . . *See* Class III.

JONES (*Sir* William). Life. (CHAMBERS'S Miscel., IX. no. 152, pp. 1 - 6.)

——— Memoir. (DISTINGUISHED Men of Mod. Times, II. 181 - 195.)

——— Life, by Henry Roscoe. (LARDNER'S Cab. Cycl., **75,** pp. 306 - 328.)

JONSON *or* JOHNSON (Ben). Life. (LARDNER'S Cab. Cycl., **96,** pp. 131 - 203.)

JOSEPH II. *Emperor of Germany.* (BROUGHAM's "Hist. Sketches of Statesmen," *etc.* 1st Ser., II. 175 – 186.)

JOSEPHINE, *Empress of the French.* History .... By John S. C. Abbott. With Engravings. New York. [1851 ?] 16°

——— Memoirs of the Empress J. By John S. Memes, LL.D. .... New York. N. D. 18° (HARPER's Fam. Libr., **28.**)

JULIUS CÆSAR (Caius). *See* CÆSAR.

KÆMPFER (Engelbert). Life. (ST. JOHN's Lives of Cel. Travellers, I. 271 – 304.)

KATHARINE *of Aragon, First Queen of Henry VIII.* Life. (STRICKLAND's Queens of England, IV. 63 – 121.)

KATHARINE HOWARD, *Fifth Queen of Henry VIII.* Life. (STRICKLAND's Queens of England, IV. 279 – 330.)

KATHARINE PARR, *Sixth Queen of Henry VIII.* Life. (STRICKLAND's Queens of England, V. 9 – 98.)

KATHERINE *of Valois, surnamed* the Fair, *Consort of Henry V.* Life. (STRICKLAND's Queens of England, III. 83 – 122.)

KEPLER (Johann). Life. [By J. E. Drinkwater Bethune.] *See* Part I. SOCIETY, *etc.* ... Lives, *etc.*

——— Life. By Sir David Brewster. *See* GALILEI (G.).

——— Memoir. (DISTINGUISHED Men of Mod. Times, I. 164 – 175.)

KING (Peter), *7th Lord King.* *See* HORNER (F.).

KIRKLAND (Samuel). Life of S. K., Missionary to the Indians; by Samuel K. Lothrop. (SPARKS's Amer. Biogr., 2d Ser., XV. 137 – 368.)

KOONG-FOO-TSE. *See* CONFUCIUS.

KOSCIUSKO (Thaddeus). Memoir. (DISTINGUISHED Men of Mod. Times, II. 263 – 272.)

LACÉPÈDE (Bernard Germain Étienne DE LA VILLE-SUR-ILLON, *Count* DE). Memoir. (JARDINE's Nat. Libr., XXVI. 17 – 32.)

LAFAYETTE (Marie Paul Joseph [*not* Jean] Roch Ives Gilbert DE MOTIER, *Marquis* DE). Sketch. (BROUGHAM's "Hist. Sketches of Statesmen," *etc.* 2d Ser., II. 141 – 158.)

LA FONTAINE (Jean DE). Life. (LARDNER's Cab. Cycl., **91**, pp. 150 – 182.)

LAMARCK (Jean Baptiste Pierre Antoine DE MONET, *Chevalier* DE). Memoir. (JARDINE's Nat. Libr., XXXI. 17 – 63.)

LA ROCHEFOUCAULD (François, *Duke* DE). Life. (LARDNER's Cab. Cycl., **91**, pp. 63 – 96.)

LA ROCHEJAQUELEIN (Henri DUVERGIER, *Count* DE). La Rochejaquelein and the War in La Vendée. (CHAMBERS's Miscel., I. no. 16.)

LA SALLE (Robert Cavelier DE). Lives of Robert Cavelier de la Salle [by Jared Sparks] and Patrick Henry. Boston. 1844. 16° (SPARKS's Amer. Biogr., 2d Ser., Vol. I.)

LAS CASAS (Bartolomé DE). *See* CASAS.

LATREILLE (Pierre André). Memoir. (JARDINE's Nat. Libr., XXXII. 17 – 60.)

LA TUDE (Henri MASERS DE). *See* MASERS DE LA TUDE.

LAURENCE *or* LAWRENCE (French). Sketch. (BROUGHAM's "Hist. Sketches of Statesmen," *etc.* 2d Ser., I. 103 – 109.)

LAVALETTE (Marie CHAMANS, *Count* DE). The Story of L. (CHAMBERS's Miscel., IV. no. 62.)

LA VILLE-SUR-ILLON (Bernard Germain Étienne DE), *Count de Lacépède. See* LACÉPÈDE.

LAWRENCE (French). *See* LAURENCE.

LAWRENCE (*Sir* Thomas). Life. (CUNNINGHAM's Lives of Brit. Painters, *etc.* V. 134 – 228.)

LEACH (*Sir* John). *See* GEORGE IV. *King of England.*

LECLERC (George Louis), *Count de Buffon. See* BUFFON.

LEDYARD (John). Life. (ST. JOHN's Lives of Cel. Travellers, II. 163 – 197.)

——— Life of J. L., the American Traveller. By Jared Sparks. Boston. 1847. 16° (SPARKS's Amer. Biogr., 2d Ser., Vol. XIV.)

LEE (*Maj.-Gen.* Charles). Lives of Charles Lee [by Jared Sparks] and Joseph Reed. Boston. 1846. 16° (SPARKS's Amer. Biogr., 2d Ser., Vol. VIII.)

LEE (Nathaniel). Life. (LARDNER's Cab. Cycl., **97**, pp. 134 – 145.)

LEE BOO, *Prince.* (CHAMBERS's Miscel., IV. no. 71.)

[LEECH (Samuel)]. The Life of a Sailor Boy. [Abridged from a work entitled "Thirty Years from Home ... being the Experience of Samuel Leech." Boston. 1843.] (CHAMBERS's Miscel., IV. no. 65.)

LEEDS, Thomas, 1*st Duke of. See* OSBORNE.

LEISLER (Jacob). The Administration of J. L., a Chapter in American History; by Charles F. Hoffman. (SPARKS's Amer. Biogr., 2d Ser., III. 179 – 238.)

LEO X. *Pope.* [GIOVANNI DE' MEDICI.] Life, by Eyre Evans Crowe. (LARDNER's Cab. Cycl., **83**, pp. 70 – 98.)

——— The Life and Pontificate of Leo the Tenth. By William Roscoe. 5th Ed. Revised by his Son, Thomas Roscoe. ... 2 vols. London. 1846. 8° (BOHN's Stand. Libr.)

LEO (Giovanni), *Africanus.* Life. (ST. JOHN's Lives of Cel. Travellers, I. 109 – 148.)

LEON (Luis Ponce DE). Life. (LARDNER's Cab. Cycl., **90**, pp. 70 – 82.)

L'ÉPÉE (Charles Michel, *the Abbé* DE). Memoir. (DISTINGUISHED Men of Mod. Times, II. 158 – 172.)

LERMA (Francisco Gomez DE ROXAS DE SANDOVAL), *Duke of.* Life, by E. E. Crowe. (LARDNER's Cab. Cycl., **83**, pp. 262 – 281.)

LE TELLIER (François Michel), *Marquis de Louvois. See* LOUVOIS.

LE VAILLANT (François). Memoir. (JARDINE's Nat. Libr., XII. 17 – 31.)

——— Life. (St. John's Lives of Cel. Travellers, III. 262 – 326.)

Leyden (John), *M.D.* Life. (Chambers's Miscel., IX. no. 152, pp. 6 – 13.)

Lincoln (*Maj.-Gen.* Benjamin). Life of B. L., Major-General in the Army of the Revolution; by Francis Bowen. (Sparks's Amer. Biogr., 2d Ser., XIII. 205 – 434.)

Linné (Carl von) [*originally* Linnæus (Carl)]. Memoir. (Distinguished Men of Mod. Times, II. 129 – 141.)

——— Anecdotes of Linnæus, translated from Fabricius, of Kiel. With a List of his Works. (Jardine's Nat. Libr., VI. i. – xv.)

——— Memoir. (Jardine's Nat. Libr., VI. 25 – 92.)

Little Captive King (The). *See* [Louis XVII.].

Liverpool, Robert Banks, 2*d Earl of. See* Jenkinson.

Liverseege (Henry). Life. (Cunningham's Lives of Brit. Painters, *etc.* V. 249 – 261.)

Locke (John). Memoir. (Distinguished Men of Mod. Times, II. 32 – 44.)

Londonderry, Robert, 2*d Marquis of. See* Stewart.

Lope de Vega. *See* Vega Carpio (Lope Felix de).

[Lopouloff (Prascovie *or* Prasca)], the Heroine of Siberia. (Chambers's Miscel., II. no. 36.)

Lorenzo de' Medici. *See* Medici.

Loughborough, Alexander, 1*st Baron. See* Wedderburn.

[Louis XVII.] *of France.* The Little Captive King. (Chambers's Miscel., III. no. 47.)

Louis-Philippe, *King of the French.* Life. (Chambers's Miscel., I. no. 1.)

L'Ouverture (Toussaint) and the Republic of Hayti. (Chambers's Miscel., III. no. 57.)

Louvois (François Michel Le Tellier, *Marquis* de). Life, by G. P. R. James. (Lardner's Cab. Cycl., **85**, pp. 282 – 320.)

Loyola *or* Loiola (Ignacio *or* Ignatius de). *See* Ignacio de Loyola.

Lulli (Jean Baptiste). Story of Baptiste Lulli. (Chambers's Miscel., II. no. 29.)

Luther (Martin). The Life of M. L. Gathered from his own Writings. By M. Michelet . . . . Translated by G. H. Smith . . . . New York. 1846. 12°

——— The Life of L.; with special reference to its Earlier Periods and the Opening Scenes of the Reformation. By Barnas Sears, D.D. Philadelphia: American Sunday School Union. [1850.] 12°

——— Luther and the Reformation. (Stephen (*Sir* J.). . . . Essays, pp. 100 – 149.)

Macdonald (Flora). Life. (Chambers's Miscel., III. no. 50.)

[MACGREGOR CAMPBELL (Rob Roy)]. Rob Roy and the Clan Macgregor. (CHAMBERS'S Miscel., VII. no. 117.)

MACHIAVELLI (Niccolò). Life. (LARDNER'S Cab. Cycl., **88**, pp. 256 - 312.)

MACKINTOSH (*Sir* James). Memoirs .... Edited by his Son, Robert James Mackintosh .... From the 2d London Ed. ... 2 vols. Boston. 1853. Large 12° (6.)

MADOC GWYNNETH. (BELKNAP'S Amer. Biogr., I. 129 - 137.)

MAHOMET. *See* MOHAMMED.

MANNY (*Sir* Walter); being a Specimen of the Military Commander during the Chivalrous Age. Life, by G. R. Gleig. (LARDNER'S Cab. Cycl., **67**, pp. 63 - 123.)

MANSEL (*Sir* Robert). Life, by Robert Bell. (LARDNER'S Cab. Cycl., **74**, pp. 39 - 65.)

MANSFIELD, William, 1*st Earl of.* *See* MURRAY.

MAN WITH THE IRON MASK. *See* [MATTHIOLI (G.)], *Count.*

MARGARET *of Anjou, Queen of Henry VI.* Life. (STRICKLAND'S Queens of England, III. 123 - 204.)

MARGUERITE *of France, Second Queen of Edward I.* Life. (STRICKLAND'S Queens of England, II. 109 - 121.)

MARIA ANTOINETTE, *Queen of France.* History .... By John S. C. Abbott. With Engravings. New York. [1849 ?] 16°

MARIA THERESA, *Empress of Germany and Queen of Hungary.* Memoir. (JAMESON'S Memoirs of Cel. Female Sovereigns, II. 126 - 198.)

MARINI (Giambattista). Life. (LARDNER'S Cab. Cycl., **89**, pp. 174 - 179.)

MARLBOROUGH, John, 1*st Duke of.* *See* CHURCHILL.

MARQUETTE (Jacques [*not* Joseph]). Life of Father M., by Jared Sparks. (SPARKS'S Amer. Biogr., X. 263 - 299.)

MARTEN (Henry *or* Harry). Life, by John Forster. (LARDNER'S Cab. Cycl., **79**, pp. 241 - 406.)

MARTYR (Peter). *See* ANGHIERA (Pietro Martire D').

MARY I. *Queen of England and Ireland.* Life. (STRICKLAND'S Queens of England, V. 99 - 295.)

MARY II. *Queen of Great Britain and Ireland.* Life. (STRICKLAND'S Queens of England, X. 185 - 315, XI. 9 - 222.)

MARY, *Queen of Scots.* History .... By Jacob Abbott. With Engravings. New York. [1848 ?] 16°

——— Life of M. .... By Henry Glassford Bell .... 2 vols. New York. 1846. [Vol. I. N. D.] 18° (HARPER'S Fam. Libr., **21, 22.**)

——— Memoir. (JAMESON'S Memoirs of Cel. Female Sovereigns, I. 171 - 213.)

——— *See* ELIZABETH, *Queen of England.*

MARY BEATRICE *of Modena, Consort of James II.* Life. (STRICKLAND'S Queens of England, IX., X. 9 – 184.)

MASERS DE LA TUDE (Henri). The Story of De la Tude. [Abridged from his own Narrative.] (CHAMBERS'S Miscel., VI. no. 105.)

MASON (John). Life of J. M., of Connecticut; by George E. Ellis. (SPARKS'S Amer. Biogr., 2d Ser., III. 307 – 438.)

MASSINGER (Philip). Life. (LARDNER'S Cab. Cycl., **96**, pp. 252 – 295.)

MATHER (Cotton). Life of C. M.; by William B. O. Peabody. (SPARKS'S Amer. Biogr., VI. 161 – 350.)

MATILDA *of Boulogne, Queen of Stephen.* Life. (STRICKLAND'S Queens of England, I. 142 – 165.)

MATILDA *of Flanders, Queen of William the Conqueror.* Life. (STRICKLAND'S Queens of England, I. 17 – 78.)

MATILDA *of Scotland, Queen of Henry I.* Life. (STRICKLAND'S Queens of England, I. 79 – 118.)

[MATTHIOLI (Girolamo)], *Count,* said to be "the Man with the Iron Mask." (CHAMBERS'S Miscel., VIII. no. 131.)

MATSYS (Quintin), the Blacksmith of Antwerp. (CHAMBERS'S Miscel., VII. no. 126.)

MAUNDRELL (Henry). Life. (ST. JOHN'S Lives of Cel. Travellers, I. 305 – 319.)

MAURICE, *Elector of Saxony.* Life. *See* GRANVELLE (A. P.), *Cardinal.*

MAXWELL (James). Heroism. (CHAMBERS'S Miscel., I. no. 12, pp. 13 – 16.)

MAZARIN (Jules), *Cardinal.* Life, by G. P. R. James. (LARDNER'S Cab. Cycl., **84**, pp. 269 – 326.)

MEDICI (Giovanni DE'), afterwards *Pope* LEO X. *See* LEO X.

MEDICI (Lorenzo DE'). Life, by Eyre Evans Crowe. (LARDNER'S Cab. Cycl., **83**, pp. 314 – 330.)

——— Lorenzo de' Medici, considered as a Poet; Marsiglio Ficino, Giovanni Pico della Mirandola, Angelo Poliziano (Politian), the Pulci (Bernardo, Luca, and Luigi), Francesco Bello *or* Cieco da Ferrara, and Domenico Burchiello. Lives. (LARDNER'S Cab. Cycl., **88**, pp. 151 – 180.)

——— The Life of L. de' M., called the Magnificent. By William Roscoe. 8th Ed., revised by his Son, Thomas Roscoe. London. 1846. 8° (BOHN'S Stand. Libr.)

MELVILLE, Henry, 1*st Viscount.* *See* DUNDAS.

MENDOZA (Diego Hurtado DE). Life. (LARDNER'S Cab. Cycl., **90**, pp. 58 – 69.)

MERIAN (Maria Sibilla), Memoir of. (JARDINE'S Nat. Libr., XXX. 17 – 46.)

METASTASIO (Pietro Antonio Domenico Buonaventura). Life. (LARDNER'S Cab. Cycl., **89**, pp. 185 – 212.)

MILTIADES. Campaigns and Character. (HERBERT'S Captains, *etc.* pp. 52 – 96. — *See* Part I.)

MILTON (John). Life, by Robert Bell. (LARDNER'S Cab. Cycl., **93**, pp. 138 – 263.)

——— Remarks on the Character and Writings of J. M. (CHANNING'S Works, I. 3 – 68.)

——— Memoir. (DISTINGUISHED Men of Mod. Times, I. 290 – 308.)

MIRABEAU (Honoré Gabriel RIQUETTI, *Marquis* DE). Life. (LARDNER'S Cab. Cycl., **92**, pp. 195 – 259.)

MIRABEAU Family. Sketch. (BROUGHAM'S "Hist. Sketches of Statesmen," *etc.* 2d Ser., II. 75 – 108.)

MOHAMMED. The Life of M. . . . . By the Rev. George Bush . . . . New York. 1847. 18° (HARPER'S Fam. Libr., **10.**)

——— Life of Mahomet. [By John A. Roebuck.] *See* Part I. SOCIETY, *etc.* . . . Lives, *etc.*

——— Mahomet and his Successors. By Washington Irving. . . . 2 vols. New-York. 1850. 12° (IRVING'S Works, Vol. XII. XIII.)

MOLIÈRE (Jean Baptiste POQUELIN DE). Life. (LARDNER'S Cab. Cycl., **91**, pp. 97 – 149.)

MOÑINO (José [Francisco Antonio ?]), *Count de Florida Blanca. See* FLORIDA BLANCA.

MONMOUTH, Charles, 1*st Earl of. See* MORDAUNT.

MONSON (*Sir* William). Life, by Robert Bell. (LARDNER'S Cab. Cycl., **74**, pp. 66 – 188.)

MONTAGUE (Edward), 1*st Earl of Sandwich.* Life, by Robert Bell. (LARDNER'S Cab. Cycl., **74**, pp. 222 – 311.)

MONTAGUE (*Lady* Mary Wortley). (CHAMBERS'S Papers, *etc.* VIII. no. 64.)

——— Life. (ST. JOHN'S Lives of Cel. Travellers, II. 72 – 100.)

MONTAIGNE (Michel DE). Life. (LARDNER'S Cab. Cycl., **91**, pp. 1 – 22.)

MONTGOMERY (*Maj.-Gen.* Richard). Life of R. M. By John Armstrong. (SPARKS'S Amer. Biogr., I. 181 – 226; — SCHOOL Libr., VI. 355 – 384.)

MONTI (Vincenzo). Life. (LARDNER'S Cab. Cycl., **89**, pp. 303 – 352.)

MONTS (Pierre DU GUAST, *Sieur* DE). De Monts, Poutrincourt, and Champlain. (BELKNAP'S Amer. Biogr., II. 15 – 46.)

MOORE (*Sir* John). Life, by G. R. Gleig. (LARDNER'S Cab. Cycl., **69**, pp. 251 – 358.)

MOORE (Thomas). (CHAMBERS'S Papers, *etc.* X. no. 80.)

MORDAUNT (Charles), 1*st Earl of Monmouth, and* 3*d Earl of Peterborough.* Life, by G. R. Gleig. (LARDNER'S Cab. Cycl., **68**, pp. 228 – 316.)

MORE (*Sir* Thomas). Life, by Sir James Mackintosh. (LARDNER'S Cab. Cycl., **76**, pp. 1 – 110.)

MORLAND (George). Life. (CUNNINGHAM'S Lives of Brit. Painters, *etc.* II. 184 – 207.)

MORTIMER (John Hamilton). Life. (CUNNINGHAM's Lives of Brit. Painters, *etc.* IV. 158 – 172.)

MOTIER (Marie Paul Joseph Roch Ives Gilbert DE), *Marquis de Lafayette.* *See* LAFAYETTE.

MOZART (Johann Chrysostomus Wolfgang Gottlieb). Memoir. (DISTINGUISHED Men of Mod. Times, II. 172 – 181.)

MURPHY (Arthur). Life. (LARDNER's Cab. Cycl., **97**, pp. 321 – 339.)

MURRAY (Alexander), *D.D.* Life. (CHAMBERS's Miscel., IX. no. 152, pp. 13 – 24.)

MURRAY (William), 1*st Earl of Mansfield.* (BROUGHAM's "Hist. Sketches of Statesmen," *etc.* 1st Ser., I. 115 – 135.)

——— Life, by Henry Roscoe. (LARDNER's Cab. Cycl., **75**, pp. 171 – 228.)

NAPOLEON I. *Emperor of the French.* Napoleon —Washington. (BROUGHAM's "Hist. Sketches of Statesmen," *etc.* 2d Ser., II. 179 – 196.

——— Remarks on the Life and Character of Napoleon Bonaparte. (CHANNING's Works, I. 69 – 166.)

——— The History of Napoleon Buonaparte. By J. G. Lockhart .... 2 vols. New-York. 1843. 18° (HARPER's Fam. Libr., **4, 5.**)

——— The Life of Napoleon. By Sir Walter Scott. Three volumes complete in one. Philadelphia. 1841. 8° (4. and 6.) pp. 702.

NECKER (Jacques). Sketch. (BROUGHAM's "Hist. Sketches of Statesmen," *etc.* 2d Ser., II. 41 – 56.)

——— Life, by G. P. R. James. (LARDNER's Cab. Cycl. **87**, pp. 240 – 314.)

NEGRO Slave. *See* [BALL (Charles)].

NELSON (Horatio), *Viscount Nelson.* The Life of Nelson. (CHAMBERS's Miscel., II. no. 22.)

——— The Life of Nelson. By Robert Southey .... New-York. N. D. 18° (HARPER's Fam. Libr., **6.**)

——— *See* JERVIS (J.), 1*st Viscount and Earl St. Vincent.*

NERO, *Emperor of Rome.* History of Nero. By Jacob Abbott. With Engravings. New York. 1853. 16°

NEWTON (*Sir* Isaac). The Life of Sir I. N. By David Brewster. .... New York. 1848. 18° (HARPER's Fam. Libr., **26.**)

——— Life. [Translated by Howard Elphinstone from that in the "Biographie Universelle," by J. B. Biot.] *See* Part I. SOCIETY, *etc.* ... Lives, *etc.*

——— Memoir. (DISTINGUISHED Men of Mod. Times, II. 72 – 87.)

NICUESA (Diego DE). Sketch of his Life. (IRVING's Life of Columbus, *etc.* III. 102 – 137.)

NIEBUHR (Carsten). Life. [By Mrs. Sarah Austin.] *See* Part I. SOCIETY, *etc.* ... Lives, *etc.*

——— Life. (ST. JOHN's Lives of Cel. Travellers, III. 99 – 154.)

NOLLEKENS (Joseph). Life. (CUNNINGHAM'S Lives of Brit. Painters and Sculptors, III. 108 – 173.)

NORTH (Francis), 1*st Earl of Guilford.* Life, by Henry Roscoe. (LARDNER'S Cab. Cycl., **75,** pp. 83 – 113.)

NORTH (Frederick), 2*d Earl of Guilford.* (BROUGHAM'S "Hist. Sketches of Statesmen," *etc.* 1st Ser., I. 61 – 79 ; comp. II. 204 – 210.)

NORTHCOTE (James). Life. (CUNNINGHAM'S Lives of Brit. Painters, *etc.* V. 48 – 117.)

NOTTINGHAM, Charles, 1*st Earl of.* *See* HOWARD.

OBERLIN (Jean Frédéric). Life. (CHAMBERS'S Miscel., V. no. 87.)

OEIRAS *or* OEYRAS (Sebastião José CARVALHO E MELLO), *Count of, and Marquis of Pombal.* *See* POMBAL.

OGLETHORPE (James). Life of J. O., the Founder of Georgia ; by William B. O. Peabody. (SPARKS'S Amer. Biogr., 2d Ser., II. 201 – 405.)

OLDEN-BARNEVELDT (Johan *or* Jan VAN). Life, by Eyre Evans Crowe. (LARDNER'S Cab. Cycl., **83,** pp. 153 – 210.)

OLIVAREZ (Gaspar DE GUZMAN), *Count, and Duke of San Lucar.* Life, by G. P. R. James. (LARDNER'S Cab. Cycl., **84,** pp. 220 – 268.)

OJEDA (Alonso DE). *See* HOJEDA.

OPIE (John). Life. (CUNNINGHAM'S Lives of Brit. Painters, *etc.* II. 156 – 183.)

OSBORNE (Thomas), 1*st Earl of Danby, and Duke of Leeds.* Life, by Thomas P. Courtenay. (LARDNER'S Cab. Cycl., **80,** pp. 198 – 375.)

OSSUÑA *or* OSSUNO (Pedro TELLEZ Y GIRON), *Duke of.* Life, by Eyre Evans Crowe. (LARDNER'S Cab. Cycl., **83,** pp. 282 – 313.)

OTIS (James). Lives of James Otis [by Francis Bowen] and James Oglethorpe. Boston. 1844. 16° (SPARKS'S Amer. Biogr., 2d Ser., Vol. II.)

OTWAY (Thomas). Life. (LARDNER'S Cab. Cycl., **97,** pp. 123 – 133.)

OWEN (William). Life. (CUNNINGHAM'S Lives of Brit. Painters, *etc.* IV. 214 – 228.)

OXENSTIERNA (Axel), *Count.* Life, by G. P. R. James. (LARDNER'S Cab. Cycl., **84,** pp. 176 – 212.)

PAINE (Robert Troup). Memoir of R. T. P. By his Parents [Martyn Paine, M.D., and Mary Ann Paine]. ... Printed for Private Distribution, especially for the Classmates of the Youth. New-York. 1852. 4°

PALFREY (William). Life of W. P., Paymaster-General in the Army of the Revolution ; by John Gorham Palfrey. (SPARKS'S Amer. Biogr., 2d Ser., VII. 355 – 448.)

PALLAS (Peter Simon). Memoir. (JARDINE'S Nat. Libr., XVIII. 17 – 76.)

——— Life. (ST. JOHN'S Lives of Cel. Travellers, III. 65 – 98.)

PARK (Mungo). Life. (ST. JOHN'S Lives of Cel. Travellers, III. 13 – 65.)

——— The Life and Travels of M. P. *See* Class XXIII. LIFE, *etc.*

PARKER (Nathan), *D.D.* Memoir. (WARE's Works, II. 25 - 84.)

PARR (Samuel), *LL.D.* Memoirs of the Life, Writings, and Opinions of the Rev. S. P. ... ; with Biographical Notices of many of his Friends, Pupils, and Contemporaries. By the Rev. William Field. ... 2 vols. London. 1828. 8°

PASCAL (Blaise). Memoir. (DISTINGUISHED Men of Mod. Times, I. 267 - 278.)

——— Life. (LARDNER's Cab. Cycl., **91**, pp. 183 - 213.)

PAUSANIAS. Campaigns and Character. (HERBERT's Captains, *etc.* pp. 137 - 171. — *See* Part I.)

PEEL (*Sir* Robert). (CHAMBERS's Papers, *etc.* IV. no. 32.)

PELLICO (Silvio). Story of S. P. [Abridged from his own Narrative, translated from the original Italian.] (CHAMBERS's Miscel., V. no. 89.)

PENN (William). Life. (BELKNAP's Amer. Biogr., III. 225 - 292.)

——— Life. (CHAMBERS's Miscel., VIII. no. 128.)

——— Memoir. (DISTINGUISHED Men of Mod. Times, II. 56 - 71.)

——— Life of W. P.; by George E. Ellis. (SPARKS's Amer. Biogr., 2d Ser., XII. 193 - 408.)

PENNANT (Thomas). Memoir. (JARDINE's Nat. Libr., VII. 1 - 65.)

PERCEVAL (Spencer). Sketch. (BROUGHAM's "Hist. Sketches of Statesmen," *etc.* 1st Ser., II. 53 - 59.)

PÉRON (François). Memoir. (JARDINE's Nat. Libr., XXV. 17 - 36.)

PERRENOT (Antoine), *Cardinal Granvelle. See* GRANVELLE.

PERRY (*Commodore* Oliver Hazard). The Life of Commodore O. H. P. By Alex. Slidell Mackenzie ... . 2 vols. New-York. [1840 ?] 18° (HARPER's Fam. Libr., **126, 127.**)

PETER *the Great, Czar of Russia.* A Memoir of the Life of Peter the Great. By John Barrow ... . New-York. 1848. 18° (HARPER's Fam. Libr., **65.**)

——— Life. (CHAMBERS's Miscel., VI. no. 104.)

PETERBOROUGH, Charles, *3d Earl of. See* MORDAUNT.

PETRARCA (Francesco). Life and Times of Petrarch. With Notices of Boccacio and his illustrious Contemporaries. By Thomas Campbell, Esq. 2d Ed. ... 2 vols. London. 1843. 8°

——— Life. (LARDNER's Cab. Cycl., **88**, pp. 61 - 115.)

PHILIPPA *of Hainault, Queen of Edward III.* Life. (STRICKLAND's Queens of England, II. 173 - 205.)

PHIPS (*Sir* William). Lives of Sir William Phips [by Francis Bowen], Israel Putnam, Lucretia Maria Davidson, and David Rittenhouse. New-York. 1845. 16° or 12° (8. and 6.) (SPARKS's Amer. Biogr., Vol. VII.)

PIKE (*Brig.-Gen.* Zebulon Montgomery). Life of Z. M. P.; by Henry Whiting. (SPARKS's Amer. Biogr., V. 217 - 314.)

PINKNEY (William). Lives of William Pinkney [by Henry Wheaton],

William Ellery, and Cotton Mather. New-York. 1844. 16° or 12° (8. and 6.) (SPARKS's Amer. Biogr., Vol. VI.)

PINKNEY (William). Life of W. P.; by Henry Wheaton. (SCHOOL Libr., VI. 1 – 54.)

PINZON (Vicente Yañez). Sketch of his Life. (IRVING's Life of Columbus, *etc.* III. 39 – 46.)

PITT (William), 1*st Earl of Chatham.* (BROUGHAM's "Hist. Sketches of Statesmen," *etc.* 1st Ser., I. 31 – 57; comp. II. 203.)

——— Memoir. (DISTINGUISHED Men of Mod. Times, II. 113 – 129.)

——— Life. (MACAULAY's Essays, II. 244 – 285.)

PITT (William), *the Younger.* (BROUGHAM's "Hist. Sketches of Statesmen," *etc.* 1st Ser., I. 211 – 223.)

——— Memoir. (DISTINGUISHED Men of Mod. Times, II. 233 – 248.)

PITTON DE TOURNEFORT (Joseph). *See* TOURNEFORT.

PLATO. Life, by William Lowndes. (ENCYCL. Metrop., X. 72 – 90.)

PLESSIS (Armand Jean DU), *Cardinal de Richelieu.* *See* RICHELIEU.

PLINIUS SECUNDUS (Caius), *the Elder.* Memoir of Pliny. (JARDINE's Nat. Libr., IX. 17 – 82.)

PLOTINUS and the later Platonists. By J. A. Jeremie. (ENCYCL. Metrop., XI. 209 – 216.)

POCOCKE (Richard). Life. (ST. JOHN's Lives of Cel. Travellers, II. 101 – 125.)

POLO (Marco). Account of M. P. (IRVING's Life of Columbus, *etc.* III. 384 – 392.)

——— Life. (ST. JOHN's Lives of Cel. Travellers, I. 30 – 69.)

POMBAL (Sebastião José CARVALHO E MELLO), *Count of Oeiras, and Marquis of.* Life, by G. P. R. James. (LARDNER's Cab. Cycl., **87**, pp. 103 – 156.)

PONCE DE LEON (Juan). Sketch of his Life. (IRVING's Life of Columbus, *etc.* III. 262 – 288.)

PONCE DE LEON (Luis). *See* LEON.

POPE (Alexander). Life, by Robert Bell. (LARDNER's Cab. Cycl., **94**, pp. 264 – 326.)

——— Life and Writings. (THACKERAY's English Humourists.)

POSEY (*Maj.-Gen.* Thomas). Life of T. P. ... Governor of Indiana; by James Hall. (SPARKS's Amer. Biogr., 2d Ser., IX. 359 – 403.)

POUTRINCOURT (Jean DE). *See* MONTS (P. DU GUAST, *Sieur* DE.)

PREBLE (*Commodore* Edward). Lives of Edward Preble [by Lorenzo Sabine] and William Penn. Boston. 1847. 16° (SPARKS's Amer. Biogr., 2d Ser., Vol. XII.)

PRIESTLEY (Joseph), *LL.D.* Life. (BROUGHAM's Lives of Men of Letters and Science, *etc.* pp. 236 – 249.)

PRING (Martin). *See* GOSNOLD (B.).

PRIOR (Matthew). Life, by Robert Bell. (LARDNER's Cab. Cycl., **94**, pp. 232 – 263.)

——— Life and Writings. (THACKERAY's English Humourists.)

PULASKI (Casimir), *Count.* Life of Count P.; by Jared Sparks. (SPARKS's Amer. Biogr., 2d Ser., IV. 365 - 446.)

PUTNAM (*Maj.-Gen.* Israel). Life of I. P.; by Oliver W. B. Peabody. (SPARKS's Amer. Biogr., VII. 103 - 218; — SCHOOL Libr., V. 239 - 312.)

PYM (John). Life, by John Forster. (LARDNER's Cab. Cycl., **78**, pp. 1 - 305.)

QUEVEDO Y VILLÉGAS (Francisco Gomez DE). Life. (LARDNER's Cab. Cycl., **90**, pp. 255 - 277.)

RABELAIS (François). Life. (LARDNER's Cab. Cycl., **91**, pp. 23 - 39.)

RACINE (Jean). Life. (LARDNER's Cab. Cycl., **91**, pp. 296 - 328.)

RADCLIFFE (James), *3d and last Earl of Derwentwater.* (CHAMBERS's Miscel., II. no. 35.)

RAEBURN (*Sir* Henry). Life. (CUNNINGHAM's Lives of Brit. Painters, *etc.* IV. 172 - 203.)

RAFFLES (*Sir* Thomas Stamford), and the Spice Islands. (CHAMBERS's Miscel., III. no. 53.)

——— Memoir. (JARDINE's Nat. Libr., VIII. 17 - 88.)

RALE, RALLE, RASLE, *or* RASLES (Sébastien). Life of Sebastian Rale, Missionary to the Indians; by Convers Francis. (SPARKS's Amer. Biogr., 2d Ser., VII. 157 - 333.)

RALEIGH *or* RALEGH (*Sir* Walter). Memoir. (DISTINGUISHED Men of Mod. Times, I. 135 - 151.)

——— Life, by Robert Southey. (LARDNER's Cab. Cycl., **73**, pp. 209 - 440.)

——— and Richard GRENVILLE. Lives. (BELKNAP's Amer. Biogr., I. 289 - 370.)

RAMSAY (Allan). Life. (CUNNINGHAM's Lives of Brit. Painters, *etc.* IV. 33 - 42.)

RASLE *or* RASLES (Sébastien). *See* RALE.

RAY (John). Memoir. (JARDINE's Nat. Libr., XXXIII. 17 - 70.)

REED (Joseph). Life of J. R.; by Henry Reed. (SPARKS's Amer. Biogr., 2d Ser., VIII. 209 - 439.)

RETZ (Jean François Paul DE GONDI, *Cardinal* DE). Life, by G. P. R. James. (LARDNER's Cab. Cycl., **85**, pp. 1 - 107.)

REYNOLDS (*Sir* Joshua). Life. (CUNNINGHAM's Lives of Brit. Painters, *etc.* I. 186 - 281.)

RIBAULT (Jean). Lives of John Ribault [comprising an account of the first attempts of the French to found a colony in North America; by Jared Sparks], Sebastian Rale, and William Palfrey. Boston. 1845. 16° (SPARKS's Amer. Biogr., 2d Ser., Vol. VII.)

RIBEIRO (Bernardim), Saa de MIRANDA, Gil VICENTE, and Antonio FERREIRA, early Poets of Portugal. (LARDNER's Cab. Cycl., **90**, pp. 288 - 294.)

RICARDO (David). *See* HORNER (F.).

RICHELIEU (Armand Jean DU PLESSIS, *Cardinal and Duke* DE). Life, by G. P. R. James. (LARDNER'S Cab. Cycl., **84**, pp. 1 – 175.)

RIPPERDA (Johan Willem), *Duke of.* Life, by G. P. R. James. (LARDNER'S Cab. Cycl., **86**, pp. 268 – 325.)

RIQUETTI (Honoré Gabriel), *Marquis de Mirabeau.* *See* MIRABEAU.

RITTENHOUSE (David). Life of D. R.; by James Renwick. (SPARKS'S Amer. Biogr., VII. 295 – 398; — SCHOOL Libr., V. 313 – 376.)

ROBERTSON (William). Life. (BROUGHAM'S Lives of Men of Letters, *etc.* pp. 157 – 193.)

ROBINSON (*Rev.* John). Life. (BELKNAP'S Amer. Biogr., II. 254 – 294.)

ROB ROY. *See* [MACGREGOR CAMPBELL (Rob Roy)].

[ROBUSTI (Marietta)]. The Tintoretto. (CHAMBERS'S Miscel., IV. no. 72.)

Note. Jacopo Robusti, the father of Marietta, was named the "Tintoretto."

ROCHEFOUCAULD (François, *Duke* DE LA). *See* LA ROCHEFOUCAULD.

ROCHEJAQUELEIN (Henri DUVERGIER, *Count* DE LA). *See* LA ROCHEJAQUELEIN.

ROLAND DE LA PLATIÈRE (Manon Jeanne PHLIPON *or* PHELIPON), *Madame.* History .... By John S. C. Abbott. With Engravings. New York. [1850 ?] 16°

——— Madame Roland and the Girondins. (CHAMBERS'S Miscel., V. no. 91.)

——— Life. (LARDNER'S Cab. Cycl., **92**, pp. 260 – 294.)

ROMILLY (*Sir* Samuel). Sketch. (BROUGHAM'S "Hist. Sketches of Statesmen," *etc.* 1st Ser., II. 105 – 112.)

——— Life, by Henry Roscoe. (LARDNER'S Cab. Cycl., **75**, 391 – 410.)

ROMNEY (George). Life. (CUNNINGHAM'S Lives of Brit. Painters, *etc.* IV. 43 – 124.)

ROMULUS. History of Romulus. By Jacob Abbott. With Engravings. New York. 1852. 16°

RONDELET (Guillaume). Memoir. (JARDINE'S Nat. Libr., XXXVI. 17 – 44.)

ROUBILIAC (Louis Francis). Life. (CUNNINGHAM'S Lives of Brit. Painters and Sculptors, III. 31 – 61.)

ROUSSEAU (Jean Jacques). Life. (BROUGHAM'S Lives of Men of Letters, *etc.* pp. 92 – 120.)

——— Life (A. H. EVERETT'S Essays, 2d Ser., pp. 301 – 324.)

——— Life. (LARDNER'S Cab. Cycl., **92**, pp. 111 – 174.)

ROXAS DE SANDOVAL (Francisco Gomez DE), *Duke of Lerma.* *See* LERMA.

RUBRUQUIS (Gulielmus *or* William DE). *See* RUYSBROEK.

RUMFORD, Benjamin, *Count.* *See* THOMPSON.

RUNCIMAN (Alexander). Life. (CUNNINGHAM'S Lives of Brit. Painters, *etc.* IV. 125 – 138.)

RUYSBROEK [*Lat.* RUBRUQUIS] (Willem DE). Life. (ST. JOHN'S Lives of Cel. Travellers, I. 17 – 29.)

SAAVEDRA (Miguel DE CERVANTES). *See* CERVANTES SAAVEDRA.

SAILOR Boy. *See* [LEECH (Samuel)].

ST. JOHN (Henry), *Viscount Bolingbroke.* Life. (Prefixed to his Works, 1841. 8° I. 13 – 107.)

ST. PIERRE (Jacques Henri Bernardin DE). Life. (A. H. EVERETT'S Essays, pp. 67 – 101.)

ST. VINCENT, John, 1*st Viscount and Earl.* *See* JERVIS.

SALISBURY, Robert, 1*st Earl of.* *See* CECIL.

SALLE (Robert Cavelier DE LA). *See* LA SALLE.

SALVIANI (Ippolito). Memoir. (JARDINE'S Nat. Libr., XXXV. 17 – 43.)

SANDWICH, Edward, 1*st Earl of.* *See* MONTAGUE.

SAN LUCAR (Gaspar DE GUZMAN), *Duke of.* *See* OLIVAREZ.

SCHILLER (Johann Christoph Friedrich VON). The Life and Writings of Schiller. (A. H. EVERETT'S Essays, pp. 102 – 138.)

SCHOMBURGK (Robert Hermann). Memoir. (JARDINE'S Nat. Libr., XXXIX. 17 – 79.)

SCHWARTZ (Christian Friedrich). Memoir. (DISTINGUISHED Men of Mod. Times, II. 208 – 221.)

SCOTT (John), 1*st Earl of Eldon.* (BROUGHAM'S "Hist. Sketches of Statesmen," *etc.* 2d Ser., I. 69 – 88.)

SCOTT (*Sir* Walter), *Bart.* Life. (CHAMBERS'S Miscel., IX. no. 144.)

——— Memoir. (DISTINGUISHED Men of Mod. Times, II. 303 – 317.)

——— Memoirs. . . . . By J. G. Lockhart. 7 vols. Philadelphia. 1839. 12°

SCOTT (*Sir* William), 1*st Baron Stowell.* Sketch. (BROUGHAM'S "Hist. Sketches of Statesmen," *etc.* 2d Ser., I. 91 – 99.)

SELDEN (John). Life, by Henry Roscoe. (LARDNER'S Cab. Cycl., **75**, pp. 43 – 59.)

SELKIRK (Alexander). Life. (CHAMBERS'S Miscel., VIII. no. 140.)

SEMIRAMIS. Memoir. (JAMESON'S Memoirs of Cel. Female Sovereigns, I. 25 – 31.)

SENECA (Lucius Annæus). Life, by William Lowndes. (ENCYCL. Metrop., X. 483 – 491.)

SÉVIGNÉ (Marie DE RABUTIN-CHANTAL, *Marchioness* DE). Madame de Sévigné; her Life and Letters. (CHAMBERS'S Repos., I. no. 4.)

——— Life. (LARDNER'S Cab. Cycl., **91**, pp. 214 – 258.)

SEXTUS EMPIRICUS and the Pyrrhonists. By J. A. Jeremie. (ENCYCL. Metrop., X. 698 – 704.)

SHADWELL (Thomas). Life. (LARDNER'S Cab. Cycl., **97**, pp. 155 – 164.)

SHAKESPEARE (William). Memoir. (DISTINGUISHED Men of Mod. Times, I. 125 - 135.)

——— Life. [With a history of the Stage immediately prior to Shakespeare, and in the time of Shakespeare; including notices of Richard Edwards, Thomas Sackville (Earl of Dorset), Thomas Norton, Thomas Preston, George Gascoyne, Robert Greene, Christopher Marlowe, Thomas Kyd, George Peele, John Lyly, Thomas Nash, Henry Chettle, and other dramatists.] (LARDNER's Cab. Cycl., **96**, pp. 1 - 130.)

——— Shakspere: his Times and Contemporaries. By George Tweddell. ... London. 1852. 18° (12. 6.)

——— *See* Class XVII. HUDSON (H. N.). Lectures on S., *etc.*

SHAW (Thomas). Life. (ST. JOHN's Lives of Cel. Travellers, II. 19 - 52.)

SHERIDAN (Richard Brinsley). Sketch. (BROUGHAM's "Hist. Sketches of Statesmen," *etc.* 1st Ser., II. 11 - 18.)

SHIRLEY (James). Life. (LARDNER's Cab. Cycl., **97**, pp. 1 - 69.)

SIBBALD (*Sir* Robert). Memoir. (JARDINE's Nat. Libr., I. 17 - 67.)

SIMSON (Robert). Life. (BROUGHAM's Lives of Men of Letters and Science, *etc.* pp. 270 - 295.)

SINCLAIR (*Sir* John), *Bart.* (CHAMBERS's Repos., II. no. 13.)

SLOANE (*Sir* Hans). Memoir. (JARDINE's Nat. Libr., XXIII. 17 - 92.)

SMELLIE (William). Memoir. (JARDINE's Nat. Libr., II. 17 - 44.)

SMITH (*Prof.* Adam), *LL.D.* Life. [By William Draper.] *See* Part I. SOCIETY, *etc.* ... Lives, *etc.*

SMITH (*Capt.* John). The Life and Adventures of Captain J. S.; by George S. Hillard. (SPARKS's Amer. Biogr., II. 171 - 407; — SCHOOL Libr., IV. 211 - 362.)

SMITH (*Sir* Thomas). Life. (BELKNAP's Amer. Biogr., II. 100 - 114.)

SMOLLETT (Tobias), *M.D.* Life and Writings. (THACKERAY's English Humourists.)

SOBIESKI (John), *King of Poland.* *See* JOHN SOBIESKI.

SOCRATES. Life, by C. J. Blomfield. (ENCYCL. Metrop., IX. 669 - 685.)

——— Xenophon's Memorabilia of S., and Wiggers's Life of S. *See* Class XVI. Part II. XENOPHON.

SOMERS (John), *Baron of Evesham, and Lord Chancellor.* Life. [By David Jardine.] *See* Part I. SOCIETY, *etc.* ... Lives, *etc.*

——— Life, by Henry Roscoe. (LARDNER's Cab. Cycl., **75**, pp. 140 - 170.)

SOTO (Ferdinando DE). Account of. (BELKNAP's Amer. Biogr., I. 258 - 271.)

SPENSER (Edmund). Life. (LARDNER's Cab. Cycl., **95**, pp. 312-351.)

STAEL-HOLSTEIN (Anne Louise Germaine NECKER, *Baroness* DE). Sketch. (BROUGHAM's "Hist. Sketches of Statesmen," *etc.* 2d Ser., II. 59 - 72.)

——— Life. (LARDNER's Cab. Cycl., **92**, pp. 295 - 344.)

STANDISH (*Capt.* Miles). Life. (BELKNAP's Amer. Biogr., III. 116 - 147.)

STARK (*Maj.-Gen.* John). Lives of John Stark [by Edward Everett], Charles Brockden Brown, Richard Montgomery, and Ethan Allen. New York. 1839. 16° (SPARKS's Amer. Biogr., Vol. I.)

——— Life of Maj.-Gen. J. S.; by Edward Everett. (SCHOOL Libr., IV. 1 - 75.)

STEELE (*Sir* Richard). Life. (SPECTATOR. Selections, *etc.* 1840. 18° II. v. - xix.)

——— Life and Writings. (THACKERAY's English Humourists.)

STERNE (*Rev.* Laurence). Life and Writings. (THACKERAY's English Humourists.)

STEUBEN (Frederic William Augustus), *Baron.* Lives of Baron Steuben [by Francis Bowen], Sebastian Cabot, and William Eaton. New-York. 1844. 16° or 12° (8. and 6.) (SPARKS's Amer. Biogr., Vol. IX.)

STEWART, Robert, *2d Marquis of Londonderry, and 2d Viscount Castlereagh.* (BROUGHAM's "Hist. Sketches of Statesmen," *etc.* 2d Ser., I. 153 - 162.)

STILES (Ezra), *D.D., LL.D., President of Yale College.* Lives of Ezra Stiles [by James L. Kingsley], John Fitch, and Anne Hutchinson. Boston. 1845. 16° (SPARKS's Amer. Biogr., 2d Ser., Vol. VI.)

STOWELL, William, 1*st Baron.* *See* SCOTT.

STRAFFORD, Thomas, *Earl of.* *See* WENTWORTH.

SWAMMERDAM (Johan). Memoir. (JARDINE's Nat. Libr., XXVIII. 17 - 58.)

SWIFT (Jonathan), *D.D., Dean of St. Patrick's.* Life and Writings. (THACKERAY's English Humourists.)

SULLIVAN (*Maj.-Gen.* John). Lives of John Sullivan [by Oliver W. B. Peabody], Jacob Leisler, Nathaniel Bacon, and John Mason. Boston. 1844. 16° (SPARKS's Amer. Biogr., 2d Ser., Vol. III.)

SULLY (Maximilien DE BÉTHUNE, *Duke* DE). Life, by Eyre Evans Crowe. (LARDNER's Cab. Cycl., **83**, pp. 211 - 261.)

TALLEYRAND-PÉRIGORD (Charles Maurice DE). Sketch. (BROUGHAM's "Hist. Sketches of Statesmen," *etc.* 2d Ser., II. 161 - 176.)

TASSO (Torquato). Memoir. (DISTINGUISHED Men of Mod. Times, I. 103 - 113.)

——— Life. (LARDNER's Cab. Cycl., **89**, pp. 96 - 162.)

TASSONI (Alessandro). Life. (LARDNER's Cab. Cycl., **89**, pp. 169 - 173.)

TAVERNIER (Jean Baptiste). Life. (ST. JOHN's Lives of Cel. Travellers, I. 180 - 205.)

TELL (Wilhelm). William Tell and Switzerland. (CHAMBERS's Miscel., I. no. 9.)

TELLEZ Y GIRON (Pedro), *Duke of Ossuña.* *See* OSSUÑA.

TELLIER (François Michel LE), *Marquis de Louvois.* *See* LOUVOIS.

TEMPLE (*Sir* William). Life and Writings. (MACAULAY'S Essays, III. 167 - 256.)

THEMISTOCLES. Campaigns and Character. (HERBERT'S Captains, *etc.* pp. 97 - 136. — *See* Part I.)

THOMAS AQUINAS [*Ital.* TOMMASO D' AQUINO], *Saint.* Life, by R. D. Hampden, D.D. (ENCYCL. Metrop., XI. 793 - 814.)

THOMPSON (Benjamin), *Count Rumford.* Life. (CHAMBERS'S Miscel., X. no. 161.)

——— Lives of Count Rumford [by James Renwick], Zebulon Montgomery Pike, and Samuel Gorton. Boston. 1845. 16° (SPARKS'S Amer. Biogr., 2d Ser., Vol. V.)

THURLOW (Edward), 1*st Baron Thurlow.* Sketch. (BROUGHAM'S "Hist. Sketches of Statesmen," *etc.* 1st Ser., I. 101 - 111.)

——— Life, by Henry Roscoe. (LARDNER'S Cab. Cycl., **75**, pp. 258 - 287.)

TIERNEY (George). Sketch. (BROUGHAM'S "Hist. Sketches of Statesmen," *etc.* 2d Ser., I. 181 - 194.)

TINTORETTO (The). *See* [ROBUSTI (M.)].

TOOKE (John HORNE). Sketch. (BROUGHAM'S "Hist. Sketches of Statesmen," *etc.* 2d Ser., I. 133 - 149.)

TOURNEFORT (Joseph PITTON DE). Life. (ST. JOHN'S Lives of Cel. Travellers, II. 7 - 19.)

TOUSSAINT L'OUVERTURE. *See* L'OUVERTURE.

TRENCK (Friedrich, *Baron* VON). Story. (CHAMBERS'S Miscel., IV. no. 76.)

TRUMBULL (John). Autobiography, Reminiscences and Letters of J. T., from 1756 to 1841. New York & London. 1841. 8°

TUCKERMAN (Joseph), *D.D.* Discourse on his Life and Character. (CHANNING'S Works, VI. 91 - 146.)

TYNDALE (William), *the Martyr.* Memoir. [By George Offor, recast by J. P. Dabney.] *See* Class II. Part II. THE NEW TESTAMENT . . . . By William Tyndale, *etc.* 1837. 12°

ULLOA (Antonio DE). Life. (ST. JOHN'S Lives of Cel. Travellers, II. 320 - 338.)

VAILLANT (François LE). *See* LE VAILLANT.

VALERIANOS (Apostolos) *or* Juan de FUCA, Account of. (BELKNAP'S Amer. Biogr., II. 7 - 14.)

VALLE (Pietro DELLA). Life. (ST. JOHN'S Lives of Cel. Travellers, I. 149 - 180.)

VANBRUGH (*Sir* John). Life. (LARDNER'S Cab. Cycl., **97**, pp. 213 - 231.)

VANE (*Sir* Henry), *the Younger.* Life, by John Forster. (LARDNER'S Cab. Cycl., **79**, pp. 1 - 240.)

——— Life of Sir H. V., Fourth Governor of Massachusetts; by Charles Wentworth Upham. (SPARKS'S Amer. Biogr., IV. 85 - 403; — SCHOOL Libr., VI. 55 - 250.)

VEGA (Garcilasso DE LA). *See* GARCILASSO DE LA VEGA.

VEGA CARPIO (Lope Felix DE). Life. (LARDNER'S Cab. Cycl., **90**, pp. 189–237.)

VESPUCCI (Amerigo) [*Lat.* VESPUCIUS (Americus)]. Life. (IRVING'S Life of Columbus, *etc.* III. 330–345.)

VILLÉGAS (Estéban Manuel DE). *See* ESPINEL (V.).

VOLNEY (Constantin François CHASSEBŒUF, *Count* DE). Life. (ST. JOHN'S Lives of Cel. Travellers, III. 219–237.)

VOLTAIRE (François Marie AROUET DE). Life. (BROUGHAM'S Lives of Men of Letters and Science, *etc.* pp. 13–91.)

——— Private Life. (A. H. EVERETT'S Essays, pp. 172–200.)

——— Life. (LARDNER'S Cab. Cycl., **92**, pp. 1–110.)

WALKER (John), *D.D.* Memoir. (JARDINE'S Nat. Libr., III. 17–50.)

WALLACE (William), and Robert BRUCE. Lives. (CHAMBERS'S Miscel., II. no. 31.)

WALLER (Edmund). Life, by Robert Bell. (LARDNER'S Cab. Cycl., **93**, pp. 91–137.)

WARD (Samuel). Life of S. W., Governor of Rhode Island; by William Gammell. (SPARKS'S Amer. Biogr., 2d Ser., IX. 231–358.)

WARE (Henry), *Jr.*, *D.D.* Memoir of the Life of H. W., Jr. By his Brother, John Ware, M.D. ... New Ed. 2 vols. Boston. 1849–46. 12°

WARE (*Mrs.* Mary Lovell [PICKARD]). Memoir of Mary L. Ware, Wife of Henry Ware, Jr. By Edward B. Hall. 5th Thousand. Boston. 1853. 12°

WARREN (*Maj.-Gen.* Joseph), *M.D.* Life of J. W., by Alexander H. Everett. (SPARKS'S Amer. Biogr., X. 91–183; — SCHOOL Libr., V. 183–238.)

WASHINGTON (George). Life of W. (CHAMBERS'S Miscel., IV. no. 60.)

——— W. and his Contemporaries. (CHAMBERS'S Papers, *etc.* II. no. 10.)

——— Entertaining Anecdotes of W.; exhibiting his Patriotism, Courage, Benevolence and Piety. New Ed. Boston. 1848. Square 16° (8.)

——— A Life of W. By James K. Paulding. ... 2 vols. New-York. [1835?] 18° (HARPER'S Fam. Libr., **75**, **76**.)

——— The Life of G. W. By Jared Sparks. ... Boston. 1846. 8°

——— *See* NAPOLEON I.

WATT (James). Life. (BROUGHAM'S Lives of Men of Letters and Science, *etc.* pp. 209–235.)

——— Life. (CHAMBERS'S Miscel., VIII. no. 136.)

WAYNE (*Maj.-Gen.* Anthony). Lives of Anthony Wayne [by John Armstrong] and Sir Henry Vane. New-York. 1844. 16° or 12° (8. and 6.) (SPARKS'S Amer. Biogr., Vol. IV.)

——— Life of A. W.; by John Armstrong. (SCHOOL Libr., VI. 251–304.)

WEBSTER (John). Life. [With sketches of the minor English dramatists, — George Chapman, Thomas Middleton, John Marston, Thomas Decker, Thomas Heywood, William Rowley, Nathaniel Field, Thomas May, Robert Davenport, and William Cartwright.] (LARDNER's Cab. Cycl., **96**, pp. 322 - 346.)

WEDDERBURN (Alexander), 1*st Baron Loughborough.* Sketch. (BROUGHAM's "Hist. Sketches of Statesmen," *etc.* 1st Ser., I. 83 - 98.)

WELLESLEY [*originally* WESLEY] (Arthur), 1*st Duke of Wellington.* The Duke of W. (CHAMBERS's Papers, *etc.* XII. no. 96.)

WELLINGTON, Arthur, 1*st Duke of. See* WELLESLEY.

WENTWORTH (Thomas), *Earl of Strafford.* Life, by John Forster. (LARDNER's Cab. Cycl., **77**, pp. 178 - 421.)

WERNER (Abraham Gottlob). *Éloge*, by Baron Cuvier. (JARDINE's Nat. Libr., XXIX. 17 - 40.)

WEST (Benjamin). Life. (CUNNINGHAM's Lives of Brit. Painters, *etc.* II. 5 - 53.)

WEST (Thomas), 3*d Baron Delaware*, Sir Thomas GATES, Sir George SOMERS, Capt. Christopher NEWPORT, Sir Thomas DALE, and Sir Ferdinando WAINMAN. Lives. (BELKNAP's Amer. Biogr., II. 115 - 147.)

WEYMOUTH (George). *See* GOSNOLD (B.).

WHITEFIELD *or* WHITFIELD (George), and Richard Hurrell FROUDE. Lives. (STEPHEN (*Sir* J.). ... Essays, pp. 58 - 99.)

WICLIF (John). *See* WYCLIFFE.

WILBERFORCE (William). Sketch. (BROUGHAM's "Hist. Sketches of Statesmen," *etc.* 1st Ser., II. 81 - 87.)

——— Memoir. (DISTINGUISHED Men of Mod. Times, II. 317 - 324.)

——— Life. (STEPHEN (*Sir* J.). ... Essays, pp. 13 - 57.)

WILLIAM I. *King of England, the Conqueror.* History. ... By Jacob Abbott. With Engravings. New York. [1849 ?] 16°

WILLIAM *of Orange* and the Netherlands. (CHAMBERS's Miscel., III. no. 42.)

WILLIAMS (Roger). Lives of Roger Williams [by William Gammell], Timothy Dwight, and Count Pulaski. Boston. 1845. 16° (SPARKS's Amer. Biogr., 2d Ser., Vol. IV.)

WILLIAMSON (Peter). Story. (CHAMBERS's Miscel., II. no. 24.)

WILLUGHBY *or* WILLOUGHBY (Francis). Memoir. (JARDINE's Nat. Libr., V. 17 - 146.)

WILMOT (*Sir* John Eardley). Life, by Henry Roscoe. (LARDNER's Cab. Cycl., **75**, pp. 229 - 240.)

WILSON (Alexander). Life. (CHAMBERS's Miscel., IX. no. 152, pp. 24 - 32.)

——— Memoir. (JARDINE's Nat. Libr., IV. 17 - 50.)

——— Lives of Alexander Wilson [by William B. O. Peabody] and Captain John Smith. Boston. 1839. 16° (SPARKS's Amer. Biogr., Vol. II.)

WILSON (Richard). Life. (CUNNINGHAM's Lives of Brit. Painters, *etc.* I. 171 - 185.)

WILTON (Joseph). Life. (CUNNINGHAM's Lives of Brit. Painters and Sculptors, III. 62 - 73.)

WINDHAM (William). Sketch. (BROUGHAM's "Hist. Sketches of Statesmen," *etc.* 1st Ser., II. 21 - 27.)

WINSLOW (Edward). Life. (BELKNAP's Amer. Biogr., III. 85 - 115.)

WINTHROP (John), *Gov. of Mass.* Life. (BELKNAP's Amer. Biogr., III. 148 - 184.)

WINTHROP (John), *Jr., Gov. of Connecticut.* Life. (BELKNAP's Amer. Biogr., III. 185 - 205.)

WITT (Johan DE), *Grand Pensionary of Holland.* Memoir. (DISTINGUISHED Men of Mod. Times, I. 278 - 290.)

——— Life, by G. P. R. James. (LARDNER's Cab. Cycl., **85**, pp. 220 - 281.)

WOLFE (*Maj.-Gen.* James). Life, by G. R. Gleig. (LARDNER's Cab. Cycl., **68**, pp. 317 - 359.)

WOLSEY (Thomas), *Cardinal.* Life. (LARDNER's Cab. Cycl., **76**, pp. 111 - 183.)

——— Life. [By Mrs. A. T. Thomson.] *See* Part I. SOCIETY, *etc.* ... Lives, *etc.*

WORCESTER (Noah), *D.D.* Tribute to his Memory. (CHANNING's Works, IV. 387 - 407.)

WORDSWORTH (William). (CHAMBERS's Papers, *etc.* V. no. 40.)

——— Memoirs of W. W., Poet-Laureate, D. C. L. By Christopher Wordsworth, D.D. .... Edited by Henry Reed. 2 vols. Boston. 1851. 16°

WREN (*Sir* Christopher). Life. [By Henry Bellenden Ker.] *See* Part I. SOCIETY, *etc.* ... Lives, *etc.*

WYAT (*Sir* Francis). Life. (BELKNAP's Amer. Biogr., II. 174 - 205.)

WYCHERLEY (William). Life. [With notices of Sir Charles Sedley, Sir George Etherege, Elkanah Settle, Thomas Durfey, John Crowne, Nahum Tate, John Banks, and Edward Ravenscroft.] (LARDNER's Cab. Cycl., **97**, pp. 165 - 212.)

WYCLIFFE *or* WICLIF (John). Memoir. (DISTINGUISHED Men of Mod. Times, I. 24 - 38.)

XENOPHON. Campaigns and Character. (HERBERT's Captains, *etc.* pp. 172 - 225. — *See* Part I.)

XERXES, *King of Persia.* History .... By Jacob Abbott. With Engravings. New York. [1850 ?] 16°

XIMENES DE CISNEROS (Francisco, *originally* Gonzales), *Cardinal.* Life, by Eyre Evans Crowe. (LARDNER's Cab. Cycl., **83**, pp. 25 - 69.)

YEARDLEY (*Sir* George). *See* ARGAL (*Sir* S.).

YOUNG (Edward), *LL.D.* Life, by Robert Bell. (LARDNER's Cab. Cycl., **94**, pp. 327 - 363.)

ZENO (Niccolò) and Antonio ZENO. (BELKNAP's Amer. Biogr., I. 138–155.)

ZENOBIA, *Queen of Palmyra.* Memoir. (JAMESON's Memoirs of Cel. Female Sovereigns, I. 57–65.)

ZINZENDORF (Philipp Ludwig, *Count* VON). Life, by G. P. R. James. (LARDNER's Cab. Cycl., **87**, pp. 69–102.)

CLASS XXV. POLITICAL HISTORY, AND WORKS ON GENERAL HISTORY; CHRONOLOGY.

Note. For *Ancient Greek and Latin Authors*, see Class XVI. Parts II. and III.

PART I. GENERAL AND INTRODUCTORY WORKS.

ARNOLD (Thomas), *D.D.* Introductory Lectures on Modern History. *See* Part III.

CREASY (*Prof.* Edward Shepherd). The Fifteen Decisive Battles of the World; from Marathon to Waterloo. ... New York. 1851. 12°

GOODRICH (Samuel Griswold). A History of all Nations, from the Earliest Periods to the Present Time ... . Illustrated by 70 Stylographic Maps, and 700 Engravings. ... 2 vols. (paged continuously). Boston. 1849–51. 4° or large 8° (4.)

HART (John S.), *LL.D.* Questions to White's Universal History. ... Philadelphia. 1844. 12° pp. 36. (Appended to WHITE.)

HAYDN (Joseph). Dictionary of Dates, and Universal Reference, relating to all Ages and Nations ... . 3d Ed. To which is added, A copious Index of leading Names. London. 1845. 8°

HOUZÉ (A.). ... Atlas Universel Historique et Géographique. *See* Class XXII. Part I.

KEIGHTLEY (Thomas). Outlines of History, from the Earliest Period to the Abdication of Napoleon. London. 8° (LARDNER's Cab. Cycl., **1.**)

LIEBER (*Prof.* Francis), *LL.D.* Great Events, described by distinguished Historians, Chroniclers, and other Writers. Collected and in part translated by F. L. Boston. [1840?] 12° (SCHOOL Libr., Vol. XVII.)

M'CULLOCH (John Ramsey). M'Culloch's Universal Gazetteer. *See* Class XXII. Part I.

MANGNALL (Richmal). Historical and Miscellaneous Questions. 1st American, from the 84th London Ed. With large Additions: embracing the Elements of Mythology, Astronomy, Architecture, Heraldry, etc. etc. Adapted for Schools in the United States by Mrs. Julia Lawrence. ... New York. 1848. 12°

MUELLER (Johannes VON). The History of the World: from the Earliest Period to the Year of our Lord 1783, with particular reference to the Affairs of Europe and her Colonies. Translated from the German of the Baron John von Müller. Compared throughout with the Original, revised, corrected, and illustrated by a Notice of the Life and Writings of the Author, by Alexander H. Everett. ... 4 vols. Boston. 1842. 12° (School Libr., Vol. XXII. - XXV.)

Nicolas (*Sir* Nicholas Harris). The Chronology of History. ... London. 8° (Lardner's Cab. Cycl., **2.**)

Oxford Chronological Tables. *See* Part II. § 1. Annales Antiquitatis, *etc.*; — Part III. Chronological Tables, *etc.*

Parker (Richard Green). Outlines of General History, in the form of Question and Answer .... New York. 1848. 12°

Peabody (Elizabeth Palmer). The Polish-American System of Chronology, reproduced, with some Modifications, from General Bem's Franco-Polish Method. Boston. 1851. 12°

——— Blank Centuries accompanying the Manual of the Polish-American System of Chronology. Boston. 1850. Oblong 4°

Pictures of War. (Chambers's Miscel., VIII. no. 137.)

Putnam (George P.). ... Hand-Book of Chronology and History. The World's Progress, a Dictionary of Dates: with Tabular Views of General History, and a Historical Chart. Edited by G. P. P. 6th Ed. New-York. 1852. 12° pp. iv. 692. + (Putnam's Home Cyclopedia, Vol. I.)

——— 1850 - - 1851. Supplement to the World's Progress .... New-York. 1852. 12° pp. 48.

Schlegel (Karl Wilhelm Friedrich von). The Philosophy of History .... With a Memoir of the Author, by James Burton Robertson, Esq. 2 vols. New-York. 1841. 12°

Taylor (William Cooke), *LL.D.* A Manual of Ancient and Modern History .... Revised, with a Chapter on the History of the United States, by C. S. Henry ..., 2d Ed. New York. 1845. 8° pp. xv., 797.

Tyson (J. W.). An Atlas of Ancient and Modern History .... [Five Charts.] Philadelphia. 1845. 4°

Tytler (Alexander Fraser), *Lord Woodhouselee.* Universal History, from the Creation of the World to the Beginning of the Eighteenth Century. ... 2 vols. Boston. 1841. 8°

——— *and* Nares (Edward), *D.D.* Universal History, from the Creation of the World to the Decease of George III., 1820. Edited by an American. ... 6 vols. New-York. 1848 - 39 - 40 - 48 - 40 - 41. 18° (Harper's Fam. Libr., **86 - 91.**)

Uses (On the) of History, as a Study; and on the Separation of the Early Facts of History from Fable. (Encycl. Metrop., IX. 3 - 72.)

Weber (*Prof.* Georg). Outlines of Universal History .... Translated from the German ... by Dr. M. Behr .... Revised and corrected, with the Addition of a History of the United States of America, by the American Editor [Prof. Francis Bowen]. Boston. 1853. Large 12° (6.)

White (Henry). Elements of Universal History .... With Additions and Questions, by John S. Hart .... Philadelphia. 1844. 12°

Note. The "Questions" are paged independently, with a distinct title.

WOODHOUSELEE, Alexander Fraser, *Lord*. *See* TYTLER.

WORCESTER (Joseph Emerson), *LL.D.* Elements of History, Ancient and Modern: with a Chart and Tables of History, included within the Volume. ... Boston. 1845. 12°

——— *The same.* A new Ed., revised and enlarged. Boston. **1850.** 12° (2 copies.)

——— An Historical Atlas. ... [Containing Charts,—I. of General History; II. Mythology; III. Sacred History; IV. Ancient Chronology; V. Modern Chronology; VI. Sovereigns of Europe; VII. Historical Chart of England; VIII. Historical Chart of France; IX. Historical Chart of the German Empire; X. Historical Chart of Spain; XI. Chart of American History; XII. Chart of Biography.] 6th Ed. Boston. [**1833** ?] fol.

——— *The same.* With Description, Illustration, and Questions ... . New and revised Ed. Cambridge. 1852. fol. Description, 12° pp. 36.

PART II. ANCIENT HISTORY.

§ 1. *General Works; Asiatic and African History.*

ANNALES Antiquitatis. Chronological Tables of Ancient History synchronistically and ethnographically arranged. Compiled from the best Authorities. Oxford. 1835. fol. pp. 44.

Note. Valuable Chronological Tables of Ancient History are appended to Smith's "Dictionary of Greek and Roman Biography and Mythology," and to his "New Classical Dictionary."

BLOSS (C. A.). Bloss' Ancient History, illustrated by colored Maps, and arranged to accompany a Chronological Chart ... . Rochester. 1845. 12°

BUCKE (Charles). Ruins of Ancient Cities; with ... Accounts of their Rise, Fall, and Present Condition. ... 2 vols. New-York. 1848. 18° (HARPER'S Fam. Libr., **134, 135.**)

CARTHAGE and the Carthaginians. (CHAMBERS'S Papers, *etc.* III. no. 20.)

HEEREN (*Prof.* Arnold Hermann Ludwig). A Manual of Ancient History, particularly with regard to the Constitutions, the Commerce, and the Colonies, of the States of Antiquity. ... Translated from the German. The 3d Ed., corrected and improved. Oxford. 1840. 8°

——— Historical Researches into the Politics, Intercourse and Trade of the Carthaginians, Ethiopians and Egyptians. Translated from the German. The 2d Ed., corrected throughout, and to which is now first added an Index, a Life of the Author, new Appendixes, and other Additions. 2 vols. Oxford. 1838. 8°

——— Historical Researches into the Politics, Intercourse and Trade of the principal Nations of Antiquity. ... Translated from the German. Vol. I. Asiatic Nations. Persians, Phœnicians, Babylonians. | Vol. II. ... Scythians, Indians, Appendixes. 2 vols. London. 1846. 8°

MOUNTAIN (*Rev.* Jacob Henry Brooke). Persia, Mithridates. (ENCYCL. Metrop., X. 120–138.)

NIEBUHR (Barthold Georg). A Dissertation on the Geography of Herodotus .... Researches into the History of the Scythians, Getæ, and Sarmatians. *See* Class XXII. Part II.

——— Lectures on Ancient History, from the Earliest Times to the taking of Alexandria by Octavianus. Comprising the History of the Asiatic Nations, the Egyptians, Greeks, Macedonians and Carthaginians. Translated from the German Ed. of Dr. Marcus Niebuhr, by Dr. Leonhard Schmitz ... with Additions and Corrections from his own MS. Notes. ... 3 vols. London. 1852. 8°

NUTTALL (P. Austin), *LL.D.* A Synoptical and Chronological View of Ancient History. (Prefixed to his "Classical and Archæological Dictionary." *See* Class XXVII.)

PUETZ (Wilhelm). Manual of Ancient Geography and History. ... Translated from the German. Edited by the Rev. Thomas Kerchever Arnold .... 2d American, revised and corrected [by George W. Greene] from the London Ed. [With a Chronological Table, B. C. 2000 — A. D. 476.] New-York. 1850. 12°

ROLLIN (Charles). The Ancient History of the Egyptians, Carthaginians, Assyrians, Babylonians, Medes and Persians, Grecians, and Macedonians; including a History of the Arts and Sciences of the Ancients. ... With a Life of the Author, by James Bell. First complete American Ed. ... 2 vols. New-York. 1841. 8°

Note. Also with engraved title-pages.

RUSSELL (Michael), *Bp. of Glasgow.* Syria, from B. C. 193 to B. C. 64. (ENCYCL. Metrop., X. 57 – 67.) Parthia, from B. C. 245 to B. C. 53. (*Ibid.* X. 204 – 209.)

——— Egypt. Ptolemy Soter. Cleopatra. (ENCYCL. Metrop., X. 337 – 354.)

§ 2. *Greece.*

CLELAND (——). Epameinondas. (ENCYCL. Metrop., IX. 589 – 610.)

CLINTON (Henry Fynes). An Epitome of the Civil and Literary Chronology of Greece, from the Earliest Accounts to the Death of Augustus. ... Oxford. 1851. 8°

GILLIES (John), *LL.D.* The History of Ancient Greece, its Colonies, and Conquests; Part the First; from the Earliest Accounts till the Division of the Macedonian Empire in the East; including the History of Literature, Philosophy, and the Fine Arts. ... The 6th Ed. ... 4 vols. London. 1820. 8°

——— *The same.* Part the Second; embracing the History of the Ancient World, from the Dominion of Alexander to that of Augustus; with a Survey of Preceding Periods, and a Continuation of the History of Arts and Letters. ... A new Ed., with Corrections and Additions. ... 4 vols. London. 1820. 8°

——— *The same.* [Part the First.] Philadelphia. 1835. 8°

GOLDSMITH (Oliver), *M.D.* Pinnock's improved Edition of Dr. Goldsmith's History of Greece, abridged for the Use of Schools. Revised

... and ... enlarged .... With Questions .... 25th American, from the 19th London Ed. Philadelphia. 1847. 12°

Grote (George). A History of Greece; I. Legendary Greece. II. Grecian History to the Reign of Peisistratus at Athens. Vol. I. – II. | History of Greece. Vol. III. – IV. 2d Ed. | Vol. V. – XI. 11 vols. London. 1846 – 53. 8°

Heeren (*Prof.* Arnold Hermann Ludwig). Ancient Greece. Translated from the German, by George Bancroft. — Also Three Historical Treatises, by the same Author. I. — Political Consequences of the Reformation. II. — The Rise, Progress, and Practical Influence of Political Theories. III. — The Rise and Growth of the Continental Interests of Great Britain. New and improved Ed. London. 1847. 8°

Keightley (Thomas). The History of Greece. To which is added, A Chronological Table of Contemporary History. By Joshua Toulmin Smith .... Boston. 1839. 8° or 12° (4. and 6.)

Lyall (William Rowe), *Archdeacon of Colchester.* Greece. (Encycl. Metrop., IX. 561, 562, 585 – 588.)

Malkin (Frederick). ... The History of Greece, from the Earliest Times to its Final Subjection to Rome. ... Published under the Superintendence of the Society for the Diffusion of Useful Knowledge. London. n. d. 8° (Libr. of Useful Knowl.)

Mitford (William). The History of Greece. ... 8 vols. Boston. 1823. 8°

——— The History of Greece, from the Earliest Period to the Death of Agesilaus. By W. M. Continued [from Chap. XXIX.] to the Death of Alexander the Great, by R. A. Davenport. ... 8 vols. London. 1835. 12°

Mountain (*Rev.* Jacob Henry Brooke). Xenophon. (Encycl. Metrop., IX. 562 – 578.) Dionysius the Elder. Dionysius the Younger. Timoleon. (*Ibid.* IX. 729 – 753.)

——— Aratus. Cleomenes. Philopœmen. (Encycl. Metrop., X. 1 – 23.)

Mueller (*Prof.* Karl Otfried). The History and Antiquities of the Doric Race .... Translated from the German by Henry Tufnell ... and George Cornewall Lewis .... 2d Ed., revised. 2 vols. London. 1839. 8°

Outlines of Grecian History. *See* Society for promoting Christian Knowledge.

Renouard (*Rev.* George Cecil). Critias. Theramenes. (Encycl. Metrop., IX. 579 – 584.) Pyrrhus. (*Ibid.* IX. 658 – 668.)

Russell (Michael), *Bp. of Glasgow.* Philip of Macedon. Alexander the Great. Alexander's Successors. (Encycl. Metrop., IX. 611 – 631, 704 – 728, 789 – 824.)

——— Syria, from B. C. 193 to B. C. 64. Perseus, King of Macedon. (Encycl. Metrop., X. 57 – 71.)

Schmitz (Leonhard). A History of Greece, from the Earliest Times to the Destruction of Corinth, B. C. **146**; mainly based upon that of Connop Thirlwall, D.D. . . . . New York. 1851. 12°

Sewell (Elizabeth M.). A First History of Greece. ... New-York. 1853. 18°

Society for promoting Christian Knowledge. Outlines of Grecian History . . . . Published under the Direction of the Committee of General Literature and Education, appointed by the Society . . . . From the latest London Ed., with Additions and Questions. Philadelphia. 1846. 18°

Thirlwall (Connop), *Bp. of St. David's.* History of Greece. 8 vols. London. 8° (Lardner's Cab. Cycl., **33 – 40.**)

——— *The same.* 2 vols. New-York. 1845. 8°

——— *See* Schmitz (L.).

§ 3. *Rome.*

Arnold (Thomas), *D.D.* On the Credibility of the Early Roman History. Hamilcar Barca. Hannibal. (Encycl. Metrop., IX. 754 – 788.)

——— The History of Rome. ... Three Volumes in Two. Reprinted entire, from the last London Ed. New-York. 1846. 8°

——— History of the Later Roman Commonwealth, from the End of the Second Punic War to the Death of Julius Cæsar; and of the Reign of Augustus: with a Life of Trajan. ... New-York. 1846. 8°

——— *The same.* (Encycl. Metrop., Vol. X.)

Elton (Charles Abraham). A History of the Roman Emperors, from the Accession of Augustus to the Fall of the last Constantine ... with Maps and Portraits. ... London. 1825. 12°

Ferguson (Adam), *LL.D.* The History of the Progress and Termination of the Roman Republic. ... Philadelphia. 1839. 8°

Note. Also with an engraved title-page, dated 1830.

——— *The same.* A new Ed., abridged. New-York. [1836 ?] 18° pp. xx., 598. (Harper's Fam. Libr., **187.**)

Gibbon (Edward). The History of the Decline and Fall of the Roman Empire. With Notes, by the Rev. H. H. Milman . . . . A new Ed., to which is added a complete Index . . . . 6 vols. Boston. 1850. 12°

Goldsmith (Oliver), *M.D.* Pinnock's improved Edition of Dr. Goldsmith's Abridgment of the History of Rome ... with ... Questions . . . . 25th American, from the 23d London Ed. Philadelphia. 1847. 12°

History (The) of Rome, from the Earliest Times to the Founding of Constantinople. [From Niebuhr, Wachsmuth, Heeren, Schlosser, and others. — With an Analytical and Chronological Table, A. U. C. 1 — A. D. 306.] 2 vols. London. 8° (Lardner's Cab. Cycl., **41, 42.**)

History (The) of Rome. [The same work.] Philadelphia. 1837. 8°

Keightley (Thomas). The History of Rome. To which is added, A

Chronological Table of Contemporary History. By Joshua Toulmin Smith .... Boston. 1839. 8° or 12° (4. and 6.)

KEIGHTLEY (Thomas). *The same.* New-York. 1848. 12° or 8° (4. and 6.)

——— History of the Roman Empire, from the Accession of Augustus to the End of the Empire of the West; being a Continuation of the History of Rome. ... Edited by Joshua Toulmin Smith .... Boston. 1841. 8° or 12° (4. and 6.)

MERIVALE (*Rev.* Charles). The Fall of the Roman Republic, a short History of the Last Century of the Commonwealth. ... London. 1853. 12°

——— History of the Romans under the Empire. ... 2d Ed. Vol. I. – II. | Vol. III. 3 vols. London. 1852. 8°

MICHELET (Jules). History of the Roman Republic. ... Translated by William Hazlitt. New York. 1847. 12°

MOUNTAIN (*Maj.* A. S. H.). Hadrianus. (ENCYCL. Metrop., X. 664 – 676.)

MOUNTAIN (*Rev.* Jacob Henry Brooke). Ancient Gaul, from B. C. 600 to B. C. 50. (ENCYCL. Metrop., X. 190 – 203.) Spain, from B. C. 234 to B. C. 73. (*Ibid.* X. 179 – 189.) Caligula. Claudius. (*Ibid.* X. 434 – 451.)

NEWMAN (*Prof.* Francis William). Regal Rome an Introduction to Roman History .... New York. 1852. 12°

NIEBUHR (Barthold Georg). The History of Rome. Translated by Julius Charles Hare ... and Connop Thirlwall .... Volume First with a Map — Volume Second from the 3d London Ed. revised. ... | Translated by William Smith, Ph.D. and Leonhard Schmitz, Ph.D. Volume Third. ... | The History of Rome from the First Punic War to the Death of Constantine. In a Series of Lectures, including an Introductory Course on the Sources and Study of Roman History. Edited by Leonhard Schmitz, Ph. D. Vol. IV. – V. Forming the Fourth — Fifth Volume of the entire History. 5 vols. (bound in 2). Philadelphia. 1844. Large 12° (6.)

——— Niebuhr's History of Rome, epitomised from the Larger Work, and adapted to the Use of Schools and Colleges. By Travers Twiss .... With Chronological Tables and an Appendix. ... [Part I.] – II. 2 pts. Oxford. 1845. 8°

——— .... Lectures on Roman History, delivered at the University of Bonn. From the Edition of Dr. M. Isler. Translated by Havilland Le M. Chepmell, M.A. and Franz C. F. Demmler, Ph.D. 3 vols. London, Edinburgh, and Dublin. 1849 – 50. 16°

OTTLEY (*Rev.* John B.). Tiberius. Antoninus Pius. Marcus Aurelius. Commodus. Pertinax. Literature of the Age of the Antonines. (ENCYCL. Metrop., X. 425 – 433, 677 – 697.)

RENOUARD (*Rev.* George Cecil). Appius Claudius. Camillus. Pyrrhus. (ENCYCL. Metrop., IX. 644 – 668.)

RUSSELL (Michael), *Bp. of Glasgow.* The Roman Emperors from Nero to Nerva, inclusive. (ENCYCL. Metrop., Vol. X.) From

Septimius Severus to Constantinus. (*Ibid.* XI. 1–80.) From the Accession of Jovian to the Extinction of the Western Empire. (*Ibid.* 217–268.)

SCHMITZ (Leonhard), *Ph. D.* A History of Rome, from the Earliest Times to the Death of Commodus, A. D. 192. ... Andover. 1847. 12°

SEWELL (Elizabeth M.) The Child's First History of Rome. ... New York. 1851. 18° (2 copies.)

SIMONDE DE SISMONDI (Jean Charles Léonard). The History of the Fall of the Roman Empire, comprising a View of the Invasion and Settlement of the Barbarians. 2 vols. London. 8° (LARDNER's Cab. Cycl., **43, 44.**)

TWISS (*Prof.* Travers), *D.C.L.* Niebuhr's History of Rome epitomised, *etc.* *See* NIEBUHR (B. G.).

PART III. THE MIDDLE AGES; GENERAL WORKS ON MODERN HISTORY, AND ON THE HISTORY OF MODERN EUROPE.

ARNOLD (Thomas), *D.D.* Introductory Lectures on Modern History, delivered in Lent Term, MDCCCXLII. With the Inaugural Lecture delivered in December, MDCCCXLI. ... Edited, from the 2d London Ed., with a Preface and Notes, by Henry Reed ... . New York. 1845. 12°

CHRONOLOGICAL Tables of Modern History from the Overthrow of the Roman Empire in the West to the Present Time. ... In a Series of Parallel Columns ... . Together with Synchronistical Tables of Modern Civilization, Science, and Literature, [a Synoptical View of Modern Painters,] Genealogical Tables of the Reigning Houses in Europe, and a complete Index. Oxford. 1840. fol. pp. 86.

Note. The Tables of the History of the Middle Ages and those of Modern History (commencing A. D. 1500) have independent title-pages, dated 1838 and 1839, respectively.

CRUSADES (The). (CHAMBERS's Miscel., X. no. 162.)

DESMICHELS (Ovide Chrysanthe). A Manual of the History of the Middle Ages, from the Invasion of the Barbarians to the Fall of Constantinople, with Genealogical Tables ... . Translated from the French ... by T. G. Jones. London. 1841. 16° (8.)

DUNHAM (S. A.), *LL.D.* A History of Europe during the Middle Ages. 4 vols. London. 8° (LARDNER's Cab. Cycl., **48–51.**)

FLORIAN (Jean Pierre CLARIS DE). History of the Moors of Spain. *See* Part IV. § 1. B. *Spain.*

GIBBON (Edward). The History of the Decline and Fall of the Roman Empire. *See* Part II. § 3.

HALLAM (Henry). View of the State of Europe during the Middle Ages. ... From the 6th London Ed. ... New-York. 1848. 8°

HEEREN (*Prof.* Arnold Hermann Ludwig). A Manual of the History of the Political System of Europe and its Colonies, from its Formation at the Close of the Fifteenth Century, to its Re-establishment upon the Fall of Napoleon. ... Translated from the 5th German Ed. London. 1846. 8°

HEEREN (*Prof.* Arnold Hermann Ludwig). Three Historical Treatises. *See* Part II. § 2. HEEREN (A. H. L.). Ancient Greece, *etc.*

IRVING (Washington). Mahomet and his Successors. ... 2 vols. New-York. 1850. 12° (Works, Vol. XII. XIII.)

JACOB (Samuel). Annals of the Greek Empire during the Ninth, Tenth, and Eleventh Centuries: of the Khalifate from the Rise of the Abassides to the End of the Eleventh Century. (ENCYCL. Metrop., XI. 556 - 570.)

JAMES (George Payne Rainsford). The History of Chivalry. ... New York. 1847. 18° (HARPER'S Fam. Libr., **20.**)

JONES (William). *Continuator. See* RUSSELL (W.). The History of Modern Europe, *etc.*

LORD (John). A Modern History, from the Time of Luther to the Fall of Napoleon. ... Philadelphia. [1849.] 12° or 8° (6. and 8.)

MICHELET (Jules). Modern History, from the French of M. Michelet. With an Introduction. By A. Potter, D.D. New-York. 1846. 18° (HARPER'S Fam. Libr., **170.**)

OCKLEY (*Prof.* Simon). The History of the Saracens; comprising the Lives of Mohammed and his Successors, to the Death of Abdalmelik, the Eleventh Caliph. ... The 4th Ed., revised, improved, and enlarged. London. 1847. 8° (BOHN'S Stand. Libr.)

PROCTER (*Col.* George). The Middle Ages, from the Fall of the Roman Empire of the West, to the End of the Eighth Century. (ENCYCL. Metrop., XI. 269, *etc.*)

——— The Feudal System. — The Crusades. (ENCYCL. Metrop., XI. 449 - 468, 584 - 612, 765 - 792, and XII. 16 - 71.)

PUETZ (Wilhelm). Handbook of Mediæval Geography and History. ... Translated from the German, by the Rev. R. B. Paul .... [Edited by Geo. W. Greene.] New-York. 1850. 12°

——— Manual of Modern Geography and History. ... Translated from the German, by the Rev. R. B. Paul .... 1st American, revised and corrected [by Jesse A. Spencer] from the London Ed. [With a Chronological Table, A. D. 1492 - 1850.] New-York. 1851. 12°

ROBERTSON (William), *D.D.* View of the Progress of Society in Europe, from the Subversion of the Roman Empire, to the Beginning of the Sixteenth Century. (Prefixed to his History of the Emperor Charles V. — *See* Part IV. § 1. B. *Austria.*)

ROSE (*Rev.* Hugh James). Annals of France, Germany, and Italy, from the Death of Charlemagne, to the End of the Thirteenth Century. (ENCYCL. Metrop., XI. 429, *etc.*)

RUSSELL (William), *LL.D.* The History of Modern Europe: with a View of the Progress of Society from the Rise of the Modern Kingdoms to the Peace of Paris in 1763. And a Continuation of the History to the Present Time. [Forming Vol. III. of the work.]

By William Jones, Esq. With Annotations by an American. ... 3 vols. New York. 1839. 8° or large 12° (8. and 12.)

Note. Also with engraved title-pages, differing from the above.

SCHLEGEL (Karl Wilhelm Friedrich VON). A Course of Lectures on Modern History; to which are added, Historical Essays on the Beginning of our History, and on Cæsar and Alexander. Translated by Lyndsey Purcell & R. H. Whitelock, Esqrs. London. 1849. 8° (BOHN's Stand. Libr.)

SCHLOSSER (*Prof.* Friedrich Christoph). History of the Eighteenth Century and of the Ninteenth till the Overthrow of the French Empire. With particular reference to Mental Cultivation and Progress. ... Translated, with a Preface and Notes, by D. Davison ... . 8 vols. London. [Vol. I. - VI.,] 1843 - 45. [Vol. VII. - VIII.,] 1850 - 52. 8°

Note. Vol. VIII. contains an Index to Vol. III. - VIII.

SECRET Societies of the Middle Ages. (CHAMBERS's Papers, *etc.* V. no. 33.)

SECRET Societies of Modern Europe. (CHAMBERS's Papers, *etc.* II. no. 15.)

THIERRY (Jacques Nicolas Augustin). The Historical Essays, published under the Title of "Dix Ans d'Études Historiques," and Narratives of the Merovingian Era; or, Scenes of the Sixth Century. With an Autobiographical Preface. ... Philadelphia. 1845. 8°

PART IV. HISTORY OF PARTICULAR COUNTRIES, NATIONS, AND RACES, NOT INCLUDED IN PARTS II. AND III.

§ 1. Europe.

A. General Works.

Note. For the General History of *Modern* Europe, see Part III.

[GOODRICH (Samuel Griswold)]. Lights and Shadows of European History; by the Author of Peter Parley's Tales. Boston. 1849. 16° or 18° (8. and 6.) (CABINET Libr., 8.)

UNGEWITTER (Francis H.), *LL.D.* Europe, Past and Present, *etc.* *See* Class XXII. Part III.

B. Particular Countries, etc.

Austria and Germany.

BROWNE (*Rev.* R. Lewis). Annals of Germany, from the Peace of Westphalia, A. D. 1648, to the Congress of Vienna, A. D. 1814. (ENCYCL. Metrop., XII. 647, *etc.* XIII. 41, *etc.*)

COXE (William), *Archdeacon of Wilts.* History of the House of Austria, from the Foundation of the Monarchy by Rhodolph of Hapsburgh, to the Death of Leopold the Second: 1218 to 1792. ... 3d Ed. ... 3 vols. London. 1847. 8° (BOHN's Stand. Libr.)

DUNHAM (S. A.), *LL.D.* The History of the Germanic Empire. **3** vols. London. 8° (LARDNER'S Cab. Cycl., **28 – 30.**)

GUSTAVUS ADOLPHUS and the Thirty Years' War. (CHAMBERS'S Miscel., VII. no. **120.**)

KOHLRAUSCH (*Prof.* Friedrich). A History of Germany; from the Earliest Period to the Present Time. ... Translated from the last German Ed., by James D. Haas. With a complete Index, prepared expressly for the American Ed. New York. **1845.** 8°

MENZEL (Wolfgang). The History of Germany, from the Earliest Period to the Present Time. Translated from the 4th German Ed., by Mrs. George Horrocks. **3** vols. London. **1848 – 49.** 8° (BOHN'S Stand. Libr.)

ORMEROD (*Rev.* T. G.). Annals of Germany, from the Diet of Worms, A. D. 1496, to the End of the Thirty Years' War, A. D. 1648. (ENCYCL. Metrop., XII. **306,** *etc.*)

PHILLIMORE (John George). Annals of Germany and Italy during the Fourteenth and Fifteenth Centuries. (ENCYCL. Metrop., XII. **103 – 122, 254 – 275.**)

ROBERTSON (William), *D.D.* The History of the Reign of the Emperor Charles V. With a View of the Progress of Society in Europe, from the Subversion of the Roman Empire, to the Beginning of the Sixteenth Century. ... Abridged Ed. With Questions ... . New-York. N. D. 18° pp. **623.** (HARPER'S Fam. Libr., **186.**)

SCHILLER (Johann Christoph Friedrich VON). The Works ... . [Vol. I.] ... History of the Thirty Years' War. *See* under *Netherlands*, below.

Denmark, Sweden, and Norway.

CRICHTON (Andrew), *LL.D. and* WHEATON (Henry), *LL.D.* Scandinavia, Ancient and Modern; being a History of Denmark, Sweden, and Norway; comprising a Description of these Countries; an Account of the Mythology, Government, Laws, Manners and Institutions of the Early Inhabitants; and of the Present State of Society, Religion, Literature, Arts and Commerce; with Illustrations of their Natural History. ... **2** vols. New-York. **1841 – 43.** 18° (HARPER'S Fam. Libr., **136, 137.**)

DUNHAM (S. A.), *LL.D.* The History of Denmark, Sweden, and Norway. **3** vols. London. 8° (LARDNER'S Cab. Cycl., **57 – 59.**)

ORMEROD (*Rev.* T. G.). Sketch of the Northern Kingdoms of Europe, from the Middle of the Sixteenth, to the Middle of the Eighteenth Century. (ENCYCL. Metrop., XII. **614 – 620, 727 – 731.**)

England and the British Empire.

ACCOUNT (An) of the Borders. (CHAMBERS'S Miscel., VI. no. **102.**)

CARLYLE (Thomas). *Editor*, etc. *See* CROMWELL (O.).

CRAIK (*Prof.* George Lillie) *and* MACFARLANE (Charles). The Pictorial History of England: being a History of the People, as well as a History of the Kingdom. Illustrated with several hundred Wood-Cuts .... By G. L. C. and C. M., assisted by other Contributors. 4 vols. New York. 1846-48. 8°

CROMWELL (Oliver). Oliver Cromwell's Letters and Speeches: with Elucidations. By Thomas Carlyle. *See* Class XXIV. Part II.

CROMWELL and his Contemporaries. (CHAMBERS's Papers, *etc.* VIII. no. 58.)

DE LOLME (John Lewis), *LL.D.* The Rise and Progress of the English Constitution: the Treatise of J. L. De Lolme, LL.D. with an Historical and Legal Introduction, and Notes, by A. J. Stephens .... 2 vols. London. 1838. 8°

Note. The two vols. are paged continuously.

DICKENS (Charles). A Child's History of England. Volume I. ... New York. 1853. 16°

GOLDSMITH (Oliver), *M.D.* Pinnock's improved Edition of Dr. Goldsmith's History of England, from the Invasion of Julius Cæsar to the Death of George II. With a Continuation to the Year 1845. With Questions .... 45th American, from the 35th English Ed. Philadelphia. 1847. 12°

GOODRICH (Samuel Griswold). A Pictorial History of England .... Philadelphia. 1846. 12°

GUIZOT (François Pierre Guillaume). History of the English Revolution of 1640, commonly called the Great Rebellion: from the Accession of Charles I. to his Death. ... Translated by William Hazlitt. New York. 1846. 12°

HALLAM (Henry). The Constitutional History of England from the Accession of Henry VII. to the Death of George II. ... From the 5th London Ed. New York. 1849. 8° pp. 737.

HISTORY of the Plague in London. (CHAMBERS's Miscel., VII. no. 124.)

HUME (David). The History of England from the Invasion of Julius Cæsar to the Abdication of James the Second, 1688. A new Ed. ... To which is prefixed a short Account of ... [the Author's] Life, written by himself. Vol. I.-V. | To which is added a complete Index .... Vol. VI. 6 vols. Boston. 1849-50. 12°

KEIGHTLEY (Thomas). The History of England. Revised and edited, with Notes and Additions, by Joshua Toulmin Smith .... 2 vols. Boston. 1840. 8° or 12° (4. and 6.)

——— The History of England, from the Earliest Period to 1839. ... From the 2d London Ed. With Notes, &c., by the American Editor. ... 5 vols. New-York. [1840 ?] 18° (HARPER's Fam. Libr., **114-118.**)

LINGARD (John), *D.D.* A History of England, from the First Invasion by the Romans to the Accession of William and Mary, in 1688. A new Ed., as enlarged by Dr. Lingard shortly before his Death. In thirteen Volumes. Vol. I.-III. 3 vols. Boston. 1853. 12° (8. 4.)

LOLME (Jean Louis DE), *LL.D.* *See* DE LOLME.

MACAULAY (Thomas Babington). The History of England from the Accession of James II. 2 vols. Boston. 1849. 12°

MACKINTOSH (*Sir* James). The History of England, from the Earliest Times, to the Year 1588. ... New Ed. Philadelphia. 1836. 8° or 12° (4. and 6.)

——— The History of England. With a Continuation from A. D. 1572, by W. Wallace and R. Bell. 10 vols. London. 8° (LARDNER'S Cab. Cycl., **3 – 12.**)

MAHON, Philip Henry, *Viscount*. *See* STANHOPE.

MARKHAM (*Mrs.* ——), *pseudon.* *See* [PENROSE (*Mrs.* Elizabeth [CARTWRIGHT])].

MEMORABILIA of the Seventeenth Century in Britain. (CHAMBERS'S Papers, *etc.* II. no. 12.)

NORMAN Conquest (The). (CHAMBERS'S Miscel., VIII. no. 132.)

[PENROSE (*Mrs.* Elizabeth [CARTWRIGHT])]. A History of England from the First Invasion by the Romans to the End of the Reign of William the Fourth with Conversations at the End of each Chapter By Mrs. Markham [*i. e.* Mrs. E. [C.] Penrose] 11th Ed. 2 vols. Paris. 1844. 12°

——— History of England, from the Invasion of Julius Cæsar to the Reign of Victoria. By Mrs. Markham. A new Ed., revised and enlarged. With Questions .... By Eliza Robbins .... New York. 1851. 12°

PROCTER (*Col.* George). Britain, from the Descent of the Saxons, to the Deposition of Richard II. (ENCYCL. Metrop., XI. 376, *etc.* XII. 16, *etc.*)

RUSSELL (Michael), *Bp. of Glasgow.* Annals of Britain, from the Accession of Henry IV. A. D. 1399, to A. D. 1815. (ENCYCL. Metrop. XII. 233, *etc.* XIII. 277, *etc.*)

SOUTHEY (Robert). The Naval History of England. *See* Class XXIV. Part I. SOUTHEY (R.) *and* BELL (R.). Lives, *etc.*

STANHOPE (Philip Henry), *Viscount Mahon.* History of England from the Peace of Utrecht to the Peace of Versailles. 1713 – 1783. By Lord Mahon. In Seven Volumes. — Vol. I. – IV. ... 3d Ed., revised. 4 vols. Boston [London]. 1853. 8° or 16° (8.)

STEPHENS (Archibald John). *See* DE LOLME (J. L.). The Rise and Progress, *etc.*

THIERRY (Jacques Nicolas Augustin). The Historical Essays, *etc.* *See* Part III., above.

——— History of the Conquest of England by the Normans; its Causes, and its Consequences, in England, Scotland, Ireland, & on the Continent. ... Translated from the 7th Paris Ed., by William Hazlitt, Esq. [With a Biographical Notice of M. Thierry.] ... 2 vols. London: D. Bogue. 1847. 8°

TURNER (Sharon). The History of the Anglo-Saxons from the Earliest

Period to the Norman Conquest. [From the 6th English Ed.] ... 3 vols. Paris. 1840. 8°

VAUGHAN (Robert), *D.D.* ... The History of England under the House of Stuart, including the Commonwealth. [A. D. 1603 – 1688.] Part I. James I. — Charles I. | Part II. Commonwealth; Charles II.; James II. Published under the Superintendence of the Society for the Diffusion of Useful Knowledge. 2 pts. London. N. D. 8° pp. xvi., 935. (LIBR. of Useful Knowl.)

WADE (John). British History, chronologically arranged; comprehending a classified Analysis of Events and Occurrences in Church and State, and of the Constitutional, Political, Commercial, Intellectual, and Social Progress of the United Kingdom, from the first Invasion by the Romans to A. D. 1847. ... 5th Ed. London. 1847. 8° pp. xii., 1240.

France.

CROWE (Eyre Evans). The History of France, from the Earliest Period to the Abdication of Napoleon. 3 vols. London. 8° (LARDNER's Cab. Cycl., **19 – 21.**)

GOODRICH (Samuel Griswold). A Pictorial History of France for Schools. ... Philadelphia. 1845. 12°

HISTORY of the Bastile. (CHAMBERS's Miscel., X. no. 166.)

INSURRECTIONS in Lyons. (CHAMBERS's Miscel., II. no. 38.)

LAMARTINE (Alphonse DE). History of the Girondists; or, Personal Memoirs of the Patriots of the French Revolution. From Unpublished Sources. ... Vol. I. – II. Translated by H. T. Ryde. | Vol. III. With a Biographical Sketch of the Author. 3 vols. London. 1848. 8° (BOHN's Stand. Libr.)

——— History of the French Revolution of 1848. ... Translated from the French. London. 1849. 8° (BOHN's Stand. Libr.)

MACPHERSON (William). Annals of France, from the Accession of Henry IV. A. D. 1589 to the Restoration, July 8, 1815. (ENCYCL. Metrop., XII. 713, *etc.* XIII. 1, *etc.*)

MICHELET (Jules). History of France ... . Translated by G. H. Smith, F. G. S. 2 vols. New York. 1847. 8°

NARRATIVE of the Russian Campaign. (CHAMBERS's Miscel., VI. no. 97.)

SÉGUR (Philippe Paul, *Count* DE). History of the Expedition to Russia, undertaken by the Emperor Napoleon in the Year 1812. ... 2 vols. New-York. [1841 ?] 18° (HARPER's Fam. Libr., **141, 142.**)

SMEDLEY (*Rev.* Edward). Annals of France from the Accession of Louis X. (A. D. 1314) to the Death of Henry III. (A. D. 1589.) (ENCYCL. Metrop., XII. 72, *etc.*)

STEPHEN (*Sir* James). Lectures on the History of France. ... New York. 1852. 8° pp. xvi., 710.

THIERRY (Jacques Nicolas Augustin). The Historical Essays, *etc.* *See* Part III.

Germany. See *Austria.*

Great Britain. See *England.*

Gypsies.

ACCOUNT of the Gipsies. (CHAMBERS's Miscel., VIII. no. 139.)

Holland. See *Netherlands.*

Iceland.

HISTORICAL (An) and Descriptive Account of Iceland, Greenland, and the Faroe Islands. *See* Class XXII. Part III.

Ireland.

MOORE (Thomas). The History of Ireland, from the Earliest Kings of that Realm down to its last Chief. 4 vols. London. 8° (LARDNER's Cab. Cycl., **15 – 18.**)

TAYLOR (William Cooke), *LL.D.* History of Ireland, from the Anglo-Norman Invasion till the Union of the Country with Great Britain. ... With Additions, by William Sampson .... 2 vols. New York. 1847. 18° (HARPER's Fam. Libr., **51, 52.**)

Italy.

MACHIAVELLI (Niccolò). The History of Florence, and of the Affairs of Italy, from the Earliest Times to the Death of Lorenzo the Magnificent; together with The Prince. And various Historical Tracts. A new Translation. London. 1847. 8° (BOHN's Stand. Libr.)

ROSCOE (Thomas). Annals of Italy, from A. D. 1648 to A. D. 1814. (ENCYCL. Metrop., XIII. 1013 – 1063.)

SFORZOSI (——). A Compendious History of Italy. Translated from the original Italian by Nathaniel Greene. New-York. 1844. 18° (HARPER's Fam. Libr., **79.**)

SIMONDE DE SISMONDI (Jean Charles Léonard). The History of the Italian Republics; or, The Origin, Progress, and Fall of Freedom in Italy, from A. D. 476 to 1805. London. 8° (LARDNER's Cab. Cycl., **47.**)

[SMEDLEY (*Rev.* Edward)]. ... Sketches from Venetian History. ... 2 vols. New-York. 1846. 18° (HARPER's Fam. Libr., **43, 44.**)

SPALDING (*Prof.* William). Italy and the Italian Islands. From the Earliest Ages to the Present Time. ... 3 vols. New-York. 1848. 18° (HARPER's Fam. Libr., **151 – 153.**)

Netherlands.

DUNHAM (S. A.), *LL.D.* Annals of the Netherlands, from B. C. 51 to A. D. 1797. (ENCYCL. Metrop., XIII. 548 – 659.)

GRATTAN (Thomas Colley). The History of the Netherlands, from the Invasion of the Romans to the Belgian Revolution in 1830. London. 8° (LARDNER's Cab. Cycl., **55.**)

SCHILLER (Johann Christoph Friedrich VON). The Works of Frederick S. [Vol. I.] Historical. History of the Thirty Years' War, complete. History of the Revolt of the Netherlands to the Confederacy of the Gueux. Translated from the German by the Rev. A. J. W. Morrison, M.A.

The Works .... [Vol. II.] Historical and Dramatic. History of the Revolt of the Netherlands continued — Trials of Counts Egmont and Horn. [Translated by Lieut. E. B. Eastwick, with corrections by A. J. W. Morrison.] Wallenstein and Wilhelm Tell, Historical Dramas. Translated from the German [by James Churchill, S. T. Coleridge, and Theodore Martin].

2 vols. London. 1846 - 47. 8° (BOHN's Stand. Libr.)

Norway. See *Denmark.*

Poland.

DUNHAM (S. A.), *LL.D.* The History of Poland from the Earliest Period to 1830. London. 8° (LARDNER's Cab. Cycl., **56.**)

FLETCHER (James). The History of Poland; from the Earliest Period to the Present Time. ... With a Narrative of the Recent Events, obtained from a Polish Patriot Nobleman. New-York. 1846. 18° (HARPER's Fam. Libr., **24.**)

HISTORY of Poland. (CHAMBERS's Miscel., IV. no. 73.)

Portugal. See *Spain.*

Russia.

BELL (Robert). The History of Russia, from the Earliest Period to the Treaty of Tilsit (1807). 3 vols. London. 8° (LARDNER's Cab. Cycl., **52 - 54.**)

STRUGGLE (The) in the Caucasus. (CHAMBERS's Repos., II. no. 9.)

Scotland.

SCOTT (*Sir* Walter), *Bart.* The History of Scotland. 2 vols. London. 8° (LARDNER's Cab. Cycl., **13, 14.**)

Spain and Portugal.

AGAPIDA (*Fray* Antonio), *pseudon.* *See* [IRVING (Washington)].

CHURCH (——). Annals of Portugal. Progress of Maritime Discovery. A. D. 1279 - 1495. (ENCYCL. Metrop., XII. 357 - 365.)

DUNHAM (S. A.), *LL.D.* The History of Spain and Portugal. 5 vols. London. 8° (LARDNER's Cab. Cycl., **23 - 27.**)

FLORIAN (Jean Pierre CLARIS DE). History of the Moors of Spain. Translated from the French Original of M. Florian. To which is added, A brief Notice of Islamism [by the Rev. S. Greene]. New-York. [1840 ?] 18° (HARPER's Fam. Libr., **177.**)

GUERILLA (The); a Story of the Peninsular War. (CHAMBERS's Miscel., X. no. 171.)

[IRVING (Washington)]. Chronicle of the Conquest of Granada. From the MSS. of Fray Antonio Agapida. New-York. 1850. 12° (Works, Vol. XIV.)

MOORS (The) in Spain. (CHAMBERS's Miscel., VI. no. 106.)

PHILLIMORE (John George). Annals of Spain, from A. D. 1407, to A. D. 1620. (ENCYCL. Metrop., XI. 454 – 467, 519 – 531.)

PRESCOTT (William Hickling). History of the Reign of Ferdinand and Isabella, the Catholic. ... 10th Ed. 3 vols. New York. 1849. 8°

ROSCOE (Thomas). Annals of Portugal, from A. D. 1495 to A. D. 1811. (ENCYCL. Metrop., XIII. 799 – 827, 983 – 1012.)

——— Annals of Spain from A. D. 1621 to A. D. 1814. (ENCYCL. Metrop., XII. 706, *etc.* XIII. 66, *etc.*)

SMEDLEY (*Rev.* Edward). Annals of Spain and Portugal during the Twelfth and Thirteenth Centuries. (ENCYCL. Metrop., XII. 1 – 15.)

Sweden. See *Denmark.*

Switzerland.

DUNHAM (S. A.), *LL.D.* Annals of Switzerland, from A. D. 418 to A. D. 1789. (ENCYCL. Metrop., XIII. 183 – 276.)

HISTORY (The) of Switzerland, from the Earliest Period to 1830. London. 8° (LARDNER's Cab. Cycl., **22.**)

WILLIAM TELL and Switzerland. (CHAMBERS's Miscel., I. no. 9.)

Turkey.

TAYLOR (William Cooke), *LL.D.* Annals of the Ottoman Empire, from the Capture of Constantinople, A. D. 1453, to the Peace of Cainarjè, A. D. 1774. (ENCYCL. Metrop., XII. 639, *etc.* XIII. 84, *etc.*)

§ 2. Asia.

A. General Works.

[GOODRICH (Samuel Griswold)]. Lights and Shadows of Asiatic History: by the Author of Peter Parley's Tales. Boston. 1849. 16° or 18° (8. and 6.) (CABINET Libr., **9.**)

B. Particular Countries, etc.

Arabia.

CRICHTON (Andrew), *LL.D.* ... The History of Arabia, Ancient and Modern. ... 2 vols. New-York. 1840 – 45. 18° (HARPER's Fam. Libr., **68, 69.**)

FLORIAN (Jean Pierre CLARIS DE). History of the Moors of Spain. ... [With] a brief Notice of Islamism, *etc.* *See* § 1. B. *Spain.*

IRVING (Washington). Mahomet and his Successors. ... 2 vols. New-York. 1850. 12° (Works, Vol. XII. XIII.)

Assyria. See *Mesopotamia.*

Hindostan.

BRITISH Conquest (The) of India. (CHAMBERS's Miscel., IX. no. 157.)

MURRAY (Hugh). Historical and Descriptive Account of British India, from the most Remote Period to the Present Time ... ; with Illustrations of the Zoology, Botany, Climate, Geology and Mineralogy. Also Medical Observations ; an Account of the Hindoo Astronomy, the Trigonometrical Surveys, and the Navigation of the Indian Seas. By Hugh Murray ... ; James Wilson ... ; R. K. Greville ... ; Professor Jameson ; Whitelaw Ainslie ... ; William Rhind ... ; Professor Wallace ; and Captain Clarence Dalrymple ... . 3 vols. New York. N. D. 18° (HARPER's Fam. Libr., **47 - 49.**)

TAYLOR (William Cooke), *LL.D.* Establishment of the Mohammedan Power in India. History of the Delhi Empire, and of Persia. (ENCYCL. Metrop., XII. 468 - 475, 696 - 705, XIII. 828 - 832.)

Japan.

EUROPEAN Intercourse with Japan. (CHAMBERS's Papers, *etc.* XII. no. 93.)

Mesopotamia and Assyria (now *Turkey in Asia*).

FRASER (James Baillie). Mesopotamia and Assyria, from the Earliest Ages to the Present Time ; with Illustrations of their Natural History. ... New-York. 1845. 18° (HARPER's Fam. Libr., **157.**)

Palestine and the Jews.

HALE (William Hale), *Archdeacon.* History of the Jews. (ENCYCL. Metrop., Vol. IX. X.)

HISTORY of the Jews in England. (CHAMBERS's Miscel., IX. no. 153.)

MILMAN (*Rev.* Henry Hart). The History of the Jews, from the Earliest Period to the Present Time. ... With Maps and Engravings. 3 vols. New-York. 1843. 18° (HARPER's Fam. Libr., **1 - 3.**)

RUSSELL (Michael), *Bp. of Glasgow.* Palestine ; or, The Holy Land, from the Earliest Period to the Present Time. ... With a Map and Nine Engravings. New York. N. D. 18° (HARPER's Fam. Libr., **27.**)

Persia.

FRASER (James Baillie). Historical and Descriptive Account of Persia, from the Earliest Ages to the Present Time ... including a Description of Afghanistan and Beloochistan. ... New-York. N. D. 18° (HARPER's Fam. Libr., **70.**)

Turkey in Asia. See *Mesopotamia.*

§ 3. Africa.

A. General Works.

[GOODRICH (Samuel Griswold)]. Lights and Shadows of African History : by the Author of Peter Parley's Tales. Boston. 1849. 16° or 18° (8. and 6.) (CABINET Libr., **10.**)

B. Particular Countries, etc.

Abyssinia. See *Nubia.*

Barbary States.

Russell (Michael), *Bp. of Glasgow.* History and Present Condition of the Barbary States .... New-York. 1846. 18° (Harper's Fam. Libr., **73.**)

Egypt.

Russell (Michael), *Bp. of Glasgow.* ... View of Ancient and Modern Egypt; with an Outline of its Natural History .... With a Map and Engravings. New-York. 1846. 18° (Harper's Fam. Libr., **23.**)

Nubia and Abyssinia.

Russell (Michael), *Bp. of Glasgow.* ... Nubia and Abyssinia: comprehending their Civil History, Antiquities, Arts, Religion, Literature, and Natural History .... Illustrated by a Map, and several Engravings. New-York. 1845. 18° (Harper's Fam. Libr., **61.**)

§ 4. America.

A. General Works; the Indians.

[Goodrich (Samuel Griswold)]. ... The First Book of History, combined with Geography; containing the History and Geography of the Western Hemisphere. ... By the Author of Peter Parley's Tales. Illustrated by Engravings and [18] Colored Maps. Revised and improved Ed., with important Additions. Boston. 1852. Square 16°

[———] History of the Indians, of North and South America: by the Author of Peter Parley's Tales. Boston. 1849. 16° or 18° (8. and 6.) (Cabinet Libr., **11.**)

[———] Lights and Shadows of American History: by the Author of Peter Parley's Tales. Boston. 1849. 16° or 18° (8. and 6.) (Cabinet Libr., **7.**)

Macgregor (John). The Progress of America, from the Discovery of Columbus to the Year 1846. ... Vol. I. Historical and Statistical. | Vol. II. Geographical and Statistical. 2 vols. London. 1847. Large 8° (4.) pp. xii., 1520, and viii., 1334, 84.

Note. Supplements to Vol. I. are appended to Vol. II.

Parley (Peter), *pseudon.* *See* [Goodrich (Samuel Griswold)].

Robertson (William), *D.D.* The History of the Discovery and Conquest of America. ... Abridged. With a Memoir of the Author from that by Dugald Stewart .... New-York. 1848. 18° (Harper's Fam. Libr., **185.**)

Stone (*Col.* William Leet). Border Wars of the American Revolution. *See* B. *a. United States.*

THACHER (Benjamin Bussey). Indian Biography. *See* Class XXIV. Part I.

WILLSON (Marcius). American History: comprising Historical Sketches of the Indian Tribes; a Description of American Antiquities, with an Inquiry into their Origin, and the Origin of the Indian Tribes; History of the United States, with Appendices showing its Connection with European History; History of the present British Provinces; History of Mexico; and History of Texas .... New York. 1847. 8° pp. 672.

B. Particular Countries, etc.

a. North America and the West India Islands.

British America.

MURRAY (Hugh). An Historical and Descriptive Account of British America. *See* Class XXII. Part III.

Hayti.

TOUSSAINT L'OUVERTURE and the Republic of Hayti. (CHAMBERS'S Miscel., III. no. 57.)

Mexico.

CONQUEST (The) of Mexico. (CHAMBERS'S Miscel., IX. no. 146.)

PRESCOTT (William Hickling). History of the Conquest of Mexico, with a Preliminary View of the Ancient Mexican Civilization, and the Life of the Conqueror, Hernando Cortés. ... 8th Ed. 3 vols. New York. 1850. 8°

United States.

(General Works.)

BANCROFT (George). History of the United States, from the Discovery of the American Continent. Vol. I.–II. 14th Ed. | Vol. III. 12th Ed. | Vol. IV.–V. 5 vols. Boston. 1848–48–46–52–52. 8°

Note. Vols. I.–III. have also the title:—"History of the Colonization of the United States." Vol. IV. has the half-title:—"The American Revolution. Epoch First. The Overthrow of the European Colonial System. 1748–1763." —— Half-title of Vol. V.:—"Epoch Second. How Great Britain estranged America. 1763–1774."

[BOWEN (*Prof.* Francis)]. History of the United States. *See* Part I. WEBER (G.). Outlines, *etc.*

CHALMERS (George). An Introduction to the History of the Revolt of the American Colonies .... 2 vols. Boston. 1845. 8°

COOPER (James Fenimore). The History of the Navy of the United States of America. ... 2 vols. London. 1839. 8°

DUNHAM (S. A.), *LL.D.* Annals of the United States of North America, from A. D. 1497 to A. D. 1814. (ENCYCL. Metrop., XIII. 847–875, 1089–1132.)

EMERSON (Joseph). Questions and Supplement to Goodrich's History of the United States. ... A new Ed., ... adapted to the enlarged Ed. of the History. Boston. 1844. 18°

FERGUS (*Rev.* Henry). The History of the United States of America, from the Discovery of America to the Election of General Jackson to the Presidency in 1829. 2 vols. London. 8° (LARDNER'S Cab. Cycl., **31, 32.**)

FROST (John). A History of the United States; for the Use of Schools and Academies. ... New Ed., with Additions and Corrections. Philadelphia. 1846. 12°

GOODRICH (Charles Augustus). A History of the United States of America, on a Plan adapted to the Capacity of Youth .... Enlarged from the 100th Ed. ... Boston. 1844. 12° or 18° (6.)

See EMERSON (J.). Questions, *etc.*

——— *The same.* Illustrated by Engravings and Colored Maps. To which are added the Constitution of the United States, and the Declaration of Independence. Revised from former Editions, and brought down to the Present Time. Boston. 1852. 12°

GRAHAME (James), *LL.D.* The History of the United States of North America, from the Plantation of the British Colonies till their Assumption of National Independence. ... 2d Ed., enlarged and amended. [Edited, with a Memoir of the Author, by Josiah Quincy.] 2 vols. Philadelphia. 1848. 8°

HALE (Salma). History of the United States, from their first Settlement as Colonies to the Close of the Administration of Mr. Madison in 1817. ... 2 vols. New-York. [1840 ?] 18° (HARPER'S Fam. Libr., **119, 120.**)

HILDRETH (Richard). The History of the United States of America, from the Discovery of the Continent to the Organization of Government under the Federal Constitution. ... 3 vols. New York. 1849. 8°

——— [Second Series.] The History of the United States of America from the Adoption of the Federal Constitution to the End of the Sixteenth Congress. In Three Volumes. Vol. I. Administration of Washington. | Vol. II. John Adams and Jefferson. | Vol. III. Madison and Monroe. 3 vols. New York. 1851 – 52. 8°

Note. Also with the title: — "The History of the United States of America." Vol. IV.–VI.

HINTON (John Howard). The History and Topography; of the United States: edited by John Howard Hinton, A.M. assisted by several Literary Gentlemen in America & England. Illustrated with a Series of Views, drawn on the Spot, and engraved on Steel, expressly for this Work. 3d Ed., brought down to 1842. 2 vols. London. 1842. 4°

PILGRIM Fathers (The). (CHAMBERS'S Repos., I. no. 7.)

STONE (*Col.* William Leet). Border Wars of the American Revolution. ... 2 vols. New-York. [1843 ?] 18° (HARPER'S Fam. Libr., **167, 168.**)

SULLIVAN (William). The Public Men of the Revolution. Including Events from the Peace of 1783 to the Peace of 1815. *See* Class XXIV. Part I.

WASHINGTON and his Contemporaries. (CHAMBERS's Papers, *etc.* II. no. 10.)

WILLARD (*Mrs.* Emma [HART]). History of the United States. ... New York. 1845. 8°

——— Abridged History of the United States. ... . New York. 1845. 12°

WILLIAMS (Edwin). The Statesman's Manual. — The Addresses and Messages of the Presidents of the United States, ... from 1789 to 1851; with a Memoir of each of the Presidents, and a History of their Administrations: also, the Constitution of the United States, and a Selection of important Documents and Statistical Information. ... Reference Ed. — enlarged. 3 vols. New York. 1852. 8°

Note. The three vols. are paged continuously. A summary of the seventh Census of the U. S. is appended to Vol. III.

WILLSON (Marcius). History of the United States, for the Use of Schools. New-York. 1846. 12° (2 copies.)

(Particular States and Territories.)

California.

CALIFORNIA. (CHAMBERS's Papers, *etc.* IV. no. 26.)

Connecticut.

DWIGHT (Theodore), *Jr.* The History of Connecticut, from the First Settlement to the Present Time. New York. [1840 ?] 18° (HARPER's Fam. Libr., **133.**)

Louisiana.

BUNNER (E.). History of Louisiana, from its First Discovery and Settlement to the Present Time. New-York. 1846. 18° (HARPER's Fam. Libr., **176.**)

Maine.

SIBLEY (John Langdon). A History of the Town of Union, in the County of Lincoln, Maine, to the Middle of the Nineteenth Century; with a Family Register of the Settlers before the Year 1800, and of their Descendants. ... Boston. 1851. 12°

Massachusetts.

PILGRIM Fathers (The). (CHAMBERS's Repos., I. no. 7.)

WHITNEY (*Rev.* Peter). The History of the County of Worcester, in the Commonwealth of Massachusetts: with a particular Account of every Town ... . To which is prefixed, A Map of the County ... . Worcester. 1793. 8°

Note. The Map is wanting.

WINTHROP (John), *Gov. of Mass.* The History of New England from 1630 to 1649. By John Winthrop, Esq. first Governour of the Colony of the Massachusetts Bay. From his Original Manuscripts. With Notes . . . . By James Savage . . . . A new Ed., with Additions and Corrections by the former Editor. . . . 2 vols. Boston. 1853. Large 12° (6.)

Michigan.

LANMAN (James H.). History of Michigan, from its Earliest Colonization to the Present Time. New-York. [1841 ?] 18° (HARPER'S Fam. Libr., **139.**)

Oregon.

IRVING (Washington). Astoria or, Anecdotes of an Enterprise beyond the Rocky Mountains. Author's revised Ed. [With a Map of the Oregon Territory.] . . . New-York. 1849. 12° (Works, Vol. VIII.)

b. South America.

Peru.

INCAS (The) of Peru. (CHAMBERS'S Papers, *etc.* XII. no. 90.)

PRESCOTT (William Hickling). History of the Conquest of Peru, with a Preliminary View of the Civilization of the Incas. . . . 2 vols. New York. 1850. 8°

§ 5. Oceania.

Note. Including *Malaysia* (otherwise called *the Asiatic*, *Eastern*, or *Indian Archipelago*), *Australia*, and *Polynesia*.

AUSTRALIA and Van Diemen's Land. (CHAMBERS'S Papers, *etc.* VI. no. 45.)

RAJAH BROOKE and Borneo. (CHAMBERS'S Papers, *etc.* V. no. 34.)

RUSSELL (Michael), *Bp. of Glasgow.* Polynesia ; or, An Historical Account of the principal Islands in the South Sea, including New Zealand ; the Introduction of Christianity ; and the Actual Condition of the Inhabitants in regard to Civilization, Commerce, and the Arts of Social Life. . . . New-York. 1848. 18° (HARPER'S Fam. Libr., **158.**)

SIR STAMFORD RAFFLES and the Spice Islands. (CHAMBERS'S Miscel., III. no. 53.)

CLASS XXVI. ECCLESIASTICAL AND SACRED HISTORY.

Note. For the History of *Various Religions and Superstitions*, see Class II. Part IV.

AUBIGNÉ (Jean Henri MERLE D'). *See* MERLE D'AUBIGNÉ.

CAMISARDS (The). [Or, The Persecution of the Protestants in France.] (CHAMBERS'S Miscel., VII. no. 114.)

CARWITHEN (*Rev.* J. B. S.). Heresies of the Fourth Century, and History of the Christian Church, from the Death of Theodosius to the End of the Eleventh Century. (ENCYCL. Metrop., Vol. XI.)

CLAIMS (Of the) and Uses of Sacred History. (ENCYCL. Metrop., IX. 73 – 80.)

CROSTHWAITE (*Rev.* John Clarke). Ecclesiastical History of the First Half of the Sixteenth Century. (ENCYCL. Metrop., XIII. 97 – 104.)

D'AUBIGNÉ (Jean Henri MERLE). *See* MERLE D'AUBIGNÉ.

DOWLING (*Rev.* John Goulter). Ecclesiastical History, from A. D. 1548 to A. D. 1700. (ENCYCL. Metrop., XIII. 475 – 495, 660 – 670.)

GAMMELL (*Prof.* William). A History of American Baptist Missions in Asia, Africa, Europe and North America. ... With Maps and an Appendix. Boston. 1849. 12°

GARNETT (*Rev.* Richard). The Christian Church, from the Death of Julian, to the End of the Fourth Century. Ecclesiastical Writers of the Fourth Century. (ENCYCL. Metrop., XI. 302 – 323.)

GLEIG (*Rev.* George Robert). The History of the Bible. ... 2 vols. New York. N. D. 18° (HARPER'S Fam. Libr., **12, 13.**)

HETHERINGTON (*Rev.* William M.) History of the Church of Scotland. From the Introduction of Christianity to the Period of the Disruption in 1843. ... 1st American, from the 3d Edinburgh Ed. New York. 1844. 8°

HINDS (Samuel), *D.D.* A History of the Rise and Early Progress of Christianity. (ENCYCL. Metrop., X. 580 – 606, 705 – 814.)

JEREMIE (James Amiraux), *D.D.* History of the Christian Church in the Second and Third Centuries, and of Rome from the Foundation of Constantinople to the Death of Julian. (ENCYCL. Metrop., XI. 81 – 208.)

LYALL (*Rev.* Alfred). The Christian Church in the Twelfth and Thirteenth Centuries. (ENCYCL. Metrop., XI. 646 – 658, 749 – 764.)

MERLE D'AUBIGNÉ (Jean Henri), *D.D.* History of the Great Reformation of the 16th Century, in Germany, Switzerland, &c. ... Vol. I. – III. 5th American from the 5th London Ed. | Assisted in the Preparation of the English Original by H. White ... . Vol. IV. | History of the Reformation of the Sixteenth Century. Volume Fifth. The Reformation in England. ... Translated by H. White ... Ph.Dr. ... . The Translation carefully revised by Dr. Merle d'Aubigné. 5 vols. New York: Robert Carter. [Vol. I. – III.,] 1843. [Vol. IV.,] 1846. [Vol. V.,] 1853. 12°

Note. The *unmutilated* edition.

MILMAN (*Rev.* Henry Hart). The History of Christianity, from the Birth of Christ to the Abolition of Paganism in the Roman Empire. ... With a Preface and Notes by James Murdoch, D.D. New-York. 1841. 8°

MIMPRISS (Robert). The Gospel History of our Lord's Life and Ministry, *etc.* *See* Class XXIV. Part II. JESUS CHRIST, *etc.*

NEANDER (*Prof.* Johann August Wilhelm). History of the Planting and Training of the Christian Church by the Apostles. ... [Vol. I.] Translated from the 3d Ed. of the original German by J. E. Ryland. | With the Author's Final Additions. Also, his Antignostikus;

or, Spirit of Tertullian. Translated from the German by J. E. Ryland. ... Vol. II. 2 vols. London. 1851. 8° (BOHN's Stand. Libr.)

Note. The "Antignostikus" has the half-title: — "Antignostikus; or the Spirit of Tertullian, and an Introduction to his Writings: a Monograph designed to be a Contribution to the History of Christian Doctrine and Morals in the First Ages. ... Translated from the 2d Ed. (*Berlin* 1849) of the Original German."

NORTON (*Prof.* Andrews). The Evidences of the Genuineness of the Gospels. *See* Class II. § 1.

Note. A large part of Vols. II. and III. relates to the history of the Gnostics.

PERSECUTIONS (The) in Scotland. (CHAMBERS's Miscel., VI. no. 109.)

RANKE (*Prof.* Franz Leopold). The History of the Popes, their Church and State, and especially of their Conflicts with Protestantism, in the Sixteenth & Seventeenth Centuries. Translated by E. Foster. Vol. I. – II. With a General Index. | Vol. III. — Appendix. 3 vols. London. 1847 – 48. 8° (BOHN's Stand. Libr.)

RELIGIOUS Impostors. *See* Class XXIV. Part I.

RIDDLE (*Rev.* Joseph Esmond). Ecclesiastical History of the Fourteenth and Fifteenth Centuries. (ENCYCL. Metrop., XII. 179 – 191, 288 – 305.)

ROSE (*Rev.* Hugh James). Ecclesiastical History from A. D. 1700 to A. D. 1815. (ENCYCL. Metrop., XIII. 1133 – 1147.)

STEBBING (*Rev.* Henry). The History of the Christian Church, from its Foundation to A. D. 1492. ... 2 vols. London. 8° (LARDNER's Cab. Cycl., **63, 64.**)

——— The History of the Reformation. 2 vols. London. 8° (LARDNER's Cab. Cycl., **65, 66.**)

TRACY (*Rev.* Joseph). History of the American Board of Commissioners for Foreign Missions. ... 2d Ed., carefully revised and enlarged. New-York. 1842. 8°

TURNER (Sharon). The Sacred History of the World, attempted to be philosophically considered, in a Series of Letters to a Son. ... 3 vols. New-York. 1846. 18° (HARPER's Fam. Libr., **32, 72, 84.**)

WHATELY (Richard), *Abp. of Dublin.* Dissertation Third: exhibiting a General View of the Rise, Progress, and Corruptions of Christianity. ... (ENCYCL. Brit., 8th Ed., I. 447 – 545.)

CLASS XXVII. HISTORY OF MORALS, MANNERS, AND CUSTOMS. — ANTIQUITIES; NUMISMATICS.

Note. Compare Classes XXII., XXIII., and Class II. Part IV.

ADAM (Alexander), *LL.D.* Roman Antiquities ... . With ... Notes ... . By James Boyd ... . 7th New York Ed., with additional Notes. By Lorenzo L. Da Ponte. ... . New York. 1837. 8°

——— Roman Antiquities ... . With numerous Notes, improved Indices, and a Series of Analytical Questions. By James Boyd ... . Illustrated by upwards of 100 Engravings on Wood and Steel. 12th Ed. London. 1843. 12° or 18° (6.) pp. xii., 528, 98.

Ancient Rites and Mysteries. (Chambers's Papers, *etc.* X. no. 73.)

Ancient Scandinavia. (Chambers's Papers, *etc.* VII. no. 50.)

Annals of Fashion. *See* Book (The) of Costume, *etc.*

Anthon (*Prof.* Charles), *LL.D.* A Manual of Grecian Antiquities. With numerous Illustrations. ... New York. 1852. 12°

——— A Manual of Roman Antiquities. With numerous Illustrations. ... New York. 1851. 12°

Becker (*Prof.* Wilhelm Adolph). Charicles: or Illustrations of the Private Life of the Ancient Greeks; with Notes and Excursus. Translated from the German ... by the Rev. Frederick Metcalfe ... . London. 1845. 12°

——— Gallus: or, Roman Scenes of the Time of Augustus; with Notes and Excursuses illustrative of the Manners and Customs of the Romans. ... Translated by the Rev. Frederick Metcalfe ... . [2d Ed., revised and enlarged, from the 2d Ed. of the original work, edited by Prof. W. Rein.] London. 1849. 12°

Boeckh (*Prof.* August). The Public Economy of Athens; to which is added, A Dissertation on the Silver Mines of Laurion. ... Translated by George Cornewall Lewis ... . 2d Ed., revised. London. 1842. 8° pp. xiii., 688. +

Bojesen (*Prof.* Ernst Frederik Christian), *Ph. D.* A Manual of Grecian Antiquities ... . Translated from the German. Edited (with occasional Notes, and a complete Series of Questions) by the Rev. Thomas Kerchever Arnold ... . Revised, with Additions and Corrections [by the Rev. J. A. Spencer]. New-York. 1848. 12°

——— A Manual of Roman Antiquities, with a short History of Roman Literature ... . Translated from the German. Edited (with occasional Notes, and a complete Series of Questions) by the Rev. Thomas Kerchever Arnold ... . Revised, with Additions and Corrections [by the Rev. J. A. Spencer]. New-York. 1848. 12°

Note. This volume and the preceding are bound together, with the common title: — "A Manual of Grecian and Roman Antiquities," etc.

Book (The) of Costume: or, Annals of Fashion, from the Earliest Period to the Present Time. By a Lady of Rank. Illustrated by upwards of Two Hundred Engravings on Wood, by the most eminent Artists. New Ed. London. 1847. 8°

Brand (John). Observations on the Popular Antiquities of Great Britain: chiefly illustrating the Origin of our Vulgar and Provincial Customs, Ceremonies, and Superstitions. ... Arranged, revised, and greatly enlarged, by Sir Henry Ellis ... . A new Ed., with further Additions. ... 3 vols. London. 1849. 8° (Bohn's Antiquarian Library.)

Carr (Thomas Swinburne). A Manual of Roman Antiquities. ... London. 1836. 12°

CHRONOLOGICAL Tables of Modern History, *etc.* *See* Class XXV. Part III.

COSTUME. *See* BOOK (The) of Costume, *etc.*

ESCHENBERG (*Prof.* Johann Joachim). Classical Antiquities; being Part of the "Manual of Classical Literature." From the German of J. J. E. . . . . With Additions. Embracing Treatises on . . . I. Classical Geography . . . . II. Classical Chronology. III. Greek and Roman Mythology. IV. Greek Antiquities. V. Roman Antiquities. By N. W. Fiske . . . . 4th Ed. Philadelphia. 1846. 8°

EVERY-DAY Life of the Greeks. (CHAMBERS's Papers, *etc.* IV. no. 29.)

FOSBROKE (*Rev.* Thomas Dudley). A Treatise on the Arts, Manufactures, Manners, and Institutions of the Greeks and Romans. 2 vols. London. 8° (LARDNER's Cab. Cycl., **45, 46.**)

FUSS (*Prof.* Jean Dominique). Roman Antiquities. . . . Translated [by the Rev. A. W. Street and the Rev. B. Street] from the last Ed. Oxford. 1840. 8° pp. xiv., 608. +

[GOODRICH (Samuel Griswold)]. The Manners, Customs, and Antiquities of the Indians of North and South America: by the Author of Peter Parley's Tales. Boston. 1849. 16° or 18° (8. and 6.) (CABINET Libr., **12.**)

GREEN (Benjamin Richard). Numismatics. (ENCYCL. Metrop., V. 619 - 650.)

HERMANN (*Prof.* Karl Friedrich). A Manual of the Political Antiquities of Greece, historically considered. From the German . . . . Oxford. 1836. 8°

HISTORY of the Slave-Trade. (CHAMBERS's Miscel., I. 19.)

JAHN (*Prof.* Johann). Jahn's Biblical Archæology. *See* Class II. Part III.

LAYARD (Austen Henry). Nineveh and its Remains, *etc.* *See* Class XXIII.

LOGAN (James). The Scotish [*sic*] Gaël; or, Celtic Manners, as preserved among the Highlanders; being an Historical and Descriptive Account of the Inhabitants, Antiquities, and National Peculiarities of Scotland . . . . 1st American Ed. Hartford. 1843. 8°

NUTTALL (P. Austin), *LL.D.* A Classical and Archæological Dictionary of the Manners, Customs, Laws, Institutions, Arts, etc. of the Celebrated Nations of Antiquity, and of the Middle Ages. To which is prefixed a Synoptical and Chronological View of Ancient History. . . . London. 1840. 8° pp. xxiv., 679.

POTTER (John), successively *Bp. of Oxford* and *Abp. of Canterbury.* Archæologia Græca, or the Antiquities of Greece . . . . A new Ed.; with a Life of the Author, by Robert Anderson, M.D. and an Appendix, containing a concise History of the Grecian States, and a short Account of the Lives and Writings of the most Celebrated Greek Authors; by George Dunbar . . . . 2 vols. Edinburgh. 1832. 8°

RUINED Cities of Central America. (CHAMBERS's Papers, *etc.* II. no. 13.)

St. John (James Augustus). The History of the Manners and Customs of Ancient Greece. 3 vols. London. 1842. 8°

Salkeld (Joseph). Classical Antiquities, or a Compendium of Roman and Grecian Antiquities; with a Sketch of Ancient Mythology. New-York. 1844. 18°

Schoemann (Georg Friedrich). A Dissertation on the Assemblies of the Athenians. Translated from the Latin of G. F. Schömann [by F. A. P.]. To which is added, A new and complete Index. Cambridge. 1838. 8°

Sepulchres (The) of Etruria. (Chambers's Papers, *etc.* I. no. 2.)

Slavery in America. (Chambers's Miscel., II. no. 27.)

Smith (Horatio). Festivals, Games, and Amusements, Ancient and Modern. ... With Additions, by Samuel Woodworth, Esq. New York. 1847. 18° (Harper's Fam. Libr., **25.**)

Smith (William), *LL.D.* A Dictionary of Greek and Roman Antiquities. Edited by W. S., Ph. D., and illustrated by numerous Engravings on Wood. First American Ed., carefully revised, and containing numerous Additional Articles relative to the Botany, Mineralogy, and Zoology of the Ancients. By Charles Anthon .... New-York. 1843. 8° pp. ix., 1124.

——— Dictionary of Greek and Roman Antiquities. Edited by W. S. .... Illustrated by numerous Engravings on Wood. 2d Ed., improved and enlarged. Boston. [Printed in London.] 1849. 8° pp. xii., 1293.

——— A School Dictionary of Greek and Roman Antiquities. Abridged from the Larger Dictionary. ... With Corrections and Improvements, by Charles Anthon .... New-York. 1846. 12°

Temperance Movement (The). (Chambers's Miscel., II. no. 23.)

Thompson (*Rev.* Henry). Heraldry. (Encycl. Metrop., V. 589 – 618.)

Wachsmuth (*Prof.* Ernst Wilhelm Gottlieb). The Historical Antiquities of the Greeks with reference to their Political Institutions ... Translated from the German by Edmund Woolrych, Esq. 2 vols. Oxford. 1837. 8°

CLASS XXVIII. HISTORY OF PHILOSOPHY, AND OF THE ARTS AND SCIENCES.

Alchemy and the Alchemists. (Chambers's Papers, *etc.* IX. no. 66.)

Ancient Philosophic Sects. (Chambers's Papers, *etc.* VIII. no. 62.)

Annual (The) of Scientific Discovery: or, Year-Book of Facts in Science and Art .... Together with a List of recent Scientific Publications; a classified List of Patents; Obituaries of eminent Scientific Men; an Index of important Papers in Scientific Journals, Reports, etc. ... Edited by David A. Wells ... and George Bliss, Jr. [Vol. I. II.] 2 vols. Boston. 1850 – 51. 12°

Beckmann (*Prof.* Johann). A History of Inventions, Discoveries, and

Origins. Translated from the German, by William Johnston. 4th Ed., carefully revised and enlarged by William Francis ... and J. W. Griffith .... 2 vols. London. 1846. 8° (BOHN's Stand. Libr.)

BLISS (George), *Jr. Editor. See* ANNUAL (The) of Scientific Discovery, *etc.*

BLOMFIELD (Charles James), successively *Bp. of Chester* and *London.* Socrates. Greek Philosophy. (ENCYCL. Metrop., IX. 669 – 685.)

BOOK (The) of Costume. *See* Class XXVII.

BRIEF View (A) of Greek Philosophy up to the Age of Pericles. Philadelphia. 1846. 24° (8. 4.) pp. 81. (SMALL Books, *etc.* II. no. 5.)

BRIEF View (A) of Greek Philosophy from the Age of Socrates to the Coming of Christ. Philadelphia. 1846. 24° (8. 4.) pp. 87. (SMALL Books, *etc.* II. no. 6.)

CELLINI (Benvenuto). Memoirs, *etc. See* Class XXIV. Part II.

CHILDHOOD of Experimental Philosophy. (CHAMBERS's Papers, *etc.* X. no. 76.)

CHRONOLOGICAL Tables of Modern History, *etc. See* Class XXV. Part III.

COUSIN (Victor). Course of the History of Modern Philosophy. Translated by O. W. Wight. [2d Ed.] ... 2 vols. New York. 1852. Large 12°

ELECTRIC Communications. (CHAMBERS's Papers, *etc.* IX. no. 71.)

ENFIELD (William), *LL.D.* The History of Philosophy, from the Earliest Periods : drawn up from Brucker's Historia Critica Philosophiæ. ... London. 1840. 8° pp. xvi., 670.

EPITOME (An) of the History of Philosophy. Being the Work adopted by the University of France for Instruction in the Colleges and High Schools. Translated from the French, with Additions, and a Continuation of the History from the Time of Reid to the Present Day. By C. S. Henry .... 2 vols. New-York. [1841 ?] 18° (HARPER's Fam. Libr., **143, 144.**)

EWBANK (Thomas). A Descriptive and Historical Account of Hydraulic and other Machines for raising Water, Ancient and Modern : with Observations on various Subjects connected with the Mechanic Arts : including the Progressive Development of the Steam Engine .... In Five Books. Illustrated by nearly Three Hundred Engravings. 2d Ed., revised ... to which is added, A Supplement. ... New York. 1847. 8° pp. xvi., 608.

Note. Also with an engraved title-page : — "Ewbank's Hydraulics and Mechanics."

FOSBROKE (*Rev.* Thomas Dudley). A Treatise on the Arts, Manufactures, *etc.* of the Greeks and Romans. *See* Class XXVII.

GREEK Philosophy. *See* BRIEF View, *etc.*

HAMPDEN (Renn Dickson), *D.D.* Thomas Aquinas and the Scholastic Philosophy. (ENCYCL. Metrop., XI. 793 – 814.)

HISTORY of Astronomy. *See* [ROTHMAN (R. W.)].

HISTORY (A) of Wonderful Inventions. Illustrated with numerous Engravings on Wood. Part I. – II. 2 pts. (bound in one vol.) New York. 1849. Square 12°

HOLLAND (John). A Treatise on the Progressive Improvement, *etc.* of the Manufactures in Metal. *See* Class XIV. Part III.

JEREMIE (James Amiraux), *D.D.* Plotinus. — The Eclectics, or later Platonists. (ENCYCL. Metrop., XI. 209 – 216.)

——— Sextus Empiricus. The Pyrrhonists. (ENCYCL. Metrop., X. 698 – 704.)

LANZI (Luigi). The History of Painting in Italy, from the Period of the Revival of the Fine Arts to the End of the Eighteenth Century: translated from the Italian of the Abate L. L. By Thomas Roscoe. ... New Ed., revised. 3 vols. London. 1847. 8° (BOHN'S Stand. Libr.)

LARDNER (Dionysius), *LL.D.* The Steam Engine, *etc.* *See* Class XI. Part II.

LESLIE (*Sir* John). Dissertation Fifth: exhibiting a General View of the Progress of Mathematical and Physical Science, chiefly during the Eighteenth Century. ... (ENCYCL. Brit., 8th Ed., I. 689 – 793.)

LOSSING (Benson J.). Outline History of the Fine Arts. ... New York. [1840?] 18° (HARPER'S Fam. Libr., **103.**)

LOWNDES (William). Plato. (ENCYCL. Metrop., X. 72 – 90.) Lucius Annæus Seneca. The Stoical Philosophy. (*Ibid.* pp. 483 – 491.)

MACKINTOSH (*Sir* James), *LL.D.* Dissertation Second: exhibiting a General View of the Progress of Ethical Philosophy chiefly during the Seventeenth and Eighteenth Centuries. With a Preface by William Whewell, D.D. ... . (ENCYCL. Brit., 8th Ed., I. 291 – 445.)

MAURICE (*Rev.* Frederick Denison). [History of] Moral and Metaphysical Philosophy. (ENCYCL. Metrop., II. 545 – 674.)

MORELL (J. D.). An Historical and Critical View of the Speculative Philosophy of Europe in the Nineteenth Century. ... From the last London Ed. New York. 1848. 8° pp. 752.

MURDOCK (James), *D.D.* Sketches of Modern Philosophy, especially among the Germans. Hartford. 1842. 16°

NEWMAN (*Rev.* John Henry). Cicero. Roman Philosophy. (ENCYCL. Metrop., X. 279 – 294.)

PLAYFAIR (*Prof.* John). Dissertation Fourth: exhibiting a General View of the Progress of Mathematical and Physical Science, since the Revival of Letters in Europe. ... (ENCYCL. Brit., 8th Ed., I. 547 – 688.)

PORTER (George Richardson). A Treatise on the Origin, Progressive Improvement, *etc.* of the Manufactures of Porcelain and Glass. *See* Class XIV. Part III.

POWELL (*Prof.* Baden). The History of Natural Philosophy from the Earliest Periods to the Present Time. London. 8° (LARDNER'S Cab. Cycl., **99.**)

RAILWAY Communications. (CHAMBERS'S Papers, *etc.* XII. no. 89.)

RECENT Decorative Art. (CHAMBERS's Papers, *etc.* IX. no. 66.)

ROLLIN (Charles). Ancient History ... including a History of the Arts and Sciences of the Ancients. *See* Class XXV. Part II. § 1.

[ROTHMAN (Richard Wellesley)], *M.D.* History of Astronomy. [London. 183–?] 8° (LIBR. of Useful Knowl., Nat. Phil., III.)

[STEPHENSON (——)]. Life of William Caxton, with an Account of the Invention of Printing, *etc.* *See* Class XXIV. Part II. CAXTON (W.).

STEWART (*Prof.* Dugald). Dissertation First: exhibiting a General View of the Progress of Metaphysical and Ethical Philosophy, since the Revival of Letters in Europe. ... (ENCYCL. Brit., 8th Ed., I. 1–289.)

TENNEMANN (Wilhelm Gottlieb). A Manual of the History of Philosophy. Translated from the German of T., by the Rev. Arthur Johnson, M.A. Revised, enlarged, and continued, by J. R. Morell. London. 1852. 8° (Bohn's Philological Library.)

WELLS (David Ames). *Editor.* *See* ANNUAL (The) of Scientific Discovery, *etc.*

WHEWELL (*Prof.* William), *D.D.* Archimedes. Greek Mathematics. (ENCYCL. Metrop., IX. 686–694.)

——— History of the Inductive Sciences, from the Earliest to the Present Time. ... A new Ed., revised and continued. ... 3 vols. London. 1847. 8°

——— Preface. *See* MACKINTOSH (*Sir* J.). Dissertation, *etc.*

YOUNG (Thomas), *M.D.* History of Mechanics — Hydraulics and Pneumatics — Music — Optics — Astronomy — and of Terrestrial Physics. (A Course of Lectures, *etc.* Lect. XX. XXX. XXXIV. XL. XLVIII. LX. — *See* Class XI. Part I.)

CLASS XXIX. HISTORY OF LITERATURE AND OF EDUCATION; BIBLIOGRAPHY.

ADELUNG (Friedrich). An Historical Sketch of Sanscrit Literature, with copious Bibliographical Notices of Sanscrit Works and Translations. From the German of A., with numerous Additions and Corrections. Oxford. 1832. 8°

ANDERSON (Christopher). The Annals of the English Bible. By C. A. Abridged and continued by Samuel Irenæus Prime ... . New York. 1849. 8°

ANTHON (*Prof.* Charles), *LL.D.* A Manual of Greek Literature, from the Earliest Authentic Periods to the Close of the Byzantine Era. ... New York. 1853. 12°

APPLETONS' Library Manual; containing a Catalogue Raisonné of upwards of Twelve Thousand of the most important Works in every Department of Knowledge, in all Modern Languages. Part I. Subjects — alphabetically arranged. Part II. Biography, Classics, Miscellanies, and Index to Part I. New-York. 1847. 8°

BRISTOL ACADEMY, *Taunton.* Historical Sketch of the Academy. *See* Class V. FELTON (C. C.). An Address, *etc.*

BRITISH MUSEUM. *See* GREAT BRITAIN — *Parliament.* Report, *etc.*

BROWN (Goold). Catalogue of English Grammars and Grammarians. (Prefixed to his "Grammar of English Grammars," *etc.* *See* Class XV. Part II. § 2. A.)

BROWN UNIVERSITY, *Providence, R. I.* A Catalogue of the Library, *etc.* *See* [JEWETT (C. C.)].

BROWNE (*Prof.* R. W.). A History of Classical Literature. ... Greek Literature. Philadelphia. 1852. 8°

BUCKINGHAM (Joseph TINKER). Specimens of [American] Newspaper Literature: with Personal Memoirs, Anecdotes, and Reminiscences. 2 vols. Boston. 1852. 12°

——— Personal Memoirs, *etc.* *See* Class XXIV. Part II.

CHAMBERS (Robert). Cyclopædia of English Literature, *etc.* *See* Class XXXI.

CHRONOLOGICAL Tables of Modern History, *etc.* *See* Class XXV. Part III.

CLEVELAND (Charles Dexter). A Compendium of English Literature, *etc.* *See* Class XXXI.

——— English Literature of the Nineteenth Century, *etc.* *See* Class XXXI.

COLERIDGE (Henry Nelson). Introductions to the Study of the Greek Classic Poets. ... Part I. containing, I. General Introduction. II. Homer. Boston. 1842. 12°

CREASY (*Prof.* Edward Shepherd). Some Account of the Foundation of Eton College and of the Past and Present Condition of the School. ... London. 1848. 12°

DANA HILL Public Schools. *See* [LIVERMORE (G.)]. A Brief Account, *etc.*

DANTE. (CHAMBERS's Repos., II. no. 16.)

D'ISRAELI (Isaac). Amenities of Literature, consisting of Sketches and Characters of English Literature. ... 2d Ed. 2 vols. New York. 1845. 12°

[———] Miscellanies of Literature. By the Author of "Curiosities of Literature." A new Ed. revised and corrected. ... Vol. I. Literary Miscellanies. Calamities of Authors. | Vol. II. Quarrels of Authors. | Vol. III. The Literary Character. Character of James the First. 3 vols. New-York. 1841. 12°

DUNLOP (John). The History of Fiction: being a Critical Account of the most celebrated Prose Works of Fiction from the Earliest Greek Romances to the Novels of the Present Age. ... 3d Ed. London. 1845. 8°

EDSON (Theodore), *D.D.* An Address delivered at the Opening of the Colburn Grammar School, in Lowell, December 13, 1848. [With a "tribute to the memory" of Warren Colburn, and historical notices of the Lowell public schools.] Lowell. 1849. 12° pp. 37.

EDUCATION Movement (The). (CHAMBERS's Papers, *etc.* V. no. 36.)

ELIOT (Samuel Atkins). A Sketch of the History of Harvard College, and of its Present State. Boston. 1848. 16°

ESCHENBERG (*Prof.* Johann Joachim). Manual of Classical Literature, *etc.* [Part V. pp. 433 - 652 of the 4th Ed. contains a *History* of Classical Literature.] *See* Class XVI. Part I.

FOSTER (*Mrs.* M. E.). A Hand-Book of Modern European Literature. ... Philadelphia. 1850. 12°

GERMAN Poets and Poetry. (CHAMBERS's Papers, *etc.* IX. no. 68.

[GOODRICH (Samuel Griswold)]. Literature, Ancient and Modern, with Specimens. By the Author of Peter Parley's Tales. Boston. 1849. 16° or 18° (8. and 6.) (CABINET Libr., 17.)

GORTON (John). Catalogue of Works ... relating to Biography and Literary History. (Appended to his Biographical Dictionary, Vol. IV. — *See* Class XXIV. Part I.)

GREAT BRITAIN — *Parliament.* Report of the Commissioners [Francis Egerton, Earl of Ellesmere, Chairman] appointed to inquire into the Constitution and Government of the British Museum ; with Minutes of Evidence. Presented to both Houses of Parliament by Command of Her Majesty. London. 1850. fol. pp. iv., 823.

——— British Museum. Index to Report and Minutes of Evidence. ... London. 1850. fol.

GRISWOLD (Rufus Wilmot). The Poets and Poetry of America. With an Historical Introduction, *etc.* *See* Class XIX.

——— The Prose Writers of America. With a Survey of the History ... of American Literature, *etc.* *See* Class XXXI.

HALLAM (Henry). Introduction to the Literature of Europe in the Fifteenth, Sixteenth, and Seventeenth Centuries. ... 2 vols. New-York. 1848. 8°

HARPER's Illustrated Catalogue of valuable Standard Works, in the several Departments of General Literature. ... New York. 1847. 8°

HORNE (R. H.). A new Spirit of the Age. ... New-York. 1844. 12°

ISRAELI (Isaac D'). *See* D'ISRAELI.

[JEWETT (*Prof.* Charles Coffin)]. A Catalogue of the Library of Brown University, Providence, Rhode-Island. With an Index of Subjects. Providence. 1843. 8°

LIBRARIES. *See* PUBLIC Libraries.

[LIVERMORE (George)]. A brief Account of the Dana Hill Public Schools, Cambridge. Cambridge. 1849. 18° ? pp. 20.

[———]. The Origin, History and Character of the New England Primer : being a Series of [eight] Articles contributed to the Cambridge Chronicle, by "The Antiquary." Cambridge. 1849. 4° *Not paged.*

Note. Twelve copies only of this very curious work were printed for private distribution.

——— Public Schools in Cambridge. Retrospective. (COMMON SCHOOL Journal, X. 228 – 234.)

——— Remarks on Public Libraries. From "The North American Review" for July, 1850. For Private Distribution only. Cambridge. 1850. 8° pp. 40.

——— Remarks on the Publication and Circulation of the Scriptures: suggested by Rev. W. P. Strickland's History of the American Bible Society, and published as a Review of that Work in the Christian Examiner for November, eighteen hundred and forty-nine. Cambridge. 1849. 8° pp. 31.

MAHON, Philip Henry, *Viscount*. *See* STANHOPE.

MECHANICS' Institutions. (CHAMBERS'S Papers, *etc.* III. no. 23.)

MONTGOMERY (James). ... Lectures on General Literature, Poetry &c. .... New-York. 1840. 18° (HARPER'S Fam. Libr., **64.**)

MUELLER (*Prof.* Karl Otfried). ... History of the Literature of Ancient Greece. ... Vol. I. [and Vol. II. Ch. XXVII. — XXXVII. pp. 1 – 128. — Translated from the German manuscript by George Cornewall Lewis.] Published under the Superintendence of the Society for the Diffusion of Useful Knowledge. London. 1840. 8° (LIBR. of Useful Knowl.)

Note. Not completed, in consequence of the author's death.

MURE (William). A Critical History of the Language and Literature of Ancient Greece. ... Vol. I. – III. 3 vols. London. 1850. 8°

NEW ENGLAND Primer. *See* [LIVERMORE (G.)]. The Origin, *etc.*

[PALFREY (John Gorham)], *LL.D.* Review of Lord Mahon's History of the American Revolution. *See* SPARKS (J.). A Reply, *etc.*

PARLEY (Peter), *pseudon.* *See* [GOODRICH (Samuel Griswold)].

POTTER (Alonzo), *D.D.* Handbook for Readers and Students .... In Three Parts. ... 4th Ed. New-York. 1847. 18° (HARPER'S Fam. Libr., **165.**)

PUBLIC Libraries. (CHAMBERS'S Papers, *etc.* VI. no. 44.)

Note. Mostly taken *verbatim*, without acknowledgment, from two articles in the North American Review for July, 1837, and July, 1850; the former by Prof. George W. Greene, the latter by George Livermore of Cambridge.

——— *See* [LIVERMORE (G.)]. Remarks on Public Libraries, *etc.*

PYCROFT (*Rev.* James). A Course of English Reading ... with Anecdotes of Men of Genius. ... With Additions, by J. G. Coggswell. New-York. 1845. 12°

RIPLEY (George) *and* TAYLOR (Bayard). ... Hand-Book of Literature and the Fine Arts, *etc.* *See* Class XIV. Part V.

SCHLEGEL (August Wilhelm VON). A Course of Lectures on Dramatic Art and Literature. Translated by John Black .... Revised according to the last German Ed., by the Rev[d]. A. J. W. Morrison, M.A. London. 1846. 8° (BOHN'S Stand. Libr.)

SCHLEGEL (Karl Wilhelm Friedrich VON). Lectures on the History of Literature, Ancient and Modern. From the German of Frederick S. New York. 1841. 12°

SCHLOSSER (*Prof.* Friedrich Christoph). History of the Eighteenth Century and of the Nineteenth till the Overthrow of the French Empire. With particular reference to Mental Cultivation and Progress. ... *See* Class XXV. Part III.

Note. Vols. I. and II. belong to Literary History.

SCHMIDT (*Prof.* H. I.), *D.D.* Education. — Part I. History of Education, Ancient and Modern. — Part II. A Plan of Culture and Instruction, based on Christian Principles, and designed to aid in the right Education of Youth, physically, intellectually, and morally. ... New York. [1842?] 18° (HARPER's Fam. Libr., **156.**)

SHAW (Thomas B.). Outlines of English Literature. ... Philadelphia. 1849. 12°

SILJESTRÖM (P. A.). The Educational Institutions of the United States, *etc.* *See* Class V.

SIMONDE DE SISMONDI (Jean Charles Léonard). Historical View of the Literature of the South of Europe ... . Translated ... with Notes, and a Life of the Author, by Thomas Roscoe. 2d Ed., including all the Notes from the last Paris Ed. 2 vols. London. 1846. 8° (BOHN's Stand. Libr.)

SPALDING (*Prof.* William). The History of English Literature; with an Outline of the Origin and Growth of the English Language: illustrated by Extracts. ... New-York. 1853. 12°

SPARKS (Jared). A Reply to the Strictures of Lord Mahon and others, on the Mode of editing the Writings of Washington. Cambridge. 1852. 8° pp. 35.

——— *The same.* — Also, A Review of Lord Mahon's History of the American Revolution. [By John G. Palfrey, LL.D.] From the North American Review for July, 1852. London. 1852. 8° pp. 89.

——— Letter to Lord Mahon, being an Answer to his Letter addressed to the Editor of Washington's Writings. Boston. 1852. 8° pp. 48.

——— Remarks on a "Reprint of the Original Letters from Washington to Joseph Reed, during the American Revolution, referred to in the Pamphlets of Lord Mahon and Mr. Sparks." Boston. 1853. 8° pp. 43.

SPIRIT of the Paradise Lost. (CHAMBERS's Repos., I. no. 8.)

STANHOPE (Philip Henry), *Viscount Mahon.* *See* SPARKS (J.). A Reply, *etc.*

STEVEN (William), *D.D.* The History of the High School of Edinburgh. ... Edinburgh. 1849. 8° pp. xx., 367, 220.

SWAINSON (William). A Bibliography of Zoology; with Biographical Sketches of the principal Authors. (LARDNER's Cab. Cycl., **122,** Part II.)

THOMSON (*Rev.* Henry). Horace. Latin Poetry. (ENCYCL. Metrop., X. 383 - 416.) Decline of Latin Poetry. (*Ibid.* pp. 455 - 579.)

TICKNOR (*Prof.* George), *LL.D.* History of Spanish Literature. ... 3 vols. New York. 1849. 8° or large 12° (4. and 6.)

TROUBADOURS and Trouvères. (CHAMBERS's Papers, *etc.* XI. no. 84.)

WARTON (Thomas). The History of English Poetry, from the Close of the Eleventh Century to the Commencement of the Eighteenth Century. To which are prefixed, Three Dissertations: 1. Of the Origin of Romantic Fiction in Europe. 2. On the Introduction of Learning into England. 3. On the Gesta Romanorum. ... From the Ed. of 1824 superintended by the late Richard Price, Esq. Including the Notes of Mr. Ritson, Dr. Ashby, Mr. Douce, and Mr. Park. Now further improved by the Corrections and Additions of several Eminent Antiquarians. [Edited by Richard Taylor.] ... 3 vols. London. 1840. 8°

WILSON (J. I.). A brief History of Christ's Hospital, from its Foundation by King Edward the Sixth. 7th Ed., with six Illustrations, and a List of the Governors. ... London. 1842. 16°

WORCESTER (Joseph Emerson), *LL.D.* History of English Lexicography, with a Catalogue of English Dictionaries, *etc.* (Prefixed to his "Universal and Critical Dictionary of the English Language." *See* Class XV. Part II. § 2. B.)

YOUNG (Thomas), *M.D.* *References to Works on various Branches of Natural Philosophy.* *See* his "Course of Lectures," *etc.* under Class XI. Part I.

ENCYCLOPÆDIAS AND POLYGRAPHY.

(Classes XXX., XXXI.)

CLASS XXX. ENCYCLOPÆDIAS, AND GENERAL WORKS ON THE ARTS AND SCIENCES.

BRANDE (*Prof.* William Thomas). A Dictionary of Science, Literature, and Art: comprising the History, Description, and Scientific Principles of every Branch of Human Knowledge; with the Derivation and Definition of all the Terms in general Use. Edited by W. T. B., ... assisted by Joseph Cauvin, Esq. The various Departments by eminent Literary and Scientific Gentlemen. Illustrated by numerous Engravings on Wood. New-York. 1845. 8° pp. iv., 1352.

BROUGHAM (Henry), *Baron Brougham and Vaux.* Objects, Advantages, and Pleasures of Science. [London. 182– ?] 8° pp. 40. (LIBR. of Useful Knowl., Nat. Phil., I.)

CONVERSATIONS-LEXICON. *See* LIEBER (F.). Encyclopædia, *etc.*

ENCYCLOPÆDIA Americana. *See* LIEBER (F.).

ENCYCLOPÆDIA Britannica (The), or Dictionary of Arts, Sciences, and General Literature. 8th Ed. With extensive Improvements and Additions; and numerous Engravings. [Edited by Prof. Thomas

Stewart Traill, M.D.] [Vol. I. Dissertations, by Dugald Stewart, Sir James Mackintosh, Archbishop Whately, John Playfair, and Sir John Leslie.] Volume II. [A — Anatomy.] 2 vols. Boston. [Printed in Edinburgh.] 1853. 4°

Note. Vol. I. has no title-page. — For the titles of the Dissertations, except the third, see Class XXVIII. under the authors' names; for the third (by Whately), see Class XXVI.

ENCYCLOPÆDIA Metropolitana. *See* SMEDLEY (E.).

LARDNER (Dionysius), *LL.D.* The Cabinet Cyclopædia. *See* Class XXXI.

LIEBER (*Prof.* Francis), *LL.D.* Encyclopædia Americana. A popular Dictionary of Arts, Sciences, Literature, History, Politics, and Biography ... including a copious Collection of Original Articles in American Biography; on the Basis of the Seventh Edition of the German Conversations-Lexicon. Edited by F. L., assisted by E. Wigglesworth and T. G. Bradford. Vol. I. – XIII. New Ed. | Encyclopædia Americana: Supplementary Volume. ... Vol. XIV. Edited by Henry Vethake, LL.D. ... 14 vols. Philadelphia. [Vol. I. – XIII.,] 1840. Large 12° (6.) [Vol. XIV.,] 1847. 8°

Note. The first 13 volumes were *stereotyped* in 1829 – 33.

LONDON Encyclopædia (The), or Universal Dictionary of Science, Art, Literature, and Practical Mechanics .... Illustrated by numerous Engravings .... By the original Editor of the Encyclopædia Metropolitana, assisted by eminent Professional and other Gentlemen. ... 22 vols. London. 1845. [1826 – 34 ?] 8°

Note. Edited, according to Worcester (Universal and Critical Dictionary, p. lxxv.), by Thomas Curtis.

[LONG (George)]. *Editor.* *See* SOCIETY, *etc.* The Penny Cyclopædia.

PENNY Cyclopædia. *See* SOCIETY FOR THE DIFFUSION OF USEFUL KNOWLEDGE.

PUTNAM'S Home Cyclopedia. In Six Volumes. Each complete in itself. I. History and Chronology. The World's Progress. [By George P. Putnam.] ... II. General Literature and the Fine Arts. By George Ripley and Bayard Taylor. ... III. The Useful Arts. By Dr. Antisell. ... IV. Universal Biography. By Parke Godwin. V. Universal Geography — a Comprehensive Gazetteer of the World. [By T. Carey Callicot.] VI. Science — including Natural History, Botany, Geology, Mineralogy, &c. By Prof. Samuel St. John, of Western Reserve College. ... [Vol. I. – V.] 5 vols. New-York: George P. Putnam. 1852 – 53. 12°

Note. Each volume has also an independent title-page.

SMEDLEY (*Rev.* Edward). Encyclopædia Metropolitana; or, Universal Dictionary of Knowledge, on an Original Plan: comprising the twofold Advantage of a Philosophical and an Alphabetical Arrangement, with appropriate Engravings. Edited [successively] by the Rev. E. S., ... the Rev. Hugh James Rose, ... and the Rev. Henry John Rose, ... Vol. I. – II. Pure Sciences .... | Vol. III. – VIII. Mixed Sciences .... | Vol. IX. – XIII. History and Biography .... | Vol. XIV. – XXV. Miscellaneous and Lexicographical

.... | Plates. Volume I. – III. | Index. 29 vols. (bound in 30). London. 1845. [1818 – 44.] 4°

SOCIETY FOR THE DIFFUSION OF USEFUL KNOWLEDGE. The Penny Cyclopædia of the Society .... [Edited by George Long.] 27 vols. (bound in 14). London. 1833 – 43. 8°

Note. A list of the contributors to the work is prefixed to the last volume.

——— The Supplement to the Penny Cyclopædia .... 2 vols. London. 1845 – 46. 8°

[TRAILL (*Prof.* Thomas Stewart)], *M.D.* *Editor.* *See* ENCYCLOPÆDIA Britannica .... 8th Ed.

VETHAKE (*Prof.* Henry), *LL.D.* Encyclopædia Americana: Supplementary Volume. *See* LIEBER (F.).

CLASS XXXI. POLYGRAPHY; OR, COLLECTED WORKS ON DIVERSE SUBJECTS; MISCELLANIES; PROVERBS; WORKS NOT INCLUDED IN ANY OTHER CLASS.

Note. Collections in this Class which have been fully *analyzed* are designated by an asterisk.

ARNOLD (Thomas), *D.D.* The Miscellaneous Works of T. A. .... 1st American Ed. With Nine Additional Essays, not included in the English Collection. New-York. 1845. 8°

AUTUMN Leaves. — Original Pieces in Prose and Verse. [Edited by Anne W. Abbot.] ... Cambridge. 1853. 16°

BARBAULD (*Mrs.* Anna Lætitia [AIKIN]). The Works of A. L. B. With a Memoir by Lucy Aikin. ... 2 vols. New-York. 1826. 12°

*[BOHN's Antiquarian Library. — vols. London: H. G. Bohn. 8°]

Brand (J.). Popular Antiquities. 3 vols. | Keightley (T.) Fairy Mythology.

*[BOHN's Illustrated Library. — vols. London: H. G. Bohn. 8°]

Lodge (E.). Portraits of Illustrious Personages of Great Britain. 8 vols.

*[BOHN's Standard Library. — vols. London: H. G. Bohn. 8°]

Beckmann (J.). History of Inventions. 2 vols.
Cellini (B.). Memoirs, by himself.
Coxe (W.). House of Austria. 3 vols.
——— Memoirs of the Duke of Marlborough. 3 vols.
Goethe (J. W. von). Auto-biography, *etc.* 2 vols.
Hall (R.). Miscellaneous Works.
Hutchinson (*Mrs.* L.). Life of Col. Hutchinson.
Junius. Letters. 2 vols.
Lamartine (A. de). French Revolution of 1848.
——— History of the Girondists.
Lanzi (L.). Painting in Italy. 3 vols.
Machiavelli (N.). Florence, *etc.*
Menzel (W.) History of Germany. 3 vols.
Milton (J.). Prose Works. Vol. I. – III.
Neander (J. *A.* W.). Planting of Christianity, and Antignostikus. 2 vols.
Ockley (S.). History of the Saracens.
Ranke (F. *L.*). The Popes. 3 vols.
Roscoe (W.). Leo X. 2 vols.
——— Lorenzo de' Medici.
Schiller (J. C. *F.* von). Works, Vol. I. – IV. *See* pp. 179 and 106, above.
Schlegel (A. W. von). On Dramatic Literature.
Schlegel (K. W. *F.* von). Æsthetic and Miscellaneous Works.
——— Philosophy of History.
——— Philosophy of Life, *etc.*
Sheridan (R. B.). Dramatic Works.
Simonde de Sismondi (J. C. L.). Literature of the South of Europe. 2 vols.
Wheatly (C.). On the Common Prayer.

BOLINGBROKE, Henry, *Viscount*. *See* ST. JOHN.

BROWN (*Sir* Thomas), *M.D.*, *Redivivus*, pseudon. An Exposition of Vulgar and Common Errors adapted to the Year of Grace MDCCCXLV. By Thomas Brown Redivivus, whilom Knt. and M.D. Philadelphia. 1846. 24° (8. 4.) pp. 97. (SMALL Books, *etc.* II. no. 8.)

*CABINET Library, Parley's. *See* GOODRICH (S. G.).

CAMBRIDGE HIGH SCHOOL. Compositions written by the Junior Class of the C. H. S. during the Spring and Summer Quarters of 1852. Arranged according to the Alphabetical Order of the Authors, and the Chronological Order of the Subjects. Vol. I. A – G. | Vol. II. H – O. | Vol. III. P – Z. | Compositions ... by the Middle Class .... Vol. IV. A – Z. | Compositions ... by the Senior Class .... Vol. V. A – Z. | Compositions ... by the College Class .... Vol. VI. A – Z. 6 vols. 4° *MS.*

CHAMBERS (Robert). Cyclopædia of English Literature: a Selection of the choicest Productions of English Authors, from the Earliest to the Present Time, connected by a Critical and Biographical History. Elegantly illustrated. ... 2 vols. Boston. 1847. 8°

*CHAMBERS's Miscellany of Useful and Entertaining Tracts 177 nos. in 10 vols. Edinburgh: William and Robert Chambers. [1845 – 47.] 16°

Note. Each number was originally published independently, and is so paged.

*CHAMBERS's Miscellany of Useful and Entertaining Knowledge. Edited by Robert Chambers [?] .... 10 vols. Boston: Gould, Kendall & Lincoln. [184–.] 16°

Note. Reprinted from the stereotype plates of the preceding.

*CHAMBERS's Papers for the People. 96 nos. in 12 vols. Philadelphia. 1851 – 52. 12°

Note. Each number was originally paged and published independently.

*CHAMBERS' Repository of Instructive and Amusing Papers. With Illustrations. Vol. I. – II. ... 2 vols. Boston. 1853. 16°

CLEVELAND (Charles Dexter). A Compendium of English Literature, chronologically arranged, from Sir John Mandeville to William Cowper. Consisting of Biographical Sketches of the Authors, choice Selections from their Works, with Notes .... Philadelphia. 1847. 8° or 16° pp. 702. (3 copies.)

——— *The same.* [Second] Stereotype Ed. Philadelphia. 1848. 8° or 12° (8. and 6.) pp. 776. (2 copies, one dated 1849.)

——— English Literature of the Nineteenth Century: on the Plan of the Author's "Compendium of English Literature," and Supplementary to it .... Philadelphia. 1851. 12° pp. 746.

ERRORS. An Exposition of Vulgar and Common Errors, *etc.* *See* BROWN (*Sir* Thomas), *M.D.*, *Redivivus*, pseudon.

EVERETT (Alexander Hill). Critical and Miscellaneous Essays. To which are added a few Poems. Boston. 1845. 12°

Containing: — Madame de Sévigné. — Who wrote Gil Blas? — The Life of Bernardin de St. Pierre. — The Life and Writings of Schiller. — Geoffroy on

French Dramatic Literature. — Private Life of Voltaire. — The Art of being Happy. — The Life and Works of Canova. — Sir James Mackintosh. — Cicero on Government. — A Dialogue on Government between Franklin and Montesquieu. — Chinese Manners. — The Sabbath. — POEMS.

——— Critical and Miscellaneous Essays .... Second Series. Boston. 1846. 12°

Containing: — Harro Harring. A Biographical Sketch. — Madame de Stael. — Musæus's Popular Tales. — Irving's Columbus. — De Gerando's History of Philosophy. — Greenough's Statue of Washington. — Stewart's Philosophy. — Life of Jean Jacques Rousseau. — Havana. — History of Intellectual Philosophy. — Lord Vapourcourt.

FRANKLIN (Benjamin), *LL.D.* Memoirs of B. F.; written by himself. With his most interesting Essays, Letters, and Miscellaneous Writings .... 2 vols. New-York. [1839?] 18° (HARPER's Fam. Libr., **92, 93.**)

GIBBON (Edward). The Miscellaneous Works of E. G., Esq., with Memoirs of his Life and Writings, composed by himself: illustrated from his Letters, with occasional Notes and Narrative, by John [Baker Holroyd], Lord Sheffield. ... London. 1837. 8° pp. xv., 848.

GOLDSMITH (Oliver), *M.D.* The Life of O. G., with Selections from his Writings. By Washington Irving. ... 2 vols. New-York. 1847. 18° (HARPER's Fam. Libr., **121, 122.**)

——— Miscellaneous Works, with an Account of his Life and Writings. Stereotyped from the Paris Ed., edited by Washington Irving. ... Philadelphia. 1839. 8°

——— Poems, Plays and Essays, by O. G. ... with an Account of his Life and Writings; to which is added a Critical Dissertation on his Poetry. By John Aikin, M.D. Boston. 1851. 12°

*GOODRICH (Samuel Griswold). Parley's Cabinet Library, for Schools and Families. 20 vols. Boston: Rand and Mann. 1849. 16° or 18° (8. and 6.)

Note. The works composing this series have no *general* title-page. The title given above is from the publishers' "Advertisement" appended to several of the volumes. The serial number of each volume appears on the margin of the signature pages, but not on the title-page. The following brief enumeration may be convenient: —

1. Famous Men of Modern Times.
2. Famous Men of Ancient Times.
3. Curiosities of Human Nature.
4. Lives of Benefactors.
5. Famous American Indians.
6. Celebrated Women.
7. American History.
8. European History.
9. Asiatic History.
10. African History.
11. History of the Indians.
12. Customs of the Indians.
13. A Glance at the Sciences.
14. Wonders of Geology.
15. Animal Kingdom.
16. A Glance at Philosophy.
17. Book of Literature.
18. Enterprise and Art of Man.
19. Customs of all Nations.
20. The World and its Inhabitants.

GRISWOLD (Rufus Wilmot). The Prose Writers of America. With a Survey of the History, Condition, and Prospects of American Literature. Illustrated with Portraits from Original Pictures. Philadelphia. 1847. 8°

HALL (*Rev.* Robert). The Miscellaneous Works and Remains of the

Rev. R. H., with a Memoir of his Life, by Olinthus Gregory ... and a Critical Estimate of his Character and Writings, by John Foster .... London. 1846. 8° (BOHN's Stand. Libr.)

*[HARPER's Family Library. 187 vols. New York: Harper and Brothers. *Various dates.* 18°]

1-3. Milman (H. H.). History of the Jews.
4, 5. Lockhart (J. G.). Life of Napoleon.
6. Southey (R.). Life of Lord Nelson.
7. Williams (J.). Alexander the Great.
8, 74. [Rennie (J.) *and* Westwood (J. O.)]. Natural History of Insects.
9. Galt (J.). Life of Lord Byron.
10. Bush (G.). Life of Mohammed.
11. Scott (*Sir* W.). Demonology, *etc.*
12, 13. Gleig (G. R.). History of the Bible.
14. Murray (H.). Polar Seas and Regions.
15. Croly (G.). Life of George IV.
16. Murray (H.). Discovery in Africa.
17-19, 66, 67. Cunningham (A.). British Painters and Sculptors.
20. James (G. P. R.). Chivalry and the Crusades.
21, 22. Bell (H. G.). Mary Queen of Scots.
23. Russell (M.). Egypt.
24. Fletcher (J.). History of Poland.
25. Smith (H.). Festivals, Games, *etc.*
26. Brewster (*Sir* D.). Life of Newton.
27. Russell (M.). History of Palestine.
28. Memes (J. S.) Empress Josephine.
29. Court and Camp of Bonaparte.
30. Lives and Voyages of Drake, Cavendish, and Dampier.
31. [Barrow (*Sir* J.)]. Pitcairn's Island and the Mutiny of the Bounty.
32, 72, 84. Turner (S.). Sacred History of the World.
33, 34. Jameson (*Mrs.* A. [M.]). Celebrated Female Sovereigns.
38-40. St. John (J. A.). Celebrated Travellers.
41, 42. Ellis (G. J. W. Agar), *Lord Dover.* Life of Frederic the Great.
43, 44. Smedley (E.). Venetian History.
45, 46. Thacher (B. B.). Lives of the Indians.
47-49. Murray (H.). British India.
50. Brewster (*Sir* D.). Natural Magic.
51, 52. Taylor (W. C.). History of Ireland.
53. Tytler (P. F.). Discovery in North America.
54. Macgillivray (W.). Humboldt's Travels.
55, 56. Euler (L.). Natural Philosophy.
57. Mudie (R.). Guide to the Observation of Nature.
58. Abercrombie (J.). The Moral Feelings.
59. Dick (T.). Improvement of Society.
60. James (G. P. R.). Charlemagne.
61. Russell (M.). Nubia and Abyssinia.
62, 63. Russell (M.). Life of Cromwell.
64. Montgomery (J.). Lectures on Literature, Poetry, *etc.*
65. Barrow (*Sir* J.). Peter the Great.
66, 67. *See* 17-19.
68, 69. Crichton (A.). History of Arabia.
70. Fraser (J. B.). Persia.
71. Combe (A.). Principles of Physiology.
72. *See* 32.
73. Russell (M.). The Barbary States.
74. *See* 8.
75, 76. Paulding (J. K.). Life of Washington.
77. Ticknor (C.). Philosophy of Living.
78. Higgins (W. M.). The Earth.
79. Sforzosi (—). History of Italy.
80, 81. Davis (*Sir* J. F.). The Chinese.
82. Circumnavigation of the Globe.
83. Dick (T.). Celestial Scenery.
84. *See* 32.
85. Griscom (J. H.). Animal Mechanism.
86-91. Tytler (A. F.). Universal History.
92, 93. Franklin (B.). Life and Writings.
94, 95. [Craik (G. L.)]. Pursuit of Knowledge under Difficulties.
96, 97. Paley (W.). Natural Theology.
98. [Rennie (J.)]. Natural History of Birds.
99. Dick (T.). The Sidereal Heavens.
100. Upham (T. C.). Disordered Mental Action.
101, 102. Murray (H.). British America.
103. Lossing (B. J.). History of the Fine Arts.
104. Natural History of Quadrupeds.
105. Life and Travels of Mungo Park.
106. [Dana (R. H.)], *Jr.* Two Years before the Mast.
107, 108. Parry (*Sir* W. E.). Three Voyages.
109, 110. Johnson (S.). Life and Writings.
111. Bryant (W. C.). Selections from the American Poets.
112, 113. [Halleck (F.-G.)]. Selections from the British Poets.
114-118. Keightley (T.). History of England.
119, 120. Hale (S.). History of the U. S.
121, 122. Goldsmith (O.). Life, and Selections from his Writings, by Irving.
123, 124. Distinguished Men of Modern Times.
125. Renwick (J.). Life of Dewitt Clinton.
126, 127. Mackenzie (A. Slidell). Life of Commodore O. H. Perry.

128. Head (*Sir* F. B.). Life of Bruce, the Traveller.
129. Renwick (H. B. *and* J.). Lives of John Jay and Alex. Hamilton.
130. Brewster (*Sir* D.). Lives of Galileo, Tycho Brahe, and Kepler.
131. Iceland, Greenland, and the Faroe Islands.
132. Manners of the Japanese.
133. Dwight (T.), *Jr.* History of Connecticut.
134, 135. Bucke (C.). Ruins of Ancient Cities.
136, 137. Crichton (A.) *and* Wheaton (H.). Denmark, Sweden, and Norway.
138. Camp (G. S.). Democracy.
139. Lanman (J. H.). Hist. of Michigan.
140. Fénelon (F. de S. de la M.). Lives of Ancient Philosophers.
141, 142. Ségur (P. P., *Count* de). Napoleon's Expedition to Russia.
143, 144. Epitome of the History of Philosophy.
145. Bucke (C.). Beauties, *etc.* of Nature.
146. Lieber (F.). On Property and Labour.
147. White (G.). Nat. Hist. of Selborne.
148. Wrangel (F. von). Expedition to the Polar Sea.
149, 150. Hazen (E.). Popular Technology.
151 - 153. Spalding (W.). Italy, *etc.*
154, 155. Allen (P.). Expedition of Lewis and Clarke.
156. Schmidt (H. I.). Education.
157. Fraser (J. B.). Mesopotamia and Assyria.
158. Russell (M.). Polynesia.
159. Davenport (R. A.). Perilous Adventures.
160. Duer (W. A.). Constitutional Jurisprudence of the U. S.
161 - 163. Belknap (J.). American Biography.
164. Natural History. The Elephant.
165. Potter (A.). Handbook for Readers and Students.
166. Graves (*Mrs.* A. J.). Woman in America.
167, 168. Stone (W. L.). Border Wars of the American Revolution.
169. Vegetable Substances used for the Food of Man.
170. Michelet (J.). Modern History.
171. Bacon (F.), *Lord.* Essays, *etc.*
172. Voyages round the World.
173. Polo (M.). Travels.
174, 175. American Adventure, *etc.*
176. Bunner (E.). History of Louisiana.
177. Florian (J. P. C. de). The Moors in Spain.
178. Lee (C. A.). Elements of Geology.
179. Brougham (H.), *Lord.* Discourses by Brougham and others.
180. Moseley (H.). Mechanics.
181, 182. Spectator. (Selections.)
183. Potter (A.). Political Economy.
184. Maury (J. S.), *Card.* On Eloquence.
185. Robertson (W.). History of America. Abridged.
186. Robertson (W.). Charles V. Abridged.
187. Ferguson (A.). History of the Roman Republic. Abridged.

*Irving (Washington). The Works of W. I. New Ed., revised. Vol. I. Knickerbocker's New-York. | Vol. II. The Sketch Book. | Vol. III. - IV. Life and Voyages of Columbus. | Vol. V. Columbus and his Companions. | Vol. VI. Bracebridge Hall. | Vol. VII. Tales of a Traveller. | Vol. VIII. Astoria. | Vol. IX. Crayon Miscellany. | Vol. X. Bonneville's Adventures. | Vol. XI. Oliver Goldsmith. | Vol. XII. - XIII. Mahomet and his Successors. | Vol. XIV. Conquest of Granada. | Vol. XV. The Alhambra. 15 vols. New-York. 1849 - 52 - 48 - 51. 12°

Note. Each volume has also a special title-page.

Johnson (Samuel), *LL.D.* The Works of S. J. ... with an Essay on his Life and Genius, by Arthur Murphy, Esq. 1st complete American Ed. ... 2 vols. New-York. 1837. 8°

*Lardner (Dionysius), *LL.D.* The Cabinet Cyclopædia. Conducted by the Rev. Dionysius Lardner, assisted by Eminent Literary and Scientific Men. 132 vols. London. 8°

Note. The volumes forming this collection are arranged as follows in a circular of the original publishers, dated August, 1839. The title-pages do not indicate their place in the series.

History.

1. Keightley (T.). Outlines of History.
2. Nicolas (*Sir* N. *H.*) Chronology of History.
3 - 12. Mackintosh (*Sir* J.). England; continued by W. Wallace and R. Bell.
13, 14. Scott (*Sir* W.). Scotland.

15-18. Moore (T.). Ireland.
19-21. Crowe (E. E.). France.
22. History of Switzerland.
23-27. Dunham (S. A.). Spain and Portugal.
28-30. Dunham (S. A.). The Germanic Empire.
31, 32. Fergus (H.). The United States of America.
33-40. Thirlwall (C.). Greece.
41, 42. History of Rome.
43, 44. Simonde de Sismondi (J. C. L.). Fall of the Roman Empire.
45, 46. Fosbroke (T. D.). Arts, Manufactures, Manners, and Institutions of the Greeks and Romans.
47. Simonde de Sismondi (J. C. L.). Italian Republics.
48-51. Dunham (S. A.). Europe during the Middle Ages.
52-54. Bell (R.). Russia.
55. Grattan (T. C.). Netherlands.
56. Dunham (S. A.). Poland.
57-59. Dunham (S. A.). Denmark, Sweden, and Norway.
60-62. Cooley (W. D.). Maritime and Inland Discovery.
63, 64. Stebbing (H.) The Christian Church, to A. D. 1492.
65, 66. Stebbing (H.). The Reformation.

BIOGRAPHY.

67-69. Gleig (G. R.). British Military Commanders.
70-74. Southey (R.). British Admirals; Vol. V. by R. Bell.
75. Roscoe (H.). British Lawyers.
76-82. Forster (J.). British Statesmen; Vol. I. by Sir J. Mackintosh, Vol. V. by T. P. Courtenay.
83-87. James (G. P. R.) *and* Crowe (E. E.). Foreign Statesmen.
88-90. Shelley (*Mrs.* M. W. [G.]). Literary and Scientific Men of Italy, Spain, and Portugal. By Mrs. Shelley, Sir D. Brewster, J. Montgomery, and others.
91, 92. Shelley (*Mrs.* M. W. [G.]). Literary and Scientific Men of France. By Mrs. Shelley, and others.
93, 94. Bell (R.). English Poets.
95. Dunham (S. A.) *and* Bell (R.). Early Writers of Great Britain.
96, 97. Dunham (S. A.). British Dramatists. By S. A. D., R. Bell, and others.

NATURAL PHILOSOPHY.

98. Herschel (*Sir* J. F. W.) Preliminary Discourse.
99. Powell (B.). History of Natural Philosophy.
100. Lardner (D.). Arithmetic.
101. Lardner (D.). Geometry.
102. Kater (H.) *and* Lardner (D.). Mechanics.
103. Lardner (D.). Hydrostatics and Pneumatics.
104. Herschel (*Sir* J. F. W.). Astronomy.
105. Brewster (*Sir* D.). Optics.
106. Lardner (D.). Heat.
107. Donovan (M.). Chemistry.
108, 109. Lardner (D.) *and* Walker (C.V.). Electricity and Magnetism, and Meteorology.
110. De Morgan (A.). Probabilities.

NATURAL HISTORY.

111. Swainson (W.). Preliminary Discourse.
112. Swainson (W.). Geography and Classification of Animals.
113. Swainson (W.). Quadrupeds.
114. Swainson (W.). Animals in Menageries.
115, 116. Swainson (W.). Birds.
117, 118. Swainson (W.). Fishes, Amphibians, and Reptiles.
119. Swainson (W.). Malacology.
120. Shuckard (W. E.) *and* Swainson (W.). Insects.
121. Swainson (W.). Habits and Instincts of Animals.
122. Swainson (W.). Taxidermy. With the Biography of Zoölogists, *etc.*
123. Henslow (J. S.). Botany.
124, 125. Phillips (J.). Geology.

THE USEFUL ARTS.

126, 127. Donovan (M.). Domestic Economy.
128. Porter (G. R.). Manufacture of Silk.
129-131. Holland (J.). Manufactures in Metal.
132. Porter (G. R.). Manufactures of Porcelain and Glass.

LEGARÉ (Hugh Swinton). Writings ...: consisting of a Diary of Brussels, and Journal of the Rhine; Extracts from his Private and Diplomatic Correspondence ; Orations and Speeches ; and Contributions to the New-York and Southern Reviews. Prefaced by a Memoir of his Life. ... With a Portrait. Edited by his Sister. ... 2 vols. Charleston, S. C. 1846. 8°

LIBRARY of Useful Knowledge. *See* SOCIETY FOR THE DIFFUSION, *etc.*

MACAULAY (Thomas Babington). Critical and Miscellaneous Essays. 5 vols. Philadelphia. 1842 - 44. 12°

Vol. I. Milton. — Machiavelli. — Dryden. — History. — Hallam's Constitutional History. — Southey's Colloquies on Society. — Moore's Life of Lord Byron. — Southey's Ed. of the Pilgrim's Progress. — Appendix [Pompeii, *and* The Battle of Ivry].

Vol. II. Croker's Ed. of Boswell's Life of Johnson. — Lord Nugent's Memorials of Hampden. — Nares's Memoirs of Lord Burghley. — Dumont's Recollections of Mirabeau. — Lord Mahon's War of the Succession. — Walpole's Letters to Sir Horace Mann. — Thackeray's History of the Earl of Chatham. — Lord Bacon.

Vol. III. Mackintosh's History of the Revolution in England, in 1688. — Sir John Malcolm's Life of Lord Clive. — Life and Writings of Sir William Temple. — Church and State. — Ranke's History of the Popes. — Cowley and Milton. — On Mitford's History of Greece. — On the Athenian Orators.

Vol. IV. Comic Dramatists of the Restoration (Wycherley and Congreve). — The late Lord Holland. — Warren Hastings. — Frederic the Great. — LAYS OF ANCIENT ROME.

Vol. V. Madame D'Arblay. — Life and Writings of Addison. — Barère's Memoirs. — Mr. Robert Montgomery's Poems. — Civil Disabilities of the Jews. — Mill's Essay on Government. — Bentham's Defence of Mill. — Utilitarian Theory of Government.

MASSACHUSETTS — *Board of Education. See* SCHOOL Library.

MILTON (John). The Prose Works of J. M. ... With a Preface, Preliminary Remarks, and Notes, by J. A. St. John. Vol. I. - III. 3 vols. London. 1848. 8° (BOHN'S Stand. Libr.)

ORCUTT (Hiram). *See* RICKARD (T.) *and* ORCUTT (H.).

PALEY (William), *D.D.*, *Archdeacon of Carlisle.* The Works, *etc. See* Class II. Part III.

PARLEY (Peter), *pseudon. See* [GOODRICH (Samuel Griswold)].

PIERPONT (*Rev.* John). Pierpont's Fifth Reader. — The American First Class Book ... . 35th Ed. New York. N. D. 12° (3 copies.)

PROVERBS. *See* SELECTION (A) of English and Scotch Proverbs, *etc.*

RICKARD (Truman) *and* ORCUTT (Hiram). Class Book of Prose and Poetry : ... Selections ... designed as Exercises in Parsing ... . Boston. 1847. 12° (8. 4.)

ST. JOHN (Henry), *Viscount Bolingbroke.* The Works of Lord B. With a Life, prepared expressly for this Ed. ... . 4 vols. Philadelphia. 1841. 8°

SCHLEGEL (Karl Wilhelm Friedrich VON). The Æsthetic and Miscellaneous Works of Frederick v. S. : comprising Letters on Christian Art — An Essay on Gothic Architecture — Remarks on the Romance-Poetry of the Middle Ages and on Shakspere — On the Limits of the Beautiful — On the Language and Wisdom of the Indians. Translated from the German by E. J. Millington. London. 1849. 8° (BOHN'S Stand. Libr.)

*SCHOOL Library (The). Published under the Sanction of the Board of Education of the State of Massachusetts. 26 vols. Boston. 1839 - [43]. 12°

Vol. I. Introductory Essay ... . Irving's Life and Voyages of Columbus, with the Author's Visit to Palos. ... 1839.

Vol. II. III. Paley's Natural Theology, with Additions from Lord Brougham, and Sir Charles Bell ... . The whole newly arranged ... by Elisha Bartlett, M.D. ... 1839.

Vol. IV. - VI. Lives of Eminent Individuals, celebrated in American History. ... 1839.

Vol. VII. - X. Sacred Philosophy of the Seasons; by the Rev. Henry Duncan, D.D. Adapted to American Readers, by F. W. P. Greenwood. ... 1839.

Vol. XI. XII. The Useful Arts, considered in Connexion with the Applications of Science. With numerous Engravings. By Jacob Bigelow, M.D. ... 1840.

Vol. XIII. A Familiar Exposition of the Constitution of the United States. With an Appendix and Glossary. By Joseph Story, LL.D. [1840 ?]

Vol. XIV. XV. Pursuit of Knowledge under Difficulties. Illustrated by Anecdotes. [By G. L. Craik.] Revised Ed., with Preface and Notes, by Francis Wayland, D.D. ... 1840 - [44].

Vol. XVI. The Farmer's Companion ... . By the late Hon. Jesse Buel. [1840 ?]

Vol. XVII. Great Events described by distinguished Historians ... . Collected and in part translated by Francis Lieber. [1840.]

Vol. XVIII. The Fireside Friend, or Female Student. ... By Mrs. A. H. L. Phelps. 1840.

Vol. XIX. Importance of Practical Education and Useful Knowledge. By Edward Everett. 1840.

Vol. XX. Letters on Astronomy, addressed to a Lady ... . By Denison Olmsted, A.M. 1842.

Vol. XXI. The Principles of Science applied to the Domestic and Mechanic Arts, and to Manufactures and Agriculture ... . By Alonzo Potter, D.D. [1840 ?]

Vol. XXII. - XXV. History of the World: from the Earliest Period to the Year of our Lord 1783. From the German of the Baron John von Müller. ... [1842.]

Vol. XXVI. A Treatise on Domestic Economy, for the Use of Young Ladies ... . By Miss Catherine E. Beecher. Revised Ed. ... [1843.]

SELECTION (A) of English and Scotch Proverbs. (CHAMBERS's Miscel., X. no. 174.)

*SMALL Books on Great Subjects. Vol. I. containing Philosophical Theories and Experience, Physiology and Intellectual Science [by the Rev. John Barlow], Prevention of Insanity [by the same], Practical Organic Chemistry. | Vol. II. containing Early Greek Philosophy, Later Greek Philosophy, Christian Doctrines in the Second Century, Exposition of Vulgar and Common Errors. | Vol. III. containing Vegetable Physiology, Criminal Law, Christian Sects in the XIX Century, Principles of Grammar. 3 vols. in 12 nos. Philadelphia. 1847. 24° (8. 4.)

Note. Each number has also a separate title-page, and is paged independently.

*SOCIETY FOR THE DIFFUSION OF USEFUL KNOWLEDGE.

Note. For the few publications of this Society which belong to the Library, see p. 15, McCULLOCH (J. R.); — p. 42, SOCIETY, *etc.*; — p. 56, VEGETABLE; — pp. 59, 124, SOCIETY, *etc.*; — p. 168, MALKIN (F.); — p. 177, VAUGHAN (R.); — p. 197, MUELLER (K. O.); — p. 201, SOCIETY, *etc.*

STEPHEN (*Sir* James). Critical and Miscellaneous Essays. Philadelphia. 1843. 12°

Containing: — Life of William Wilberforce. — The Lives of Whitfield and Froude. — D'Aubigné's History of the Great Reformation. — Life and Times of Richard Baxter. — Physical Theory of another Life. — The Port-Royalists. — Ignatius Loyola and his Associates. — Taylor's Edwin the Fair.

VULGAR and Common Errors. *See* BROWN (*Sir* Thomas), *M.D.*, *Redivivus*, pseudon.

WALSH (Robert), *LL.D.* Didactics: Social, Literary, and Political. ... 2 vols. Philadelphia. 1836. 12°

WARE (Henry), *Jr.*, *D.D.* The Miscellaneous Works, *etc.* *See* Class II. Part III.

WILCOX (*Rev.* Carlos). Remains ... . With a Memoir of his Life [by Lavius Hyde]. Hartford. 1828. 8°

WIRT (William), *LL.D.* The Letters of the British Spy. ... 10th Ed., revised and corrected. To which is prefixed, A Biographical Sketch of the Author. New-York. 1848. 12°

WONDERS (The) of Human Folly. (CHAMBERS's Papers, *etc.* VIII. no. 63.)

ADDITIONS AND CORRECTIONS.

Page 2, after line 3, insert

HAMILTON (*Sir* William), *Bart.* Discussions on Philosophy and Literature, Education and University Reform. Chiefly from the Edinburgh Review; corrected, vindicated, enlarged, in Notes and Appendices. With an Introductory Essay by Robert Turnbull, D.D. New York. 1853. 8° pp. xlviii., 764.

Page 11, after line 13 from the bottom, insert

BROUGHAM (Henry), *Baron Brougham and Vaux.* ... Political Philosophy ... Part I Principles of Government Monarchical Government | Part II Of Aristocracy Aristocratic Governments | Part III Of Democracy Mixed Monarchy 2d Ed. 3 pts. London. 1849. 8° (Under the Superintendence of the Society for the Diffusion of Useful Knowledge.)

Page 19, after the last reference under BARNARD, insert

——— *Editor.* *See* RHODE ISLAND INSTITUTE OF INSTRUCTION. Journal, *etc.*

Page 30, "SOCIETY," *etc.* The Schoolmaster, Vol. I. and II. — By a strange oversight, only part of the contents of these volumes is specified.

Page 52, line 8 from the bottom, for "Muckle" read "Mucklé."

Page 59, after line 17, insert

SPENCE (William). *See* KIRBY (W.) *and* SPENCE (W.)

Page 60, line 10 from the bottom, for "*M.D.*" read "M.D."

Page 61, line 20, for "Class XXVII." read "Class XXVIII."

Page 77, last line, add "pp. 52."

Page 85, after line 5, insert

EUCLIDES. Geometry. *See* Class IX.

Page 86, after line 24, insert

COLERIDGE (Henry Nelson). Introductions, *etc.* *See* Class XXIX.

Page 91, line 17 from the bottom, for "SALLUSTIUS (Caius Crispus)" read "SALLUSTIUS CRISPUS (Caius)."

Page 99, line 19, *dele* the words "*and* THOMSON (James)," and place the title first in order under COWPER.

Page 115, after line 24, insert

LOGAN (James). The Scotish Gaël, *etc.* *See* Class XXVII.

Page 117, after line 12, insert

COOLEY (William Desborough). The History of Maritime and Inland Discovery. 3 vols. London. 8° (LARDNER's Cab. Cycl., **60 - 62.**)

Page 119, line 8 from the bottom. "AMERICAN Adventure," *etc.* — This anonymous work was written by Epes Sargent.

Page 121, line 7, inclose the dash in brackets.

Page 125, bottom, insert

THOMPSON (*Rev.* Henry). Heraldry. (ENCYCL. Metrop. V. 589 - 618.)

Page 139, line 13, for "Weldore" read "Welbore."

Page 161, after line 6 from the bottom, insert

——— Memoir. *See* Class XI. Part II. LARDNER (D.). The Steam Engine, *etc.*

Page 176, line 21, inclose the dash in brackets.

Page 178, line 18 from the bottom, read "[SFORZOSI (——)]."

Page 208, line 3 from the bottom, for "p. 42," read "pp. 30, 42."

ALPHABETICAL INDEX.

Note. The following Index is principally intended to show at once where each work is entered in the Catalogue. It contains the names of authors, including translators, editors, and commentators, followed by a very brief indication of their literary labors. The titles of anonymous publications are also referred to, except the anonymous tracts in Chambers's "Miscellany," "Papers for the People," and "Repository," which belong to Class XXI. (PROSE FICTION) and to Class XXIV. Part II. (INDIVIDUAL BIOGRAPHY). For the description of different editions, and other particulars, the Catalogue itself must be consulted.

The abbreviation "*trans.*" is used for "translator"; "*edit.*" for "editor"; "*annot.*" for "annotator"; and "*biogr.*" for "biographer." When the initial of a Christian name is followed by a period in the Index, the full name will be found in the Catalogue; when the full name is not known, two dots are placed after the initial. Italicized initials belong to names printed in spaced letters (for a reason explained in the Preface) in the preceding part of the Catalogue. When a word is printed in small capitals, that is the word to be sought on the page referred to.

PHILOSOPHICAL APPARATUS

BELONGING TO THE HIGH SCHOOL.

Mechanics.

Set of Mechanical Powers, . .	$35.00
Set of Ivory Reaction Balls, and Frame, ...	8.00
Apparatus for illustrating Centrifugal Force, ...	8.00
Centre of Gravity Apparatus, . .	7.00
Atwood's Machine, . . .	35.00
	$93.00

Hydrostatics and Hydraulics.

Hydrostatic Press, ...	$25.00
Hydrostatic Bellows and Fixtures, .	8.00
Hydrostatic Paradox Apparatus,	8.00
Hydrostatic Balloon, . . .	5.00
Equilibrium Tubes, . . .	5.00
Barker's Centrifugal Mill, . .	1.25
Specific Gravity Apparatus, .	12.00
	$64.25

Pneumatics.

Chamberlain's American Air-Pump, ...	$85.00
Chamberlain's Double-acting Exhauster and Condenser, . .	8.00
Swelled Open-Top Bell-Glass, .	3.50
Eight-Inch Bell-Glass, Brass-capped, (duplicates,) . . .	6.00
Five-Inch Bell-Glass with Brass Cap, ...	2.00
Tall Bell-Glass and Jar, . .	3.00
Bell-Glass, Jar, and Bolthead, .	1.00
Open-Top Bell-Glass, with Glass Stopper, ...	1.25
Small Open-Top Bell-Glass and Jar,	2.00
Swelled Hand-Glass, . . .	1.00
Mercury Tunnel used with do., .	1.00
Glass Cup " " " .	.50
Bladder-Cup, with Cap and Cock,	2.00
Cupping-Glass, with Cap and Cock,	1.50
Magdeburg Hemispheres, . .	$7.00
Upward Pressure Apparatus, . .	12.00
Artificial Fountain and Jets, .	5.00
Treble Globe Transferrer, . .	3.00
Large Bolthead and Cup, . .	1.50
Torricellian Tube, ...	1.00
Siphon Gauge for Pump, . .	2.50
Pear Gauge for Vacuum Test, .	3.00
Barometer Apparatus, . .	7.00
Large heavy Siphon for Barometric Purposes, ...	5.00
Pair of Working Models of Lifting and Forcing Pumps, . .	12.00
Siphon in Vacuo, ...	3.00
Bell in Vacuo, ...	1.50
Vane and Mill in Vacuo, . .	7.00
Water Hammer, ...	3.00
Guinea and Feather Tube, . .	7.00
Expansion Apparatus, . .	1.00
Sheet Rubber Bag, Cap, Cork, and Hook, ...	2.00
Glass Bursting Squares, . . .	1.50
Valve Cap for " . .	.33
Guard Cap for " . . .	1.00
Condensing Syringe, . . .	5.00
Glass Condensing Chamber, . .	10.00
Copper Condensing Chamber and Fixtures, ...	3.50
Pair of Condensing Gauges by Bulk of Air, ...	2.00
Mercury Siphon Gauge, . .	2.50
Crushing Squares for Condenser, .	1.00
Sinking Glass Balls, . . .	.50
Air-Gun Barrel, ...	1.00
Revolving Jet, ...	1.25
Weighing Air Apparatus, . .	12.00
Double Transferrer, . . .	10.00
Pneumatic Paradox, ...	1.00
Pipe Paradox, ...	1.00
Set of Screw Couplings, . . .	2.50
Set of Hose and Screws, . .	2.00
Cock with Interior and Exterior Jets, ...	2.90
Straight Brass Jet, ...	.50
Hose Brass Jet, ...	1.00
Sliding Rod and Packing Screw, (duplicates,)	1.50

Working Model of the Steam-Engine,	$ 50.00
Wollaston's Steam Globe,	3.00
Pair of Gasometers with Fixtures, (large size,)	60.00
Compound Blow-Pipe and Fixtures,	3.00
Pneumatic Cistern,	20.00
Apparatus for making Oxygen,	4.00
Apparatus for making Hydrogen,	1.50
Hydrogen Balloon,	3.00
Bottle Imps,	4.00
	$ 413.73

Optics.

Set of Eye Models,	$ 12.00
Set of Mounted Lenses,	13.00
Prism,	3.00
Compound Microscope and Fixtures,	50.00
Magic Lantern with Solar Lamp, &c.,	25.00
	$ 103.00

Magneto-Electricity and Galvanism.

Case of Bar Magnets,	$ 4.00
Steel U and Rolling Armature,	3.00
Pair of Small Magnetic Needles,	2.00
Dipping Needle,	4.00
Galvanic Battery,	50.00
Grove's Battery, (four cups,)	8.00
Cylindrical Sulphate of Copper Battery,	6.00
Smee's Battery,	2.00
Daniel's Battery,	2.00
Ampère's Battery,	8.00
De la Rive's Ring,	1.25
Helix and Stand,	2.50
Lifting Coil and Bars,	2.00
Large Electro-Magnet,	2.25
Revolving Electro-Magnet,	5.00
Magic Circle and Armatures,	3.00
Revolving Circle,	12.00
Revolving Coil,	6.00
Revolving Needle,	6.00
Revolving Magnet, (Registering,)	10.00
Armature Engine,	6.00
Double-Beam Axial Engine,	18.00
Electro-Magnetic Railway,	35.00
Magnetic Telegraph,	35.00
Simple form of Telegraph,	5.00
Small Decomposer,	1.50
Decomposing Apparatus,	4.00
Decomposer and Recomposer,	12.00
Galvanic Lamp,	2.50
Powder Cup,	.50
Thermo-Electrical Rectangle,	5.00
Magneto-Electrical Machine,	45.00
Compound Magnet and Electrotome,	$ 18.00
Pair of Shocking Handles,	1.50
Set of Connecting Wires,	.50
Contracting Helix,	3.50
Galvanometer,	3.50
Astatic Galvanometer,	7.00
Horizontal Galvanometer,	4.00
Apparatus for analyzing Shocks,	12.00
	$ 358.50

Electricity.

Electrical Machine, (Thirty-Inch Plate,)	$ 85.00
Glass Friction Cylinder,	2.00
Wax Friction Cylinder,	1.50
Two-Quart Leyden Jar,	2.00
Two-Quart Electrometer Jar,	2.50
Two-Quart Diamond Jar,	3.00
Two-Quart Suspension Jar,	3.00
One-Quart Hand Jar,	1.25
Jar with Movable Coatings,	3.00
Electrical Battery,	12.00
Jointed Discharger,	3.50
Universal Discharger,	7.00
Directing Rod,	2.00
Insulating Stool,	6.00
Electrical Bells,	3.00
Dancing Images and Plates,	3.50
Spiral Tube,	3.50
Abbé Nollet's Globe,	5.00
Thunder House and Fixtures,	5.00
Gas Pistol,	2.50
Electrical Wheel and Point,	1.25
Electrical Inclined Plane and Wheel,	4.00
Electrical Orrery,	3.00
Long-haired Man,	.75
Electrical Swing,	2.00
Ether Spoon,	1.00
Powder Bomb,	1.25
Decomposing Bomb,	1.75
Electrophorus and Fixtures,	8.00
Pith-ball Electrometer,	.75
Gold-leaf Electrometer with Condenser,	7.00
Silver-leaf Electrometer,	5.00
Ball Electrometer,	.75
Balance Electrometer,	6.00
Kinnersley's Electrometer,	7.00
	$ 205.75

Thermotics.

Air Thermometer,	$ 2.00
Fahrenheit's Thermometer, (triplicates,)	3.75
Extra-finished Thermometer,	6.00
Rosewood-cased Barometer and Thermometer,	18.00

Thermometer for Chemical Purposes,	$ 5.00
Differential Thermometer,	2.50
Pyrometer,	3.00
Cryophorus,	6.00
Radiating and Absorbing Cubes,	2.00
Reflectors in Cases,	7.00
Iron Ball and Stand for the Reflectors,	1.00
Conductometer with Six Rods,	2.00
Freezing Apparatus,	8.00
Bell-Glass for Freezing Apparatus,	1.50
Marcet's Steam Globe and Fixtures,	20.00
Chamberlain's Steam Boiler and Fixtures,	8.00
Spirit Lamp, (duplicates,)	.62
Lamp Stand,	2.00
Wire Gauze for Gas Flame,	.50
Fire Syringe,	1.50
Dobereiner's Hydrogen Lamp,	4.00
	$ 104.37

Miscellaneous.

Philosophical Diagrams,	$ 6.00
Swain's Planetarium,	50.00
Tellurion,	12.00
Pair of Globes,	45.00
Geometrical Solids, (two sets,)	10.00
Theodolite,	150.00
Level,	75.00
Surveyor's Compass,	25.00
	$ 373.00

Mural Maps.

Ancient.

Kiepert's Wandkarte des Römischen Reichs, 1852,	$12.00
Imperium Romanum,	8.00
Kiepert's Wandkarte von Alt-Italien, 1850,	12.00
Italia Antiqua,	8.00
Kiepert's Wandkarte von Alt-Griechenland, 1847,	12.00
Græcia Antiqua,	8 00
Greece and its Colonies,	8.00
Athenæ Antiquæ,	$ 8.00
Gallia Antiqua,	8.00
Plan of Rome,	5.00
Plan of the Capitoline and Palatine Hills,	10.00
Roman Forum, (in Perspective,)	4.00

Modern.

Mitchell's Map of the World on Mercator's Projection,	$ 10.00
Guyot's Mural Map of the World,	10.00
Bidwell's Map of the Eastern Hemisphere,	6.00
Bidwell's Map of the Western Hemisphere,	6.00
Bidwell's Map of Western Asia,	4.00
Mitchell's Map of the United States,	10.00
Colton's Map of the United States,	5.00
Topographical Map of Massachusetts,	5.00
Wilson's Comprehensive Chart of American History,	7.00
Lyman's Historical Chart,	10.00
Mattison's Astronomical Maps, (16,)	20.00
Cutter's Anatomical Outline Maps, (9,)	17.50
Map indicating the proposed Course of the Steam Navigation between San Francisco and Shanghae. Baltimore. [1852?]	

Bauerkeller's Maps in Relief.

L'Empire Ottoman,	$ 4.00
La France et la Belgique,	4.00
La Suisse et les Pays limitrophes,	4.00
La Grande Bretagne et l'Irlande,	4.00
Les États-Unis de l'Amérique du Nord,	4.00
	$ 233.50

Mechanics,	93.00
Hydrostatics and Hydraulics,	64.25
Pneumatics,	413.73
Optics,	103.00
Magneto-Electricity and Galvanism,	358.50
Electricity,	205.75
Thermotics,	104.37
Miscellaneous,	373.00
	$1,949.10

THE END.

www.ingramcontent.com/pod-product-compliance
Lightning Source LLC
LaVergne TN
LVHW010252110826
845151LV00004B/1456

* 9 7 8 1 4 2 5 5 2 2 8 0 3 *